Thom

For Leonard, Dorsey and Rena

Patricia Taylor

THOMAS BLAIKIE (1751–1838)
The 'Capability' Brown of France

TUCKWELL PRESS

First published in Great Britain by
Tuckwell Press
The Mill House
Phantassie
East Linton
East Lothian EH40 3DG
Scotland

Copyright © Patricia Taylor, 2001

ISBN 1 86232 110 8

British Library Cataloguing-in-Publication Data
A catalogue record for this book is available
on request from the British Library

The right of Patricia Taylor to be identified
as the author of this work has been asserted by her
in accordance with the Copyright, Design and
Patent Act 1988

Typeset by Carnegie Publishing Ltd, Lancaster
Printed by The Cromwell Press, Trowbridge

Contents

Illustrations

Acknowledgements

THIS BOOK could not have been written without generous assistance from the Stanley Smith Horticultural Trust, which contributed to the cost of my research and that of publication, and I would like to express my gratitude to the Trust and to its Director, Dr James Cullen.

In addition to Leonard and Dorsey Baynham, whom I can never thank enough for their kindness and hospitality, I am grateful to Leonard's daughters, Cynthia, Daphne and Meredith, for sharing their mementos of Blaikie with me. Cynthia, in particular, has kindly allowed me to use and photograph the diaries and all the Blaikie material in her possession. To Rose and Matthew Freeman and Eileen and Emmanuel Rimbert my thanks for their unstinting hospitality during my research in Cambridge and Paris respectively, with additional thanks to Emmanuel for refining my inelegant French in many an official letter.

I am indebted to Dr John Edmondson and Claire Smith of the Botany Department of the National Museums & Galleries on Merseyside who kindly collated Blaikie's alpine list with the Haller numbers on the list, and gave me information and advice on all things botanical, although I hasten to add that any botanical errors are my own.

To Dr Weber of the Landschaftsverband Rheinland I cannot sufficiently express my thanks for answering so patiently my many queries on Salm Dyck. In respect of Salm Dyck I would also like to thank Professor Dr Wilhelm Barthlott of the University of Bonn Botanic Institute, Countess Ursula Dohna and Count Metternich.

So many people and institutions deserve my thanks that it is impossible to mention more than a handful. In France, I would like to thank the staff of the Archives Nationales, particularly M. Emmanuel Rousseau and M. Jackie Plault, and those of the Bibliothèque Nationale de France. I am also grateful to Mme Roslyn Hurel and M. Christian Leribault at the Musée Carnavalet. My favourite small library in Paris is the Bibliothèque Historique de la Ville de Paris, whose staff have always been unfailingly helpful, as have those at the Bibliothèque du Muséum d'Histoire Naturelle. I am most grateful also to M. Bernard Chevallier and M. Eric Pautrel of the Musée National des Châteaux de Malmaison et Bois-Préau, Madame Marianne de Meyenbourg, Librarian at the Musée de l'Ile de France, M. Raymond Dartevelle and Mme Bénédicte Leconte of the Fondation de la Haute Banque, and Madame Anne de Thoisy, Conservateur of the Musée Municipale de la Toile de Jouy. The Directors and staff of the following Departmental Archives have been particularly helpful; the Archives Départementales de Calvados, the Archives des Yvelines, the Archives Départementales du Val de Marne, de la Seine et Marne, La Nièvre and the Archives de Loiret. Also the Archives Municipales of Chauny and those of Saint-Quentin.

In the UK I am indebted to the Director and staff of the University of Liverpool

Botanic Gardens, Ness, for allowing me to use the facilities of their library; to Mr
Peter Cunnington, the Curator, and Dr Hugh McAllister who have never complained
of having their work interrupted by elementary questions from a non-botanist, my
special thanks. At the Museum of Natural History, I would like to thank Dr Charles
Jarvis who first pointed out to me that one of Blaikie's alpine specimens still existed
in the A. E. Smith Collection.

My thanks are also due to Dr Robin Will and the staff of the Edinburgh Botanic
Garden Library, the Librarian of the Cambridge Botanic Gardens Library, the staff of
the Cambridge University Library, and the British Library, Marion Robertson of the
Midlothian Library Service, Christine McGilly of the Mitchell Library, Glasgow, Pat
Underwood and the staff of the Cheshire Libraries, Jane Kimber and the staff of the
Hammersmith and Fulham Archives, the late Louise M. Rose, Head of the Archive
Service, St Helier, Jersey, Mrs Margaret Eccleston and Mr Bob Lawford of the Alpine
Club Library and Mr B. D. Keefe of Dollond & Aitchison.

Of the many individuals who helped me in my long search for Blaikie, I would
especially like to thank Miss A. S. Cowper for her generosity in passing on to me her
own research on Blaikie and for her friendship and encouragement over the years.

I am indebted to M. le comte Jean-Marc de La Bédoyère, who allowed me the
freedom of Raray, and its archives, and to Madame Genevieve Mazel, archivist at
Raray, whose kindness in providing me with information and photographs from the
archives has been exceptional. My thanks to M. le Baron de Pontalba, for permitting
me to roam around Mont l'Evêque, and to my friend and fellow garden enthusiast
Gabrielle Joudiou, my companion there and on many a garden visit whose knowledge
and enthusiasm made the eighteenth-century gardens of Bagatelle and Saint-James
come to life for me even in the icy cold of a February day. I am grateful to Mme
Léonard de Maupeou who gave me information from treasured family sketch books
on Montcel and to the Duc de Rohan for information on his ancestor the Duchesse
de Rohan-Chabot. To Alain de la Guiche, descendant of Lauraguais, to Mme Jacqueline
Bougon who showed me round Le Raincy, M. Luc Degonville my guide at Manicamp,
and M. Pierre-Emile Renard who brought the ghosts of the Désert de Retz to life for
a group of friends one fine October Saturday. Rodolphe Trouilleux has not only helped
me find my way around various archives and libraries but from strolls with him and
his wife Catherine, I have painlessly learned the history of eighteenth-century Paris,
its streets and its buildings. I would also like to thank Mrs Christine Warren, Librarian
at the British Embassy, who showed me round the Embassy and its library, Mr Emil
Wittmer without whose help I might never have discovered some of these gardens,
Martine Constans, Conservateur en chef at the Archives Nationales, my guide and
mentor at the Archives who gave me the benefit of her own research on the Household
of Artois and M. J. C. Cappronnier, now at the Archives Nationales, who kindly
provided me with information on the Château of Caulaincourt. I am indebted also
to the Maison de France, the Comte Louis-Amédée de Moustier and the Comtesse
de Nicolay for allowing me access to their private archives.

I would like also to mention M. Gaston Briant of the Société Dunoise, M. François
Callais of the Société Historique de Compiègne, Mme Paulette Cavailler, Secrétaire

générale of the Société Historique et Archéologique de Corbeil, d'Etampes et de Hurepoix, Mme Monique Severin of the Fédération des Sociétés d'Histoire et d'Archéologie de l'Aisne, and Mr Allan Dumayne, historian of Southgate.

Others whose help and encouragement have smoothed my path are

Daniel Catan, Ray Desmond, M. Patrice Leperlier, Pat Marsh, Sigrid Peel, Olivia Ract-Madoux, Professor Forbes Robertson, Eliane Roux, Barbara Tchertoff, Michel Traversat, Miss E. J. Willson, and Jennifer Woods.

Finally to my husband, Douglas, who has uncomplainingly followed Blaikie's path over the years, and willingly taken on the task of cook, and proof reader, my loving thanks.

Introduction

I N 1931, some 94 years after his death, the diary of a forgotten Scottish botanist and gardener called Thomas Blaikie was published under the title of *Diary of a Scotch Gardener at the French Court* (ed. Francis Birrell).[1] The diary covered the years 1775 to 1792 and dealt with the months he had spent in 1775 as Britain's first professional plant collector in the Alps, together with his subsequent career as a gardener and landscaper to the French royal family in the period before the Revolution.

It revealed him as a man of undoubted charm, shrewd, frank, single-minded and with extraordinary physical stamina. Equally at home in peasant's hut or in the gardens of Versailles, he was, as one reviewer put it, 'one of those remarkable Scotsmen who not only make themselves at home anywhere but achieve success by sheer force of character'.[2] His idiosyncratic style of writing with its scattering of French and Scottish words and its bizarre spelling, together with the freshness of his descriptions, also gave his diary a naive quality leavened by a dry humour, which added to its charm. He was even hailed as 'a second Pepys'.[3]

Henri Montagnier, in an article, 'Thomas Blaikie and Michel-Gabriel Paccard' (*The Alpine Journal* May 1933), used his profound knowledge of Alpine history to illuminate the Swiss section of the diary, highlighting the originality and historical importance of Blaikie's account of his travels, both from the point of view of mountaineering and his descriptions of alpine life and landscape. In an indirect rebuttal of a review in *Le Figaro*[4] claiming that, as the diaries were not written day by day, their value as historical documents was reduced, Montagnier felt strongly that, although events described in the diaries may have been transcribed at a later date, the journal of this 'shrewd and conscientious' Scot was 'the record of what is probably the most remarkable series of expeditions in the Alps that has come down to us from the pen of a British traveller of the eighteenth century'.

Two eminent writers and historians, Eleanor Sinclair Rhodes and Peter Quennell, emphasised in their reviews[5] the diary's importance for the history of gardening in France and England and for the way it gave the curious flavour of a period when modern gardens were diversified by grottoes, temples and other exotic buildings. The distinguished French garden historian, Ernest de Ganay, did not share their view. He saw Blaikie as no more than a well-qualified artisan. His diary, a behind-the-scenes

---

1. Published by Routledge, Kegan & Paul.
2. *The Spectator*, 9 January 1932.
3. *The Boston Transcript*, 17 August 1932.
4. Eliane Engel, *Figaro*, 25 February 1932.
5. Peter Quennell, *New Statesman and Nation*, 9 January 1932; Eleanor Sinclair Rhodes, *The Spectator*, 9 January 1932.

glimpse of gardens hitherto described by their lordly owners or gardening amateurs, smacked of the tittle tattle of the servants' quarters.⁶ Blaikie's distinctively Scottish type of humour he saw as 'subtle malice'. Its target was often the French, and Blaikie's comments can scarcely have endeared him to French readers of the diary. This, combined with the way Blaikie gives us the inside information on his clients together with his uneducated style of writing, partly explains De Ganay's view. On the other hand, such attitudes are historic and not confined to France. They account for the way in which the part played by Blaikie and men like him – botanists, gardeners and nurserymen – in the creation of eighteenth-century gardens was largely overlooked in favour of the architects, painters and poets connected with them. The term 'gardener' in the eighteenth century covered a whole range of gardening activities from a 'Capability' Brown to a garden labourer who could neither read nor write. The term 'landscape gardener', which first came into general circulation in England around 1827, raised the status of those who planned, laid out and planted gardens in the nineteenth century. For lack of such a label, Blaikie ensured the respect of his later clients by calling himself *'ingénieur des jardins'*.⁷

In spite of the publication of *The Diary* in 1931 and of a French translation of the Swiss part of it in 1935, Blaikie once more faded into obscurity, although now at least he was credited with the plant introductions that had previously been attributed to his patrons Drs Pitcairn and Fothergill.⁸ It was almost another fifty years before he began to be considered worthy of more than a line or two in garden history publications.⁹ More recently the role played by this Scottish gardener in important French gardens has been acknowledged with greater frequency. In 1981 the Association Franco-Ecossaise initiated an exhibition held at the Musée Cernuschi in Paris that, for the first time, recognised the Scotsman's role at Monceau. Called *Grandes et Petites Heures du Parc Monceau*, it bore the sub-title, *Hommage à Thomas Blaikie* as *'jardinier écossais du duc d'Orléans'*. Finally, in 1997, in the introduction to the first complete French translation of *The Diary of a Scotch Gardener*, Blaikie has been recognised by a leading French garden historian, Mme Monique Mosser, as the most influential figure in the understanding of the art of gardening in France at the end of the 1770s.¹⁰

6. Ernest de Ganay, 'L'Architecte Bélanger et le jardinier Blaikie', *L'Architecture*, XLIV, 12 December 1931, pp. 445–54.
7. *Journal des champs*, unpublished diary of the Comtesse Ambroisine de La Bédoyère, refers to Blaikie as *'ingénieur Anglais'*, Raray, Private Archive.
8. Dr William Pitcairn (1711–1791). President of the Royal College of Physicians in 1775 and Dr John Fothergill (1712–1780). A Quaker philanthropist and a highly successful physician, Dr Fothergill was probably the leading amateur botanist of his day. See Chapter 2, notes 52, 53.
9. William Howard Adams, *The French Garden 1500–1800* (London, 1979). Christopher Thacker, *The History of Gardens* (London, 1979).
10. Janine Barrier and Monique Mosser, *Sur les terres d'un jardinier, journal de voyages 1775–1792* (Besançon, 1997), Introduction, p. 31. For a discussion of the part played by 'gardeners' in the eighteenth-century landscape garden, see Douglas Chambers, *The Planters of the English Landscape Garden* (Yale, 1993).

When editing Blaikie's diary, Francis Birrell also had access to a 'considerable quantity' of Blaikie's papers.[11] However, these and Blaikie's account book, together with his claims against the French government after 1815, proved profoundly uninteresting to Birrell. Consequently, he concluded that 'for us and for him his real life ended with the Revolution'. In the absence of the papers and diaries which have long been presumed lost, this judgement became received wisdom.

I first heard the name of *le Sieur Blaikie* in 1991 during a lecture at the château of Bagatelle just outside Paris and as a Scot was intrigued by what I heard. *The Diary of a Scotch Gardener*, although deeply interesting, left a number of unanswered questions. What was Blaikie's background? Where did he train? How could I find out more about the part he played in the gardens mentioned in the diary? What did happen to him after the Revolution?

In his Introduction, Francis Birrell stated that the diary which he edited was in the possession of a Mrs Baynham of Tonbridge. Blaikie's wife died in Paris in 1850 and left her personal belongings, including the diaries, papers, furniture paintings and various *objets de vertu*, to her friend Dr Burnett through whom they were eventually passed on to Mrs Baynham. Here, therefore was the obvious starting point of my search. Mrs Baynham had died in 1935, as had Francis Birrell, and there was no trace of the whereabouts of the legacy. However, with perseverance and a good deal of luck, I finally made contact with Colonel Brian Baynham who very kindly put me in touch with his cousin Leonard, Mrs Baynham's elder son, living in America, to whom Mrs Baynham had bequeathed the Blaikie legacy. Leonard and Dorsey, his wife, invited me to America to see Blaikie's papers and some of Blaikie's belongings, and I shall never forget their warmth and hospitality. Sadly, the diary, which apparently had been mislaid, still eluded me and it was not until 1997 that, thanks to Cynthia Baynham Geerstema, Leonard's daughter, I eventually held the two books of the diary and Blaikie's account book in my hands.

Thomas Blaikie wrote his diaries in two, cream-coloured, vellum-bound notebooks. The first volume, begun on 13 April 1775, contains 274 pages of which 190 are devoted to his eight months in Switzerland. It carries on its spine the handwritten title 'Blaikie's Travels'. The second begins in October 1781. A number of pages have been torn out at the beginning of volume two and the diary ends after only 91 pages in August 1792. The back of this notebook has been used to jot down his personal expenses during his early years in France. Nowhere in his private papers does he explain why he kept his diary but it seems that during the years 1777 to around 1781, Blaikie retained the habit, required of him during his period as a botanical collector, of recording, more or less day by day, the progress of his work at Bagatelle and elsewhere. From 1783 onwards, he condenses, not always accurately, a whole year's events without specific dates and, towards the end of his diary, seems to rely entirely on random recollections. The major Revolutionary events of 1789–92 are evidently seared into his memory and, even if recalled at a distance in time, remain as vivid as the day he experienced them.

---

11. *The Diary of a Scotch Gardener*, Introduction, p. 17.

Perhaps he felt impelled to write about these experiences or more likely was asked by his family and friends to record them.

Blaikie's spelling, and his rather tortured syntax, occasionally makes the sense almost impenetrable. It sometimes distracts the reader and has led to Blaikie's being dismissed, wrongly, as an illiterate. A fresh transcription of the original diary produced even more spelling idiosyncrasies than those in the Birrell edition and varied from it in one important respect: Blaikie's original is virtually without punctuation, while the Birrell edition makes extensive use of semi-colons to clarify the text. Faced with the dilemma of whether to sacrifice some of the charm of the original in the interest of accessibility, I reluctantly decided that since the diary has already been published in nearly its original form, I would modernise the spelling while conserving words that are specifically French. The franglais I have treated as English. The only Scottish words that Blaikie used were *doun* for down and *toun* for town. I have also modified slightly Blaikie's almost indiscriminate use of capitals. As to punctuation, I have kept what there is of Blaikie's, and otherwise punctuated to give my own understanding of the text.

There is also the question of the date of Blaikie's birth. Until 1752 Britain adhered to the Julian or Old Style Calendar, which counted the beginning of the year as 25 March not 1 January. As France and almost all of Europe had adopted the New Style or Gregorian Calendar much earlier, and the birth dates of the French people mentioned in this biography are calculated by the New Style Calendar, I have reckoned Blaikie's birth date according to it as well.

Despite Birrell's dismissal of Blaikie's life after the Revolution, the accounts revealed that Blaikie had enjoyed a distinguished career during the Napoleonic period and that, until two or three years before his death, he continued to design gardens for the French nobility. Most of the 70 or so gardens mentioned in his accounts were situated to the north of Paris and were destroyed in the course of the First World War or earlier. Others have disappeared in later developments. Consequently, it is difficult to assess Blaikie's work since, of the large gardens, only Schloss Dyck near Düsseldorf remains to some extent as he conceived it. Nevertheless, I have tried to summarise what was distinctive about his style in the last chapter. It would have been a lifetime's task to study more than a handful of the gardens mentioned but I hope that this book will prove a basis for further research on French gardens and on Blaikie himself.

CHAPTER I

The Fete at Bagatelle

' THE 20 May, the Count gave a great fete at Bagatelle to the King and Queen and the court, which was at this time at La Muette. Here was a *Superbe* Band of Musick placed upon a scaffold on a thicket of trees which, as the company walked round to see the Gardens, played, which, with the echo of the trees, made an enchanting effect. And in different parts of the wood was Booths made of the Branches of trees in which there were actors who acted different pieces agreeable to the scene. On the further side towards Longchamp, there was erected a *pyramide* by which was a Marble tomb. This part of the wood being newly taken in to the grounds, there remained the wall of the Bois de Boulogne and, to *rendre* this scene more agreeable, Mr Bélanger had an invention which made a singular effect by undermining the wall on the outside and placing people with ropes to pull the wall down at a word. At this *pyramide* there was an *acteur* who acted the part of a magician, who asked their Majesties how they liked the Gardens and what a beautiful *vue* there was towards the plain if that wall did not obstruct it, but that their Majesties need only give the word that he with his enchanting wand would make that wall disappear. The Queen, not knowing, told him with a laugh, "Very well I should wish to see it disappear," and in the instant, the signal was given and above 200 yards, opposite where the company stood, fell flat to the ground, which surprised them all.' [1]

The fete that Thomas Blaikie described with naive pleasure in his diary was held in May 1780 for Marie Antoinette, Queen of France, by her brother-in-law, the Comte d'Artois, Louis XVI's youngest brother. The setting was the garden of Bagatelle, still in the process of being laid out around a small, neo-classical villa [2] in the Bois de Boulogne, as a country retreat and hunting lodge near Paris for the 22-year-old Count.

The new building owed its existence to a famous wager of 100,000 livres [3] between the Count and Marie Antoinette that the prince could demolish the old house on this small estate and build another one in 64 days before the Court returned from its sojourn at Fontainebleau in November 1777. [4] Under the direction of his principal

---

1. Diary, 20 May 1780.
2. 'Villa' in the eighteenth-century sense means a Palladian house, of relatively small proportions, surrounded by its estate, in the countryside but within a few miles of a town.
3. Approximately £44,000. 10 livres equalled 8s. 9d. according to Arthur Young, *Travels during the years 1787, 1788 and 1789 etc.* (Bury St Edmunds, 1792; 2nd edn, 1794; ed. Constantia Maxwell Cambridge, 1929).
4. Bachaumont Louis, Petit de, *Mémoires secrets pour servir à l'histoire de la République des lettres en France, depuis MDCCLXII jusqu'à nos jours, ou Journal d'un Observateur* (London, 1780), vol. X, p. 259 (22 October 1777).

architect, François-Joseph Bélanger,[5] at least 800 men worked in shifts day and night by the light of lamps, to ensure that the Count won his bet. The shortages and delays that bedevil most building projects were not a problem. Carts making their way in and out of the city, laden with building materials for other owners, were seized and brought to Bagatelle by the Swiss guard, whose Commander-in-Chief was Artois. The people subjected to this high-handed treatment were compensated but, naturally, they were aggrieved.[6] Bélanger worked fast, but he did not sacrifice quality to speed. The list of the craftsmen and artists he employed was a roll call of the outstanding artists of the period: painters, sculptors, gilders, cabinet makers, clock-makers, musical instrument makers and decorators. The building was finished on time and was acclaimed a masterpiece.

Before the dust of the construction work had settled, Bélanger created a small formal French garden reached by a terrace behind the house. The rest of the park, including new ground to be taken from the Bois de Boulogne, was to be laid out as an informal English garden, a green and leafy glade through which to approach the house, and the fashionable choice for a generation of wealthy European landowners newly awakened to the beauties of nature. Bélanger engaged Thomas Blaikie to make the English garden at Bagatelle in December 1778; hence the Scot's attendance on the day of the long-postponed fete to celebrate the completion of the project. The garden Blaikie had constructed, as yet unfinished, had been transformed, as if by sleight of hand, into a fairy landscape. Invisible musicians played ethereal music and, as dusk fell, the glimmer of thousands of lanterns gilded the green branches of the trees.

The day of the fete had dawned fine with a light breeze.[7] Artois waited at the foot of the steps in front of the pavilion to greet his royal visitors and conduct them round his small château. Deeply competitive by nature, he had been determined that in its modernity of architectural style and its decorative refinement his *'folie'* [8] would outshine those of his more wealthy rivals.[9] Satisfied that his object had been achieved, this was a moment for self congratulation. Behind him, the façade with its air of elegant restraint gave nothing away of the luxuriously furnished interior. His bedroom, for example, detailed in a series of water colour drawings by Bélanger, was decorated as a canopied campaign tent where the theme was military. Yet it was no austerely martial room any more than its owner, although Commander in chief of the Artillery, was a great warrior. The silk tented walls and ceiling were of a tender blue and white, picked out with gold. Deep cushions filled the armchairs, and the dressing table, with its exquisite bottles and flasks, worked in gold, was covered with the finest lace. The Comte was a libertine, and the most notorious room at Bagatelle was fitted between

5. François Joseph Bélanger (1744–1818).
6. Bachaumont, vol. X, p. 281 (18 November 1777).
7. *Journal de Paris*, 23 May 1780, the date usually given for this fête.
8. A corruption of *feuillé* or leafy and the generic name for a host of little country retreats around the capital. Later, the immense sums spent on these buildings justified the modern meaning of the word.
9. In particular that of his cousin, the Duc de Chartres, at Monceau. For others see *De Bagatelle à Monceau, 1778–1978: les Folies du XVIIIe siècle à Paris*, exhibition catalogue, 1978.

the ground and first floor with access from his bedroom and with a window overlooking the salon below. The *boudoir de l'entresol*, as it was called, was painted in '*rose tendre*'. It was decorated with '*ornements de fantaisie*', described as '*peu orthodoxe*' in a memoir of the period,[10] where there is also a reference to the mirrors which supposedly lined its walls, ceiling and floor.[11] To afford the prince privacy, and relief from the constant presence of servants and attendants, his staff was housed in the *Pavilion des Pages*, a building joined by a covered archway to the identically designed *Communs* or domestic quarters and offices, the whole serving as a monumental entrance through which the carriages with their royal cargo would reach the *cour d'honneur* in front of the château. The food was brought by underground passage from the kitchens to the dining room.

During the Ball that evening, Blaikie was free to enter the house. The domed, circular salon, its walls decorated with arabesques inspired by the frescoes of Pompeii, its windows opening on to the terrace that overlooked the little formal garden, was the setting for the dance. But dancing and theatricals, the most popular pastimes at court held no appeal for the ungainly King. Happier out of doors than at a ball, he had walked over that morning on foot from his hunting lodge nearby at La Muette and watched indulgently as, in a tent in the garden, Artois and the Queen entertained their guests before dinner with *Rose et Colas*, a comic opera by Sedaine. Marie Antoinette had played the soubrette, Rose, and Artois had acted the part of Colas, the simple country swain, while the pretty Duchesse de Polignac and one or two others of the Queen's closest friends filled the supporting roles. That night, as the Queen moved with distinctive grace in the dance, Blaikie found himself a corner in the billiard room to watch the King playing billiards at half a crown a game and reflected with native dryness that, 'at this rate he could never ruin his fortune'. The final event of the celebration was a magnificent display of fireworks. Cascades of light threw the pavilion, the pyramid and the gardens into momentary relief against the illuminated sky, the trees and copses a dark mass in the background. Then, the spectacle over, the garden was left to Blaikie who noted with Presbyterian approval in his diary that 'this fete was conducted with great order and decorum with mirth'.[12]

Apart from his enjoyment of the fete itself, Blaikie had two particular reasons for feeling happy that day. For the last eighteen months he had thrown himself into the making of the garden with little reward in the way of encouragement and now, for the first time, he enjoyed the pleasure of hearing his work praised by a large number of people. His second cause for gratification was that 'this day I was presented to the King and Queen as Inspector of the Count's Gardens, who complimented me upon what I had already done'.

10. Theibault, General, Baron P., *Mémoires* (Paris, 1894). In spite of what he writes, the floor, according to the records (AN., R1 332) were of oak. Quoted in Martine Constans, 'Le château du comte d'Artois' p. 74 in *Bagatelle dans ses jardins* (Paris, 1997).

11. See Martine Constans, p. 74. and Christian Baulez, 'L'Ameublement du comte d'Artois', p. 96, in *Bagatelle dans ses jardins* (Paris, 1997).

12. Blaikie's testimony counters the often scurrilous suggestions about the behaviour of the Queen and her coterie, at the fetes held here and at the Petit Trianon.

At the time of the inaugural fete at Bagatelle, Blaikie had been in France for three and a half years. The garden's success was to make him the most fashionable garden designer in France during the last golden days of the Ancien Régime when, hand in hand with anglomania, garden mania flourished. Women wore hats covered with blooms. They carried fans depicting garden scenes, while the buttons on a man's frock-coat might be painted with views of his garden. Almost every rich aristocrat fancied himself as a botanist, importing rare plants to ornament his hothouses and acquiring choice American evergreens as trophies to display in his park. Fortunes were thrown away and financiers bankrupted themselves in pursuit of the perfect garden. Blaikie's employment at Bagatelle came at an opportune moment but he was not an opportunist. To understand how he came to be there we have to turn to a very different and apparently unlikely world, the village of Corstorphine, three miles west of Edinburgh in the year 1751.

CHAPTER 2

Corstorphine to London

I N 1826, the year after Thomas Blaikie's last visit to his birthplace, Sir Walter Scott published his *Provincial Antiquities and Picturesque Scenery of Scotland*. For it he commissioned a painting of the view of Edinburgh from Corstorphine Hill, which he described as 'one of the most magnificent in the neighbourhood of Edinburgh'.[1] To the north across the Firth of Forth lay the coastline of Fife, to the east the dramatic skyline of Edinburgh, and below to the south west the picturesque village of Corstorphine with its medieval church and fifteenth-century fortified castle. Thomas Blaikie's father owned a market garden of four and a half acres on the favourable southfacing slope of Corstorphine Hill where Blaikie was born on 2 March 1751.

Each part of the hill had its own character; gentle slopes to the south and west, precipitate to the east, and rising in a crested ridge to the north. This part was heavily wooded with ash, horsechestnut, oak, birch, holly, rowan and Scots pine, the habitat of birds as rare as the blackcock[2] and a shelter for small wild animals. Below, in complete contrast to the wildness of the hillside, lay fields of wheat, gentlemen's estates with ordered gardens and cherry orchards, farms, nurseries and market gardens, all typical of the prosperous agricultural county of Midlothian whose landlords had been agricultural improvers since the beginning of the eighteenth century.[3] The nurseries around Corstorphine supplied imps (tree grafts) and other plants for the surrounding areas, and its market gardens provided Edinburgh with fruit, green vegetables and the new crop, potatoes.[4]

The mid eighteenth century, after the Jacobite defeat at Culloden, was a period of burgeoning affluence in the Scottish Lowlands and Edinburgh's Old Town was bursting at the seams. Blaikie's father was particularly well placed to provide the fast growing and increasingly prosperous population with fruit and vegetables. The

---

1. Rev. John Thomson of Duddingston, *View of Edinburgh from Corstorphine Hill*, painted for and engraved for inclusion in Sir Walter Scott's *Provincial Antiquities and Picturesque Scenery of Scotland* Edinburgh, 1826. (Quoted in A. S. Cowper, *Corstorphine and Roundabout* Part 2 p. 98.) Sir J. Sinclair, *The Statistical Account of Scotland* (Edinburgh, 1791–92), vol. XIV, p. 447 also praises the beauty of the area.
2. Cowper, Part 2, p. 97.
3. Priscilla Minay, 'Early Improvements in the Eighteenth Century Lothians' in *Bulletin of the Scottish Georgian Society* 1973, vol. 2. *Statistical Account*, vol. XIV, p. 452.
4. R. N. Salaman, *The History and Social Influence of the Potato* (Cambridge, 1949), p 390. See also p. 392, quoted in Smout T. C., *A Social History of Scotland* p. 270, and H. Arnott, *History of Edinburgh* (Edinburgh, 1779), p. 347. *Statistical Account*, vol. XIV, p. 452 confirms that particular attention was paid to the raising of potatoes in Corstorphine. The potato did not became a common vegetable in France until after the Revolution and Blaikie would become one of its promoters.

turnpike road skirted the foot of his small holding and ran from Edinburgh by the Haymarket and Roseburn towards Glasgow.[5] Then, it was little more than a rough track scarcely passable by carriage in winter, when streams running off the hillside turned it into a quagmire and icy weather left it stiff and rutted. Today it is the main A8/M8 from Edinburgh to Glasgow and the village of Corstorphine, once so distinct from the city, has been absorbed by its suburbs.

For a while, during the eighteenth century, Corstorphine was a fashionable watering place visited for the healing properties of its mineral well. The sick were sent there to get 'the benefite of the waters', the air being kept pure by the strong south and south-west winds. In Edinburgh, 10 per cent of the adult population died of smallpox, and infant mortality from the disease was as high as 20 per cent. Crowding and lack of hygiene meant that epidemic diseases were rife in the city, but were never experienced in virulent form at Corstorphine.[6] In the years before the building of the New Town, the rising merchant and professional classes looked to the countryside as an escape from the teeming, insanitary tenements of the old city. At the same time, the purchase of a country estate satisfied their social ambitions. Thomas Blaikie senior's first post was as gardener to just such a man, John Dickie, an Edinburgh merchant and later Accountant General of Excise.[7] In 1721, Dickie purchased most of the south facing slope of Corstorphine Hill. In 1740[8] he sold four and a half acres together with a house and outbuildings on the eastern edge of his estate to an Edinburgh merchant, John Inglis. In 1744 Inglis conveyed the small property to Dickie's gardener, Thomas Blaikie, who started a market garden there.[9] How Blaikie senior had sufficient savings to buy the property, which was first known as Corstorphine Hill, and later Pinkhill, remains a mystery. As a gardener the most he could have earned in a year was £18 with perhaps a peck of meal weekly and one pair of shoes, although occasionally a landowner might cede some land to his gardener in lieu of wages. That the purchase took place so soon after his marriage in 1743 suggests that his wife may have brought a small inheritance with her and that Inglis, faced with a cash crisis, sold the property he had so recently acquired, at a bargain price.

Thomas married Janet Fiddes, a fellow servant at Dickie's, at Corstorphine Church in 1743. She was probably the Janet Fiddes born in 1719 in the neighbouring village of Gogar, one of the three daughters of the Gogar miller, Robert Fiddes, whose tombstone at Gogar bears the admonitory epitaph, *My Glass is run/Yours is running Be/Feared to Sin for Iud/gements Coming.*

Four children are recorded in the Parish register as having been born to the couple. Their eldest, John, was baptised in 1744 and two daughters, Agnes and Isabel, followed

---

5. Turnpike roads were introduced around 1713 in the Edinburgh area.
6. *Statistical Account*, vol. XIV, Corstorphine, p. 462. *New Statistical Account of Scotland*, vol. 1, p. 207, in which the minister of Corstorphine, the Rev. David Horne, wrote in 1839 'when the cholera was prevalent in this country there were no cases in the village of Corstorphine'.
7. A. S. Cowper, Part 2, p. 89.
8. Scottish Record Office, B22/8/212.
9. *Ibid.*

in 1746 and 1748. Their last child, Thomas, was born on 2 March 1751 and baptised six days later.[10]

To be a landowner, feuar of Corstorphine Hill,[11] enhanced the father's social standing but the reality of the gardener's existence was plain living and unremitting toil, a way of life reinforced by the teaching of the Presbyterian church, which governed every aspect of the people's moral life. Its insistence on habits of self discipline, frugality and hard work, together with its insistence on the importance of universal education through parish schools, formed the Scottish lowland character and as a by-product equipped its flock to take advantage of the emerging economic opportunities in the second half of the eighteenth century.[12]

Every member of the Blaikie family shared in the work of the household and the gardens. It was a hard life in a harsh climate and few concessions were made to childhood.[13] From an early age, Thomas would have been expected to be up at dawn and help pick the crops in season. Later, school would take second place to his work in the market garden or hay-making for neighbours. It was a pattern familiar in rural areas until the twentieth century. Indulgence at home or demonstrations of affection within the family were rare. Parents and schoolmasters alike brought up children on the principle of 'Spare the rod and spoil the child'. Living conditions were over-crowded and primitive, the Blaikies' original house probably no more than a but and ben [single storey house with two rooms], and the stream their washing place. But, at least the Blaikie children could escape to the freedom of the hillside with its rocks and copses, its wild flowers and Scots pines and, having had the good fortune to survive infancy, they grew up strong and healthy, free from the infection of the city, its stench and its contaminated water supplies.[14]

A childhood spent in a setting remarkable for its beauty[15] gave Blaikie an intrinsic feeling for natural scenery. Later, he wrote in his diary that Nature was the key to creating a beautiful garden and that every place possessed natural beauties which the seeing eye could develop.[16] His later travels in Switzerland and his exposure to the great parks and gardens of England and France would complete his education as a gardener but his love of nature and his interest in agriculture was rooted in the world of his childhood.

---

10. OPR 678 Corstorphine, which gives both the date of his birth and the date of his christening.
11. Scots legal term for the owner of the land. The phrase appears as his father's occupation on Blaikie's baptismal record but not on those of his older siblings.
12. Smout, pp. 97–9.
13. 'Children ... may now at an age not very advanced, be made useful, and contribute assistance to their parents for supporting them, without impairing their vigour, or stinting their growth.' *Statistical Account*, vol. XIV, pp. 459–60.
14. As late as 1789, Sir Francis Burdett in a letter to his aunt described Paris as 'the most ill-contrived, ill-built, dirty, stinking Town that can possibly be imagined; as for the inhabitants they are ten times more nasty than the inhabitants of Edinburgh'. Thompson, *English Witnesses of the French Revolution* (Oxford, 1938).
15. *Statistical Account*, p. 447.
16. Diary, undated entry 1785/86.

Corstorphine offered another important advantage. It had a parish school.[17] Education was not compulsory but moral and social pressures ensured that most children would attend. No records of the pupils exist but two pieces of evidence suggest that Blaikie attended it. The first relates to a contemporary of Blaikie's, Andrew Fyfe (1752–1824). Fyfe attended the parish school and later became a loved and eccentric figure in the University Medical School. (He was one of the last people in Edinburgh to wear the pigtail.) [18] As dissector in the department of Anatomy, he served two generations of professors of the same family, the Munroes. All called Andrew, they held the Chair of Anatomy for three generations in succession from 1720 to 1846. In addition, Fyfe wrote numerous medical text books. His own son, also Andrew, became Professor of Chemistry at Aberdeen. In his later years, through Blaikie's family,[19] he enquired after Blaikie as an old school friend, and when he died in 1824, Blaikie's nephew wrote to inform his uncle. The second indication that Blaikie had a parish education appears in his Diary when he describes how he was mistaken for an American spy and imprisoned briefly in Jersey in June 1777. The chief surgeon on the island visited him and vouched for him on the grounds that they had been to school together. Blaikie's father could not have paid for private schooling and the only alternative was the parish school where the children of the professional classes and even the gentry sat side by side.[20]

All ages were taught together in the same room. Attendance was irregular, learning was by rote and the brutal schoolmaster was a common figure in the memoirs of the period. The tawse, a peculiarly Scottish instrument of punishment known to generations of the nation's schoolchildren, was liberally used as a teaching aid.[21] School began at 9 each morning. It finished at 5 in the summer, and 2 o'clock in the winter. From April to October the children were allowed two breaks of an hour in the day but in winter, when school finished earlier, only one hour's respite from lessons was permitted. Yet, in spite of its drawbacks, the system produced a literate and often intellectually curious working class with a love of reading.

Fetes, pageants or colourful religious displays were outside their experience. Public opportunities for childish amusements or high spirits were rare. The Church condemned the celebration of holy days as smacking of papistry; only Candlemas (2 February) was traditionally a holiday. That day the children brought gifts to school

17. The city of Edinburgh had no parish schools (Smout, pp. 451, 468 and 469). A. Law, *Education in Edinburgh in the 18th Century* (London, 1965), p. 29.
18. Sir Robert Christison, *The Life of Sir Robert Christison*, 2 vols (1885), vol. 2, p. 68; and John Struthers, *Historical Sketch of the Edinburgh Anatomical School* (Edinburgh, 1869). I would like to thank Miss Janet Ferguson for drawing my attention to these accounts.
19. Letters from Blaikie's relatives. Blaikie Papers, Private Archive.
20. Smout, p. 290.
21. The tawse was a thick leather belt or strap, fringed at the striking end. For an account of the rigours of a parish school education see Thomas Somerville, *My Own Life and Times* (Edinburgh, 1861), p. 347. The Scottish judge, Henry Cockburn (1779–1854) in *Henry Cockburn. Memorials of His Time* (Edinburgh, 1856), p. 4, describing his years at the Edinburgh High School writes, 'Out of the whole four years of my attendance there were probably not ten days in which I was not flogged at least once'.

for the schoolmaster who, after receiving the geese and hens and coins they offered him, would declare a holiday. The pupils then paraded the streets in procession with their 'king' or 'queen', the giver of the most valuable gift! The celebrations finished with the 'bleeze', a large bonfire. On Shrove Tuesday, the master was able to increase his income by holding cock fights, a sport popular with all classes in Scotland during the eighteenth century.[22] From Blaikie's comments subsequently about cock fighting at Vincennes,[23] he detested the brutal contest. His strong antipathy to it may signal an underlying disgust with the harsh regime of his schoolmasters and explain how such an intelligent child escaped the system that might have given him a university education.

Corstorphine records show that Blaikie's first schoolmaster was a young man called Ralph Drummond. Both he and his successor Alexander Bannatyne were Divinity students, and both taught Latin, writing, arithmetic and English to the children of Corstorphine. The fees were a crown per quarter for Latin, half a crown for writing or arithmetic and two shillings sterling for English.[24] No examples of the handwriting of Thomas's brother, John, survive but from his sisters' few remaining letters,[25] it is clear that the Blaikie sisters were almost illiterate. Only two letters of Agnes's still exist and, for the most part, Isabel relied on her children to write for her, so it seems that she, in common with most girls, received a more rudimentary education than her brother.

The nucleus of the Corstorphine Blaikie knew survives today; the medieval parish kirk that looked like 'three or four little ones put together',[26] with its walls of grey stone and its slabbed roof, beneath which the tombs of knights in armour are a reminder of its Catholic, collegiate past; the restored building in the High Street that housed the local inn and the tall, harled house called the Dower House. The castle was an important landmark in Blaikie's day. It stood on a headland between two lochs, and was already uninhabited by the mid eighteenth century and beginning its slow decay. The lochs have long been drained and the castle's 100 ft. long curtain walls with a round tower in each corner have disappeared completely. It is commemorated now only in a street name. Today, all that remains of the Corstorphine castle dependencies is the restored circular dovecot. Close to it, on what was once the shore of the loch, stood, until recently, another well known landmark, an ancient sycamore tree.[27] Fifty five feet tall with a girth of twelve and a half feet, it was the sole survivor of an avenue of trees planted as an approach to the castle in the sixteenth century. Beneath its boughs, in 1679, a young woman stabbed and killed the laird, who was both her uncle and her unfaithful lover, and the father of her child. She was hanged for her crime and was said to haunt the tree in the white robe she wore for her execution. In 1795 the Corstorphine sycamore was described as being 'the largest in

22. See Smout, opp. p. 249.
23. Diary, Saturday 15 April 1780.
24. A. S. Cowper, Part 1, p. 66.
25. Blaikie Papers.
26. Robert Southey, *Journal of a Tour in Scotland in 1819* (London, 1829).
27. It survived until 26 December 1998 when it was split in two by a 90 m.p.h. gale and its demise was lamented in the *Scotsman*, the *Edinburgh Evening News* of the same date and *The Times*, 31 December 1998.

Scotland, which in the end of May and beginning of June exhibits an appearance of the most striking beauty'.[28] Certainly, its magnificent height and spread together with the green-gold shimmer of its young leaves gave pleasure to generations of Edinburgh people. It was remarkable also as a unique subspecies of Acer, *Acer pseudoplantanus corstorphinensis*. Perhaps this noble tree inspired Blaikie's love of trees and led him to observe and describe them till the end of his life.[29]

At what age Blaikie left the parish school and what he did afterwards are not known. All instruction at University was in Latin and youths from the parish schools sometimes spent a preliminary year or two at the High School to improve their proficiency in the language, but Blaikie's name does not appear in the school lists. There is no record of his attendance at university either. From his spelling and syntax, bizarre even for the times, one has to conclude that his education was limited. He was certainly intelligent. His diary demonstrates that his curiosity embraced agricultural improvement, the structure of rocks, botany and poetry[30] and he learnt French quickly. His writing is vivid and funny and full of direct observation. Its rhythms, at least in the early part of the diary, are Scottish and throughout its pages he uses the Scottish words 'doun' and 'toun' for 'down' and 'town', reflecting the fact that, although the King James Bible would have been preached to him from the pulpit and used to teach him English at school, he would have spoken Scots, the common language amongst ordinary people.

Had he been considered 'a lad o' pairts', a Latin scholar and good material for the ministry, the Church would have financed his university career, or a local patron might have funded him. The neighbouring parish of Kirkliston produced a Professor of Greek at Edinburgh University in Andrew Dalzel (1742–1806) and a successful diplomat and ambassador in Robert Liston (1742–1836), later Sir Robert. Dalzel, the son of a carpenter, was adopted by his uncle, a minister, and sent to the university as preparation for the ministry. Liston, son of a tenant farmer, had a patron in the Earl of Lauderdale. Without such support, a man of Blaikie's father's resources would have been unable to pay the fees of £25 per year.

That is not to say, however, that Blaikie's education stopped when he left the parish school. Although no records have been found of the next few years of his life, he would have been apprenticed about the age of eleven as a gardener in Edinburgh.[31] By the

---

28. *Statistical Account*, vol. 14, pp. 447–8.
29. J. C. Loudon, *Arboretum et Fruticetum* (London, 1838). Loudon sent out over 3000 question-naires seeking information on the largest or oldest trees of each genus grown in Europe. Blaikie was among his correspondents and supplied him with descriptions and measure-ments mostly of trees he himself had planted in the past 40 or so years.
30. He left a collection of books at his death, a number of which were poetry books. Amongst them were Pope's translation of the *Illiad* and James Macpherson's *Ossian*, two of the most influential poems of the eighteenth century. Also, the strong impression certain Alpine views made on him led him to quote two poetic extracts in his diary record of 10 June and 27 July 1775, see pp. 48, 59. I have been unable to identify either of these quotations.
31. His name does not appear in apprenticeship records held at the Guildhall Library, London. I am grateful to the librarian for this information.

time of his expedition to the Alps, he was almost certainly a master gardener and a proficient botanist. He mentions in his diary an uncle in Southgate, to whom it is possible he might have been sent in his youth, but no one by the name of Blaikie or Fiddes appears in the surviving Southgate records of the time.[32] One strong possibility is that he was employed at the new Edinburgh Botanic Garden, founded in 1763 by Dr John Hope of Edinburgh University.[33] Hope (1725–1786) was one of the secondary figures of the remarkable Scottish Enlightenment which gave giants like Hume and Adam Smith to the world. Doctor of Physic and Professor of Botany and Medicine at Edinburgh, he devoted his life to the foundation and development of an outstanding botanical garden at Edinburgh. He was responsible for the introduction of many new plants to Scotland and as a man was respected for his goodness of heart.[34]

There are three elements in the diary which suggest employment at the Edinburgh Botanic Garden and another two in Blaikie's private papers seem to bear them out. The first element in the diary is his familiarity with different systems of botanical nomenclature.

Today, when Linnaeus's binomial system [35] is universally followed, it is difficult to understand the passions which methods of identifying and naming plants aroused in the eighteenth century when the almost daily discovery of new plants made the introduction of a foolproof method of identifying and classifying them a matter of urgency. Every major botanist swore by his own system and each had his own supporters. Most medical schools, however, laid out their gardens according to the medicinal uses of plants without reference to any particular system of identification. At Edinburgh, Professor John Hope was one of Linnaeus's most ardent followers. He made an early decision to abandon the apothecary style of botanical garden and to set out the beds in his botanical school according to Linnaeus's system. Only Cambridge followed a similar course at such an early date. His determination to adopt this new type of botanical school resulted from a visit he had paid in 1749 to the King's Garden

---

32. My thanks to Mr Alan Dumayne of Southgate for this information.

33. John Hope (1725–86). Scottish botanist and FRS. For an account of his life see A. G. Morton, *John Hope 1725–1786 Scottish Botanist* (Edinburgh Botanic Garden Trust, 1986).

34. Edinburgh Royal Botanic Gardens Library. Professor Daniel Rutherford (1749–1819), *Miscellaneous papers and correspondence*. Contains a letter from the most famous of Hope's protégés, Archibald Menzies written to Hope's successor, Rutherford, in 1789. It describes Hope as 'my best and only friend whose sincere attachment and disinterested kindness towards me I shall ever venerate with a grateful remembrance'.

35. Carl von Linné or Linnaeus (1707–1778). Professor of Botany at the Swedish university of Uppsala is considered the founder of modern botany since he invented the system of nomenclature we use today of identifying plants by a single generic or 'family' name followed by a single specific name. In his *Species Plantarum* published in 1753, he classified plants by their 'sexual' characteristics, dividing them into 24 classes according to their number of stamens. Each class was subdivided into orders according to the number of pistils. It was objected to as an artificial method of identifying plants by those who favoured more 'natural' systems of classification and has gradually given way to identification by other characters. At the time, it represented a breakthrough in the search for a universal system.

in Paris (today's *Jardin des Plantes*) where he had seen the plants laid out according to the system of the French botanist, Tournefort.[36] The clarity of the Linnaean system made it his choice for Edinburgh but one of the characteristics of Hope's teaching was the way in which he encouraged his students to become familiar with other more 'natural' ways of categorising plants.[37]

It is his familiarity with at least three systems of identifying and naming plants which makes it likely that Blaikie had been a student gardener at Edinburgh. From his diary we learn that he often passed his free time in the evenings during his months in Switzerland 'translating' the names of plants from the Linnaean system to Haller's.[38] Blaikie's field guide on his Swiss journey was an abridged version of Haller's *History of the Plants of Switzerland*.[39] It contained a brief description of each plant in Latin but very rarely the Linnaean name. Instead, Haller gave each plant an identifying number, useful shorthand in communicating with Swiss botanists and collectors. Later on in the diary we find him in the company of his friend, Albert-Henry Gosse, a young bookseller in Geneva, pouring over the works of Jacquin, an Austrian botanist, whose system of describing plants was different from the other two.[40] Blaikie appears to have no difficulty with this system or that of the French botanists, Jussieu and Adanson.[41]

In the Edinburgh Botanic Gardens Library is a small, green, leather-bound notebook containing a Linnean catalogue of the plants in the *Jardin du Roi* in Paris. It is written in Blaikie's hand, signed by him, and dated 1777.[42] Its presence at Edinburgh suggests that Blaikie may have sent it to Hope, knowing, as a protégé of the professor, how interesting he would find it.[43] Blaikie also gave a copy to Sir Joseph Banks and later wrote to Banks making corrections to his original list.[44]

36. Joseph Pitton de Tournefort (1656–1708). Distinguished French botanist who collected plants in the Levant. He developed a system of nomenclature which defined plants by families or genera according to their flowers, so was an important forerunner of Linnaeus.
37. A description of Dr Hope's course of botany with its emphasis on the Linnean system is given in H. Arnot, *History of Edinburgh* (Edinburgh, 1779), pp. 402–3.
38. Diary, 20 May 1775, '. . . in the evening went to Bourdigny where I stayed next day writing the Linnaean names to the nomenclature of Haller for the convenience of the mountains'.
39. Albrecht von Haller, *Nomenclator ex Historia Plantarum Indigenarum Helvetiae Excerptus* (Berne, 1769).
40. Nicolaus Joseph von Jacquin (1727–1817), Professor of Chemistry at Vienna. He published text books of Medicine and Pharmacopoeia and many beautifully illustrated folios of botany. In his youth he had travelled and collected in the Caribbean.
41. *Adanson in His Familles des Plantes* (Paris, 1763), divided plants into 58 families in which were included 1615 'genres'. Blaikie lists a book in his collection by Adanson entitled *Flore de France*, but I have been unable to find this title.
42. Edinburgh Royal Botanic Library, G 5980/F86f. My thanks to Mrs Jennifer Woods for drawing my attention to this notebook.
43. It is also possible, but unlikely, that the book was brought back to Scotland by Blaikie's nephew Thomas Mackie after Blaikie's death and given to Patrick Neill, Blaikie's friend and Secretary of the Caledonian Horticultural Society, who will be mentioned later. However, Neill was a meticulous man who would have given an account of the gift to the Caledonian Society in its *Transactions*. No such record appears to exist.
44. Letter dated 6 December 1777. (Kew: B.C.I. 67).

Hope's involvement with the Botanic Garden extended to assisting young gardeners of promise by training them in botany. His kindness, however, was not wholly disinterested. His aim was to recruit collectors whom he could recommend to others and who would contribute to Edinburgh's stock of rare plants. In addition, it was his ambition to publish a Scottish *Flora* and he employed at least one of the gardeners he had educated to collect all over Scotland for him.[45] Hope also encouraged his medical students to become field botanists. Each year he presented a gold medal for the best dried collection of native plants (*hortus siccus*) and organised excursions to collect them. Sir J. E. Smith, founder of the Linnean Society, describes finding 'a great number of rare plants' on one such expedition to the top of Ben Lomond.[46] It was also the practice for Hope's student botanist-gardeners as part of their training to keep a *hortus siccus* mounted in a heavy volume that served as a kind of scrap book, and among Blaikie's possessions is an index in his handwriting to two volumes of dried plants.[47] The volumes themselves were probably jettisoned a long time ago but the existence of the index suggests that Blaikie was trained in a botanical school. In addition, in relation to Hope's emphasis in his teaching on field botany, and the flora of Scotland, a remark in Blaikie's diary becomes significant.

During an excursion around Chamonix on 31 August 1775, he tells of 'finding plenty of the *Sibbaldia procumbens'*[48] along the border of the River Arveyron and goes on, 'thus meeting with a country man in the midst of this desert'.[49] He means a 'fellow' countryman[50] which implies that he recognises the plant, the Mountain Cinquefoil, as a native of Scotland. Its habitat is high places, such as Ben Lomond or Ben Lawers and it is very unlikely indeed that Blaikie would have undertaken botanical excursions alone to these places. Such expeditions were almost certainly organised by Professor Hope.

Blaikie's diary also suggests a third influence which the professor may have had on him. Hope was interested in the practical application of botany, in the discovery

---

45. James Robertson (*c.* 1747–1796). Hope, in a letter to Joseph Banks in February 1767, mentions that he had sent 'a young man, one of the gardeners whom I had educated myself on a botanical expedition' as far as Inverness'. (*The Banks Letters; a calendar of the manuscript correspondence of Sir Joseph Banks, preserved in the British Museum, the British Museum (Natural History) and other collections in Great Britain* (London, 1958). Robertson's travels in Scotland are described in D. M. Henderson and J. H. Dickson, *A Naturalist in the Highlands* (Edinburgh, 1994).

46. Sir James Edward Smith (1759–1828). *Memoirs and Correspondence of the late Sir James Edward Smith MD*. Edited by Lady Smith, 2 vols (London, 1832), vol. 1, p. 54.

47. Blaikie Papers.

48. *Sibbaldia procumbens* is named in honour of Sir Robert Sibbald (1641–1772), Professor of Medicine at Edinburgh and founder of an earlier botanic garden in the city. An insignificant little flower, it is today the logo of the Edinburgh Botanic Gardens.

49. Diary, 31 August 1775.

50. There is the same use of the word countryman for fellow countryman in *Henry, Elizabeth and George (1734–80). Letters and Diaries of Henry, 10th Earl of Pembroke and his Circle* (London, 1939), p. 473, 'Singleton would not even open one Single Stable Door for a Countray [sic] man'.

of plants of economic as well as medicinal value for Scotland. Blaikie, it seems, followed his principles when he noted, and later carried back with him, silkworms that he found growing in Switzerland on a pine identical to the Scots pine. The silkworms' adaptation to the harsh climate of Switzerland convinced him that they might equally well be used to start a silk-manufactory in Scotland.[51]

Hope was so successful in his aim to make the new botanic garden at Leith Walk one of the best in Europe that by the time of his death, Edinburgh was second only to Uppsala, the university of Linnaeus. He corresponded assiduously with botanists at home and abroad. Amongst his English correspondents were Sir Joseph Banks, the most powerful figure in the botanical world of the time and, significantly, Dr William Pitcairn,[52] and Dr John Fothergill,[53] two distinguished amateur botanists. In his garden at Upton in Essex,[54] Dr Fothergill had amassed a magnificent collection of 'exotics' the name given to foreign plants, particularly trees and shrubs from North America, while his greenhouses were second only to those of Kew. Both men exchanged seeds with collectors around the world and financed botanical expeditions. Pitcairn and Fothergill were generous benefactors of the Botanic Gardens in Edinburgh, as Hope always acknowledged in his first botany lecture to his students each session. He began by informing them that, 'This garden exists by the Royal bounty of his Majesty – next to his Majesty I must mention the bounty of the Earl of Bute,[55] who is passionately fond of all parts of Natural History but most of Botany. I must mention also two others, Dr Pitcairn and Dr Fothergil [sic], who possesses Gardens the next to this Royal garden in goodness'.[56]

In autumn 1766, Hope set out for London, visiting nurseries and gardens on the way,[57] intending to add to Edinburgh's stock of plants and note others for future acquisition. In the capital he met his correspondents and a number of prominent

---

51. Diary, 14 June 1775.

52. Dr William Pitcairn (1711–1791). President of the Royal College of Physicians in 1775. Friend of Fothergill and of Dr John Hope. His name appears in Dr Hope's records as receiving seeds from Hope. SRO, Hope Papers. Copies of these are kept in the library of the Edinburgh Botanic Gardens.

53. Dr John Fothergill (1712–1780). A Quaker philanthropist and a highly successful physician, Dr Fothergill was probably the leading amateur botanist of his day. He spent vast sums obtaining the rarest plants from every corner of the world. His garden at Upton in Essex was famous for its collections of plants and he sponsored collectors in different parts of the world. See J. C. Lettsom, 'Hortus Uptonensis', vol. III, *The Works of John Fothergill* (1783–84). Introduction, pp. xxxvii–xl.

54. In the diary entry for 1 January 1776, the day after his arrival in London at the end of his period in Switzerland, Blaikie tells us that he set out to see his old acquaintances at Upton and that he remained there.

55. John Stuart, 3rd Earl of Bute (1713–1792), friend of Frederick Prince of Wales and later of George III, Prime Minister 1762–1763. An enthusiastic botanist and gardener responsible for the development of Princess Augusta's garden at Kew.

56. Library of the Royal Botanical Gardens, Edinburgh University. MS entitled *Lectures in Botany by John Hope in the Royal botanick garden Edinburgh, 1777–1778*.

57. John Harvey 'A Scottish Botanist in London in 1766'. *Garden History* (1981), vol. 9, No. 1.

nurserymen like James Lee, of the Vineyard Nursery of Kennedy and Lee at Hammer-smith.[58] It is possible that he may at that time have recommended the sixteen year old Blaikie to his contacts as a bright young gardener who might one day make a collector.[59]

As a Scot, and especially one who came well recommended, Blaikie would have had no problem in securing employment in England. Throughout the eighteenth century, a Scottish 'mafia' ensured that Scots held almost a monopoly of the top gardening posts in Britain. English gardeners deeply resented the 'invasion' of these 'Northern lads' and complained bitterly that 'by the help of a little learning and a great deal of Impudence, they invade these Southern Provinces'.[60] Philip Miller,[61] head of the Chelsea Physic Garden, was particularly resented for seeming to employ only his fellow countrymen.[62] A group of English gardeners formed a society pledged to refuse employment to Scots, but their resolution had little effect.[63] Scotland was a small country which produced an educated peasantry, the products of its Presbyterian parish schools. The more enterprising left home and walked south to find employment. Used to a harsh rural economy and inured to hardship, they accepted long hours and poor pay. Once installed and successful themselves, they would naturally recruit ambitious, literate and hard working young Scots as apprentices.

Miller had trained William Aiton,[64] a Scot from Lanarkshire, Princess Augusta's head gardener at Kew and, later, the manager of its botanic garden. Both men made major contributions to horticulture by their writings; Miller published *The Gardener's and Florist's Dictionary* in 1724 and Aiton his dictionary of plants, *Hortus Kewensis*, in 1789. James Lee of Hammersmith,[65] the most famous nurseryman of his day, was also a Scot. He had walked from his native Selkirk to find work in London and became gardener to the Duke of Argyll on his estate at Twickenham before going into partnership with Lewis Kennedy at the Vineyard Nursery, Hammersmith in 1745. He was a skilled propagator and nurseryman with an extensive catalogue[66] who

58. Harvey, *op cit.*
59. Some 23 of his letters to Banks survive, among them one recommending the botanist Adam Freer as a collector, 7 April 1776 (BC.1.1) and another, 14 February 1767 (BC. 1.3) describing botanical excursions by Freer and other pupils. Although no evidence survives, it is possible that Blaikie was one of these.
60. S. Switzer, *Iconographia Rustica or The nobleman, Gentleman and Gardener's Recreation*, 3 vols (London, 1742), vol. i, p xxiv.
61. Philip Miller (1691–1771). For an account of his life see Hazel Le Rougetel, *The Chelsea Gardener Philip Miller 1691–1771* (London, 1990).
62. DNB, referring to *Gentleman's Magazine*, liii, 332.
63. *Adam Armed*, Guildhall Library, MSS 3389/2 Quoted in E. J. Willson, *James Lee and the Vineyard Nursery, Hammersmith* (London, 1961).
64. William Aiton (1731–1793). Appointed to the management of Princess Augusta's garden at Kew and in 1789 when the two gardens were united, he became manager of the Royal Gardens there as well.
65. James Lee (1715–1795). See E. J. Willson *James Lee and the Vineyard Nursery Hammersmith* (Hammersmith Local History Group, London, 1961).
66. Kennedy & Lee's catalogue of 1774 is preserved in the Archives Department of the Hammersmith and Fulham Library.

introduced around 135 plants to cultivation in England.[67] His *Introduction to Botany* published in 1766 ran to many editions. Aiton and Lee were Blaikie's mentors and he kept in touch with both of them. Other influential Scottish nurserymen were Gordon of Milend, supplier of plants for Marie Antoinette's Trianon, and Fraser of Chelsea, a plant collector who provided plants for Catherine the Great.

The initial stage in the English career of a Scottish gardener who came South with a first class recommendation might be a training at Kew, where the hothouses contained the finest collection of 'exotics' in the country under Aiton's skilled management. Blaikie's respect for Aiton is evident from his diary and the older man must have liked him. When Blaikie went to France to work for a French count, the Comte de Lauraguais, in September 1776, Aiton gave him a collection of 26 American plants to take as a gift to his employer, the sort of action that suggests the kindly patronage of a master for his apprentice. Each time Blaikie returned to England he visited Aiton at Kew and they exchanged seeds and plants. A single letter from Aiton to Blaikie remains amongst Blaikie's papers. It is dated 1789 and after listing plants which he has sent to Blaikie via a Mr Gerard,[68] Aiton writes, 'Your last letter I received about a fortnight ago. – Give me leave to return you my sincere and best thanks for your kind present of Buttons, they are most beautiful, and really I value them highly.' Next, after some words about the severity of the winter, he concludes, 'Mrs Aiton unites with me in best wishes and kind Compts. to you & beleive [sic] me ever Yours W. Aiton'.[69]

Buttons in the eighteenth century could be extremely valuable and exquisite objects in themselves. They were highly fashionable at the French court. The Count d'Artois had his decorated with diamonds and Blaikie's other main employer, the Duke of Orléans, adorned the front of his *frac* (frockcoat) with buttons portraying mythological and erotic subjects. These particular buttons, which, typically, were larger than those of today (almost 6 cm. in diameter), created a stir when he wore them in English drawing rooms[70] and it is unlikely that Blaikie would have sent such subjects to the elderly Aiton. What he probably gave him were what are described today as 'architectural' buttons. These buttons were miniatures painted on ivory or paper, covered with glass and edged with gilt. They showed scenes of the Duke's gardens either at Monceau or at Raincy and, since Blaikie was employed in the refurbishment of both these gardens, views of either would have made appropriate if expensive presents. Two sets showing Le Raincy are known to exist in private collections[71] Both sets are

67. My thanks to Dr John Edmondson, Curator of Botany at the Liverpool Museum, for providing me with a list of Lee's introductions.

68. Gerard is probably the same Gerard who had worked for Gordon of Milend and was put in charge of the nursery at Le Raincy (Diary, undated entry). The plants requested as listed by Aiton were *Protea argentea*, *P. strobalina*, *P. salicifolia*, *P. myrtifolia*, *Geranium betulianum* and *Erica petiveria*.

69. Blaikie Papers.

70. A Britsch, *La Jeunesse de Philippe Egalité* (Paris, 1926).

71. See *En Aulnoye Jadis*, No. 3 (1974). J. Astruc, 'Des boutons d'habit extraordinaires', pp. 13–17, and same journal, No. 13 (1983). J. Bougon, 'Des boutons d'habit extraordinaires', pp. 50–4. These describe sets of the Raincy buttons in France. There are four also at the Smithsonian Institute in New York.

based on paintings by Carmontelle, the original designer of Monceau. What seems
to confirm that it was a set of these architectural or landscape buttons that Blaikie
sent Aiton is that James Lee of the Vineyard Nursery, Hammersmith, listed a set of
Monceau buttons[72] as an item in his will. There is no indication of how Lee came
by them but given Lee's connection with Blaikie, evident throughout the diaries, it
seems likely that he, too, received them from Blaikie. Such tokens would be a way
for Blaikie to pay tribute to his old masters and at the same time show them how
successful he had become.

Blaikie's diary with its references to visiting old friends at Kew, Hammersmith and
Upton[73] seems to indicate that his first employment was at Kew and that he may
have moved from there to work for Lee at Hammersmith. Dr John Fothergill's garden
at Upton was the scene of the final phase of his training as a botanist and it was from
here that the Scot set out on his Swiss expedition in April 1775, a month after his 25th
birthday.

Until the second quarter of the eighteenth century, the Alps had for the most part
been regarded with something approaching horror. As a distant backdrop, they came
to be admired for their grim beauty but most travellers on the Grand Tour considered
them more as an obstacle to be overcome on the route south to Italy. They dreaded
the journey over the Mount Cenis Pass and their letters and diaries are full of the
bleakness and discomfort they had to endure. The ladies, and sometimes the men,
were carried over the pass in 'little seats of twisted osiers, fixed upon poles upon
men's shoulders; their chaises taken to pieces and laid upon mules'. They complained
of the extreme cold and arrived 'half dead' at their destinations.[74] And there were
other dangers besides the cold. Thomas Gray, in 1739, described the savagery and
horror of winter on Mount Cenis and was appalled when a wolf suddenly appeared
on the track, seized a little fat black spaniel, the pet of his travelling companion
Horace Walpole, and loped away with it before a shot could be fired.[75]

Attitudes to the high mountains began slowly to change after William Windham
made an excursion to Chamonix to visit the glaciers in June 1741 and published an
account of his expedition in 1744. During the summer of 1770, Henry Temple, the
2nd Viscount Palmerston, spent six weeks in the Alps accompanied by the painter,
William Pars (1742–1782) and, at the Royal Academy the following year, Pars exhibited
a group of seven water-colours of Alpine scenes. These, which admirably portrayed

72. E. J. Willson mentions the buttons, p. 39, as being as yet unidentified. My thanks to Mr Peter
   Hayden of the Garden History Society for the information that they depict Monceau and
   to Miss Willson who has kindly sent me prints of several of them. My thanks also to Miss
   Lois Pool, Secretary of the American National Button Society, for an article by MWS,
   'The Story Behind the Buttons' from the *Bulletin of the Button Society of America*, February
   1986.
73. Diary for October/November 1777.
74. Lady Mary Wortley Montague, *The Complete Letters*, ed. R. Halsband (Oxford, 1965–67),
   vol. I, pp. 434–5.
75. Thomas Gray, *Letters* (1971 edn, ed. Paget Toynbee and L. Whibley), vol. 1, p. 125. Letter
   to his mother from Turin, 7 November 1739.

the grand scale and beauty of the mountains, were speedily engraved and were a further encouragement to visit the region.[76]

The publication in 1761 of Rousseau's novel, *La Nouvelle Héloise*, set in the area round the lake of Geneva, was to introduce the region to a huge new audience. The book's subject was the doomed love between a young woman and the young man who was her tutor, where social difference made marriage between them impossible. The painful victory of virtue over the torments of passion and Rousseau's lyrical portrayals of the scenery around the lakeside were the main factors in the book's phenomenal popularity, with 72 French editions and ten English ones before the turn of the century. Rousseau's inference that nobility of scenery nurtured nobility of soul and that the pure air of the mountains brought well-being and peace to those who breathed it provided an additional reason for visiting the Alps.

This was not the first time that such a view had been expressed. Albrecht von Haller of Berne was a scientist, administrator and naturalist. In his long poem, 'Die Alpen' published in 1731[77] he celebrated the beauty of the mountains, the rich Alpine flora and the region's mineral wealth, but his central message, like that of Rousseau later, was that such noble surroundings, far from the corruption of cities, fostered noble qualities in its inhabitants.

Drs John Fothergill and William Pitcairn, were more interested in a later publication of Haller's, his *Historia stirpium indigenarum Helvetiae inchoata* (Berne 1768) which revealed a treasure house of Alpine flora. The prospect of being the first to introduce many of these plants into England probably encouraged the doctors to make enquiries amongst the fraternity of Swiss botanists for a collector. Among Blaikie's papers, an unsigned document in French,[78] written in an unidentified hand and entitled *Réflexions pour ceux qui souhaitent faire des collections des plantes Alpines*, reads like a response to such a request.[79] It describes the problems the writer's correspondent and his friends would face. It dwells on the expense (a Swiss botanist would probably charge one louis, just under one pound sterling, a day), the vast extent of the Alps, the difficulty of locating species and, should several botanists be employed, the almost insurmountable problem of assembling the plants from different parts of the region for sending to London. The author describes himself as '*un vieux valétudinaire*' who has not long to live and says the same is true of his '*directeur*' whom he does not name, but who may have been Haller himself. Consequently, the writer urges his correspondent to make up his mind quickly. In the introduction to his Swiss flora, Haller had acknowledged the collectors, peasants as well as educated amateurs of botany, who had scoured the mountains to bring him specimens, but the anonymous botanist points out that such peasants do not know any Latin plant names and Linnaeus is out of

---

76. Peter Barber, *Switzerland 700* (British Museum, 1991), pp. 51–6.

77. *Poésies de M. Haller*, trans. V. B. Tscharner, 2 vols in one (Berne, 1760).

78. This is a document consisting of eight pages of hand-written text. Blaikie Papers.

79. It is not addressed to any one person, but its reference to 'you' and 'your friends' gives the impression that it has been enclosed in a letter to an individual, perhaps with the intention of passing it on to several interested parties.

the question as far as they are concerned. Anyone unfamiliar with the local patois would be unable to tell them which plants to collect.

It may have been this missive that gave the two physicians the idea of sending their own collector to the Alps. Fothergill already financed Bartram [80] in North America and here was the opportunity to acquire plants, not yet introduced to England, at a cheaper cost than that incurred using a Swiss botanist, and infinitesimal compared with the sum required to finance an expedition to South Africa or North America.

They discussed their project with Joseph Banks.[81] Banks, who was to dominate the scientific scene for the next fifty years as President of the Royal Society, had sailed at the age of 24 with Captain Cook in the Royal Navy vessel, *The Endeavour*, on its historic voyage to the Pacific in 1768. In 1772, the year after his return from the Pacific, he had chartered another ship and made an expedition to Iceland and the Hebrides. He would be elected President of the Royal Society in 1778 and given a baronetcy by his friend George III in 1781. Rich, practical and forceful, with contacts all over Europe and beyond, he could be relied upon to forward any worthwhile botanical scheme. He had persuaded the king to send Francis Masson, a Scottish gardener at Kew, as Kew's first collector to South Africa in 1772 and was constantly on the look out for other suitable young men who might become collectors for him in distant parts of the world. He particularly favoured Scots for this demanding and often dangerous employment for he was convinced that, 'So well does the Seriousness of a Scotch Education fit the mind of a Scotsman to the habits of industry, attention and frugality that they rarely abandon them at any time of life and I may say never while they are young'.[82] For the post of plant collector in Switzerland, Thomas Blaikie was his choice.

Fothergill and Pitcairn financed Blaikie's tour of Switzerland, but it was Banks who laid down his duties and decided what he should be paid. As well as some knowledge of botany, of soil types and how to preserve specimens, the autocratic Banks required a collector to be 'active and healthy, able to write a good hand and willing to write down such observations as he may make'.[83] The personal qualities he demanded were honesty, sobriety, diligence, activity, humility and civility. Whether Blaikie could ever have been described as humble is doubtful, but his Scottish background, his stamina and strong physique plus the fact that he had taken part in excursions to the Scottish Highlands made him an ideal candidate for this expedition, and the training it would give him could be useful for future botanical expeditions. The letter from Banks setting out Blaikie's terms of employment covers three foolscap sheets. First, it gives detailed

---

80. William Bartram (1739–1823) had accompanied his father, the botanist and collector, John Bartram, on his expedition to Florida. In 1773, he undertook a journey to the south east of North America as a collector for Dr Fothergill and published the record of his journey, *Travels through North and South Carolina* etc. in 1791. The Bartrams also ran a famous nursery in Philadelphia whose catalogue was available in Europe.

81. Joseph Banks (1744–1820).

82. Quoted in H. C. Cameron, *Sir Joseph Banks* (London, 1966 edn), chapter II, p. 100, n. 52. Warren Dawson Col, III, 41.

83. Bank's criteria for a collector for HMS *Nautilus*'s survey of the West Coast of Africa, quoted in Ray Desmond, *Kew: The History of the Royal Botanic Gardens* (London, 1995).

instructions for drying and preserving specimens. This part is written in an unknown hand. The last paragraph, written and signed by Banks himself, is headed 'Terms'. For each complete species collected (i.e. specimens of flowers, seeds, fruits and leaves) Blaikie was to receive a shilling, or five pounds per hundred. Each incomplete species would earn only two pounds ten pence per hundred. He was not to gather common English plants and Banks specifies that, 'if many species of alpine plants are found in the collection and but few common English ones I shall allow a premium for your honesty and diligence according to my judgement'.[84] On that reckoning, Blaikie would have earned all of twenty pounds in his eight months expedition provided, of course, that his specimens of each species were complete and did not include many native English plants. For Blaikie, as Banks knew, the money would not have been a consideration. The Swiss journey was an opportunity to prove that he was a capable botanist and collector. It was an adventure.

An expedition to Switzerland would not have been considered hazardous in 1775. Every year, especially after the end of the Seven Years' War in 1763, an increasing number of visitors toured the Alps.[85] The difference between them and Blaikie was that, by and large, they kept to known routes, travelling on horseback or in carriages. Rousseau's St Preux, the despairing lover in *La Nouvelle Heloise*, had spent several days wandering in the Haut Valais, the mountainous region near Berne, accompanied by a guide but, although it was now fashionable to admire mountain scenery, Rousseau's readers were not yet ready to follow their hero's example. They remained ignorant of the life of the peasants in the higher mountain regions around them. Inevitably, their contact was with innkeepers and guides, their visits to known beauty spots. Other botanists had visited the region[86] but it seems they mainly relied on collectors, either amateur or professional to supply them with plants and seeds from habitats high in the mountains.[87] Blaikie's expedition was unique in that he was the first foreigner, certainly the first British subject, to spend days and weeks completely alone in remote areas sharing the life of the shepherds and chamois hunters of the region. His vividly observed account of the separate world of the people and the mountains is probably the first ever recorded by a foreigner.[88]

---

84. Blaikie Papers.

85. By 1780 Thomas Brand describes the inn at Chamonix as so crowded 'that we met with but indifferent [service]'. In the afternoon he set out on foot and the ladies in 'charabancs' to the 'glacier de Buissons'. Berne, 1 August 1780 (Cambridge University Library, Brand MS Add 8670). These charabancs were planks on wheels with a chain on which the passenger could rest his or her feet, with an awning overhead in bad weather.

86. Amongst them Antoine Richard (1735–1807), the botanist-gardener at the Trianon.

87. In *Reflexions* etc. quoted above, the author complains, 'Nothing is more disagreeable or annoying than the view held by almost all foreigners that these plants can be found without moving from ones door, at every step one takes and in every variety one wishes'.

88. H. Montagnier, 'Thomas Blaikie and Michel-Gabriel Paccard', in *The Alpine Journal*, no. 246, May 1933.

CHAPTER 3

The Plant Collector

The bearer Thomas Blakey, Gardener by Profession and Botanist, travels into Swisserland, in our service, in search of rare and curious plants. Should he by sickness, or any accident stand in need of assistance all reasonable demands on this account will be gratefully paid, by applying either to: Dr William Pitcairn, Fellow of the college of Physicians in London and F. R. S. Warwick Court, or to Dr John Fothergill in Harpur Street London.

London, 11 April 1775 [1]

THE FIRST ENTRY in Thomas Blaikie's diary is dated 13 April 1775, two days before the start of his expedition. The journey from London to Geneva would take almost three weeks; two days to cross the Channel and a six day coach ride to Paris where he was obliged to wait for a place on the coach to Chalon-sur-Saône. From there he boarded the water coach for Lyon and from Lyon reached Geneva by post chaise on 5 May.

Like the hero of some picaresque novel, Blaikie's thoughts at the start of his journey are entirely on the future. If any friends gathered to see him off, he does not mention them and he describes none of his preparations, except that he has provided himself 'with what I thought necessary for the journey'. As he spoke no French, he probably took a rather primitive crash course in the language before leaving England. In his own hand, at the back of his diary is a series of French lessons graded, to begin with, according to the length of the sentences and later by the inclusion in each lesson of words of an ascending number of syllables. Each page is divided in two, on one side the French and on the other Blaikie's sometimes laborious English translations. Very little seems appropriate for a travelling botanist. For example, the concluding sentence in the final lesson, lesson number 4, points out, using words of six syllables, the merits of the Epistle to the Thessalonians!

The London to Boulogne packet commanded by its master, Henry Meriton,[2] slipped its moorings at St Katharine's dock just below the Tower of London about one o'clock in the afternoon of the 15th and began its sail down the Thames. They reached Boulogne on the morning of the 17th but the ship had to wait until 11.30 for a favourable tide, when a pilot came on board and conducted them into the port. The landing in Boulogne was a culture shock for most English Protestants but especially for a Presbyterian, like Blaikie, whose religion condemned sacred images as blasphemy. There, dominating the pier, was a wooden Cross about 20 ft high 'with our Saviour

---

1. Blaikie Papers.
2. Also mentioned by name in Smollett's *Travels through France and Italy* (World Classics edn), p. 9.

upon the same in wood, as large as nature and I, being ignorant of the Roman Catholic religion and having never seen such a sight before, served me very much to gaze at in entering the port'.[3] In spite of finding great difficulty in making himself understood, he retrieved his luggage from the Custom House, found lodgings for the night, strolled around Boulogne and booked himself a place on the morning coach to Paris. His fare cost him 5 crowns[4] and like most other English visitors, he was disappointed to find the *diligence* was more like a wagon than the fine French coach of his imagination. Large 'baskets' were attached to it for the luggage and for the outside passengers, with room for eight inside.

For six days, the time it took to travel the 160 miles from Boulogne to Paris, he sat, miserably confined in the narrow, jolting coach, unable to speak or understand a word his fellow passengers uttered. The inns were filthy and the countryside dull so it was with relief that he reached Paris on 24 April. While he waited for a place on the coach to Chalon, he spent three days visiting the sights. He mentions only two of them; Notre Dame, in the then unfashionable Gothic style, he dismissed as making 'no great appearance' although he admired its interior, especially the fine paintings and the 'exceeding rich' high altar; Les Invalides impressed him as 'a magnificent building', its chapel 'one of the finest in Europe'.[5] Most of his time was spent dodging the coaches that drove furiously through the narrow dirty streets, spattering those on foot with mud. The streets were lit by *réverbétoires* suspended from pulleys in the middle of the street, something he had not seen before. Another novelty was the *brouette*, a kind of poor man's sedan chair, which carried passengers in what Blaikie called 'a sort of wheelbarrow which a man draws and another pushes behind'. He was unable to decide who deserved more sympathy, the poor Christian horses, as he calls them, who suffered greatly when the streets were steep, or the passenger who required Christian patience to endure the slowness of the journey.

The next stage of his journey proved much more congenial than the first. He left Paris by diligence at midnight on 27 April. As this coach changed horses every five leagues, it reached Chalon-sur-Saône in two days. For the remainder of the journey to Lyon, the passengers transferred to a *coche d'eau*, 'a sort of barge drawn by horses'. From the deck, Blaikie was able enjoy the fine, warm weather and the countryside on either bank of the river. He was charmed by the lighthearted way the French entertained themselves on board, 'There is a pretty smart cabin for the better sort of passengers, where they amuse themselves playing at cards, and some of the Ladies sung a remarkable good song with some Gentlemen that played upon different sorts of musical instruments, which upon the water made it very agreeable'.[6] With two days to wait for the coach from Lyon to Geneva, there was time to attend the

---

3. Diary, 17 April 1775.

4. A crown was worth 5 English shillings.

5. Its construction was begun in 1670 by Libéral Bruant on the orders of Louis XIV to house war wounded. The architect of the chapel, begun in 1677, was Hardouin-Mansard, and the fine esplanade was laid out in 1704 by Robert de Cotte.

6. Diary, 29–30 April 1775.

theatre[7] and visit the School of Anatomy[8] 'exceeding entertaining for the curiosity'. From Lyon, he shared a chaise on 2 May with two other young men. The first leg of the journey opened up to them a prospect of the River Rhone and 'stupendous' mountains, whose lower slopes were covered with box trees. The inn at Montluel, their first stop, proved even more filthy than the norm. Although he must have noticed them earlier in his travels, it was here he drew attention to the absence of knives at table in French inns, every traveller being expected to carry his own. Another custom that caught his attention was the 'monstrous large' jackboots that horsemen wore in France The rider, he writes, 'is placed as if his legs were in two baskets. These boots is made of the strongest bend[9] leather and besides, to strengthen them, there is two or three iron hoops, one at the top and one about the middle of the leg, and fixed to the boots is a large pair of spurs. Those boots they wear with their shoes, and when they alight from horseback, they leave their boots at the door as it is impossible to walk with them. But yet, there is a convenience in those boots. If their horse falls, as they frequently do, the rider runs no risk of breaking his leg, as the weight of the horse cannot squeeze the boot.'[10]

At midday the next day, they stopped at the village of Coupy situated about a mile above the Poste at Vanchy.[11] There, travellers were invited to examine the spot where the Rhône disappeared in a narrow channel so that a man could stand with his feet on either bank, one side of which belonged to France and the other to Savoy. The next day, the 4 May, at Fort de L'Écluse, the French border, he had to show the passport he had, with foresight, obtained from the British Ambassador in Paris. They reached Geneva about 5 o'clock the same day.

Geneva at that time was a strongly fortified town of around 24,000 inhabitants with a garrison, of some 700 men on constant alert against sudden attack from its neighbour, the Duchy of Savoy. Blaikie noted his first impressions in his diary, 'In entering the town there is three draw bridges which is drawn every night at sun set and opened in the morning at sun rise and likewise shut every Sunday [during] the time of service. Neither is there any person allowed to be in the streets the time of Divine service. In entering the town all strangers is examined; what they are and where they are going'.[12] The three gates marked the entrances from France, Savoy and Switzerland and, since attack was not expected from the other two sides, only on the Savoy side were the fortifications up-to-date. He heard English voices all around him at his inn, The *Hôtel de la Balance*, the best hostelry in the town. Permanent English colonies had existed at both Geneva and Lausanne virtually since the beginning of the century and by 1775 Geneva was 'brimful of English'.

---

7. The first of the great theatres of eighteenth-century France. The architect was J.-G. Soufflot (1713–1780), who was born in Lyons. See Allan Braham, *The Architecture of the French Enlightenment* (London, 1980).

8. Founded 1761 and considered one of the foremost of the time.

9. Leather from the thick part of the butt, cut lengthways.

10. Diary, 2 May 1775.

11. Horace-Benedict de Saussure, *Voyage dans les Alpes et le Jura* (Neuchatel, 1779), vol. 1, pp. 325–6.

12. Diary, 4 May 1775.

The next morning Blaikie presented himself, with a letter of introduction from Dr Pitcairn, at the house of Mr Paul Gaussen, a banker and amateur botanist.[13] Gaussen was at his country estate, and the next day, 6 May, one of the Mr Gaussen's servants escorted Blaikie to Chapeaurouge, the banker's country house at Bourdigny, two miles or so to the west of the town where he cultivated exotic trees and plants in his garden and hot-house. Gaussen greeted Blaikie warmly and, to Thomas's intense relief, spoke perfect English. The young man's Scottish accent must have rekindled memories for the Swiss. His first wife, who died in 1773, had been a Miss Jane Ogilvie 'a hearty Aberdeenshire woman' according to James Boswell who met her on a visit to Geneva in December 1764.[14] Throughout Blaikie's stay in the Alps, Gaussen was to supply him with funds and act as his mentor and friend. They kept in touch for many years and, until the Revolution, Blaikie regularly sent Gaussen seeds and plants from the gardens of Monceau.[15] It is clear from the diary that people liked Blaikie and he must have had an attractive personality and a pleasing appearance but no portrait or sketch of him has been found. The only clue to his looks comes from the minimal details on a passport, granted in 1802 when he was 51. This describes him as 1.88 m. tall, an exceptional height for the period, with brown eyes, brown eyebrows, and brown hair; his face was oval and his brow domed.[16]

Eager to begin collecting at once, Blaikie began searching for plants in Gaussen's meadows. First he found some orchids, then *Genista germanica*, a plant he had never seen before, a member of the broom family from Central and Eastern Europe.[17] Straightaway, he made a bed for them in a corner of Mr Gaussen's garden, pleased to have completed his first day's excursion. but the plants were not his only interest. He noted that the land was enclosed here, that walnut trees were a major crop and that the method of cultivating the vine was very different from that he had observed in France. Here the ground was laid out in ridges about nine feet wide. Fruit trees were planted between the ridges and vines were grown close to the trees, the young vine shoots being trained from tree to tree. Corn was sown in the ground between the trees, and the vines, held well above the corn, did not deprive the crop of light.

Blaikie's alpine expedition can be divided into three distinct stages. The first was centred on Geneva, in the Salève and the Jura and marked his apprenticeship period. The second took him further afield on a long and physically demanding trip along

13. Paul Gaussen (1720–1806). Gaussen's brother Jean-Pierre Gaussen was a Governor of the Bank of England and a Director of the East India Company. According to J. C. Loudon, *Arboretum et Fruticetum*, vol. I, p. 163, Gaussen began his garden in 1767.

14. *Boswell on the Grand Tour; Switzerland and Italy*, ed E. A. Pottle (1953), p. 279.

15. The garden of the Duc d'Orléans in Paris. A letter of thanks from Gaussen, dated 1790, survives amongst Blaikie's papers.

16. Blaikie Papers, Private Archive. There is an etching of a painting by Moreau in Georges Wildenstein, *Un peintre de paysage au XVIIIe Louis Moreau* (Paris, 1922) entitled 'Le comte d'Artois et son jardinier'. The man is comical, turning and bent almost double in a clumsy effort to bring himself down to the height of the dainty Count, so it may well have been Blaikie, but it is impossible to decipher his features.

17. Introduced to England by the Earl of Bute, 1773.

the south shore of Lake Geneva and on to Berne, then via Bienne and La Ferrière back to his headquarters at St Genis about seven miles to the north west of Geneva. The third was the most testing and exhilarating part of his whole stay in the Alps, his excursion to Chamonix and his days spent with Michel-Gabriel Paccard, the first man to climb Mont Blanc. All three phases were not without their moments of extreme danger. As far as pace was concerned, his expedition began slowly and gathered momentum until, at the end, he was rushing up the wintry mountains doggedly digging plants out of the icy ground in an effort to replace those he had lost from his collection.

His first priority was to ensure that the plants he collected were planted and cared for during his absence on excursions. As well as the plot he had selected at Bourdingy, he arranged another at an inn at St Genis, towards the Jura, to receive his collections. It was always difficult to make sure that the people he entrusted with transporting his plants back to base bothered to do so speedily enough to preserve them. The rare plants which he had collected on Mont Blanc and dispatched from there on 6 September took 15 days to reach Bourdigny and many of them were spoilt.

The trouble was that, at first, there was little scope for collecting. He had arrived too early in the season and had to pass his time exploring the lower slopes of the Jura. Snow still covered the upper pastures and the mountains were deserted as the herdsmen did not take their cattle to the mountains until the first of June. On his initial foray into the mountains on 10 May, he found 'little vegetation unless some crocuses, and in the warmer lying places there is great quantities of the *Scilla bifolia*, both blue and white, which make a very good appearance and, likewise, some Narcissus ... At this time, spent 3 days upon the mountains only returning in the evening to St Genis with the plants I procured, and planted them in the garden in purpose to preserve them until the Autumn.' [18]

The flowering season in the Alps is short and he must have been worried that he would run out of time before he could carry out all his instructions for collecting.[19] These were quite specific and detailed. He could bring back seeds, and plants grown in earth. He was also to secure branches with flowers 'in perfect condition', picked on a day free from rain. Flowers which opened in the morning should be picked when they were widest open at an hour when the sun had dried the dew, while evening flowering plants were to be gathered at the right moment for them, presumably before the evening moisture attacked them. He was also required to bring back branches with fruit attached, gathered when the fruit was at its fullest. All of these had to be dried according to a lengthy procedure involving laying the branches, leaves, flowers and fruit between sheets of paper to be pressed in books which were then placed on top of each other, with a heavy weight of at least 10 lb. laid upon the pile. The papers were changed several times at 12 hourly intervals until the plants were completely dry. After that, the books were to be exposed to the sunshine or

---

18. Diary, 10 May 1775.
19. Laid out at the beginning of his contract under the heading 'Rules for collecting and Preserving Specimens of Plants', Blaikie Papers.

the warmth of a fire from time to time so that the plants did not grow damp and deteriorate. Plants (or berries) too juicy or succulent to press without damage were to be wrapped in a linen rag and then sealed in a brandy bottle. If he was to obtain flowers, fruits and seeds, it was essential to make the most of his time, and without expert direction he hardly knew where to begin.

He was to spend the next two solitary and rather aimless weeks between the slopes of the Jura and visits to Bourdigny and Beaulieu, an estate near the lakeside where the head gardener showed him the treasures of his hothouses. On these early desultory excursions, he was struck by the intensely blue-flowered *Viola calcarata* and two gentians, *Gentiana verna* and *G. acaulis*, this latter 'so beautiful as to be past description'. However, the pace of his life was to change after he visited Geneva on 22 May to order a suit of clothes for his expeditions to the mountains. In the town he had the good fortune to strike up a conversation with a young bookseller called Henri Albert Gosse.[20] At the time of his meeting with Blaikie, Gosse was a young man of 22, and an enthusiastic botanist. He and Blaikie became friends at once and spent the evening together communicating as best they could and studying the works of the botanist, Jacquin.[21] Unable to tear himself away, Blaikie put up at an inexpensive inn called the *Petit Maure* where the accommodation was in dormitories,[22] and the next morning, the 23rd May, his new friend did him an act of the greatest kindness; he took him to visit de Saussure, Switzerland's foremost scientist and an authority on Swiss plants. Saussure[23] was the natural scientist who had 'discovered' Chamonix and would give an account of the whole Alpine region in his four volume *Voyage dans les Alpes*. His first excursions at the age of 16 were to the Salève, the white limestone ridge, rich in alpine flora, to the south east of Geneva. By 1758 he had climbed the Dôle, the highest peak in the Jura, where the sight of the high Alps made him long to explore them. Then, in 1760, when he was 20, he arrived in Chamonix which he described as little frequented at that time. It became his obsession to reach the summit of Mont Blanc and he offered a reward to the first person who would conquer the majestic peak which had so captured his imagination. In 1787, one year after Dr Michel-Gabriel

20. Henri-Albert Gosse (1753–1816) assisted his father Jean Gosse in his Geneva book shop. His uncle was also a bookseller in the city. Gosse was passionately interested in the Natural Sciences and, shortly after Blaikie's visit, left for Paris where he distinguished himself by winning prizes in chemistry, pharmacy and botany. As a result of his success he won the friendship of Lavoisier, Lacepède and Parmentier. On his return to Switzerland he established a pharmacy, became a founder of the *Société Helvétique de Physique et d'Histoire Naturelle*, the oldest learned society in Switzerland. Later, he followed a career in politics.
21. Nicolaus Joseph von Jacquin (1727–1817); see ch, 2, n. 40.
22. L. Seylac, *Excursions d'un botaniste écossais dans les Alpes et le Jura* (Neuchatel, 1935), p. 39.
23. Horace Benedict de Saussure (1740–1799), Professor of Philosophy at the Academy of Geneva and Switzerland's leading scientist and botanist. He had a country house at Conche on a curve of the River Arve near Geneva. *Voyage dans les Alpes*, 4 vols (Neuchatel, 1779) was his most famous work. Montagnier (p. 5) remarks how strange it is that in the *Diary of a Scotch Gardener*, pp. 34, 35, Blaikie does not mention Saussure by name. This is an omission in the published version; Saussure's name does appear in the original diary.

Paccard with his guide, Jacques Balmat, had made the first ascent, the Professor finally achieved his ambition to make the ascent himself.

Saussure must, like Joseph Banks, have recognised in Blaikie the qualities which make a good plant collector. He showed him his herbarium and gave him detailed instructions on where to find plants. He probably also inspired him with this advice; that to observe and benefit from the mountains, he must leave the roads, which almost always wound their way along the bottoms of the valleys or crossed the lowest and easiest passes, to climb to the highest summits and there view a multitude of objects at once. Such excursions were difficult. The true observer would travel on foot, not on horseback. His powers of endurance would be tested to the limits and he would sometimes be exposed to danger and often suffer disappointments, but the fresh, invigorating air of the Alps would act like a restoring balm to his body while the great spectacle of nature would renew his spirit and his courage.[24]

Fired by his meeting with the professor, Blaikie set out immediately across country for the Salève, where de Saussure himself first started collecting plants. Following the naturalist's instructions, he discovered some of the rarer plants at once, *Daphne alpina* and *Anthyllis montana* amongst them. Still relatively unfit, he found 'the rocks very steep'. On that first day in the Salève he made friends with a Scottish doctor, a Jacobite who had fled his country in 1745.[25] He had settled either in Monnetier or its twin village, Mornex,[26] where he had married a local woman and raised a family. Through him Blaikie found comfortable lodgings at Monnetier, near the church embowered in lime trees, at an inn run by a Mme Laurence,[27] a good cook and motherly woman.

After a week collecting in the Salève, he returned to his base at St Genis and, on 4 June, began searching for plants on the north side of the Jura. He paints an atmospheric picture of the desolate countryside of the Franche Comté. Snow was lying thick 'in many places, and some dismal Rocks shaded by the lofty spruce firs render those scenes melancholy and lonesome. In those woods grows great plenty of the Ciprepidium. In the plain to the north of this mountain there is some cottages and small fields[28] where the inhabitants lives more upon the produce of their cattle than the produce of their Agriculture … there is many of the Summer huts but all empty, the inhabitants being not yet arrived with their cattle. In many of those declivities, the verdure is exceeding fine, the grass intermixed with Narcissus, *Viola calcara (ta)*, *Gentiana verna* and numbers of other flowers. Found upon some of the

24. De Saussure, Introduction, pp. x–xi.
25. After the defeat of Charles Edward Stuart, the Young Pretender, son of James III, the Old Pretender, at the Battle of Culloden.
26. Montagnier, 'Thomas Blaikie and Michel-Gabriel Paccard', in *The Alpine Journal*, no. 246, May 1933, suggests that from village information the Doctor's name may have been Bain. He identifies Monnetier-Mornex as the place where he lived and Monnetier nearby as the location of the inn. See also Beckford, *The Travel Diaries of William Beckford*, ed. G. Chapman, 2 vols (London, 1928), which describes Monnetier as a straggling village with its church tower 'embosomed in gigantic limes'.
27. L. Seylac, p. 40.
28. Probably Valmijoux.

watering troughs at the bottom of the Mountain plenty of the *Swertia perennis*. Returned in the evening and lodged at St Genix.'[29]

Saussure had undoubtedly told him to climb the Dôle and at the beginning of June, the season for going to the mountains at last arrived. Gaussen's herds set out for their summer transhumance at Mont Pierre Olivier, an unidentified mountain pasturage to the south of the Lac des Rousses between Mont Dôle and Mont Tendre.[30] Blaikie arrived at the same time as the herdsmen and took part in the traditional festivities associated with the move to the mountains. He describes in one of the most attractive parts of his diary (7 June 1775) how companies of herdsmen with as many as two hundred heads of cattle made their way up the mountain, and continues, 'This is a great fete[31] for the people. Their cows' horns is adorned with flowers, and [the cows are] followed with the herds[32] and others playing upon the music and dancing. They have sometimes a horse to carry their different luggage such as pots &c for making cheese and milk dishes. This is most of their furniture. Some of their cows carry part of this furniture. Each herd is provided with a one-footed stool for milking which, with a strap and buckle, they buckle round their loins so when they sit down, they balance upon their legs ... as if their body was placed upon three legs. This, by means of [a] girth is buckled to the person so that he walks easily with his stool at his backside, the foot of which, at a distance, appears as if the man had a tail ... this seems very convenient.' He observed them milking and noted, 'Their manner of straining their milk is very clever and well adapted to these Mountains. It is a funnel shaped pail in which, at the bottom, they put a handful of spruce branches with the tops upwards. This fills up the strainer, and the leaves all standing upwards, prevents all hairs or any thing to pass, and strains the milk better than any cloth. This is changed every milking so that they are always clean and fresh ... Here', he adds, 'I stayed very happy with the cowherds, lived upon good milk and cream'.[33] The men would only let him pay for his lodging if he promised to return for their feast two nights later. He passed the time in between fruitfully on Mount Dôle finding *Tozzia alpina*, *Vaccinium uliginosum* and *Mespilus alpinus*, none of them rare.

Most of all, he enjoyed the 'noble and striking *vue* of the other hills and over the Lake of Geneva to Savoy'. As he descended the mountain, a thunder storm raged beneath him and he witnessed 'several trees tore with the lightning. The echo of the Rocks makes the noise awful.' He was late in reaching the lower slopes and, as it was almost night, he lodged in a little cottage where the people gave him some eggs, the best fare that they could provide. The next day, he collected once more on Mount Dôle before returning to keep his promise to the herdsmen. His last night with them, 'was spent very merry in dancing and drinking, one of the company played upon the fiddle and the others danced, I joined likewise and so we danced all barefooted ...

29. Diary, 4 June 1775.
30. It is likely that the name Pierre Olivier refers to the lessee of the pastures.
31. For a description of other festivities on Mount Dole see De Saussure, *Voyage dans les Alpes*, vol. 1, p. 289.
32. Herdsmen.
33. Diary, 7 June 1775.

At last when we was tired and the wine finished we retired to rest upon our beds of spruce branches and hay where we slept comfortably.'[34]

From here he set out for Mount Dôle once again. *Rhododendron ferrugineum*, the Mountain Rose, made a fine sight on the slopes and drew from him the following quotation:

> In the wild waste remote from human toil
> There Rocks bring forth and desolation smile
> Here blooms the Rose where human face ne'er shone
> And spreads its beauties to the Sun alone.[35]

He was to return here several times and later, on 18 August, he lingered at the summit to watch the sun set upon the mountain. The view was magnificent. The whole range of mountains was visible, from the Dauphiné as far as St Gothard, and in its centre towered Mont Blanc. Far below lay the lake of Geneva surrounded by its cultivated fields and vineyards and with a multitude of little villages and towns scattered over the fields and slopes. Blaikie describes in his diary how, 'in the afternoon went to the top of Mont Dolle this being the highest of all the Mountains of the Jura. The weather being very clear, I amused myself amongst the different clefts of the rocks in seeking after plants, in purpose to see the sun set from the top of this high Mountain and indeed it is beautiful to see how quick the shadow of those mountains lengthens. And you upon the highest centre of the horizon. The sight is really noble, as is the different shades of the Mountains.' When he recovers from the emotion which the beauty of the scene inspires in him, the practical Scot is almost ashamed of the intensity of feeling it has aroused in him and goes on, 'This I was happy to see but when I found the night coming on and the Distance I had to descend the mountain, [it] made me regret my curiosity. However, I made shift to arrive at my shepherds' huts although late.'[36] Although this area had been explored by Swiss botanists, Blaikie's is probably the first description in English of a view from the top of the Dôle,[37] a view that became famous later from Goethe's account of it on his visit there in June 1777.[38] The scene gave Goethe a sense of how futile it is to try to grasp the infinite when the finite is so incomprehensible and he paints a dramatic picture of the red glow of the sun fading from the peaks and leaving them a cold greenish grey. At last only Mont Blanc retains a faint flush of life which one is reluctant to see depart, as if it were the last sign of life at the death of a loved one. Goethe's picture is a compelling one yet Blaikie's simple expression 'and you upon the highest centre of the horizon' conveys immediately that sense of wonder, almost ecstasy, which the individual occasionally experiences, alone with the awesome beauty of nature; a feeling that was to find expression in Wordsworth's *Descriptive Sketches*, written seventeen years later:

---

34. Diary, 10 June 1775.
35. Diary, 11 June 1775.
36. Diary, 18 August 1775.
37. Montagnier, p. 8.
38. Albert Bielshowsky, *The Life of Goethe* (New York, 1905–8), vol. 1, p. 350.

> But now with other mind I stand alone
> Upon the summit of this naked cone

But this was still June, and Blaikie determined to make one more visit to the Salève before he ventured further afield. It was during this excursion that his confidence was shaken by a nearly fatal accident. On returning from the south-west tip of the range after visiting a monastery called La Pommière, he decided to cross over to the east side by climbing up over the top. The Salève was known for its huge boulders and, high up on the mountain, he found his path blocked by two enormous rocks. Rather than go back, he attempted to scramble over them. He describes what happened next, 'the bush upon which I stood began to crack and give way, which frighted me, that I began to look about. But when I looked behind me and saw the precipice over the under Rock, I began soon to think I was lost and threw away my Box and plants and every thing, to the bottom which, however, did not fall over the second precipice. Here I clung to the bushes as well as I could and descended gradually from bush to bush until I got down, and so recovered myself as well as I could. However, sat down for some time, for when I had reflected of the danger and examined the rocks, I trembled, no body being near me to give any assistance. Even if I had fallen and broke a leg I must have remained there and perished.[39] So, after comforting myself in the best manner I could, I concluded to return back by the road I came.'

His trials were not over. Night was drawing in and he dare not attempt to go any further. He found the entrance to a large cave and having examined the interior as carefully as he could in the fading light, he writes, 'I found it a good comfortable lodging, about ten feet wide and above 30 in length. Began cutting down Branches of trees to stop up the entrance of the cave. This I soon effectuated, and with some other branches formed my bed. Here I slept but very little, dreadin[g] the wolves which is common in those woods.' The next morning (20 June) he left his shelter at first light and he continues, 'I began to move and continued searching after some plants, but more particularly the road to return to my former lodgings [at Monnetier] in purpose to procure victuals having no provision with me, expecting to return home yesterday.'

Before he reached the inn, a man ran out to meet him, taking hold of his hand and asking him how he was and where he had been. And when he arrived, he found the landlady in tears, convinced that he had been murdered. On hearing of his ordeal, the kindly couple kissed and embraced him. Two men had been murdered on the mountains and, from the description of one of them, they had been convinced it was Blaikie.

On his return to St Genis after his near accident in the Salève, he received on the 24 June, a visit from the region's most distinguished resident, Voltaire, who came to view his plants. That the great man should have taken the trouble to visit him is proof of the stir his presence had caused. And had he realised how many visitors

---

39. Diary, 19 June 1775. Probably more climbers have been killed on the Salève according to Montagnier (p. 6) than on any other summit of the western Alps.

plotted and schemed for letters of introduction to the philosopher, or crowded into the ante-chamber at Ferney to catch a glimpse of him, he might have been more impressed.[40] He describes the meeting in his diary, 'This day had a visit from the famous Voltaire who came to see my collection of plants. He speaks English.[41] He is esteemed one of the greatest men in Europe and of the most universal knowledge. He lives upon the borders of the Lake of Geneva [42] where he has a very fine château. He has been exiled from France,[43] his native country, for writing against their government. However, he was very well pleased with my collection and surprised to find that in the numbering of my plants I had adopted Haller. Voltaire is rather tall but very thin. They tell me he is about 80 years old and has been continually writing and publishing.'[44] Voltaire was 81 years old at the time he came to look at Blaikie's collection. Many of his visitors described his skeletal appearance but also noted his piercing eyes and their expression of spirit and vivacity.[45] Voltaire's observation about Blaikie's use of Haller's numbering system showed his up to date knowledge of botany and was no doubt intended to do so.[46]

During the first half of July, Blaikie made several trips into the north-east Jura. The rock formations in this part of the mountains fascinated him. One enormous rock, about half a mile in circumference, held his attention for hours and he spent a great part of the day 'in examining round this wonderful rock'. His French had now improved to the point where he could communicate easily with the herdsmen in their summer pasturage. They showed him the plants they picked, leading him to any they considered unusual and described which ones they used as remedies for themselves or their cattle, quizzing him at the same time about those that he considered beneficial. He noticed they kept no goats in the mountain and they explained this was because the animals would be killed by wolves, which were common in the Jura. From this particular expedition he returned across the Dôle making his way to Aubonne and reaching Geneva by the lakeside. In gravel amongst the small channels that fed into the lake, he discovered one of the plants that he was

40. The Rev. William Cox, tutor to the son of the Earl of Pembroke reported to Lady Pembroke in a letter dated Berne, 15 September 1776, that Voltaire had refused to see the young Lord Herbert and is reported to have said, 'Voilà Milord Pembroke qui m'envoye son fils qui a 17 ans et moi j'ai 82. Nous sommes pas d'accord, et je souffre comme un malheureux; je ne peux pas le voir'. *Pembroke Papers* (1780–94), ed. Lord Herbert (1950), p. 91.

41. He preferred not to and told Boswell in 1764 that English required the tongue to press against the teeth and he had no teeth. *Boswell on the Grand Tour*, ed. F. A. Pottle (1953), p. 279, Sunday 23 December 1764.

42. Ferney.

43. Ferney was just inside the French border but so near Switzerland that it didn't matter.

44. Diary, 24 June 1775.

45. Dr John Moore, *A view of Society and Manners in France, Switzerland etc.* (8th edn, London, 1793), pp. 179–80. Voltaire was in his 81st year. Mme de Genlis, the famous French blue-stocking, visited him in August 1775 and, although he did not receive her very graciously, declared that his eyes were the most spiritual she had ever seen. Gabriel de Broglie, *Madame de Genlis* (Paris, 1985), p. 83.

46. See comments on systems of nomenclature, chapter 3.

to introduce to England, *Epilobium dodonaei*. Its characteristically strong roots burrowed so deep into the gravel that he had difficulty in digging it up. He also noted silk-worms colonising the local pine trees, and would bring some back to England in the hope of starting silk manufacture.[47] The French Pays de Gex to the east of the Fort de l'Écluse was the wildest of any he had yet passed, and so empty that he could walk for an entire day through a country of woods, mountains and lakes without meeting a soul. In some places the spruce firs grew so thick and close that, he wrote, 'hardly any thing grows under them for there is hardly light, although in other places there is steep rocks out of which gushes falls of water which seem really enchanting amidst those gloomy and melancholy regions'. Towards evening, he would come across a little hut where the herdsmen would share what they had with him, usually milk or cheese with some hay for a bed.[48]

Blaikie had now grown familiar with the mountains and felt a bond of comradeship with its people. Physically more fit, he was ready for the challenge of a longer excursion.

---

47. See chapter 2.
48. Reminiscent of the lines describing St Preux's excursion to the Haut Valais in *La Nouvelle Héloise* Part I, Letter XXIII. 'Sometimes great rocks hung in ruins above my head. Sometimes from above, roaring waterfalls covered me with their thick mists of spray. Sometimes an unending torrent opened before me an abyss into whose depths I dared not look. Sometimes I found I was lost in the gloom of thick woods. Sometimes in emerging from a deep gorge a smiling meadow would refresh my eyes.'

CHAPTER 4

Berne and Beyond

O N 19 July 1775, armed with a letter of introduction from Monsieur Gaussen, Blaikie set off east along the wilder southern shore of the lake of Geneva, part of the beautiful but more backward region of Chablais. At Thonon he dined and at Evian he procured a guide to lead him south down the steep Drance d'Abondance valley. They spent the first night at Châtel, the highest village in the valley, just below the Pas de Morgins. Then, for the next three days, Blaikie collected tirelessly from morning to night, sleeping in shepherds' huts and living on their diet of cheese and milk. Bread, in this poor region, was a luxury they did not possess. He noted in his diary that he 'found those mountains rich in plants which gave me great satisfaction. Found plenty of the *Senecio nova*, No. 63[1] of Haller and several other plants'.[2] For the first time, he saw the chamois nimbly scaling the tops of the rocks 'so that there is no coming nigh them. There was some of them upon those precipices where it is hardly possible to imagine any animal without wings could go'.

His guide's insistence on following the paths at the foot of the valley irritated Blaikie whose heart was set on climbing the mountains. The guide grew tired and indignant at the pace he was expected to keep up and objected to the lack of bread in this impoverished region, complaining that 'he could not climb, walk and live at that rate and if I intended to break my neck he would not break his'.[3] One has some sympathy with the guide, constantly on the move and deprived of bread and a good bed. Eventually, he would go no farther. They were obliged to descend on the Sunday morning to a village (possibly Troistorrents) where the guide attended Mass. At mid-day they dined at the village of Monthey whose tall, obelisk-like steeple could be seen for miles amidst a wood of chestnut trees. As they sat outside the inn, they watched a man, a gypsy or an Italian entertain the crowd. He had, as Blaikie describes, 'a rope fastened to the steeple and the other end fixed to a tree. 'Upon this rope,' Blaikie tells us, 'he was to fly from the steeple to the ground. All the people in the village was assembled. The actor began at the top and, after he had descended about 10 feet upon the rope, he tied himself, sometimes by one foot, and let himself hang down from the rope a great way, and sometimes by one hand, and then recovered himself back upon the great rope. But he had not long begun this before the rope broke in the middle, but luckily for him he was tied fast to the upper part where he recovered himself, and so climbed up and got in at the window of the steeple.' The

---

1. Haller No. 63 refers to *Senecio subalpinus* Koch. Blaikie's original specimen is preserved in the A. E. Smith Collection at the Linnean Society.
2. Diary, 21 July 1775.
3. On leaving Chatel Blaikie appears to have gone by the Pas de Morgins to one of the villages of the Troistorrents and then travelled back up towards Monthey.

near disaster caused consternation. 'The people was all in an uproar for every one thought that the poor fellow would fall to the ground and be dashed to pieces. After the fright, he wanted to begin, but the people opposed and so this sport finished which is their Sunday's recreation, although there is not one of them will work,' he added bitterly, obviously smarting from his guide's refusal to continue collecting.[4]

Blaikie's objective was the town of Aigle but when they reached Vouvry in the Rhône valley on 24 July, his patience with his guide ran out and he dismissed him, engaging him instead to carry his collection of plants back to Evian and thence by carrier to Monsieur Gaussen's at Bourdigny. He continued along the side of the Rhône to Porte de Sex where he caught a ferry across the River. The passage cost him a 'demi bash'.[5] Finding no road at the other side, he walked across the fen-like water meadows to the town, collecting plants of the marshes as he went along. At Aigle, he tried to deliver a letter to the pastor, Abraham-Louis De Coppet,[6] but finding him not at home, took a room at 'the Signe de la Ville de Berne',[7] and called upon the pastor the next day, the 25 July.

De Coppet was a distinguished botanist, a friend and collaborator of Haller who had assisted him in his great work *Historia Stirpium indigenarum Helvetiae* (1768).[8] He was also a much loved and respected local figure. The 69 year old and the 25 year old took to each other immediately. United in their enthusiasm for botany, they set off together to examine the flora of the neighbouring mountainside, carrying home specimens of *Astragalus monspessulanus* and several other plants which Blaikie had not as yet found. However, fit as he was for his age, De Coppet realised that Blaikie's pace was too much for him and arranged for him to have as his guide Abraham Thomas, a man whose stamina and agility was unsurpassed and whose legendary knowledge of plants and their habitats had made him, and his father before him, Haller's favourite collectors.[9] Haller had chosen Abraham Thomas's father as a plant collector for his acute powers of observation, his outstanding memory and his intelligence. These qualities, and an extraordinary flair for botany, were inherited in even greater measure by his son and together father and son collected all over the alpine regions of Switzerland, the Valais, Italy and the Grisons, contributing greatly to Haller's collections and supplying universites and botanical collections also. Walkers of exceptional stamina, like Blaikie himself, excursions of up to eighteen hours at a

4. Diary, 23 July 1775. Blaikie calls the village 'Mante'.
5. A batz, was worth about 3 sous in 1787. See Thomas Martyn, *Sketch of a Tour through Swisserland* (London, 1787). Martyn paid 25 batz for a guide and a mule in 1787 and reckoned one batz equalled 1½d.
6. Abraham-Louis De Coppet (1706–1785).
7. The inn was the Maison de Ville. See J. G. Ebel, *Manuel du Voyageur en Suisse*, 4th edn (Zurich, 1819).
8. Haller acknowledges the help of '*Abrahamus Ludovicus de Coppet, vir venerabilis*' in the Preface to his work, p. xvii.
9. Haller, *Historia stirpium*. In his introduction p. xvii refers to Abrahamus Thomas and gives a list of the places where Thomas had collected. Petrus Thomas is mentioned on p xviii.

time were normal for them. They were also renowned for their generous and hospitable natures and it is no wonder that Blaikie found them kindred spirits.

They lived near Bex close to the Gryonne torrent where the cliffs of the 9000 ft Grand Mourveran towered above them, an appropriate dwelling place, wrote Blaikie for such a 'curious man.' He goes on to describe it as 'situated at the bottom of those prodigious Rocks at the bottom of which there is lofty spruce firs with a rivulet running over the rocks which form its bottom. The sides is covered with long moss. Betwixt the house and the mountain there are some fields for hay and corn.' The next day, 27 July, he and Abraham Thomas made a long excursion from Bex to Sion.[10] The 'terrible' scenery of the Diablerets, an area devastated by landslides, affected him powerfully. 'The Mountain on the left,' he wrote in his diary, 'is cleft in two and the one part of it is fallen into the valley. The other side stands almost perpendicular where you can perceive all the stratum of the ground ... In some places there is stones or rather rocks of a prodigious size thrown across this valley by this eruption into the woods, where they have cleared avenues of those large firs and in some others [the trees lie] with their roots in the air and their tops buried in the ground. This place may be called the Valley of Desolation because Desolation appears on all sides. This is what they call La Montagne du Diable [Diableret][11] which was clove by an earthquake about 30 years ago.' Then he goes on to quote these lines:

> Dire Earthquakes rent the solid alps below
> And from the summits shook the eternal snow [12]

The havoc Blaikie describes had been caused by two landslides. The first in 1713 had swept down upon the villages on a clear sunny afternoon without warning, killing many people and destroying many houses and cattle. The second, in 1749, for which it had been possible to give a warning, took no lives but cast the debris further over the mountain.[13] Blaikie, always fascinated by the structure of rocks, wanted to stay and examine the various strata of exposed rock, but they had a long day ahead and could not delay.

Next, they made their way by the Pas de Cheville (6695 ft), 'a narrow path cut in the rock with the mountain over your head on the left hand and steep rock on your right'. They saw chamoix and Thomas pointed out a vulture to Blaikie. After dining at Avens sur Conthey they reached the 'pretty little town' of Sion about seven that evening. Huge goitres swelled the necks of some of the women of the town and a fair proportion of the people they saw were cretins. The reason for the condition was

---

10. There were, according to the Doyen Bridel's 'Excursions de Bex à Sion' in the *Conservateur suisse* 1786 (vol. 2), two routes from Bex to Sion. The first by Mont Avançon was the easier and would have been chosen by Thomas because of its rich flora. The two routes joined at the foot of the Anxeinde and then the path descended by the Pas de Cheville, which Bridel said would have been described as a precipice anywhere else, to Deborence, then down the valley of Triquent by the side of the River Lizière to Avens and thence to Sion.
11. 10,476 ft.
12. Diary, 27 July 1775. I would be pleased to hear from anyone who can identify these lines.

not known at the time but it was sometimes ascribed to the dirt and filth of the inhabitants of the Haut Valais of which Sion was the capital. Blaikie accepted that it was caused by the water though he also thought that it might be hereditary.

At Sion he left Thomas with regret, and with a new guide set out for Berne. The spa town of Leukerbad where they stopped on 29 July was crowded with visitors. Blaikie tasted the waters, then saw evidence of the restorative properties of the hot stream when a withered lettuce, immersed for a few moments, was brought out as fresh 'as if newly cut'. Disappointingly, there were no new plants here and they set out after dinner for the Gemmi pass. The Gemmi, with its narrow dangerous paths, its steep precipices and deep, sheer drops had caused even seasoned travellers to quake with fright before its refurbishment in the eighteenth century by the cantons of Berne and the Valais.[14] This refurbishment, between 1736 and 1741 marked a triumph of engineering for the time; 2.5 miles of rock were blown up by gunpowder to create a sharply winding path about 9 ft wide which zigzagged up the mountain, sometimes through a tunnel of rock and at others on the brink of a precipice, presenting the walker with a continually changing scene. Horses and mules could not be used, either in the ascent or the descent, but were left loose to find their own way. At certain places ladders were fixed to the rock to make it easier to climb.[15] Blaikie's description of the ascent seems to be the earliest one written in English, although the pass was used frequently in the summer by travellers to the baths.

He writes, 'We set out towards the Mount Gemmi where there is a road cut where the people go up a perpendicular rock amazing high, and in some places there is ladders tied from rock to rock where the people passes. Here we can see the people, like little birds upon the top of these rocks, beginning to come down or going up, but from the top you can hardly discern the houses in the valley. Here, going up this road, or rather ladder, there is upon one of the opposite rocks a sort of sentry box but I could not discover how it was placed nor how they could get to it as it seems to be fixed upon the sides of the rock. Neither could I discover the use of it but to guard this passage which might easily be intercepted, [for] by breaking one of those ladders none can pass. It is indeed very surprising how this road stands; it seems only tied slightly to those rocks with branches.'[16]

At the top of the pass, he collected several sorts of salixes, *Diapensia helvetica*[17] and *Cherleria sedoides*,[18] all new to him, and he resolved to stay at the only inn, the Schwarrenbach, for an extra day in the hope of finding more. The inn, open for no more than a few months each year, was buried under 18 ft of snow in the winter and even in summer a keen north wind blew. The terrain was beautiful but snow still

13. Bourrit M-J, *Description des Cols* 1803 (p. 24).
14. See G. R. DeBeer, *Early Travellers in the Alps* (London, 1930), p. 38.
15. The Rev William Coxe describes the Gemmi in *Sketches of the Natural State of Swisserland*, 1779, pp. 225–7. He was in Switzerland in 1776.
16. Diary, 29 July 1775.
17. *Androsace vandelli.*
18. *Minuartia sedoides.*

lay to the north. Nothing, however, could deter Blaikie from setting out next morning, not even his guide who, after a few minutes' walk, refused to go any further but followed as Blaikie tells us 'into a valley in this mountain by a little wood'. He goes on, 'I was astonished to find my man rush out of this thicket with another, armed with an axe, almost naked with a beard like an old Rabbin [Rabbi]. They both approached to me with threats, as I could see, but could not understand what he said. But when he perceived that I was armed he began, as it appeared, to beg of me not to go any further for, as I went towards the mountain to go up, the man kept before me. At last, when he saw that he could make nothing of me, the[n] they both sat down and let me go on. So I left them, although, as I went up, for a long way they called after me but I could not understand what they said, they some times shaking their fists at me and I in return did the same to them until we lost sight of one another.' [19]

Rhododendron hirsutum was in full bloom on the slopes. In places, he wrote, 'the sides of the mountain were entirely red with it but there is none of the *R. ferrugineum* to be found'. As he climbed higher, the plants grew fewer and fewer and he abandoned plant hunting for the sheer challenge of reaching the top and surveying the vista. The snow was thick and banked now but he pushed on, cutting steps in the snow for his feet until he reached the summit which he found 'entirely bare'. The view, however was impressive. 'From the north of this mountain there is an extensive valley [20] which seems to be surrounded by those rock or precipices ... I could see no sort of vegetable, but the bottom [was] entirely covered with huge pieces of the adjacent rocks which time had tumbled down.' His next observation is typical of the kind of visual experience which would influence his plantings later. 'Here the *vue* is remarkable to observe all the adjacent Mountains which surrounds you, the bottoms of which is entirely covered with tall firs. Then begins larix, and higher the *Pinus cembra*, but the degree of height every plant takes according to their height upon the Mountain, till at last it dwindles into the smallest sort and at last all vegetation ceases.'

A thick mist hampered his descent and, as he came near the inn, the landlord ran out and, to his surprise, shook him by the hand. Once they were inside the building, the guide appeared 'skulking' and Blaikie turned on him but, before he could say more than a few words, the landlord felled the man with a blow and, afraid the guide would be killed, Blaikie felt obliged to defend him. It transpired that the man had tried to steal Blaikie's belongings and although the people at the inn warned him against it, Blaikie was forced, since he could not find the way himself, to continue with the same guide on the journey down the Kanderstal valley to Frutigen, one of the most beautiful villages of the canton of Berne.

Here, on 1 August, he paid off the man and left the town with another guide in the direction of Berne. At the village of Aeschi they enjoyed the fine view of the whole lake of Thoune and part of the lake of Bienne. They tasted the cherry liqueur for which

---

19. Diary, 30 July 1775.
20. According to Montagnier, this is probably the upper ridge of the Ueschninthal, to the north-west of the Daubensee.

the place was famous. Blaikie noted that the fruit in the orchards was small, scarcely bigger than the wild cherry, but nonetheless it was grafted. Perhaps thinking of the cherry orchards of Corstorphine, he tried unsuccessfully to find out which species it was. Then, finding scarce plants all the way, they carried on through the rich vale of Frutigen to Lessigen on the bank of the lake of Thoune. Here, they crossed the lake (probably to Neuhaus) with the object of reaching Grindelwald that evening but rain forced them to stop at Wilderswil for the night. Next morning, they set out early for the Grindelwald glaciers through wooded mountains where, at the edge of the spruce trees, Blaikie gathered a number of plants which were new to him.[21]

At last they came to the glaciers. Blaikie was enchanted to see 'this valley entirely covered with ice. It is not a level ice like a river that is froze but snow that has froze for Ages and converted as into hard rocks with large cracks running all across of a prodigious depth, so that in many places you walk upon this ice as if upon the top of a house. All around this valley is surrounded with huge rocks and pyramids of ice which is one of the most striking Landscapes that can be imagined.'[22] Great was his disappointment when the guide refused to take him across the glacier but there was nothing he could do since it was too dangerous to traverse alone. The Rev William Coxe was to have the same experience when he visited the glacier on 14 August the following year; his guide assuring him that it was impossible to proceed on the ice and that no traveller had penetrated farther.[23]

Reluctantly, Blaikie descended and, with his guide, took a boat at the lakeside to sail the length of the lake to Thoune. The three hour passage on the lake was enjoyable, for the views were picturesque, the borders edged by steep mountains with here and there tall pyramids of rock rising vertically from the edge of the water. They reached Berne at around seven that evening after a long and exhausting day in which they had walked an incredible thirty nine miles.[24]

At Berne, Blaikie paid off his latest guide, whom he found 'only an encumbrance', and continued on his own. As he walked through the streets, he remarked on a strange sight, 'a great many people chained to a cart with iron chains round their waist and leg'. They were criminals who served their sentence cleaning the streets. 'The women sweep and have an iron collar about their necks with a bar of iron standing out about a foot or 16 inches that every body may see them. Here, every cart has its number with a conductor. However, I did not see them so mortified with their situation as might be expected, for all along the street while they stop to load,

---

21. *Satyrium repens* L., *Pyrola uniflora* L. and *Ophrys corallorhiza* (possibly *Corallorhiza innata* R. Br.). *Ophrys corallorhiza* is not mentioned in his alpine list so he may have had difficulty with its identification.

22. Diary, 1 August 1775.

23. Coxe, *Sketches of the Natural State of Swisserland*, vol. 1, pp. 204–6. An earlier visitor was William Burnett, son of Bishop Gilbert Burnett, whose letter to the Royal Society 'concerning the Icy Mountains of Switzerland was published in the *Philosophical Transactions* of the Royal Society in March and April 1709. He also took only a few steps on the ice.

24. Montagnier, p. 16, n. 18, gives the distance from Wilderswil to Grindelwald as 9¾ miles; from Grindelwald to Thoune 11¾ miles and from Thoune to Berne 17½ miles.

I saw them dealing with the people in buying and selling shoes or other old cloths which they bought up and mended, to sell at their spare times, as undoubtedly there was amongst them some good workmen of different trades.' [25]

He had a letter of introduction to a M. Samuel Engel [26] in Berne and next morning delivered it at his house. Engel took him to Hindelbank, [27] about 6 miles away, to visit the château built in 1730 by a M. d'Erlach. The farms on the domain were considered model ones, hence, presumably, Mr Engel's particular interest. Engel, who was to have introduced Blaikie to Haller, had to disappoint him as the great man was seriously ill and by way of consolation he gave Blaikie a letter for a Dr Gagnebin at La Ferrière in the Bernese Oberland. Gagnebin, [28] an army surgeon who had retired to La Ferrière and established a practice there, was a friend of both Rousseau and Haller and reputed to be equally as good a botanist as the latter. [29]

After packing up his plants and arranging for them to be carried to Bourdigny, Blaikie set out to the north-west of Berne towards La Ferrière. He spent the night of 4 August at Bienne and reached La Ferrière the next afternoon. Gagnebin showed him his botanical and mineral collections and then together they went plant collecting in the general direction of the Jura, Blaikie's goal. They walked together for three days botanising, and Gagnebin showed Blaikie the unusual sights of the region. They attended a wedding together in one of the villages and enjoyed the dancing afterwards. They climbed La Corbatière and the Tête de Ran where Gagnebin had to admit, to his chagrin, and to Blaikie's scarcely concealed amusement, since the Dr prided himself on his knowledge of the region, that he was completely lost. They spent the night in a shepherd's hut and the next morning, having rediscovered their location, the disgruntled Gagnebin put Blaikie on his road and returned home. Over the next few days Blaikie made his way alone back to his familiar haunts in the Jura. While he was collecting near Cottens, he met another botanist. They showed each other the plants they had collected and the botanist, whose name was Jean Laurent Garcin, [30] invited Blaikie to dine with him at his small château nearby. [31] Garcin was the son of

---

25. Diary, 3 August 1775.

26. Samuel Engel (1702–1784). Librarian of the city of Berne. Distinguished magistrate, one of the founders of the Economic Society of Berne. An agronomist who is credited with having introduced the culture of the potato in the Noyon region.

27. Gibbon singles out the estate for praise as being in great good taste. See DeBeer, *Miscellanea Gibboniana* (London, 1951), p. 59. Hindelbank was also a popular place with late eighteenth-century visitors who came to consult an internationally famous doctor, Schupbach (or Schuppach), who diagnosed by examining the patient's urine. Coxe, *Sketches of the Natural State of Swisserland*, pp. 429–30.

28. Abraham Gagnebin (1707–1800). His collections of botany and minerals attracted many visitors. He collaborated with Haller in his great work.

29. He is mentioned twice in Haller's preface.

30. Jean Laurent Garcin (1733–1781). After a life of varied careers he had returned to Aubonne. His marriage brought him the estate of Cottens-sur Aubonne where he settled in 1771 and devoted himself to scientific studies. It is here that Blaikie visited him.

31. In the *Gardener's Magazine* (1836), vol. 12, p 690, Blaikie gives further details of his meeting with Garcin, 'When I was rambling upon Mt Jura, I met one day a gentleman, who, like

an eminent botanist, after whom Linnaeus had named the genus Garcinia, a family of tender evergreens.[32] Together Garcin and Blaikie studied the page of Linnaeus's *Species Plantarum* in which the Garcinia appeared and, on discovering, as Blaikie recounts, that 'the plant before that is the Blakea,[33] he asked me if it was not named after my father. I told him *surement* so we concluded we was very nearly related in the Linnean System and so we must go together to the mountains and spend a day or two.' However, Garcin, a man in poor health, lasted only a single day at Blaikie's pace and Blaikie continued alone. He was back in St Genis on 24 August after an absence of 34 days.

This period of his stay in the Alps had been particularly valuable to him as a botanist. He had been able to learn from the very collectors who had contributed to Haller's work and had visited some of the rarest Alpine plant habitats with them. More importantly, in the light of what was to come, he had reached the peak of his physical condition.

One week later he was off again, this time on the journey that was to prove the highlight of his whole expedition and the one of most interest to alpine historians for the early picture it gives of the Paccard family and in particular of Michel-Gabriel Paccard, who in 1786 was the first person to reach the summit of Mont Blanc. Paccard had been born in 1757 and was 18 years old at the time of Blaikie's visit. The excursions which he undertook with the young Scot demonstrate his early ability as a mountaineer, and Blaikie's potential as one. Together they made mountaineering history.[34]

---

myself was looking after plants. We soon got acquainted, and showed each other what we had discovered. We afterwards walked together to a little château, situated at the foot of the mountain.' Garcin went on to tell Blaikie a rather tall tale about having served with two Scotsmen in Russia. One day they were surrounded and carried off by Tartars but the two Scots by speaking Celtic made themselves perfectly understood, 'this people speaking nearly the same language as themselves'. As a result they were treated most kindly and released.

32. Named after Laurent Garcin MD (1683–1751), French botanist and traveller in India. A genus of 180 species of leathery-leafed evergreen trees, many of which produce valuable fruits. Natives of tropical Africa, Asia and Polynesia.

33. Named in honour of Martin Blake of Antigua. A genus of around 16 species of evergreen trees and shrubs, natives of tropical America. They possess large, showy red flowers and the leathery, smooth and shiny leaves are from 2.5 to 4 inches long.

34. See Montagnier, pp. 22–3.

CHAPTER 5

The Wondrous Vale of Chamonix

O N THE EVENING of 29 August the mail coach deposited Blaikie at Bonneville, about 26 kilometres from Geneva, on the first stage of his journey to Chamonix. Here he collected a letter of introduction to a Monsieur Joseph Paccard of Chamonix and around eight o'clock next morning, set off on foot for Sallanches. His route took him across the Arve by a narrow stone bridge and along a wide road shaded by fine walnut trees. After the village of Cluse the road grew narrower, bounded by the river on one side and rocky heights on the other. Waterfalls cascaded down the rock face from a 'prodigious' height, and he notes that, 'where the road serpents through this narrow opening [it] forms at every step a different Landscape beyond all imagination'. Amidst this delightful scenery he discovered many 'curious' plants.

Next day at dawn, after an 'indifferent' night's lodging at Sallanches, he set off again, marvelling at the height of the mountains that surrounded him on every side, the view always dominated by Mont Blanc, 'which,' he wrote, 'stands superior as a King over all the others in the form of a cone entirely covered by snow'. He arrived in Chamonix sometime in the late morning of the 31 August.

At that time, the valley of Chamonix was remarkable for the contrast between its cornfields and meadows, its neat fenced gardens and the giant fingers of ice that descended among the woods of larch and spruce and plucked at the fields themselves. Both valley and mountains were rich in fertile pastures and, as well as farming, the people augmented their income by selling their honey, reputed 'the most delicious in the world'.[1] They also traded in the crystals they excavated in the high mountains.

When William Windham and his party of friends rode into Chamonix on 21 June 1741, they were the first foreigners to ask to be taken to the Mer de Glace. Because of the remoteness of the place and rumours of the dangers to be faced in the mountains, they came heavily armed, with rifles slung across their shoulders and pistols and swords in their belts. They travelled with five servants and a baggage train laden with provisions and both their appearance and their request astonished the villagers. By 1773, about a dozen Englishmen visited the glacier each season.[2] But, in 1775 when Blaikie arrived in Chamonix, visitors were more common. Mostly, after a few steps on the ice, they were content to leave the mountains to the peasants, to Swiss scientists and botanists and to the occasional foreigner like Sir George Shuckburgh who travelled in Switzerland taking barometric measurements of the height of the mountains in July 1775[3] while Blaikie was plant hunting in the region. Local guides made an attempt on Mont Blanc that same month and a few amateurs also aspired to conquer the

---

1. Martyn, Thomas, *Sketch of a Tour through Swisserland* (London, 1787), pp. 86–8.
2. Montagnier, p. 18.
3. Sir George Shuckburgh, *Observations made in Savoy* (London, 1777).

mountain. Such were Dr Paccard's sons and Marc-Theodore Bourrit, the Precentor of the Cathedral of Geneva. By 1780, tourists would become numerous enough to be carried to the foot of the mountain in 'charabancs'[4] consisting of three or four planks fastened between four low wheels on which the traveller sat sideways about thirty inches from the ground, his or her feet resting on a board suspended below by a chain. In wet weather a canvas roof was attached and supported by four sticks.[5]

Blaikie found M. Paccard[6] at home with his three sons, 'very genteel young men'. M. Paccard himself, Blaikie adds, 'seems to be a man of respect in this place'. Paccard was a notary and secretary of the parish of Chamonix, the most important public servant in the region. He had been educated in Paris and was a cultivated man. His eldest son was a priest,[7] the second training as a lawyer,[8] and the youngest, Michel-Gabriel,[9] a medical student in Turin. Michel-Gabriel and one of his brothers, agreed to act as Blaikie's guides while Blaikie promised to teach them about plants. Then, although Blaikie had already walked about 16 miles that morning, they set off at once, ascending through fir trees and copses of *Rhododendron ferrugineum* to the Glacier des Bois, the name given at that time to the middle portion of the Mer de Glace. The glacier was an impressive sight: a valley of ice nearly a mile wide, stretching towards Mont Blanc on one side and down to the valley of Chamonix on the other, surrounded by peaks rising boldly above the clouds, many of them bare rock and others covered with snow.

Blaikie describes, in his diary, his first venture on the ice, making what was probably the first reference by a writer to the Grande Jorasse.[10] It was usual for visitors to carry a long pole spiked with iron to steady them on the ice. Primitive crampons with four small spikes were also attached to their shoes but, if Blaikie was equipped with these, he does not mention them. He writes, 'This is the Most considerable tract of ice. It lies to the left of Mount Blanc. This terminates in very considerable rocks called the Grande and petite Jorasse. From betwixt those rocks, which they call needles, this *glacière* takes its course downwards forming a vast plain of ice which in some places

---

4. Thomas Brand, in a letter dated Berne, August 1780. C.U.L., Add. MS 8670.
5. Berry, Miss Mary, *Extracts from the Journal and Correspondence of Miss Berry*, ed. Lady Theresa Lewis. 1865, vol. i, p. 29, 12 July 1783.
6. Joseph Paccard (1712–1787). He was drowned in a torrent in July 1787 while waiting with Saussure for the heavy rains that delayed the start of the professor's first successful expedition to the summit of Mont Blanc. See Douglas W. Freshfield, *The Life of Horace-Benedict de Saussure* (London, 1920), p. 223.
7. Abbé Pierre-Joseph Paccard, curé of Pontchy, who died in 1833.
8. Local tradition has it that he emigrated to America where his descendants founded Paccard motors.
9. Michel-Gabriel Paccard (1757–1827), the conqueror of Mont Blanc. He was 18 years old in 1775 and the climbs he undertook with Blaikie show him to have been a skilful mountaineer from an early age. He became a doctor after studying in Turin and returned to Chamonix where, fascinated by the idea of climbing Mont Blanc from the side of the Glacier de Bossons, he made many preparatory climbs before reaching the summit in 1786 accompanied by the guide, Jacques Balmat.
10. H. Montagnier, p. 20, n. 29.

is very steep and in other precipices. Here, about the middle, we crossed. In many places there is great openings in the ice which runs mostly across and so deep that you cannot see the Bottom. This ice seems exceeding hard and firm.' He goes on, 'The middle of this *glacière* is a most frightful and amazing landscape, all the ground work white, surrounded with high precipices of frightful rocks many of them in form of Chinese obelisks as if growing through the ice. Those, the inhabitants call needles.' His reading of the landscape is highly 'picturesque' with his description of the foreground as 'groundwork', his emphasis on the sublime [11] or 'frightful' and his introduction of a 'Chinese' element into the picture. He continues, 'Here we descended along the east side of this *glacière* which runs down almost to a little town called the Hameau de Bois. From the bottom of this *glacière* the *rivière de l'Arveiron* [Arveyron] begins coming from under the Ice, which forms a great arch of ice and runs along the Valley of Chamouni and joins the Rhône at Geneva.' [12] Blaikie was probably the first foreigner to cross the glacier and descend on the eastern side and his is the first known record of such an expedition written in English. [13] It was along the bank of the Arveyron that Blaikie found, growing in profusion, *Sibbaldia procumbens*, the little plant which reminded him of Scotland and gave him a momentary pang of home-sickness. [14]

On 1 September Gabriel Paccard and Blaikie set off together on a two day excursion, the highlight of Blaikie's alpine expedition. They ascended by La Coudraz on the south side of the valley to the Lac du Plan de l'Aiguille (7342 ft.) where Blaikie was delighted to find 'many curious plants'. [15] He was particularly taken by a small white four-petalled flower, the Alpine Bitter Cress, *Cardamine alpina*, growing alone at the edge of the lake 'in flower and about an inch and a half high, beautiful'. Next, they scrambled up behind the Aiguille de Blaitière, where Blaikie found, growing on the surface of the rocks, the buttercup, *Ranunculus glacialis*, a plant he was to introduce to Britain. It is one of the most beautiful of Alpine flowers with its cluster of golden stamens and large white petals turning pink in maturity. In the same area he collected *Ranunculus aconitifolius, Artemisia rupestris*, [16] *A. glacialis*, and *A. genipi*, [17] the staple diet of the marmots and thought to possess many beneficial properties. As they climbed higher and higher, 'examining,' as Blaikie notes, 'this solitary region', they heard the unmistakable and terrifying roar of an avalanche close by, 'as if the whole Mountains was going to fall about our ears'. This was not the first time Blaikie had heard the sound but never so close. Darkness was falling and, fearful of another avalanche, they descended by the dismal Lac de Nantillon, a feature which has disappeared along with

---

11. Edmund Burke, *Enquiry into the Sublime and Beautiful* (London, 1756). 'Sublime' equalled terrifying or awful. 'Beauty' meant calm and tranquillity.

12. Diary, 21 August 1775.

13. Montagnier, p. 21.

14. See chapter 2.

15. *Saxifraga bryoides* L., *Veronica alpina* L., *Veronica bellidioides* L.

16. *A. spicata* Wulfen ex Jacq.

17. According to Saussure, vol. 2, p. 13, Linnaeus confused this plant with *A. atrata*.

the retreat of the glacier of the same name, and took refuge in the Chalet de Blaitière [18] where they spent the night with the herdsmen.

The next day, very early, they made their way through meadows and woods of pine and larch by the Plan de l'Aiguille and the Pavillon du Pierre Pointu to the edge of the Glacier des Bossons. Rhodendron *ferrugineum* grew right to the edge of the glacier and Blaikie regretted it was too late to see its fine scarlet flowers in bloom against the whiteness of the ice. They crossed the ice, probably in the area of the Pierre de l'Échelle (not named at that time), to the Montagne de la Côte. From here, a few weeks earlier, a group of guides, among them two cousins of Paccard, had made an unsuccessful attempt on Mont Blanc. The great plain of snow and ice were of a whiteness that fatigued the eyes and Mont Blanc, Blaikie wrote, appeared 'a desert mass of eternal snow'. They pressed on to the Aiguille du Gouter and had climbed some way up the Mountain when Paccard called a halt to the day's excursion. Unbeknown to Blaikie, Paccard was reconnoitring one of the routes that might lead to the summit of Mont Blanc.[19] As it was, he and Blaikie had followed a route which in 1775 no guide or explorer had so far attempted, a remarkable expedition for this early date and in all likelihood, according to Montagnier, the first attempt at serious climbing by a visitor to the Chamonix valley. Blaikie finishes his account of the day, unfatigued and in high spirits, with probably the first description of glissading in English.[20] 'Here,' he wrote, 'is an exceeding good way to descend the Ice by means of a Stick with an Iron pick at the end which you place behind and leans upon and so slides down the steepest ice. Arrived in the evening at Chamonix.'[21] No wonder Montagnier felt that the Scot was a loss to mountaineering.

The next day Paccard, the future conqueror of Mont Blanc, complaining of tiredness, had to be persuaded to join his father and brother for the ascent of the Brevent with Blaikie. This was the most frequently climbed peak in the range and there is an account in French of an ascent of it by Colonel Augustus Hervey (later the 3rd Duke of Bristol) in July 1775. Hervey took two days, leaving in the afternoon and spending the night on the mountain to observe the night sky.[22] Other men may have climbed it, but Blaikie's is the earliest known description of the view from the summit written in English. In his account he uses an archaic name, the Brouvanar, for the mountain, out-of-date even in 1775, but one he may have heard from M. Paccard. Their route took them up the south side of the mountain by the Planpraz, stopping at the herdsmen's hut called the Chalet de Planpraz. After giving the height of the chalet as 6466 feet above sea level, Blaikie writes, 'Here we continued our road towards the top of the Brouvannar which is exceeding steep, and high. Upon the top of the peak

18. Montagnier suggests that since they were so close to the avalanche they must have climbed fairly high above the Aiguille and probably stayed the night at Blaitière-dessus, adopted as his headquarters by Saussure in 1784.
19. C. E. Engel, *A History of Mountaineering in the Alps* (London, 1948), p. 47.
20. Montagnier, p. 20.
21. Diary, 2 September 1775.
22. Bourrit, M.-T., *Nouvelles Descriptions des Glaciers de Savoie*, 3 vols (1787), vol. 1, p. 134.

du Breven[t] there is a Cross placed ... Here the air from the north is keen and sharp. This peak is 1311 toises high.[23] From the summit of this mountain is perhaps the most noble perspective in the universe; here you are right over against Mont Blanc and command a *vue* of all the Valley of Chamouni from it[s] beginning towards the right hand where this Chain of Alps runs almost in a straight line for Many miles towards the left. The top of this ragged ridge of Alps is surprisingly covered with sharp Rocks which seems as if growing throw the Snow. Above all is the Majestic appearance of Mont Blanc whose huge, colossal bulk makes the Others appear as nothing.'[24] The near accurate measurement of mountains by the barometric method was new and the Scot delights in noting the height of most of the peaks. Mont Blanc, he tells us is 15214 feet high, '2874 feet higher than the famous peak of Tenerife which is only 12340 feet perpendicular'. Although the top of the Brevent is 7,079 feet lower than Mont Blanc according to his calculations, 'yet', he goes on, 'you seem to be in a level with the great Mass of snow and ice which seems to run down like six great rivers down the side of the Mountains Opposite, issuing from the eternal mass of ice which covers at the upper half of these Mountains, intermixed with those huge dark rocks which seems like stone pillars ... About the top of the Breven[t] near the cross are many curious plants.'[25] As usual, he was interested in the geology of the mountains and while they were on the Breven, his companions, to satisfy his curiosity, took him to see an ancient gold mine, long unworked. They told him that gold dust was occasionally extracted from the sand where the river Arve entered the Rhône.

The next day, 4 September, Blaikie made his final expedition with the Paccards. He set off with Michel-Gabriel and his brother Pierre-Joseph, the priest, for the Montenvers and across the Mer de Glace. From there they explored the lac de Tacul, a little lake rich in plants. The lake no longer exists but it lay in the angle formed by the lateral moraines of the Glaciers of Le Géant and Lescheaux and even as late as 1802 when visitors to the Mer de Glace could be counted in thousands, only a handful had ventured as far as the lake, to enjoy its fine views.[26] Blaikie and his companions pressed on further to the glacier of Talèvre where Blaikie was fascinated by the strange phenomenon of the Jardin de Talèvre. He describes it as 'a little triangular piece of ground called the Courtil, a sort of natural rock garden, and goes on, 'this remarkable spot which seems to have no connection with any other part of the vegetable world is surrounded on every side with rocks and ice. Here grows the *Hieracium alpinum* and the *Hieracium* Haller 41,[27] the *Artemisia glacialis* &

23. 8138 ft. The Michelin Guide gives the height as 8288 ft. Blaikie's figures are probably based on Shuckburgh's recent barometrical measurements which Paccard would have received from Saussure. In a note on the height of Mont Blanc amongst his papers, Blaikie equates one toise to roughly 6 ft.

24. Diary, 3 September 1775.

25. *Bupleurum stellatum* L., *Senecio incanus* L., *Veronica aphylla* L., *Aretia alpina* (*Androsace alpina* (L.) Lam)., *Primula minima* L., *Gentiana bavarica* L. and 'many others'.

26. Shuckburgh walked on the ice but 'found it impossible to go to the Lac de Tacul, it being three hours' walk' (p. 155). Same comment made by E. A. Smith, vol. 3, p. 157.

27. *Hieracium intybaceum* All.

(A.)*rupestris*,[28] *Geum reptans* and many of the scarce Alpine plants.' The name 'Courtil' was the word for 'garden' in Savoyard and old French. It was a flat rock, lying a little above the level of the glacier and surrounded by a 'wall' of stones and pebbles, deposited there by the movement of the glacier. As Spring came very late to this high altitude, in August, the garden was covered by a green turf, studded with alpine flowers. Unfrequented by all except crystal hunters, it was almost unknown, even to Blaikie's guides who had never been there before. Blaikie's is the first mention of it, but a detailed description of it is given by De Saussure in his *Voyage dans les Alpes* (1779) in which he remarked, 'when the snows have melted it is neither dangerous or difficult of access'.[29]

Doubt has been cast on Blaikie's account of the next part of their journey on the grounds that the descent he describes from the Jardin de Talèvre to Chamonix by the valley of the Glacier d'Argentière and the Chalets de la Pendant would appear to have been beyond the capabilities of mountaineering at the period.[30] It has been suggested that Blaikie may have inadvertently combined two expeditions. However, among his papers, a brief note of his daily itineraries during his stay at Chamonix shows that this cannot be so. He spent part of the following day, 5 September, reconnoitring his intended route for his return to Geneva the next day. This took him by Planpraz to the Lac Cornu, a lake situated to the north of the chalet of Planpraz and so called because of the horned rocks that surround it. For his excursion on the 4th, he has scribbled in his rough note the words 'Les Charmos, sur Montanvert, le Mouret et Bounanay'. Neither Le Mouret (which may have been les Montets) or Bounanay appear on any maps of the area and may be obsolete names or errors arising from Blaikie's inadequate French. What is more likely is that he may have taken the slightly easier though still demanding and hazardous way by the east side of the Mer de Glace, across the col des Grands Montets and down to Chamonix via Lognan.[31] Another reason given for doubting his account of his excursion of 4 September[32] is his mention of having passed en route 'a little house called l'Hospital de Blair', a building believed to have replaced an earlier hut on the same spot at a date after his visit in 1775.[33] However, if he was mistaken, there is a simple explanation suggested by Montagnier, namely that at sometime later, when transcribing his diary,

---

28. Now *A. spicata* Wulfen ex Jacq.

29. Saussure, vol. 2, p. 33.

30. M. Bourrit, *Nouvelle Description des Glacières, vallées de Glace et Glaciers* (Geneva, 1787). 'I am unaware of anyone who has undertaken to cross from the one to the other' (Glacier d'Argentière to Talevre), p. 172.

31. Montagnier, p. 27, suggests that even this would have taxed Blaikie's 'extraordinary powers of endurance'.

32. In Eliane Engel's review *of The Diary of a Scotch Gardener at the French Court at the end of the 18th Century*, ed. Francis Birrell (London, 1931); *Figaro*, 25 February 1932.

33. William Coxe, *Travels in Switzerland in a Series of Letters to William Melmoth Esq. from William Coxe*, 2 vols (Dublin, 1789). Letter 37, p. 367, gives the date of Blair's hut as after 1776, but he dates the July 1775 attempt on Mont Blanc as July 1776.

Blaikie imagined that the hut he had seen and the well known Blair's hut were one and the same.

Blaikie's diary entry for 5 September records that he spent the day ordering a box for his plants and collecting seeds in the woods around Chamonix, without any mention of his visit to the Lac Cornu. The morning of the 6th was spent packing up his plants for the carrier and identifying specimens for Gabriel Paccard. He left Chamonix in the afternoon, having decided to make his way alone over the mountains to Geneva. Today, Blaikie's excursions may seem little more than strenuous mountain walks but at that time climbers were poorly equipped. In addition, little was known about the dangers of climbing after midday because of the possibility of avalanches. Even now 40 people die on average each year climbing Mont Blanc and 160 are seriously injured. Blaikie and Michel-Gabriel Paccard, one of the founders of Alpinism, broke new ground together during those five days in Chamonix and this, as well as his descriptions of the mountains, have earned the botanist a place among British pioneers of mountaineering.[34] Blaikie's legacy to his companion was a love of botany that distinguished Paccard from other mountaineers.[35]

In electing to return to his base near Geneva through the region called the Chablais, Blaikie chose a 'long and precarious way' over wild and unfrequented countryside. The reason he gave was, 'that I might procure many plants, as I had to pass over some of the most ragged Mountains of Savoy'. But he must also have found the challenge of such a journey irresistible after the exhilaration of his expeditions in the mountains. At the chalets at Planpraz, he stopped and drank some milk by the fire with an old herdsman who knew about plants. Although the nights were already exceedingly cold, he decided to carry on farther up the Brevent to those huge pyramids of red granite, the Aiguilles Rouges, and to make again for Lake Cornu, remarkable for its crystal clear waters in their rocky setting amongst dark red columns of stone. There was no vegetation here so his attraction to the place was entirely due to its harsh beauty. Shortly after leaving the lake, he realised that he was lost. With no map to guide him, he pressed on, seeing no one and hearing nothing but the rushing sound of mountain torrents and the shrill cry of marmots, 'almost like a man that whistles'. With no prospect of a bed for the night, he made do with a cleft in the rock but the bitter cold kept him awake. Very early next day, he left the spot he ironically christened his 'Hotel du Rocher' and took an eastward direction guided by the rising sun. Still he met no one and saw no sign of habitation, yet, in spite of fatigue and lack of food, the discovery of a number of plants, he writes, 'gave me fresh spirits'.[36] His provisions were exhausted and, after climbing ridge after ridge in an attempt to find his way, he had almost resigned himself to another night on the

---

34. Blaikie's name is recorded after those of Windham and Pococke in *Les Anglais à Chamonix aux 18ème et 19ème siècles*, an exhibition held at the Musée Alpin-Chamonix in September 1984.

35. Douglas Freshfield, p. 201.

36. *Onosma echiodes* L., *Campanula barbata* L., *Hedysarum alpinum* L., *Phaca alpina* (*Astragalus alpinus* L.), *Sonchus alpinus* (*Cicerbita alpina* (L.) Wallr.).

mountain when, from the top of the highest point he could find, he saw a huddle of lighted cabins some two miles distant.[37] 'Hither,' he writes, 'I marched with speed, as it was almost evening.' When he reached the huts, he found, to his surprise, that 'this company was all women, not one man amongst them'. The woman who received him with kindness gave him milk and, since there was not a single house within an eight hour's walk, she told him he might stay the night. 'To this,' Blaikie adds, 'I most willingly agreed and indeed was treated very hospitable and had the best she could afford, which was milk, cheese and cream and a hay bed upon the floor.'[38] The women's chalets were the chalets d'Anterne and Blaikie was not the only one to have been glad of their hospitality.[39]

Next day after a breakfast of curds and cream, the herdswoman walked a mile with him to set him on his way via the Cascade du Rouget, a spectacular beauty spot, in the Vallée des Fonds near Sixt. This he describes as an immense waterfall which cascaded out of the rocks 400 feet above him. Half way down it fell into a rocky basin and burst forth again to disappear in a spectacular mist of spray amongst huge pines.

About seven o'clock the following evening, he reached the village of Tanninges where an incident occurred that made him wish he were back in his cheerless bed among the rocks, and tested his courage and cool-headedness to their limit. Two men approached him at his table in the inn and advised him to leave at once or else, Blaikie recounts 'the people would perhaps murder me'. He could extract from them no reason for their hostility and, in spite of his offer to take his papers from Geneva to a local magistrate, they refused to believe that he was not a German. One of them, who professed friendly feelings towards the German people, assured him that he would be very sorry to see him suffer the same fate as his comrades had a few days earlier and urged him to make his escape. Seeing a mob armed with sticks crowding around the entrance to the inn, Blaikie decided to play for time. He writes, 'I found there was no way to go to leave this house and to go out to the street, the[y] would

---

37. Seylac, p. 131 suggests that after leaving the lac Cornu he made his way down to the bottom of the Diosaz valley where he should have followed the stream in a southerly direction. Instead he scaled the crest between the Pointe Noire de Pormenaz and the Col de l'Échaud from where he spied the Chalets d'Anterne.

38. Diary, 7 September 1775.

39. Dentand and Deluc, *Relations de Différents Voyages dans les Alpes du Faucigny* (Maestricht, 1776), pp. 108–10. Lost in the vallée d'Anterne, they perceived lights glimmering through the chinks in some cabins a little distance away. They chose the cabin whose light they had first noticed and knocked. The single-roomed dwelling belonged to two women who were gathered around the fire with their friends. At first they were astonished to see strangers in a place frequented only by hunters and shepherds, but they received them with the kindest hospitality, offered them all that they had which consisted of milk and cheese, spread out beds of hay for them on the floor and retired to their own beds for the night without any awkwardness. The next morning the two men saw that they were in a valley bounded by high mountains on all sides except to the south. This was not the first time they had been lost in this wild and lonely area in spite of being accompanied by hunters as guides.

soon have knock't me down. Neither was I certain of my companion although he seemed my friend. I told him I was determined to stay there that night as I had offended nobody. I would defend myself as long as I could but begged him to drink a glass of wine which he accepted. Here we drank a bottle of wine while the woman of the house trembled. I begged something for supper but with great difficulty I got an omelette of eggs. When the people without saw me appear so unconcerned, they began not to be not so outrageous and my companion began to be a little merry, ... After supper my companion and I parted but I made him promise to come and breakfast with me next morning, which he did. As soon as he was gone out, all the people about the house went with him, I suppose to inquire what he had learn'd of Me.' After Blaikie had paid his bill, the innkeeper showed him his lodging, 'a sort of a hog sty' behind the house. Here, he adds, 'I bethought my best way was to leave this place and get into the wood which was just behind'.[40]

The night was one of profound blackness but he found a mountain road made by the people to drag their wood or bring their cattle down from the mountain. He writes, 'After getting up a considerable way ... I came to a steep rock upon which I sat down to rest a little'. Noises floated up to him from the village below and as he peered down, he writes, 'I could plainly see by some lights which I saw the people carry round about my cabin, which I had so lately left, and in an instant I saw it all in flames. This struck me with terror to think how narrowly I had escaped, as I saw those people by the light of the fire standing round this place with sticks and forks, expecting I was there. This scene made me think of getting of[f] as fast as I could from this bloody place. Although the night was dark and the road through a thick wood, I continually kept upwards until at last I got clear of the wood and near the top of [the mountain].' After another night sleeping in a deserted hut and by day keeping away from the villages, Blaikie skirted the Mole [41] and reached the Salève. He sought out his old friend, the Scottish doctor, who assured him of his good fortune in escaping as two men had been murdered a few days earlier in the same village 'under pretext of Religion'. It seems such horrifying events were common enough as the earlier tale of two men murdered in the Salève demonstrated.

Back at Bourdigny, Blaikie concentrated his search for plants around the Jura. With the plant hunting season drawing to a close, his major expeditions were now almost over. He made, however, one final visit along the north side of Lake Geneva to Aigle and Bex to seek the assistance of his friends in replacing some of the plants he had lost from his collection. He stopped on the way at Lausanne, noting there were so many English there that they were able to form a cricket team and arrange horse races. The countryside to the east of Lausanne near Vevey, was one of the most beautiful on the lakeside, and its gentle, vine clad slopes were a welcome change for Blaikie after the inhospitable mountains of Savoy. At Aigle he spent part of Saturday and Sunday, 7 and 8 October, with his friend M. De Coppet, the pastor. They made a valedictory excursion together to gather seeds, then, on Sunday morning, Blaikie

---

40. Diary, 8 September 1775.
41. Erroneously transcribed in *The Diary*, ed. Francis Birrell, as the Dôle.

attended the minister's service, finding it little different from the Presbyterian one he knew in Scotland. Next, with the Thomases, he searched the mountains near Bex for plants, full of admiration for Abraham's father who at 80 could walk as well as the two younger men. As the season was too advanced to spend the night on the mountains, Abraham and Blaikie, who could now hold his own for stamina with anyone, made a last heroic journey together. They started out from Bex at one a.m. on the 13 October and returned, laden with many 'strange and curious plants',[42] around eleven o'clock, twenty two hours later, from an excursion which normally lasted two days.[43] The two returned to Bex laden with plants at around 11 p. m., 'hungry for supper'. Then Blaikie took his leave of the father and son, describing them as 'the only two people I have met with that is worth travelling upon the Mountains'.[44]

He retraced his steps to Geneva along the opposite side of the lake. The weather was worsening but, in spite of snow and icy winds, he returned daily to the Salève and the Jura where he describes his last visit to the mountain above the town of Thoiry. 'Left Gex and ascended the Thuirry [Turet].[45] The snow continued to fall. Here I found the passage very difficult over the rocks, as they were covered with snow and [it was] impossible to distinguish where to step and even the bushes [were] almost hid. This was the first day I had suffered upon those Mountains; the wind and snow blowing in such a Manner that it was with difficulty in some places I could keep hold of the Bushes to keep my self from slipping over the precipices. After a great deal of difficulty, I gained the top of the Mountain where the wind blew so keen and strong, with the snow which seized me in such a Manner that I almost fainted away. However, observing one of the Summer huts, I took courage and got thither. So this movement of running brought about, with the shelter of this hut, a Glow over me which, after refreshing a little, I was quite recovered. After getting some sticks and with a pistol lighted a fire. I warmed myself as well as possible in this solitary house for I believe I was the Only person upon those Mountains at this season. As the day was far spent and having a sort of a house, and fire, I resolved to stay in this place all night, fixed the doors, got some of the rafters and wood for my fire. Although I kept a tolerable good fire, yet the night in this place was so excessively

42. Blaikie noted among his finds *Astragalus tragacantha* (*Astragalus sempervirens* Lam. subsp. *sempervirens*), *Selinum acaulis* (not identified), *Azalea* (*Loiseleuria*) *procumbens* (L.) Desv., *Gentiana punctata* L., *G. bavarica* L., *Androsace carnea* L., *Achillea genipi* (*Artemisia erba-rotta All.* ssp. *moschata*), *Anemone* (*Pulsatilla*) *alpina* (L.) Delarbre, *Diapensia helvatica* (*Androsace vandellii* (Turra) Clov.), *Plantago alpina* L., *Juniperus sabina* L., *Lonicera coerulea* L. Here, he found *Bupleurum stellatum* L., *B. longifolium* L., *Campanula thyrsoides* L., *Eryngium alpinum* L., *Astrantia minor* L., and *Laserpitium panax* (*L. halleri* Crantz, subsp. *halleri*).
43. Montagnier gives the route as climbing from the Rhone valley to the pastures above the hamlet of Morcles. Next they proceeded via the Gran' Vire by the west face of the Dent de de Morcles to the Creux de Dzéman and crossed the ridge by the Col Demètre from which they descended into the Fully valley. They dined at the Portail de Fully and descended by the Allezes to Dorénas.
44. Diary, 14 October 1775.
45. Range of mountains above the town of Thoiry from The Reculet to the Crêt de la Neige.

cold that I passed a very disagreeable night.'[46] The next day, 26 October, as soon as daylight dawned, he left the hut. The conditions were treacherous, with an icy north wind which blew the snow into deep and dangerous drifts, but he persevered, going westward along the mountain, and spent the whole day searching for plants missing from his collection before returning to the inn at St Genis.

During November, he catalogued his plants and prepared them for their journey to England, dividing them equally between the Drs Fothergill and Pitcairn before packing them in a single box. This done, and having braced his box with pieces of wood, he sent it to the customs at Collonge to be sealed with lead so that it could not be opened and spoiled on the way to London. He also commissioned a wooden box to hold the silkworms he had seen on the pine trees and which he felt might be suitable to start a silk industry in Scotland.

At this point in the diary he lists the plants sent from Bourdigny to Doctor Fothergill and Doctor Pitcairn, directed to Dr Pitcairn's address at Warwick Court, Warwick Lane, London. This list can be found in Appendix 1.

Then, on 27 November, he breakfasted with his 'good friend, Monsieur Gaussen in Geneva for the last time and boarded the coach for Lyon. At Lyon, he sent his luggage by coach to Paris and sailed up the Loire from Roanne to Orléans. At Nevers, the boat ran against the bridge and the boatman would have fallen overboard had not Blaikie and another passenger seized him by his feet as he disappeared over the side. From Orléans he set off on foot for Paris, noting as he went the name of each town and village he passed. He reached Paris on 13 December 1775.

Determined to make the most of his visit, he stayed in the city until 23 December. He lodged at the *Hotel de Picardie* in the rue St Jacques on the left bank of the Seine near the magnificent church of St Geneviève (later the Panthéon) still unfinished at the time Blaikie was in Paris.[47] At his hotel, he made friends with a French medical student who took him to a secret dissecting room, a garret, amongst the rooftops of the city where he was shocked at the sight and smell of twelve 'dead corpses' in the process of dissection by students who took him for a fellow surgeon. The activities of the medical students were of necessity clandestine for they were refused cadavers and either bought them or stole them.[48] He attended a lecture and demonstration at the *Académie royale de Chirugiens* in the rue des Cordeliers with its impressive anatomy theatre, where it was the custom to lay out a corpse on a black marble table at the front of the lecture theatre and dissect it before an audience of 800 students.[49] He visited the *Jardin du Roi*, today's *Jardin des Plantes*, and made the acquaintance of André

---

46. Diary, 26 October 1775.
47. The building had been dogged by controversy from the beginning. Its first design, by the architect, Soufflot (1713–1780), was engraved in 1757 but it was not till 1764 that the King laid the foundation stone and in 1775 when Blaikie saw it, work had just begun on the dome. It was not fully completed until 1790 and a year later it was secularised as the Pantheon.
48. See Rétif de la Bretonne, *Les Nuits de Paris* (folio edn 1986), *trente et unieme nuit*, p. 67.
49. Louis Sebastien Mercier, *The Picture of Paris before and after the Revolution*, trans. W. and E. Jackson (London, 1929), p. 95.

Thouin, the head gardener who was to become a lifelong friend. He found time to visit the *Bibliothèque du Roi* in the rue de Richelieu (*Bibliothèque Nationale*) where he marvelled at the free public access to this vast library of books and longed to be able to spend some time there.

From Paris, he walked to Calais, stopping at Chantilly on the way. In the forest of Chantilly he remarked how, 'the ground in some places is entirely covered with flocks of partridges and pheasants by hundreds together'.[50] Like every other visitor he admired the Prince of Condé's palace-like stables even more than the château and its grounds. He was delayed a little by his sightseeing and bad weather but made up some time when, on the last day, an Englishman in a post chaise, whom he had passed several times on the road, was so curious about the weather-beaten, solitary walker that he invited him to complete the journey to Calais in his carriage. Blaikie's journey had taken six days and, on his arrival, he treated himself to the luxury of a night at Dessein's hotel, a comfortable refuge much appreciated by English travellers. On 31 December he reached London. Here he tells us he 'Dined at Dr Fothergill's where I was well received by him and all the family. Here ended a long and troublesome journey accompanied with many hardships'. The next day he received his greatest accolade: he became one of the privileged people invited to breakfast with Mr Banks.

Blaikie's Swiss odyssey, particularly in its last phase, had tested his good judgement and courage and had demonstrated his extraordinary stamina and indifference to physical discomfort. The few scientists and travellers who ventured off the main roads complained of being tormented by fleas as they slept on the stinking palliasses of straw in the herdsmen's huts, of the smoke from the chimneyless fire and the gaps in the wooden walls through which entered snow and sleet,[51] but Blaikie took them in his stride describing humorously that to make himself ready for the day after a night in one of these huts all he had to do was shake himself. Of the two parts of his diary, the Swiss one reveals most sympathetically his sense of humour and his capacity to empathise with all classes of people. His last expeditions with the Thomases and his final days on the mountains in deteriorating weather underline his single-mindedness in the pursuit of plants for his employers. Indeed, his diary and his copy of Haller's field guide to Swiss plants,[52] with its margin notes in Blaikie's hand, reveal that he collected more plants than he brought home. In particular, almost all the specimens he collected at Chamonix were spoilt by the length of time it took the carter to deliver them to Bourdigny. Nevertheless, he succeeded in collecting over 3500 plants and numerous 'tufts' and cuttings of 440 species. Of these, the first edition of *Hortus Kewensis*, published in 1789, attributed the introduction of around 40 to Doctor Fothergill and Doctor Pitcairn. Blaikie as 'Thomas Blackie', is credited with two. The second edition, published in 1810–12, ascribed a number of the Pitcairn and Fothergill introductions to other people, notably to Philip Miller, and it credited others

---

50. Diary, 24 December 1775.

51. M. B(ordier), *Voyage pittoresque aux glacières de Savoie fait en 1772* (Geneva, 1773), pp. 169–70.

52. Haller, *Nomenclator ex Historia Plantarum indigenarum Helvetiae excerptus* (Berne, 1769).

to people who introduced them at a later date. The general consensus is that he introduced 32 or 33 new plants to Britain[53] but he was to remain anonymous, unrecognised as a collector, except by a very few of his contemporaries, until the publication of his diary in 1931 set the record straight. However, as far as his employers and Sir Joseph Banks were concerned, he had shown sufficient prowess as a botanist to be considered for a major expedition.

Apart from the mind-opening experience of visiting another country, there were three other important consequences for his future career of his months in Switzerland. The first was that he could now speak fluent French; the second was the experience, so enlightening for a gardener-botanist, of seeing the flora of Switzerland in its natural setting. He was moved by the beauty of whole hillsides self-sown with *Rhododendron hirsutum* and during difficult moments in his travels the sight of rare Alpine plants growing in the crevices along the top of steep precipices refreshed his spirit. The third benefit was the impetus the alpine experience itself would give to his subsequent career as a landscape gardener, since the savage scenery of the Alps was one of the key influences in the gardens of the late eighteenth century and in the early part of the nineteenth.[54] Rocks in the form of an immense pile or *rocher*, or as part of an underground cavern or grotto, were an important feature of the gardens designed by Bélanger, the architect who was to employ Blaikie at Bagatelle, not for their picturesque qualities alone but as symbols of the primeval force of nature in the eighteenth-century passion for the natural world. Blaikie himself, although not a geologist, took a sensuous pleasure in studying rock formations, lingering half a day to trace with his hands the girth of a huge and 'wonderful' rock that obstructed his path in the Salève. He was fascinated by the rock strata in the Diablerets and the fantastic pyramids and columns of ice upon the glaciers, while the tortuous mountain passes educated his eye in the art of creating dramatic vistas. The rugged precipices, the roaring cataracts and rocky streams, the still lakes, the sunset over Mont Blanc viewed from the top of the Dôle, awakened in his soul those feelings of being alone and in harmony with nature, that we associate with the Romantics some ten years later.

Botanical collector, practical gardener or landscape artist? At this stage in his life he would probably have opted for the first, but his immediate future lay in the hands of two men, Banks and Lee.

53. Graham Stuart Thomas, *The Rock Garden and its Plants* (London, 1989), credits him with 32. Fox Hingston, *Doctor Fothergill and His Friends* (1919) attributes the introduction of 33 Swiss plants to Fothergill and Pitcairn *c.* 1775. Blaikie annotates his alpine plant list with the attributions in Aiton's *Hortus Kewensis*, 1789, in which Fothergill and Pitcairn together in 1775 are credited with 39 introductions and Blaikie with four, although his are given for a later date.
54. Marie Antoinette imported only Swiss cattle and goats for her farm at the Trianon since, in the love of the natural, all things Swiss were considered best. A.N. o1 1880 quoted in Annick Heitzmann, *Trianon La ferme du hameau* (Paris, 1991). See also A. De Laborde *Descriptions des Nouvelles Jardins* (Paris, 1808).

CHAPTER 6

Normandy and the Comte de Lauraguais

O N 25 April 1776 James Lee of the Vineyard Nursery, Hammersmith, wrote a letter
to Joseph Banks which was to change the course of Thomas Blaikie's life. In it
he recommended a young, self-effacing Scotsman, David Nelson, as botanist on
Captain Cook's last voyage to the Pacific which was to leave Plymouth on 12 July
1776.[1] To his letter, Lee added the following postscript:

> P. S. I have a better opinion of this man than B——kie, which is with other
> Reasons that I shall tell you at meeting – the Reason I did not send him.[2]

Blaikie does not seem to have known that he was considered for the post with
Cook. He recorded in his diary during the first six months of 1776 that Banks 'had
the project of sending me upon an expedition to the East Indies but the American
war and Many other Objections hindered this undertaking.' Banks had long been
aware of the benefits of the breadfruit tree (*Artocarpus altilis*) as a food. As early as
1772, a West Indies landowner had written to him for help in procuring the tree as
a more reliable plant than the native plantain, the staple food of the West Indies. By
1775, in spite of offers of financial rewards, the planters had failed to persuade traders
to the East Indies to obtain the plants for them and Banks may have considered
sending Blaikie to the East Indies with the purpose of collecting this and other plants.
There is no way of knowing why Lee preferred Nelson to Blaikie, or what his other
'Reasons' were for not sending him to Banks but Lee may, unwittingly, have done
Blaikie a good turn, for David Nelson, after his return from the Pacific, served on the
Bounty with Captain Bligh.[3] The mutineers, in April 1789 consigned Bligh, and those
who remained loyal to him, Nelson amongst them, to the ship's launch. Nelson
survived weeks at sea only to die shortly after they reached land. Even without the
hazards of adventure at sea, the life of a plant collector was scarcely to be envied.
Exploited by their employers, the majority of plant hunters faced disease, accidental
death or murder; most of them were Scots.

The more prudent career option was to rise to the position of head gardener on
some great noble's estate where a gifted gardener might just be given the opportunity
to develop his talent for landscaping. Lancelot 'Capability' Brown (1716–1783) had

---

1. Richard Hough, *Captain James Cook, a Biography* (London, 1994). For Nelson's character,
   see pbk edn, p. 443.
2. *Banks' Correspondence*, vol. 1, Add. mss. 33977. Quoted in E. J. Willson, *James Lee and the
   Vineyard Nursery Hammersmith* (London, 1961), p. 43.
3. William Bligh (c. 1753–1817). Served with Cook (1772–78). As captain of the *Bounty* sailed to
   Tahiti to collect plants of the bread-fruit tree. He and a number of his crew were cast
   adrift by mutineers and, after 47 days, by a tremendous feat of navigation without compass
   or charts, he succeeded in reaching Timor, near Java.

begun his career as gardener to Sir William Loraine at Kirlharle Towers in North-umberland. Generally, the more intelligent head gardeners distinguished themselves by contributing papers to the transactions of the Horticultural Society of London or by winning prizes for the newest and largest melons or the sweetest strawberries in the name of their masters, just as Blaikie's plant introductions would be attributed to Fothergill and Pitcairn. As Blaikie had no capital, and his brother was, at that time, the inheritor of the small family nursery, the trade of nurseryman could be discounted.

Unaware of the decisions of Banks and Lee, Blaikie, with a sense of anticlimax, whiled away his time at Dr Fothergill's at Upton, nursing the plants he had brought back from Switzerland and perfecting himself in botany in preparation for an offer from Banks. The highlight of the uneventful summer was a visit to his friend Mr Hoy,[4] gardener to Sir Topham Beauclerk[5] at Mill Hill; the pretext was to watch an eclipse of the moon with his friend at Beauclerk's observatory on 30 June. The two young men also made an outing to Luton Hoo, the still uncompleted garden designed for the Earl of Bute[6] by 'Capability' Brown and spent the rest of their time together in the conservatory at Muswell Hill examining the collection of ericas, almost all recently introduced, and debating the rival merits of sand, dung and tan[7] for growing pineapples. Otherwise, as Blaikie recorded in his diary, 'nothing very material happened'.[8]

On Friday 13 September 1776 he received a letter from Lee enclosing a note from the Comte de Lauraguais. Both men engaged him to travel to France. The Count instructed him 'to get trees from Mr Lee, as he expected a little vessel of his from France which was to carry the whole to his seat, Mont Canisy, in Normandy'. Glad to be active again, Blaikie at once set about preparing for his journey and visiting those places where he could obtain interesting plants. At Kew, William Aiton made him a gift for Lauraguais of 26 sorts of American plants. By 5 October, the trees and plants were packed and ready to be put on board the Count's sloop,[9] the *Polly Jones*, which lay in the Thames below St Katherine's stairs. On 13 November he embarked once more for France. The adventures of the journey were an omen of what life would be like in the service of his new employer.

---

4. J. Thomas Hoy (*c.* 1750–1822). Hoy was later to become head gardener at Sion for the Duke of Northumberland. Ray Desmond, *Dictionary of British Botanists and Horticulturists* (London, 1994), p. 361.
5. Topham Beauclerk (1739–1780). Described variously as descendant of Charles II and Nell Gwynn and illegitimate son of George II. He was a dandy and a friend of Samuel Johnson.
6. John Stuart, 3rd Earl of Bute (1713–1792). His strong influence on George III secured him the office of prime minister in May 1762. As a Scotsman and the confidant of the king, he was particularly unpopular and his government lasted a little less than a year.
7. Tan or tanner's bark was usually the bark of oak reduced to a coarse powder for use in the tanning of leather. Once this process was completed, the tan was removed and utilised to make hotbeds for germinating or growing on tender plants or exotics such as pineapples; a procedure introduced to England from the Netherlands early in the eighteenth century.
8. Undated diary entry between 30 June and 13 September 1776.
9. A small, one masted, fore-and-aft rigged vessel, differing from a cutter in having a jib-stay and standing bow-sprit (O.E.D.).

His fellow voyagers were the Count's steward, a Mr Louard, and two French fishermen acting as the crew. Also, concealed on board, were two sailors, fugitives from the Press Gang, whom they put on board a Dutch East Indian vessel opposite Gravesend. Next morning, it became apparent that the crew had no idea where they were, nor in which direction to steer. Furthermore, no one except Blaikie could understand the charts of the Channel kept on board. They had taken on no provisions and Blaikie had to go ashore with one of them in a rowing boat to purchase meat and bread. Worse was to come. Becalmed one moment and storm-tossed the next, they lurched towards Calais, Blaikie at the helm. He berthed at the port about 3 o'clock on Friday 15 November, almost wrecking the boat against the pier in the high wind. Determined to sail no farther, he engaged an English sailor, a smuggler who spoke 'tolerable French', to take the charge of the vessel and bring it round to the port of Touques. Even then, his troubles were not quite over. The Customs Officers were intent on seizing the vessel because no one on the Count's staff had thought to take out a Bill of Lading. The matter was dropped, however, when it was discovered that the sloop belonged to the Count, and Blaikie experienced for the first time 'that the nobleman in France is very powerful'.

He and Luard hired horses for the rest of the way. The weather was wet and windy and, on the last leg of his journey from Honfleur to Mont Canisy, the road 'exceeding bad'. He reached the château on 21 November at about two o'clock in the afternoon and was disappointed at the sight of it. 'This house, which they call the château, stands upon the top of a little hill ... From this house there is indeed a fine view, as the house stands naked to the north-west and south, not a tree.' To the north-east he could see as far as Le Havre and the mouth of the Seine and, to the south-east, a river, navigable to the port of Touques, wound its way through a fine valley, while to the south, in the direction of Pont l'Eveque, stretched lush dairy meadows. His verdict, 'This place might be made beautiful, as the situation and *vues* on every side is fine but I hardly ever saw a Gentleman's Seat so out of the way of all communication.'[10]

The hill called Mont Canisy still exists but the château has long since vanished and the lands of the Count form part of the town of Deauville and its golf course. Lauraguais' grandfather, the Marquis de Lassay had built the château in the style of Louis XIV, using a local white stone prized for retaining its original whiteness longer than most others.[11] Lauraguais added features to bring it into line with his own taste but abandoned it, either through boredom or lack of money, to his brother Bufile de Brancas in 1778. The Brancas family sold the domain around 1830. By that time the château was already dilapidated and the intention of the new owner was to sell off the land in lots for building. He proceeded to demolish the castle but the State intervened and insisted that two walls should remain standing as an aid to navigation.[12] It was about this time that the writer, Gustave Flaubert (1821–1880), whose family

10. Diary, 21–22 November, 1776.

11. J. Chennebenoist, 'St Arnoult' in the revue *Athena sur la Touques*, May 1969.

12. *Promenade sur le Mont Canisy. Bénerville, Tourgeville, Deauville, Saint-Arnaut*, by Gérard Gailly (Brussels, 1960), p. 134.

had bought some of the land, came there from time to time in search of peace and tranquillity to read poetry. By that stage all that survived of the château was 'a great Louis XV staircase, a few windows without any glass, a wall where the wind blew all the time. It was situated on a plateau overlooking the sea'.[13] It seems that Blaikie's brief efforts had little permanent effect on the estate. A visitor writing about 1835 praises the fine view but describes Mont Canisy as 'un peu aride et sans eau' and the countryside around having few attractions.[14] However, a small memento of the Scotsman's work there was still in evidence in 1840 when another visitor remarked on the existence of two or three *'bosquets'* (groves) of foreign trees which were badly maintained.[15] In the 1914–18 war, English soldiers bivouacked on the mount[16] and today it is still the scene of German gun emplacements and bunkers remaining from the 2nd World War. Nothing is left of the château.

Blaikie was puzzled at the contradictions he found at Mont Canisy. The Count had English carriages and phaetons but the roads around the château were so poor that these could not be driven half a mile without overturning. He had imported expensive English race horses and enough English grooms to start a stud but there were no stables.[17] The whole place was in complete disorder. Mme Jones, the Count's English mistress (probably the Polly Jones after whom the sloop was named) was ignorant and insolent with almost everyone, but Blaikie found the Count 'a tolerable good sort of a man'.

Charles Louis Félicité de Brancas, Comte de Lauraguais (1733–1824) was a man driven by his enthusiasms, original to the point of eccentricity and, some would say, even madness.[18] He devoted himself intemperately in turn to almost all the pursuits, literary, scientific, and political of the day. Pamphlets on a myriad of subjects poured from his pen. He produced two dramas, *Clytemnestre* in 1761 and *Jocaste* twenty years later. Neither of his plays was performed but he did make his name in the theatre for ending an abuse which had caused much irritation for actors and audiences alike, namely the right enjoyed by certain of the nobility to seats on stage during performances. De Lauraguais bought out all the seats, and so delighted Voltaire that he dedicated his play *l'Écossaise* to him in recognition of his action.

One of his more useless and financially ruinous scientific experiments was an attempt to dissolve diamonds, but his search for a porcelain that would be more

---

13. From a letter of 1853 quoted in Gailly, pp. 135–6.
14. Caumont A de, *Statistique monumentale de l'arrondissement de Pont l'Eveque* (1859) (written about 1835–40).
15. La Butte A, *Essai historique sur Honfleur et l'arrondissement de Pont l'Eveque* (1840).
16. Paul YVON, 'Un Ecossais en Normandie à la fin du XVIIIme Siecle', *Normannia* (1933), p. 432.
17. The architect Bélanger writes in an autobiographical fragment in Ottomeyer H., 'Autobiographies d'architectes parisiens', *Bulletin de la Société de l'Histoire de Paris*, vol. 98–100, pp. 145–9, that he constructed a stable block for 200 horses in Normandy. See also plan at BN Estampes. However, Blaikie makes it clear that when he arrived at Mont Canisy in the autumn of 1776, there were no stables.
18. E. and J. de Goncourt, *Sophie Arnould d'apres sa Correspondance* (Geneva, 1967–68 edn), p. 34.

resistant to the heat of the kiln won him election to the *Académie des Sciences* in 1758, while his championing of the parlements against the king made him unpopular at court and led several times to his imprisonment and exile. He took up the cause of inoculation against smallpox in spite of Louis XV's disapproval of the procedure, and a pamphlet he wrote attacking the Parlement of Paris for banning it and ridiculing the clergy for their support of the ban was the cause of one of his imprisonments.[19] Always he embraced what was new in political and economic ideas, and in the arts, particularly architecture. His passion for everything English, from government to gardening, made him one of the foremost figures in the tide of anglomania which broke over France in the years before the Revolution and persisted even when the countries were at war.

With his fellow anglophiles, the Duc de Chartres (later the Duc d'Orléans), cousin to Louis XVI, and the Comte d'Artois, the King's brother, both of whom were later to employ Blaikie, he took up racing and the breeding of horses, a science much more advanced in England than in France. The first ever race using the English style of course and run according to English rules was held on 25 February 1766 by de Lauraguais at the Plaine des Sablons, an arid piece of land near the Bois de Boulogne. As a spectacle it was a sensational success and over two thousand carriages descended upon the Plain to view it. What impressed the spectators most, apart from the sheer beauty of the scene, was the lightness and speed of the horses bearing their undersized and skinny jockeys. For de Lauraguais only one thing slightly marred the success of the day. His specially bred French horse was obviously ill and could barely make its way round the track, having, it turned out, been poisoned by one of the English grooms who in a fit of patriotism was determined that it would not win against an English horse. From then on racing and betting on horses became the rage at court.[20] Huge sums of money were spent on buying horses, bringing English jockeys to France and laying bets on them.[21] The Duc de Chartres even started a fashion for dressing as a jockey. Lauraguais who had his own horses at Newmarket,[22] invited the English breeder Robert Tattershall to start a venture with him, breeding horses on the slopes of Mont Canisy.[23] They imported large numbers of horses and English servants and jockeys and it was these which Blaikie had observed with astonishment on his first day at the château.

Fascinated by the voyage of Captain Cook, Lauraguais had corresponded with Joseph Banks and the two men became friends. Banks, who had accompanied Cook on his historic voyage, wrote Lauraguais an account of his stay on Tahiti and invited him on board the *Sir Lawrence*, the vessel he had charted for a voyage to Iceland in

19. Rodolphe Trouilleux, *N'oubliez pas Iphigénie. Biographie de la cantatrice et épistolaire Arnould* (Grenoble, 1999), p. 51.

20. Grouchy and Cottin (eds), *Journal inédit du duc de Croy (1718–1784)*, 4 vols (Paris, 1906–7), vol. 2, p. 223.

21. He bought the famous horse Gimcrack which was much painted by Stubbs. See B. Taylor, *Stubbs* (London, 1971), p. 207.

22. R. Black, *Horse Racing in France* (1886), pp. 8–10.

23. Archives Départementales de Calvados, 8E 16086.

1772. Lauraguais joined the ship and its company at Gravesend, the evening of its departure, for the sail down the Thames, and was put ashore in the morning at Deal.[24] He had the idea of creating a botanical garden and a *jardin anglais* at his estate in Normandy and it was because of this that Blaikie found himself in his employment.

Lauraguais was 43 when Blaikie met him and their association was to last thirty years. The son of Louis, duc de Villars-Brancas, and his third wife Adelaide Geneviève Félicité d'O, the young Lauraguais inherited his estates in Normandy through his mother. He began his adult life with a career in the army, as was the custom for one of his rank, but the army was not to his taste and he gave up after only one campaign. Having conducted himself with bravery he was delighted to put up his sword permanently. At the age of 22, he married Elisabeth-Pauline de Gand de Middlebourg, a member of one of the richest and most noble families in what is now Belgium. However, he had no intention of submitting to the restraints of marriage. Within two years, posing as a simple clerk by the name of Dorval, and lodging at their home, he had abducted Sophie, the daughter of Monsieur and Madame Arnould.[25] The 'divine' Sophie was at the start of her career and was to become one of the leading singers of the Paris opera, chosen by Gluck to introduce the part of Iphigénie to Paris. Lauraguais became the first of her many lovers. She bore him four children[26] but the relationship was tempestuous and was often the subject of ribald comment in the journals of the time. She broke with him at the end of 1761 and Bachaumont, the leading chronicler of Parisian society commented, 'Mlle Arnoux having had enough of the jealousy of M. de Lauraguais has profited by his absence to break with him. She has sent to Mme la Comtesse de Lauraguais all the jewels which the lady's husband has given her, including a coach with two children inside it which she received from him.'[27] The long suffering Countess was obliged by de Lauraguais to bring up the children as her own.

In 1766 he spent six months in prison after a quarrel with a Monsieur de Villette on the subject of racing. Transferred to the prison of Dijon, he escaped to England where, in 1769, the most scandalous and bizarre of his numerous sexual escapades occurred. He married off one of his servants, who was also his mistress, to his secretary in London and then abducted her and smuggled her back to France. He was taken to court by the secretary for enticing his wife away from him. The outcome of the court case is unknown but it is likely that Lauraguais lost because he attacked the English legal system and defended himself in a strange way by pleading his case in a book which he published in London in 1773 entitled *Mémoire pour moi par moi Louis de Brancas comte de Lauraguais*. Witty and charming de Lauraguais may have been but,

---

24. H. B. Carter, *Sir Joseph Banks* (London, 1988), p. 104.
25. Madeleine-Sophie Arnould (1740–1802). Celebrated as a singer, an *amoureuse* and a wit. Admired by the Bavarian composer, Gluck (1714–1787), she was the first to play Iphigénie and Eurydice in 1774, her crowning year. Thereafter her style of singing went out of fashion. In 1778 she gave up the theatre and began to fall into debt. She survived the Revolution without persecution but suffered much illness before her death.
26. The children were later legitimised.
27. Bachaumont, *Memoires secrets*, vol. V, p. 9 (1 January 1762).

in the end, he was more often than not bad news to those who were closest to him. Sophie Arnould vowed that he had given her two million kisses and made her shed four million tears.[28] His wife, whom he treated abominably, eventually obtained a separation from him on the grounds of his cruelty, claiming that he beat her. He betrayed the trust of Joseph Banks by publishing without Banks' consent, and much to his annoyance, an abstract of the voyage of the *Endeavour* based on Banks's letter describing his voyage with Cook to Tahiti.[29] And Blaikie, who owed his career to Lauraguais' early patronage, would in the end, bitterly regret their association.

Lauraguais' projects and adventures eventually ate up his large fortune and Blaikie was perhaps unlucky to be drawn into his orbit just at the time when his money began to run out. Blaikie's cautious judgement that the count seemed 'a tolerable good sort of a man' suggests that he found de Lauraguais sympathetic in spite of the disorder of his affairs. Although their station in life was so different, Blaike was just the sort of man to appeal to the Count; one who shared his employer's curiosity of spirit, a botanist who had travelled on foot to the peaks of the Alps and been visited by Voltaire, who had attended medical dissections in Paris and was also interested in agricultural improvement, as well as such esoteric subjects as the commercial breeding of silk worms on pine trees for the manufacture of silk in Scotland. In his own sphere of life Blaikie was an original also.

Lauraguais was avid for the new 'exotic' trees and shrubs. Even money could not procure them all and Blaikie with his 26 American plants from William Aiton had already demonstrated his value. He was on friendly terms with the foremost horti-culturists, nurserymen and garden managers in England. In consequence, he could obtain newly introduced plants from them at a time when such introductions were generally unobtainable in France, and he could lay out the garden to display them to best advantage. That he was practical and capable also soon became evident. Finding the botanical garden in which he was supposed to plant his trees non-existent, he set about planting them in a temporary home while he began preparing the ground. Before long, he was ordering hay and corn for the horses and managing the farm when the new English farm manager, Mr Longdon, proved a disappointment. The contacts he soon established with French botanists like Varin[30] at Rouen and

28. Quoted in J. Stern, *A l'ombre de Sophie Arnould, François-Joseph Bélanger, architecte des Menus Plaisirs. Premier architecte du comte d'Artois* (Paris, 1930), vol. I, p. 16.

29. In a letter to Banks written in 1772, after finding him not at home, Lauraguais pleads that he does not deserve Banks' reproaches. See History of Science and Technology, Part 4: Correspondence and Papers relating to Voyages of Discovery 1767–1819. From the State Library of New South Wales (Microform, Reel 56). See also H. C. Cameron, *Sir Joseph Banks* (London, 1952), who relates that on Lauraguais' manuscript, Banks had written, 'Abstract of Endeavour's voyage written for Count Lauraguais who printed it. I seized the impression and burn'd it' (Appendix G, pp. 313–20). It was published in French in 1772 by A. F. de Fréville as a supplement to the voyage of Bougainville. See E. D. Cox, *A Reference Guide to the Literature of Travel* (University of Washington, 1935).

30. Varin was head gardener at the botanical gardens of Rouen. He was noted particularly for his work on the hybridisation of lilacs.

particularly André Thouin[31] in Paris at the *Jardin du Roi* (*Jardin des Plantes*) meant that he established a source of rare plants in France also. Lastly, and most importantly, by employing a botanist and a plant collector Lauraguais was adding to his own prestige, since very few gardeners possessed this double qualification.[32]

With Mr Longdon, the farm manager, Blaikie made a few excursions in the spring of 1777 to the area round about Mont Canisy. He found Caen 'a clean neat town' and was so impressed by the riding academy, that he reluctantly acknowledged the French as superior in ridng to the English. In May, he and Longdon set out to buy seeds and seed potatoes and they took a Sunday afternoon off to stroll about the harbour in Le Havre where Blaikie's observant and appreciative eye was turned upon the appearance of the women of the area in their traditional costume and he noted in his diary how their dress set off their beauty. Their hair was drawn back under caps with a silver or gold lace band that fitted close to the front of the forehead. At the back two fine linen strips were attached, each about a yard long. These trails of linen waved in the air behind them in a most attractive way as they walked and as they turned their heads from side to side. A tight corset or stays with a shortish petticoat completed their appearance and showed off their handsome figures. In the Swiss part of his diary he had described the traditional dress of both the men and women in the various districts but this was the only one he found aesthetically appealing. Blaikie and Longdon's enquiries about seed potatoes drew a blank. The French did not appear to cultivate them and knew little about them. In June 1776, on the instructions of the Count, he set off with Longdon for Jersey, via Cherbourg, to buy implements for the farm.

At this stage the diary gives an account of one of the many extremely bizarre situations into which Blaikie stumbled during the course of his life. Fraught with almost incredible coincidence, it makes hilarious reading, although at the time the experience must have been extremely distressing. First, Blaikie was mistaken for an American spy and imprisoned in Jersey. From there he was released through the good offices of a school friend, who just happened to be the chief surgeon of the island. A few days later he was allowed to leave for Guernsey where he was again imprisoned as a spy. When he obtained his freedom from there, he made his way via Alderney back to Cherbourg where he was immediately seized as a British spy and arrested again, being released only on the intervention of the Count. The episode, as well as being interesting in itself, throws light on the tensions existing in the period before France and England declared war over American Independence.

In the summer of 1776, the relationship between the two countries was deteriorating because of French support for the rebellious American colonies. Although war with England was not officially declared until 1778, French popular sympathies were entirely with the Americans. Blaikie had noted on his visit to Le Havre in May 1777 that, in its small harbour, they were busy building 36-gun frigates and shipping off ammunition for America. Hostilities between Britain and her American colonists had existed since

---

31. André Thouin (1747–1824), head gardener at the *Jardin du Roi*.
32. Antoine Richard, the Queen's gardener at the Trianon was one.

April 1775 and the Continental Congress of the 13 States authorised privateering operations against British vessels in 1776. These privateers were allowed to dock in French ports and bring into harbour the English ships they captured as prizes.

Such was the case of an American schooner, the *Montgomery*, which, on 5 June 1777, had captured an English merchant ship, *The Good Intent*, with its cargo of oil, fruit and gin, within sight of its destination, Guernsey, and brought the vessel, a brigantine,[33] prisoner into Cherbourg. The *Montgomery's* captain, one Brunnel or Brunnell, set out for Paris at once to seek advice from the American representative[34] there as to how he could get permission to sell his prize and her cargo, for, as France and Britain were not yet officially at war, such action was still officially illegal.[35] Amazingly, on 7 June, Blaikie and Longdon met up with Brunnel outside Cherbourg. Travelling in the same postchaise was also the landlord of an hotel in Cherbourg. This man knew Mr Longdon and invited the farm manager and his companion to lodge at his inn. Blaikie's natural curiosity about the Americans was not in the least diminished by the fact that they had taken an English vessel captive, and he describes how, on his arrival at the hotel, they became acquainted with the crew of the privateer and were invited on board. To his surprise he found it, 'one of the smallest vessels[36] that ever tried to pass the Atlantic ocean'. No bigger than a fishing boat, it carried two swivel guns, one on either side in the middle of the boat and lay so low in the water that in action the crew were never visible above deck. According to Blaikie, the Captain, Mate and Gunner were decent fellows but the crew, numbering about twenty, was a set of young ragamuffins. The privateer, with its prize, a brig from Jersey lying alongside it, lay in the newly constructed harbour, and Blaikie learnt that the brig's crew was at liberty to return home after having had the 'hard fortune' to lose both ship and cargo.

Blaikie and Longdon had hoped to find a passage from Cherbourg to Jersey but were advised that there was a boat ready to leave at Carteret, further along the coast. As a result of a number of minor mishaps they were not able to leave Carteret until the evening of the 9th when they succeeded in hiring a small fishing boat to take them to St Helier. Until the last minute, they had doubts about the wisdom of their journey in such unsettled times, especially since Longdon had forgotten or lost his letter of introduction from the Count to the governor of Jersey, but they pressed on and set sail with some other passengers for St Helier. Towards morning a storm of hurricane proportions overtook them. The half rotten ropes and sails gave way and

---

33. A merchant ship with two masts, square-rigged (O.E.D.).

34. There was not yet an American ambassador in Paris but there were three Commissioners, Deane, Lee and Benjamin Franklin. The latter was already considered as an ambassador in effect if not in title.

35. PRO, Kew, SP 47.

36. It was described in a letter dated 7 July from the Lieut. Governor of Jersey, Moyse Corbet to Lord Weymouth as a 25-ton schooner originating in Maryland, armed with 2 carriage and 6 swivel guns, long built but very low, and possessing 32 muskets and 26 men on board. A later letter in the same file describes it as a converted Virginia pilot boat and its captain as a Devonshire man.

the boat was driven amongst the rocks at the south-east point of the island. Some of the women passengers started to cry. Others prayed or fainted away while poor Mr Longdon, Blaikie tells us, was as terrified as the women. It was touch and go but somehow the sails were raised and although the sea was running 'prodigeous high' they succeeded in running the boat ashore on the the north side of the Island about 11 o'clock in the morning. As they had landed some distance from St Helier, it took the bedraggled passengers and crew about four hours to walk across the fields to the town, so that it was evening before Blaikie and his companion could enjoy the comforts of the *The Golden Lion*, whose landlord was a Scotsman called Mr Horn. There, unfortunately, the two were spotted by some members of the crew of the *Good Intent* who had returned to Jersey. The next morning, Blaikie was surprised to find himself with Mr Longdon under guard as American spies. Later, they were summoned to what Blaikie calls the town house to appear, accompanied by their guards, before the assembled council and all the principal people of the town.

Blaikie and his companion could not have been aware that the Channel Isles were in ferment over the seizure of the *Good Intent*, a Jersey vessel with a Jersey captain, Paul Bienvenu, and a Jersey crew. Letters sped from the islands' governors to Lord Weymouth, the Secretary of State, with rumours of other privateers, French skulduggery and espionage. That supposed British subjects had been seen aboard the American schooner was enough to condemn them in the eyes of the islanders. After being interrogated separately, the two men were allowed to return under house arrest to the hotel and many visitors came to inspect the 'spies'. Amongst them was the Chief Surgeon of the island. Since he possessed some knowledge of botany, he had been sent by the Governor to check Longdon's claim that his companion was a botanist. In the course of conversation, Blaikie and the surgeon realised that they had been to school together, presumably at Corstorphine Parish School, and that their parents were acquainted.[37] A remarkable coincidence and a piece of luck for Blaikie.

At once the Surgeon requested Blaikie's release but the Governor would only allow him to take Blaikie to dine at his house. The terrified Longdon had to remain at the hotel. This situation lasted until Monday 16 June, when the two men were escorted to the harbour to board a boat going to Guernsey. Feeling was still running high against them and there were repeated requests to the Governor that they should be detained. In Guernsey, they were again arrested but allowed to continue to Alderney on 18 June and were relieved at the civil reception they received from the governor, John Le Mesurier, who did believe their story. Here they met one other stranger, an elderly hairdresser whose son had died on the island and who had arranged to return to England on board a smuggler's lugger[38] leaving Alderney on the same tide as the boat which was to take Blaikie and Longdon to Cherbourg.

No sooner had Longdon and Blaikie reached Cherbourg and were on the way to their hotel with thoughts of a good supper and a comfortable night's sleep, than they

---

37. See chapter 2.
38. A small vessel with four corner cut sails set fore and aft and may have two or three masts (O.E.D.).

heard a great deal of noise and were suddenly surrounded by a patrol of some 24 soldiers who seized them at bayonet point crying out *'La voila encore de ces coquins'*. (Here are some more of these rogues.) Blaikie asked them in French why they were treating him in this manner and, on hearing French spoken, their officer intervened and asked him who he was. Blaikie told him and gave him the name of his hotel and the officer agreed to go with a group of his men to the hotel to confirm the Scot's story. It looked as if all would be well but, when the soldiers accompanying Blaikie and Longdon realised that Longdon spoke no French, they shouted at the two men calling them liars and rogues and began to drag them forcibly along, pushing them from behind with their guns and bayonets. Blaikie protested but, before long, he was glad of the troops for protection from the hostile crowd that surrounded them. Jostled and abused by the mob and, thinking that a declaration of war between France and England was the explanation for the violence, they were marched to the guard-house, where the first person Blaikie saw was the poor old hairdresser from Alderney sitting on a bench, with several of the crew of the smuggler's boat lying wounded on the floor beside him. There was no time to ask the old man what had happened. The soldiers pushed Blaikie and Longdon towards the upper end of the crowded prison shouting at the same time, 'There you are, see what's happened to your compatriots'.

Fortunately, Mr Druet, the landlord was found and he was allowed to take them to the hotel as prisoners under house arrest. It was Drouet who filled in the missing details of the story which had caused Blaikie's arrest in Cherbourg. Apparently, and this is confirmed in the official correspondence of the event,[39] on 14 June, the officers of a Sherborne cutter [40] lying outside the harbour, persuaded the American Captain and the Mate of the *Montgomery* to go aboard their ship for a drink, captured them and took them off as prisoners to England or Jersey. A few days later, around 22 June according to one report, but on the 19th according to Blaikie, the smuggler's lugger arrived from Alderney with the hairdresser on board. A fight broke out when a priest reported that he had overheard the sailors insulting the Americans. The smugglers were attacked and thrown into prison. It was at this stage that Blaikie and Longdon had arrived and been taken prisoner.

Nor was the episode entirely over. The day after his release and his detention at the hotel, Blaikie heard that the remaining Americans, with a number of other boats, had set out that morning, the 20th, to take the lugger as a prize and were bringing her into port. Unable to control his curiosity, Blaikie went along to see what was happening. He was spotted and had to make a run for it to his hotel. In fact the boat was so obviously a smuggler's lugger that it was released, but the crew of the lugger and the captain of *The Good Intent* were held for another two weeks. Blaikie's and Longdon's ordeal ended on the 28th when the governor received a note from the Count to whom Blaikie had managed to send a message, and they left Cherbourg with relief. The brig was eventually declared by a court to be the property of its

---

39. PRO, SP47.
40. A cutter is a small single-masted vessel with a straight running bowsprit and rigged much like a sloop, carrying a fore-and-aft main sail, gaff-top-sail, stay-foresail and jib (O.E.D.).

master and the cargo owners, but when their agent went to claim it, he found that it had been sold with false papers at Dunkerque and its cargo had vanished.[41]

Blaikie spent the next two months quietly at Mont Canisy before being sent by de Lauraguais to Paris on 14 September. He returned briefly at the beginning of October en route from Paris to London and put the finishing touches to the walks and enclosures he had designed. While he was in Paris he had been offered the post of head gardener at Maisons, where he was to lay out an English garden at the Comte d'Artois' estate outside Paris, with instructions to go to England to purchase trees. He agreed with de Lauraguais to engage a new gardener as a replacement for himself in England, and in November, he brought back Archibald Macmaster to take over his work at Mont Canisy. Archibald became his trusted aide and Blaikie acted as his patron over the years, finding him employment and watching over his career.[42]

In January 1778 Lauraguais, hearing that Blaikie had refused the terms of employment offered by the Comte d'Artois, asked him to return and take over the running of his estate in Normandy as Longdon had departed. Having put together a new collection of trees for Mont Canisy, Blaikie took up his old employment again, finding a post for Archibald in Paris with his friend André Thouin, head gardener at the *Jardin du Roi* (*Jardin des Plantes*). However, in August 1778 the Count, probably short of funds, sold Mont Canisy to his brother and he and Blaikie set off to take a look at his château at Lassay to see if he could go there to live.

Lauraguais owned three châteaux; Lassay, between the town of Bagnoles-de-L'Orne and the town of Mayenne in the Department of the Orne; Mont Canisy in the little commune of St Arnoult in Calvados; and Manicamp near the town of Chauny in the Department of the Oise. Blaikie disapproved of Lassay, a heavily fortified castle which he likened to a prison, and gave it the thumbs down by declaring that he had never seen a more disagreeable situation. They then set off together on a tour of the countryside visiting the Count's various properties and dining with his friends and neighbours. As he went along, Blaikie remarked on the state of agriculture and the condition of the people. He admired the rich pasture and the King's stud at Argentan (Orme) and was appalled at the distressing poverty and wretchedness of the people of Picardy, 'most of them without shoes or stockings and some hardly any clothes'. They spent three days at Manicamp which was to become the Count's eventual choice of a new home, and a place that Blaikie was one day to know very well. Although the house was ruinous, Blaikie thought it a paradise compared to Lassay and considered its situation agreeable.

At Noyon, where, without identifying themselves, they visited an estate belonging to Lauraguais' wife they heard from the steward that 'the Count had been dead many years and what a fool he had been and what a good woman his wife was'. Another

---

41. PRO, SP47.
42. Macmaster became head gardener to the Duke of Vaux Praslin at Vaux le Vicomte. There was an Archbald McMaster christened in Straiton, Ayrshire on 6 February 1743 whose age would fit in with the date of Archibald's retirement to Chessy sur Lagny around 1816. The record of his death has not been found.

incident which caused them some amusement was the day they met an Irish officer who took them for a pair of horse traders and offered to buy one of their horses. This confusion must have delighted de Lauraguais with his passion for horses and his affectation of the sporting, English style of dressing in which a noble and his servant were almost indistinguishable. Finally having spent most of September and October touring the region with Blaikie, the Count went to Paris leaving instructions to take up all the trees in the botanic garden at Mont Canisy and transport some to Manicamp, preparing the rest for sale in Paris. This Blaikie did and on 12 November left for Paris to attend to the trees which he had sent on ahead of him.

The Count's companionship during their tour together of Normandy and Picardy engaged Blaikie's strong loyalty. On 26 October, soon after their return to Paris, when both the Count and Blaikie were at de Lauraguais' house, Blaikie was handed a *lettre de cachet* intended for the Count who had offended the King's Minister Necker. The messenger demanded to know where his master was but Blaikie, afraid that de Lauraguais would be arrested and imprisoned, refused to tell him. The Count took off immediately for Mainz and told Blaikie to go to Manicamp till the affair passed over. The order in fact only banished de Lauraguais to a distance of 10 leagues (30 miles) from Paris[43] and Blaikie was able to return to Paris on 21 December.

From then on Blaikie, occupied at Bagatelle, returned to Manicamp only occasionally. He spent about six weeks in the spring of 1779 planting the gardens, and came back for a few days at the end of 1780 to make new plantings and check on the success of the work of the year before. In May 1782, he laid out a garden for Lauraguais at his new Paris town house in the *rue des Vieilles Tuileries*. On a visit in 1783 he showed mild disillusionment with the Count's ever changing schemes, commenting, 'he has great projects both in gardening and horses but seems to succeed little in either, for he is so unsettled in his ideas that his new works have not time to show their effects'. Nevertheless, he took time on a visit to England in 1785 to procure yet another gardener for Lauraguais and accompanied the young man, whose name was Brough, to Manicamp.[44] The Count was still immersed in grandiose projects for hothouses and Blaikie agreed to furnish plants and trees for them at £100 per quarter. All Blaikie's original plantations were thriving but the Count, he commented wryly, was 'still changing and frequently for the worse as he cannot have any idea of Nature'. After 1785 Blaikie ceases to mention Lauraguais or Manicamp in his diary. The Count's contract with him was never honoured.

As for Manicamp, the only contemporary record of it is a short description in the memoirs of Mme Ducrest, Josephine's lady-in-waiting. When she visited it during the Empire, Manicamp belonged to Lauraguais' nephew, Buffile de Brancas, an insignifi-

---

43. Bachaumont *Memoires secrets*, vol. XII, p. 145.
44. On 4 April 1785 Lauraguais wrote to Banks. After commiserating with him on the disputes that racked the R.S. at that time, he asked Banks to provide him with rare plants from Kew, with instructions to label them clearly to be given to him; an imputation that Blaikie might appropriate them. This perhaps says more about de Lauraguais than Blaikie, since Blaikie appears always to have been honest in his dealings.

cant man, extraordinarily niggardly in his hospitality compared with de Lauraguais, who, she tells us, had spent considerable sums in turning his park into a *jardin anglais*. He had, reported Mme Ducrest, succeeded in creating something very beautiful, in which magnificent stretches of water already there played a part.[45]

There is a rough plan, the sole one among Blaikie's papers, which may delineate the park of Manicamp. It does indeed show much water. It also indicates two châteaux on the site, one old and one new. What is certain is that Blaikie, although he did not know it, was not finished with Manicamp and would later spend many unhappy years there.

45. Georgette Ducrest, *Mémoires sur l'Impératrice Joséphine*, 3 vols (Paris, 1828), vol. II, pp. 186–7.

CHAPTER 7

Blaikie, Bélanger and the *Jardin Anglais*

B LAIKIE's first, short spell of employment, as a gardener in the service of the Comte
d'Artois, lasted from 19 September to early December 1777. It came about through
de Lauraguais who, on Blaikie's going to Paris, gave him a letter of introduction to
François-Joseph Bélanger,[1] the recently appointed Principal Architect to the Comte
d'Artois, at his house in the *rue de Poissonière* (*rue du Faubourg-Poissonière* near the *rue
Bergère*). A successful architect and designer, Bélanger (1744–1818) was also a landscape
artist and engineer. He studied at the *École de l'Académie royal d'architecture*[2] and, after
leaving the School in 1765, is thought to have spent part of the following year in
England, at the invitation of Lord Shelburne, to provide drawings for the decoration
of a gallery in his London residence, Lansdowne House.[3] On his return to France, he
obtained a post in the department of *Menus Plaisirs*, a government department responsible for all ceremonies and fetes relating to the royal house. He rose through the
ranks of the *Menus Plaisirs* purchasing the post of Principal Architect to the Comte
D'Artois in 1777.

De Lauraguais had met Bélanger eight years earlier, when he commissioned the
architect to design a bath house in the grounds of his mansion in the *rue de l'Université*
near the Palais Bourbon.[4] For its richly decorated interior Bélanger employed the
sculptor l'Huillier recently returned from Rome after studying the decorative style of
Pompeii and Paestum and with the drawings of Piranesi in his luggage. In 1774, the
architect drew up impressive plans for stables at Mont Canisy.[5] Lauraguais was the
perfect client for Bélanger; ahead of his time in his tastes and extravagant in his
enthusiasms, happy to employ the best and most expensive craftsmen and materials.
However, the Count's choice of Bélanger as his architect came about not through a
shared appreciation of Palladio and Piranesi but by the intervention of Sophie Arnould,
Lauraguais' former mistress.

Around 1769 when her long, turbulent association with de Lauraguais finally ended,
Sophie was at the zenith of her brief career as a singer, and a central figure in the

---

1. See Jean Stern, *A l'ombre de Sophie Arnould François-Joseph Bélanger Architecte des Menus-Plaisirs
Premier Architecte du Comte d'Artois*, 2 vols (Paris, 1930).
2. Bélanger together with Soufflot, Ledoux, Brogniart, De Wailly and others were products
of the teaching of Blondel whose interest was aesthetics rather than technical training. In
particular Blondel taught that there was a particularly French way of doing things which
reflected the country's greatness established in the reign of Louis XIV. See David Watkins,
'Architectural Education, Patronage and Practise in Ancien Regime France', Georgian
Architectual Practice, *Symposium of the Georgian Group* (1991), pp. 18–23.
3. Jean Stern, vol. I, p. 4.
4. Bélanger drawing, BN Estampes.
5. BN Estampes. See chapter 6, n. 17.

world of artists and aristocrats. Neither her bust by the sculptor, Houdon, nor an unfinished portrait of her in the Wallace Collection,[6] fully captures her famous charm, intelligence and vitality. According to the court painter, Elizabeth Vigée Le Brun, she was no beauty; her mouth spoiled her face and only her eyes revealed the cleverness which made her famous. Yet such was her presence on stage that Mme de Genlis, writer, mistress of the Duc de Chartres, and governess of his children, never forgot the first time Arnould appeared in performance at the Opera wearing a lilac and silver gown over a large hoop or panier.[7] In 1770, as a star of the Opera, she featured in several highly acclaimed performances to celebrate the marriage of the Dauphin and the fifteen year old Marie Antoinette of Austria.[8] During the preparations for the brilliant fetes and dramatic entertainments to mark the occasion, Sophie met Bélanger, then 24 year old, in his first post as a draughtsman at the *Menus Plaisirs*. The young man was handsome, witty and amusing and she embarked on a light-hearted affair with him. The affair turned to love and although the grand passion faded, and many lovers succeeded him, their friendship endured till her death in 1802.

As her 'bel ange' was penniless, she set out to garner commissions for him from her admirers. De Lauraguais, who came occasionally to see Sophie, was introduced to Bélanger, as was the Prince de Ligne,[9] the most important client she sent him. He commissioned Bélanger to remodel his château at Beloeil in May 1769 and to design an English garden for him. The architect's appointment, in March 1777, as Principal Architect to the Comte d'Artois was secured through Sophie's influence with her protector, the Prince d'Henin, captain of Artois' guard. Some six months later de Lauraguais recommended Blaikie to the architect thus introducing him to the most fashionable artistic coterie in Paris and the circle of the Comte d'Artois.

At this time Artois had a number of building projects in hand. The King had made him a gift of the château of St Germain with funds to renovate and repair it, and he had purchased for himself the old château of Maisons, today known as the château Maisons-Laffitte. It was here that a new *jardin anglais* was planned. Bélanger asked Blaikie to meet him and Artois' Treasurer, Radix de Sainte-Foy,[10] with some others, at Maisons on 20 September 1777 with the intention of employing him as *jardinier anglais*.[11] The meeting was not a success. Blaikie's year in the service of de Lauraguais

6. Manchester Square, London.

7. Mme de Genlis, *Mémoires* (Paris, 1825), vol. I, p. 70. There is a similar painting by Carmontelle in the Musée Condé, Chantilly.

8. See also Grouchy and Cottin, vol. 2, p. 423, 9 June 1770. 'Le neuf juin on donne à Versailles la première représentation de Castor et Pollux ... L'opéra bien joué et du plus grand effet. Mlle Arnould excéllente actrice, joua au mieux.'

9. Charles-Joseph, Prince de Ligne (1735–1814). For a translation of his writings, with extensive notes and bibliography, see Basil Guy, *Coup d'Oeil at Beloeil and a Great Number of European Gardens* (California, 1992).

10. Radix de Sainte-Foy (1736–1810), Treasurer General of the Navy, Superintendent of the Finances and Buildings of the Comte d'Artois, later imprisoned for financial corruption.

11. Diary, 19 September 1777.

had not taught him the ways of a courtier. Opinionated by nature, coping with the count's extravagant, confused and impractical schemes had encouraged him to rely on his own judgement and to offer his views freely. Of the château, he writes, 'This place is finely situated upon the Banks of the River [the Seine] and might be made beautiful but,' he goes on, 'their ideas seems so contracted that they only showed a piece of ground about four or five acres which they said they wanted to make an English garden of'. His response was blunt: 'I told them that was not what was meant by English gardens, that the whole ground round the house ought to correspond, else they never could think of having any thing beautiful but,' he adds, 'this they had no ideas of'. He meant, of course, that the house should be the central feature of the garden and that the lawns should come right up to its windows without being cut off by terraces and parterres. He concedes that, 'Mr Bélanger who had been in England understood better than the others,' and adds, 'he told me to have patience and to do as well as we could until they saw something and that their intention was to send me to England to buy trees in a few days.'[12]

The 'few days' stretched into weeks, giving Blaikie time to sightsee around Paris with a London nurseryman, James Hairs,[13] and to make a catalogue of the plants at the Jardin du Roi. It was not until Tuesday, 8 October, that he received permission to leave. He set off for Normandy, taking with him with some plants for Mr Lee. Then, after a few days putting the finishing touches to Lauraguais' gardens, he boarded the packet from Dieppe to Brighton. He reached London on the 21st where he lodged at Mr Hairs. He called on Dr Fothergill, then on Mr Banks and spent the time until 4 November amongst his old friends at Upton, Kew and Hammersmith.[14]

Blaikie's outspokenness over the planned English garden at Maisons probably lost him that particular post, for when he returned from England with the trees at the end of November, he was angered to find another gardener in his place.[15] Bélanger attempted to persuade him to stay on as *jardinier anglais* responsible for the new part of the garden but he had too much pride to settle for such a compromise and, although Bélanger talked to him about an English garden he planned 'at a place called Bagatelle', Blaikie refused adamantly to consider it. He had sent Banks a copy of the catalogue

12. Diary, Friday 20 September 1777.
13. Hairs had a nursery at Ranelagh, Chelsea, and at Ham Common, Surrey. Blaikie stayed with him in London at St James, Haymarket, when he went to England to buy the Count's trees. See ref to him in E. J. Willson, *West London Nursery Gardens* (London, 1982). His presence in Paris suggests Hairs had a French as well as an English clientèle.
14. In addition to the £50 which he received to pay for trees before his departure, his bill for expenses shows that he spent £28 19s. 4d. at Lee's nursery, £3 4s. 6d. at Thoburn's, £2 10s. at Hairs', and £4 10s. at Wilson's. Account dated 28 October 1777, AN., R1 310. For this period of employment he was paid 1204 livres, AN., R1 309. For information on these nurseries see Ray Desmond, *Dictionary of English and Irish Botanists* (London, 1994), and E. J. Willson, as above.
15. Bélanger's plan for the garden had been delivered to Maisons on 1 November, four days before Blaikie left London. A gardener called Durand was instructed to carry it out. Stern, vol. I, p. 78.

he had drawn up of the plants in the *Jardin du Roi*, and now, perhaps with thoughts of a return to a career as a botanist, he wrote to him again on the pretext of correcting some of the plant names he had given wrongly in his catalogue. He told his patron that he was dissatisfied with his working conditions in Paris, but there is no record of Banks' reply.[16]

Although Bélanger had replaced Blaikie as *jardinier anglais* at Maisons, he must have been impressed by the gardener's commitment to the English garden. Lauraguais' recommendation, too, carried particular weight with him, for Lauraguais had been one of the first to adopt the fashion for the English garden. He had visited England many times, was familiar with Sir William Chambers' influential *Dissertation on Oriental Gardening* (1772)[17] and had himself created a most unusual *jardin anglais* in which he had begun the construction of a volcano.[18] Blaikie's strong views on the features of an English garden, although inconvenient at Maisons, were interesting in relation to Bagatelle, where the English garden was to be the most important feature. He invited Blaikie several times to his house that December, no doubt to discuss what each understood by an English garden and where their conception differed.

The first accounts of the *jardin anglais* in France probably date from about the late 1760s[19] and although French and English writers still differ in their views as to its origin,[20] they agree about its main purpose. It was essentially a place where the individual, or a small group of people, could enjoy a variety of the different aspects of 'Nature', in hidden dells, leafy glades and by meandering streams. This was in strong contrast to formal French gardens as exemplified by Versailles,[21] designed to be viewed in one panorama as the setting for the public life of a splendid court, with nature geometrically controlled. The features of the *jardin anglais* were easily

---

16. 6 December 1777, Kew: B.C. 1.67.
17. Lauraguais offered Chambers a French translation of his work. J. Barrier et M. Mosser, *Sur les terres d'un jardinier* (Paris, 1997), p. 26.
18. Grouchy and Cottin, vol. 2, p. 328. 'I saw that at the Petit Palais Bourbon M. de Lauraguais was selling to the Prince de Condé, a *jardin anglais* in perfect taste, that he finished and abandoned at the same moment and where he had begun to construct a volcano which made a fine effect.'
19. Grouchy and Cottin, vol. 2, p. 272 (14 April 1767). The Duc de Cröy describes a family party at Boulogne where the amusing Countess Montmorency had profited from a visit to England to make an English garden. He thought that it was a fashion that might catch on, possibly avec fureur like other English fashions. Also, vol. 4, p. 259 (28 May 1782). Describing the garden of the Duchesse de Bouffleurs which was probably created between 1765 and 1768 he writes that, 'Quite a while ago she created the most truly beautiful *jardin anglais* that we have in France, resembling a real English one'.
20. For differing points of view see Oswald Siren, *China and the Gardens of Europe of the 18th Century* (New York, 1950), and David Jacques, 'On the Supposed Chineseness of the English Landscape Garden', *Garden History*, 18, vol. 2 (Autumn 1990), pp. 181–91. See also Jacques Moulin 'Le Château d'Aunoy et l'apparition en France du Jardin à l'Anglaise' *Bulletin Monumental* (1991), Tome 149 II, pp. 221–4.
21. Laid out by Le Notre (1613–1700), but not so rigidly geometric as is sometimes thought. See Pierre-André Lablaude, *The Gardens of Versailles* (London, 1995).

recognised and in pedestrian hands became a cliché; the winding avenue to the house which appeared in view as a 'surprise' at the last moment; the serpentine river, the irregularly shaped lake, the groups or clumps of trees and the wide expanse of lawn. Garden structures or *fabriques* were an essential part of this landscape. They took many forms, of which the most popular was the Temple with its association with ancient Greece or Italy. Exotic countries inspired buildings, such as pyramids, Chinese pavilions, Turkish or Tartar tents. Gothic ruins and grottoes, romantic symbols of a national past, also became popular, as did thatched cottages, or hermitages representing the simple pleasures of rustic life.

Features associated with these gardens had existed in earlier parks, but it was the English designer, William Kent (1685–1748), whose work at the gardens at Chiswick, Rousham and Stowe defined the style in the 1730s and 40s. A painter and stage designer strongly influenced by ten years' sojourn in Italy, his gardens, laid out as a series of three dimensional 'pictures' had immense visual appeal. Together with the architect, William Chambers (1723–1796), designer of gardens and buildings for the Prince and Princess of Wales at Kew, Kent had a stronger influence in France than any other English designer. Leasowes, the poet William Shenstone's[22] 'Arcadian farm' at Halesowen in the Midlands, was also important for the French as an example of what could be contrived in a much smaller area than great estates like Stowe. It was described with the other major English gardens in Thomas Whately's *Observations on Modern Gardening*,[23] the essential reference book for the garden maker and garden visitor alike. Jefferson admired it and the Marquis de Girardin acknowledged the influence of the poet when he made his famous garden at Ermenonville. Both the Leasowes and Painshill in Surrey, the work of its owner Charles Hamilton between 1740 and 1773, featured in Bélanger's sketch book or *carnet de voyage*, the record he kept of his visits to England.[24]

These earlier gardens with their classical allusions were fully accessible only to an educated élite, and English taste began to move towards the idea of a garden where knowledge of Greek and Latin authors was no longer a prerequisite for its appreciation. Instead it aimed to appeal to the emotions and imagination of the individual. This development reached its apotheosis with Lancelot 'Capability' Brown (1716–1783). In designing his gardens, Brown sought, by accentuating the natural contours of the ground, to imitate and enhance Nature itself. Since there were no straight lines in Nature, long, serpentine drives and walks traversed the landscape. Differences in the levels of ground were united by gentle undulating slopes, the predominant feeling being one of tranquillity with no rude 'shock' of the kind occasioned by imported

---

22. William Shenstone (1714–1763). For a description of the gardens, see Robert Dodsley, 'A description of the Leasowes' in William Shenstone, *Works in Verse and Prose*, 2 vols (London, 1764), vol. II, p. 364. See also Mavis Batey and David Lambert, *The English Garden Tour* (London, 1990), pp. 181–5.

23. First published in 1770 and translated into French by F. de Paule Latapie as *L'Art de former les jardins modernes* (Paris, 1771).

24. Library of the École Nationale Supérieure des Beaux-Arts, Paris, ms. PC 12760.

rocks and artificial precipices. Trees were planted in belts or strips around the perimeters of an estate to 'conceal the bounds' and were grouped at specific spots to direct the eye towards particular features inside the park. In the larger gardens, the middle distance, when viewed from the house, was embellished by a extensive, irregular expanse of water. Garden buildings were still important but they were fewer in number and the house with lawns stretching right up to the windows became an essential part of the Arcadian scene. No wall restricted the views near the house. As in earlier grounds, a ha-ha separated the garden from the wider park with its sheep and cattle. Cedars of Lebanon and other specimen trees planted alone or in clumps broke up the wide expanse of green, and landowners began to incorporate new trees from North America in the landscape, either as individual specimens, or in clumps, or within a woodland of native trees, great subtlety being employed in combining their colours and masses. Blenheim was the triumph of Brown's style, but he remodelled many earlier gardens and became the King's gardener at Richmond and Kew in 1764. There he made significant alterations to the landscape and it is certain that Blaikie would have seen his work along the west side of today's gardens, as well as at Luton Hoo and other gardens near London. It is possible also, since Brown worked at Kew until his death in 1783, that Blaikie had the opportunity to study his methods by watching him directing changes there.

Brown's achievements met with less favour in France[25] for three main reasons. Firstly the English landscape lent itself much more to his type of improvement since its scenery was naturally more varied than in France. English estate owners spent a large part of their time in the country. The landlord's interest in new methods of cultivation, and in enclosing the land, gave the countryside a generally more attractive, prosperous appearance than that of France. Secondly, different methods of hunting in the two countries also had an effect on the countryside. The French chase required wide allées through vast tracts of forest and much land was left uncultivated to allow game to proliferate. The Englishman, on the other hand, when he changed from stag to fox hunting, chased the fox over fields and woods and managed his shooting coverts more tightly.[26] The third and greatest distinction between the two nations' landowners was one of scale. Blaikie had put his finger on it when, at Maisons, he rejected the idea that four acres was adequate for an English garden. Voltaire summed it up when he told an English visitor at Ferney, 'The French make a parody of English gardens by cramming 30 acres into three'.[27] French nobility preferred the town, where space was limited. They wanted their experience of 'Nature' near Paris where, without a

---

25. Brown summarises his principles in landscape making and acknowledges that the French 'do not rightly comprehend our ideas about Gardening and Place-making' in a draft of a letter he wrote in response to a request received in 1775 from the Rev Thomas Dyer of Marylebone, writing on behalf of a French friend who wanted to lay out his garden in the English style. Quoted in Dorothy Stroud, *Capability Brown* (London, 1984), pp. 156–7.

26. See Christopher Hussey, *English Landscapes and Gardens*, p. 27.

27. Nat. Library of Scotland, *Intimate Society Letters of the 18th Century*, edited by the Duke of Argyll (London, 1910), vol. ii, p. 364, quoted in G. R. DeBeer and A. M. Rousseau, *Voltaire's English Visitors* (Geneva, 1967), April 1776, p. 181.

great deal of tiresome walking, men and women could together enjoy scenes that appealed both to the eye and the sentiments. Not for them the separation of the sexes demonstrated at Stowe by Cobham's exclusively male Temple of Friendship half a mile distant from the Queen's Temple where the ladies passed their time alone at embroidery or other female occupations. The preponderance of trees in the English scene appeared melancholy to the French, and its tranquil landscape of vast lakes and green spaces so like unadorned nature as to be tedious[28], but they did admire the velvety, close cropped texture of English lawns. Bélanger understood and shared the tastes of his countrymen and, at the same time, aimed to capture their imaginations with something new, a small park planted in the English way.

The architect never quite lost his own fondness for classical French gardens. At Bagatelle, he laid out a formal garden near the house and at the Folie St James, another of his creations, there were also distinct, formal elements. His *carnet de voyage* is the best indicator of his taste in gardening.[29] He visited at least a dozen country houses, amongst them Painshill, Hagley, Wilton and Stourhead, and his sketches were of Palladian villas, temples, bridges and water pumps rather than of the gardens themselves. Only Leasowes interested him sufficiently for him to draw a plan of the gardens and he also sketched the cascade and other scenes there. There are no notes on planting, nor on the types of trees, or the different effects they create, except that there were 'too many trees' around a temple of Victory (probably Kew) and insufficient *'percées'* and *'claireries'*. Several sketches of the rocky gorges at Dovedale were to influence his rock building at Bagatelle and the Folie Saint James.[30]

Blaikie speaks highly of only two French gardens, both 'English' in conception but of very different types; Ermenonville belonging to the Marquis de Girardin, and Guiscard, the property of the Duc D'Aumont (1709–1782). His description of the latter makes his Brownian views clear; 'this place was done by Mr Morelle,[31] an Architect

---

28. The French architect, Blondel, writing in 1771 saw the English garden as part of the character of a people 'serious by nature who bring to it a simplicity no doubt praiseworthy but often sad and monotonous and when they deploy their resources in this area of art they turn their genius to composing walks so solitary as to be frightening'. Blondel, *Cours d'architecture civile* (Paris, 1771), vol. 1, Introduction. Quoted in Jacques Moulin. Brown also had English critics, notably Sir William Chambers, who disliked his gardens for the same reasons.

29. Kenneth Woodbridge, 'Bélanger Son Carnet de Voyage', *Architectural History*, 25 (1982), gives an account of each of the drawings in Bélanger's Carnet. With regard to Blaikie, Woodbridge asserts that 'a man with such positive views can hardly have failed to have affected Bélanger's ideas'. See also Janine Barrier, 'Bélanger et l'Angleterre' in *Bagatelle dans ses jardins* (Paris, 1997).

30. In view of the wealth of sketches in the carnet, it is difficult to know what credence to give Mme de Genlis who, in her *Mémoires*, vol. IV, p. 115, insists categorically that he had visited England only once, some time before the Revolution, that he had never visited Dovedale in Derbyshire and that the paintings he showed her of the gorges were ones he had copied.

31. Jean Marie Morel (1728–1810). Painter, architect and garden designer. Designed the gardens of the Duc d'Aumont at Guiscard, is believed to have aided the Marquis de Girardin at

in Paris, and is the only place I have seen in France where there is any mark of taste. Here, they have followed a noble simplicity in the slopes of their grass Lawns.[32] There is a piece of water in form of a river very well laid out, which is about two miles in length and about 200 yards over. This joins agreeably the adjacent country.' He approves the way the estate embodies the agricultural principles as well as the aesthetics of the English garden, so much so that he is moved to quote Pope's *Epistle to Lord Burlington*, 'Here it may be said,

> Whose ample Lawns are not ashamed to feed
> The milky heifer and deserving Steed.[33]

The Duc de Cröy's reaction to this garden was probably much more typical of French taste. He regretted the destruction of the old formal garden and, for him, the Duc d'Aumont's English garden had 'too much the air of a prairie'.[34]

One French garden artist for whom Blaikie had little admiration was the painter Hubert Robert,[35] known particularly for his paintings of Italian landscapes with ruins. Robert was responsible for most of the construction of Méréville, the last of the great pre-Revolutionary gardens; he was Director of the King's gardens of Versailles and is credited with having had a hand in almost every well known garden of the day. Blaikie is scathing about his skills as a landscaper, 'those pretended great painters can see beauties in a Landscape without imagining how they are formed or the effects of time upon those objects'. Such comments are to some extent sour grapes, since Robert was a fine painter, but Blaikie's general contention, that the landscape artist captures only one moment in the evolution of a scene is indisputable. It was left to men like Blaikie to 'translate' the painter's vision, however fanciful, into a permanent landscape.[36]

Ermenonville was the most admired garden in France of its time. Although it is seriously in need of restoration, it can still be visited and its magic lingers on. The château, with the gardens behind it, and those between it and the road, is now a hotel. The part of the original garden that is open to the public lies on the opposite side of the road from the château. Blaikie visited Ermenonville more than once and attributed its realisation to the architect Morel.[37] The first time he saw it, as he records in his diary, was in April 1779, the spring after he had begun work at Bagatelle. He describes the gardens as, 'in some places beautiful though more in a Romantick than an elegant style' and records enthusiastically, 'There is plenty of wood and water.

Ermenonville and was called out of retirement to advise Joséphine on Malmaison. Reckoned to be the most skilful exponent of the English garden, he disapproved of gardens crowded with fabriques. He set out his views in *Théorie des Jardins* (Paris, 1774).

32. The lawns were tended by 'a band of Scottish gardeners' Martin-Decaen, *Le dernier ami de Jean-Jacques Rousseau Le Marquis René de Girardin* (Paris, 1912), p. 18.
33. *Epistle IV to Lord Burlington*, lines 185–6.
34. Grouchy and Cottin, vol. 3, p. 148.
35. Hubert Robert (1733–1808). See Jean de Cayeux, *Hubert Robert et les jardins* (Paris, 1987).
36. See C. C. L. Hirshfeld, *Théorie de l'art des Jardins* (Amsterdam, 1779), vol. I, pp. 171, 175.
37. The Marquis de Girardin insisted that he had designed it himself.

The house stands surrounded with the ancient *fosse* [moat or ditch] which is agreeably united with the rest of the La[n]dscape. Towards the south there is a noble cascade which falls from a fine Lake fronting the house. [This] forms a River which serpents to the left hand; forms another cascade falling into the *fosse* which surrounds the house.' He praises the way the road to the village is incorporated into the view to render the scene more lively. And goes on, 'at the extremity of this Landscape, upon the hill to the right hand stands a temple [38] surrounded by the forest'. Of the part of the garden behind the château, he writes, 'The other side of the house, the Landscape is level but more extensive. Here, we have a fine *vue* of the river which runs serpentin[g] along this valley surrounded by the rising ground and wood in each side. In the middle of this plain stands a tower dedicated to the Belle Gabrielle, Henry IV's mistress.' His greatest enthusiasm is reserved for the best known feature of the garden, the great lake, 'which is a beautiful piece of water. At the further end stands an Island planted with poplars where is buried the famous J. J. Rousseau which lately died here'.[39]

One day was insufficient to view the garden attentively and the next day he continued his tour, with the desert 'a mountainous heath full of large stones and rocks upon which they have sown Bordeaux and Scotch pins which thrives amazingly. The entry to this desert from the forest is through a sort of a house made of roots &c called the Maison du Charbonnier.'[40] The rocks or stones in the desert and the surrounding woods carried inscriptions in English, French and Latin in the manner of the Leasowes but not always well adapted to their situation, according to Blaikie. The desert is obviously something new for him and he would use this mixture of two sorts of pines at Bagatelle. Other English visitors like Sir J. E. Smith[41] and Arthur Young[42] were also complimentary about Ermenonville, the garden which most resembled their idea of an English garden.

Blaikie had visited Versailles in October 1777 with Mr Hairs and found the gardens both at the palace of Versailles and the Trianon in a state of upheaval. At Versailles, the original *bosquets* (groves) planted by Le Nôtre had outgrown their situation and the King had initiated a controversial programme to remove them and replace the entire area with saplings. Blaikie found the gardens 'all in disorder ... All the statues is displaced some of theme exceeding fine' All the basins and canals were dry and the

---

38. The Temple of Philosophy. A comprehensive, recent account of Ermenonville can be found in Geneviève Mazel, 'Le château et les jardins du marquis de Girardin. Le souvenir de Jean-Jacques Rousseau', in *Groupe d'étude des Monuments et Oeuvres d'art de l'Oise et du Beauvaisis* (1996), Bulletin No. 73–5.

39. Rousseau died on 2 July 1778. His body was removed to the Panthéon on 9 October 1794.

40. Charcoal-maker.

41. J. E. Smith (1759–1826), English botanist, purchaser of Linnaeus's herbarium and founder of the Linnean Society of which he was first President. In *Sketch of a Tour on the Continent in the Year 1786–87* (London, 1793), vol. 1, p. 98, he praises the turf at Ermenonville, the work of a Scottish gardener whom Blaikie tells us was called Murray.

42. Arthur Young (1741–1820), English agriculturist. Describes Ermenonville in an entry for September 1787, *Travels in France during the Years 1787, 1788, 1789.*

'fabulous monsters' who 'threw water out of their mouths' were being repaired.[43] Next he visited the Trianon where Louis XV's botanic garden was being removed to make way for a garden *à l'anglaise* for the Queen, to a plan conceived by one of her courtiers and implemented by her architect, Mique. Blaikie describes his meeting with the head gardener 'Monr. Richard'[44] who' he continues, 'showed us very civilly the gardens which formerly was one of the first Botanick gardens in Europe. There is still a great many rare and curious plants but, as this belongs to the Queen who is not fond of plants, they are turning it all into a sort of English garden. What a pity such a valuable collection should be destroyed. This seems much to affect old Mr Richard.'

One of the first gardens that Blaikie saw in the autumn of 1777, as he awaited instructions to go to England and purchase trees for Maisons, was the garden of Monceau in Paris (today's Parc Monceau), owned by the Duc de Chartres (later Duc d'Orléans). He found it 'a confusion of Ruins, Temples &c crowded one upon another. In one place you see a gothic ruin, just by that a Grecian and next a Chinese temple or Pavilion finely guilted [gilded?] which makes a most singular contrast in so small a compass.' It was a view shared by most English visitors[45] and Blaikie would later alter the gardens himself.

Back in 1777, however, he had not yet had the opportunity to try his skills on any of the gardens of Paris and it looked as if he was destined to spend the rest of his time in France at Mont Canisy where the Count had asked him to return and manage the estate. He remained there until September 1778, when he was again given the opportunity to take on the post of English gardener at Bagatelle. This time he did not refuse.

---

43. Diary, Saturday 4 October 1777.
44. Antoine Richard (1735–1807), botanist and gardener to the Queen at the Trianon, had also been on a botanical excursion in Switzerland and had visited England. Old M. Richard is Claude Richard, and later, Blaikie also mentions 'young Richard', Louis, Claude Marie (1754–1821).
45. Some of their comments are quoted in the chapter on Monceau.

CHAPTER 8

A Place Called Bagatelle – Part I

T HE PAVILION OF BAGATELLE with its gardens, although much changed from its eighteenth-century appearance, is still today one of the major attractions on the outskirts of the Bois de Boulogne and its history is an unusual one, to say the least.

The Comte d'Artois purchased the lease of this small Crown property on the road from Neuilly to Longchamps in November 1775.[1] The house on the site was already called Bagatelle, perhaps from the Italian word *bagato*, a little house, and its diminutive, *bagatello*. The French expression *'petite maison'* implied a retreat for amorous encounters and Bagatelle had served this purpose for the young Maréchale d'Estrées,[2] the first owner of the property.[3] During the tenancy of her successor, Madame de Monconseil, Bagatelle became famous for its fetes and theatrical performances but Madame de Monconseil had insufficient income to maintain the fabric of the building, so by the time Artois acquired it, the house was dilapidated, its foundations undermined by floods. For 36,000 livres, the cost of the lease and the furnishings,[4] Artois gained, without having to purchase the property outright, an ideal location for his *folie*. Enjoying views over the Seine and Mount Valérian, and close to the hunting ground of the Bois de Boulogne, it was near Paris, yet within easy reach of Versailles and his other properties at Maisons and St Germain-en-Laye (the Château of Saint Germain). The press of the day saw his bet with the Queen as a ploy to help pay for the rebuilding of Bagatelle.[5] 100,000 livres was an enormous sum[6] but the bills of the contractors alone amounted to 1.2 million livres, more than ten times the amount of the bet.[7]

Betting was a pastime imported from England along with English racing, English horses, the game of whist, and gentlemen's clubs. The fashionable Parisian male rode out in an English high-sprung two wheeled carriage called a *whiski*; he wore a *frac* (frock-coat), a *chapeau jockey*, and a *redingote* (a triple collared English overcoat or

---

1. AN., MC, LIII 521, 1 November 1775, quoted in Martine Constans, 'Le château du comte d'Artois', *Bagatelle dans ses jardins* (Paris, 1997).
2. This use of Bagatelle is confirmed in R-L D'Argenson, *Journal et Memoires du Marquis* (Paris, 1858), quoted in Robert Hénard 'Les Jardins de Bagatelle', p. 442. *La Grande Revue*, 10 May 1907.
3. It was built at a cost of at least 100,000 livres by her eldery but understanding husband around 1720 as a retreat to which she and her friends could escape from the formalities of the court. See Jean -Pierre Jouve, 'La maison avant le comte d'Artois' in *Bagatelle dans ses jardins* (Paris, 1997).
4. Jean-Pierre Jouve, *op. cit.*
5. Bachaumont L., Petit de, *Mémoires secrets* (London, 1780), vol. X, p. 259, 22 October 1777.
6. Approx. 24 livres to the pound at that time.
7. Stern, vol. I, p. 60. In the end the project cost more than three million.

riding coat). An English coachman drove his wife's carriage, while she had abandoned elaborate hoops, underskirts and sleeved bodices for a simple robe à l'anglaise. This was set off, for the first time in France, by a hat, either of straw or an elaborate brimmed confection of ribbons and feathers perched to one side of her head and finished with a turned up brim.[8] This passion for all things English, labelled pejoratively anglomania,[9] included English politics, freemasonry and neo-Palladian architecture, and reached its apogee in the craze for English gardens. Artois, like his cousin, the Duc de Chartres, and Blaikie's employer, de Lauraguais, was one of the leaders of this movement although, unlike them, he stopped short of embracing English constitutional ideas. As the third son of the heir to the throne, he had been given a large allowance and encouraged to take up princely pleasures with the aim of keeping him out of politics. Horses, hunting, mistresses, building, the purchase of works of art were the diversions of almost every great noble in the eighteenth century and Artois, conscious of his rank, was determined to keep his pre-eminence amongst them. Marriage in 1773 to Marie Thérèse, daughter of the king of Sardinia, and the birth of his first child, the Duc d'Angoulême, in 1775, made little impact on his life. Unlike his two older brothers, Artois was 'as handsome as an angel'.[10] With a graceful form and a pleasing manner, he was reckoned in later life 'one of the most charming men of his age'[11] but his reputation as a libertine and spendthrift, and his huge debts, met time and time again by the long suffering King, turned the people of Paris against him. Most reprehensible of all, in many eyes, was the damage he unwittingly inflicted on the Queen's reputation by encouraging her in trivial pastimes. As her popularity waned, scurrilous pamphlets depicting the two as depraved lovers circulated in Paris. However, as yet, only three years after the coronation, the complaints were fairly muted and life at the youthful court was carefree.

Artois' intention in building Bagatelle had been to divert and amuse the Queen and, at the same time, to create a pied à terre where he could entertain his latest mistress, the actress Rosalie Duthé (1752–1820), whose appetite for luxury was such that Mme Vigée-Le Brun claimed 'elle a mangé des millions'.[12] The faces of the sphinxes at the top of the steps in the forecourt of Bagatelle are said to be modelled on her.[13] Artois was delighted by the praise showered on the newly completed Palladian villa, but there was one disadvantage. Its site of only five or six hectares was narrow and restricted on the river side and to the south by the road to Longchamps and to

---

8. For an insight into eighteenth-century fashion see Aileen Ribeiro, *Dress in 18th-Century Europe 1715–1789* (London, 1984).

9. Mercier, *Le Tableau de Paris* (Amsterdam, 1782), vol. 7, p. 44. J. Grieder, *Anglomania in France 1740–89, Fact, Fiction and Political Discourse* (Geneva, 1985). *Escape from the Terror. The Journal of Madame de la Tour du Pin*, ed. and trans. Felice Harcourt (London, 1979).

10. Mme du Deffand, *Lettres à Horace Walpole (1766–1788)*, ed. Paget Toynbee, vol. 3, Lettre 686, p. 812.

11. Philip Mansel, *The Court of France 1789–1830* (Cambridge, 1988).

12. Elisabeth Vigée Le Brun, *Souvenirs*, 2 vols (Paris, 1869).

13. Barbara Scott, 'Bagatelle Folie of the comte d'Artois', *Apollo*, (June 1972), pp. 476–85.

the north by the château of Madrid, but it could be extended to the east by taking in part of the Bois de Boulogne, thus making room for a *jardin anglais*.

When Thomas Blaikie turned down the post of English gardener at Bagatelle on 30 December 1777, he must have been almost the only person in the city completely unaware of the celebrity of the building, having been absent first in Normandy and then in England from 8 October until 29 November.[14] The Pavilion had taken six weeks to build and was completed on 26 November 1777 so that he had heard none of the gossip concerning its construction, neither the Count's bet, nor the incredible speed with which Bélanger had executed his plan. However, when he returned to the city some eleven months after his first refusal of the post, his appointment was a foregone conclusion. He had already agreed to reserve some of the surplus trees from Mont Canisy and Manicamp for Artois' gardens[15] and on his arrival in Paris on 16 November, he went straight to see Bélanger. From Bélanger's house he slipped out to Bagatelle on his own to look at the site and sketch out a rough plan of the gardens. Then, on 22 December, he accompanied Bélanger to Bagatelle. Here, as at Maisons before, they met the Count's corrupt Superintendent of Finances, Radix de Sainte Foye, an important figure in the garden equation since he held the purse strings.

Blaikie undertook to prepare a plan and lay out the *jardin anglais*, as well as to supply the trees. He was to direct the felling and uprooting of trees from the Bois de Boulogne to leave an agreable outlook over different parts of the garden and to be responsible for the movement of earth around the garden but not its cost. Sainte Foy was to provide the workmen and the whole was to be completed in three years.[16] The ground was poor and Blaikie was irked to find that a road was already designated to run through the garden 'at great expense'. He recorded in his diary, 'This ridiculous affair was the plan of Mr Bélanger which had cost at least 30,000 livres. He begged of me not to change that in the plan I was making, although he agreed that it was bad, but he said it might be changed later as the French was very fond of changes and this pleased them for the moment.'[17] It was obvious he was not to be given the free hand he would have wished in laying out the garden, except in the plantations, but would work under the supervision of Bélanger whose designs he frequently criticised in his diary on the grounds of inappropriateness and extravagance. However, his influence on Bélanger's thinking was considerable, for although he was obliged to include it in his plan, the offending road does not appear in later ones.

Several plans for the garden exist. The first by Bélanger dated 1777 shows a relatively small area with a formal French garden at the north end.[18] The park was extended when the Count received permission from the King to take in some 18 arpents

14. Diary, 29 November 1777. He arrived in Paris and went at once to see Bélanger.
15. Lauraguais had made him a gift of them. Blaikie Papers.
16. AN., R1 320. The document was signed by Blaikie as *'jardinier choisi pour la formation et plantation du dit jardin'*. Drawn up by Chalgrin, Intendant des Batiments and witnessed by one of the Inspectors.
17. Diary, 22 December 1778.
18. *Plan général du pavillon et du jardin à la française*, dated 1 September 1777 by Bélanger. Archives Nationales.

(approximately 20 acres) of the Bois in March 1779.[19] There were to be further appropriations of the woodland all of which would be incorporated in the English garden. The formal garden, the earliest part of the garden to be completed, was designed and planted by Bélanger, although Blaikie worked in it while he prepared the plan of the English garden,[20] and later he planted the beds with ornamental creeping brambles recently imported from North America.[21]

The second plan and the first showing the *jardin anglais* was probably that which Blaikie gave Bélanger at the end of 1778, a beautifully executed water-colour now in the French National Archives with the word 'bon' scribbled across it denoting the Count's approval.[22] It shows a tranquil parkland, roughly trapezoid in shape, with the house towards the north corner. Irregular plantations of trees obscure the boundary, so that sometimes the serpentine path that encircles it leads through thick wood and at others opens out to give a view over the rest of the gardens. The area of the *jardin anglais* is more or less dissected diagonally by a road leading to the house, a very un-Brownian concept, and presumably Bélanger's original road to which Blaikie had taken such exception. This drive widens about the middle of the route to incorporate three almost circular 'islands' of woodland. Roughly parallel to this main approach lie winding paths connecting with those around the perimeter. Clumps of trees or single specimens clothe the lawned area and the buildings are few. Just distinguishable on the plan is the drawing of what looks like a bed, surmounted by a metal work baldaquin (canopy) in rococo style, placed at the edge of one of the paths. Bélanger's *carnet* contains a sketch of a bed with a baldaquin similar to the one on the plan so he may have doodled this one or perhaps it was intended as a garden conceit to be used for displaying special collections of plants.[23] To Bélanger, Blaikie's 'natural' English scheme lacked visual excitement and it was not until the beginning of the nineteenth century that the peaceful, late eighteenth-century English landscape park with its emphasis on trees and shrubs began to be truly appreciated in France.[24]

The vestiges of Blaikie's plan are still visible on a third plan, an undated sketch that appears to show a slightly later stage in the development of Bagatelle.[25] This one,

19. H.-G. Duchesne, *Le château de Bagatelle (1715–1908) d'après les documents inédits des Archives Nationales, des Archives de la Seine et des Mémoires manuscrits ou imprimés* (Paris, 1909), p. 136, quoting from Extracts of registers of the *Conseil d'Etat*, Archives Nationales.

20. Diary, 21 December 1778.

21. Probably *Rubus hispidus*, which features in the nursery acounts. The description comes from C.-L. Hirschfeld, *Théorie de l'art des jardins*, (Amsterdam, 1779).

22. AN., NIII Seine 586 Blaikie mentions a plan in his diary for week beginning Monday 21 December 1778.

23. There is a sketch of a four poster bed used to display plants in John Evelyn's unpublished *Elysium Britannicum* (c. 1666). Trustees of the John Evelyn Collection, Christchurch Oxford. Reproduced in John Harris, *A Garden Alphabet* (1979).

24. David Watkin, *The English Vision. The Picturesque in Architecture, Landscape and Garden Design* (London, 1982). This change is evident in De Laborde's comments. A. De Laborde, *Description des nouveaux jardins* (Paris, 1808), p. 49–50.

25. BN Estampes.

in contrast to Blaikie's restrained scheme,[26] contains many more paths rather too intricately winding for English tastes. As well as a much larger number of buildings, there is an amphitheatre reminiscent of William Kent's at Claremont in Surrey and stables are projected for a corner near the main entrance route which now winds to the right (when viewed from the house). The original main allée, so disliked by Blaikie, has been suppressed. The circular plantations of trees are still visible but a river, a lake and paths wind around them. This plan in turn seems very different from those of Lerouge in 1784[27] and of Krafft's in 1812.[28] The map which best shows the final state of the garden that Bélanger and Blaikie created is that of Boucher and Nicolas dated 1814 and reproduced here.[29]

Blaikie was to have three major problems in making the garden at Bagatelle. The first was the difficulty in obtaining a sufficient quantity of 'exotic' trees and shrubs. The second was the parlous state of Artois' finances which caused so many delays to the work that Blaikie sometimes despaired of completing the garden at all. And the third was the poor sandy soil of Bagatelle.

The nurseries in and around Paris proved disappointing to Blaikie after the high standard he had been used to in England. Paris's leading nurseryman, Henri of the rue de la Roquette, conducted his business from the public house and his clients had to select and pack up the plants themselves. On the several occasions he was there, Blaikie tells us, 'I always found him at his bottle'.[30] The other nurserymen in the city, Blaikie dismissed as 'much the same'. An important source of plants for the Royal gardens was the King's nurseries (*les Pépinières du Roi*). These, under the direction of the Abbé Nolin,[31] consisted of nineteen royal nurseries at various sites[32] mostly around Versailles, supplying trees and shrubs for royal gardens and those of the royal princes, as well as other privileged people approved by the Comte d'Angiviller, Director General of the Royal Buildings. In 1778 Sainte Foye submitted a list of plants for Maisons and Artois' other gardens but, with thousands of trees and shrubs requested

26. 'Where the landscape itself should arouse emotion based on Hogarth's principle of curves and Burke's conception of beauty in gentle undulations.' Christopher Hussey, *The Picturesque* (1927, repr. 1967), p. 137.
27. LeRouge, Plan du jardin de Bagatelle, 1784, *Détails de nouveaux jardins à la mode*, cahier XII pl. 2.
28. Krafft, *Plan général du parc de Bagatelle*, in *Receuil d'architecture civile* 1812, pl. 119.
29. Musée Carnavalet.
30. Yet, in spite of these criticisms, the accounts show that Henri did supply trees for Bagatelle in 1779. AN., R1 309.
31. Abbé Pierre-Charles Nolin (1717–1796). In 1764 he was nominated Controller of the King's Nurseries at which time the Bishop of Orléans allowed him to give up his duties as a priest. Considered to be one, if not the first, to naturalise the new exotic species of trees in France. From 1785 to 1790 he created a nursery at Rambouillet for the American trees introduced by André Michaux. He also obtained plants from Charles Hamilton of Painshill. See Michael Symes, 'Charles Hamilton's Plantings at Painshill', *Garden History*, vol. 11, no. 2, based on the correspondence between the two men in the collection of the Earl of Abercorn (Northern Ireland Record Office).
32. Marie Blanche d'Arneville, *Parcs et jardins sous le 1er Empire* (Paris, 1981), p. 128, n. 17.

for Marie Antoinette's garden at the Trianon, Nolin claimed he could not meet the Prince's demand.[33] Even Mique,[34] Marie Antoinette's architect at the Trianon, had to order evergreens from English nurserymen in April 1777.[35] France was recognised as 'the cradle of botany' but new and rare plants were, by and large, grown as specimens in botanic gardens. The custom of planting exotics in large numbers as part of the garden scene began later than it did in England. In addition, the French climate with its severe frosts was less conducive to the survival of young evergreens. As a result, there was a dearth of large commercial nurseries like that of Kennedy and Lee in England whose owners were experts in mass propagation of 'exotics'.[36] For his rarest trees Blaikie had to turn to botanists like Thouin or rich amateurs of botany.

The doyen of private collectors of 'exotics' was the Chevalier Janssen, an Englishman[37] who owned a celebrated garden in the area of the Champs Elysées.[38] De Lauraguais took Blaikie to see Janssen in 1777,[39] and the Chevalier's garden provided a temporary home for the trees Blaikie brought with him from Manicamp. Janssen and Blaikie became friends. They exchanged plants and the young man often visited the old one until the latter's death in December 1780.[40] Janssen also introduced him to another eminent botanist, a M. Trochereau, a friend of Rousseau, who possessed a 'curious' collection of American plants at his property of Feuillancourt[41] near St Germain-en-Laye.

Whenever the opportunity arose, Blaikie augmented his supply of plants with English ones. He exchanged rarities with Aiton.[42] Before his death in 1781, James Morrison, head gardener to Dr Fothergill at Upton, sent Blaikie seeds, and Banks made sure he received some from the last Cook expedition. Archibald Macmaster, the old friend he had recommended to the Comte de Lauraguais, went more than once to London and brought a great number of plants back, both for the Duke of Orléans and for Blaikie at Bagatelle. Such was the enormous enthusiasm for horti-culture that botanists, both professional and amateur, corresponded with each other exchanging seeds and plants. This passion transcended international conflicts. Exchanges between France and England carried on all through the American War of

33. AN., O1 2111.
34. Richard Mique (1728–1794), pupil of Blondel. 1775, Became first architect to Louis XVI. 1782, Director of the Academy of Architecture. Subsequently worked entirely for Marie Antoinette. Executed 1794 for his supposed part in a conspiracy on behalf of the queen. Michel Gallet, *Les architectes parisiens au XVIIIe siècle* (Paris, 1995), p. 464.
35. AN., O1 1876. I am indebted to M. Michel Traversat for drawing my attention to this source.
36. See E. J. Willson, *James Lee and the Vineyard Nursery, Hammersmith* (Hammersmith, 1961).
37. Robert Janssen was an Englishman who had accompanied James II to France.
38. His garden of Marbeuf was situated between today's rue de Marbeuf, Quentin Bauchard, Francois I and the Champs Elysées.
39. Diary, 12 January 1778.
40. Bachaumont gives an obituary of Janssen, 28 December 1780 (vol. 16, p. 121).
41. E. de Ganay *Les Jardins de France* (Paris, 1949), p. 221.
42. Letter from Aiton to Blaikie, Blaikie Papers.

Independence, in spite of the fact that hostilities between the two countries had begun in 1778 and lasted till the treaty of Versailles in September 1783. For instance, one of Blaikie's messengers to Banks was a Captain Curry, master of a privateer, the *Lady's Adventure* whose ship had been taken as a prize by the French in the Bay of Biscay in 1780. The captain was released and Blaikie met him in Paris on his way home.[43] Archibald Macmaster had been to England and back via Holland in 1781 without any mishap. Banks and Thouin also corresponded and exchanged seed during this time[44] just as, during the Napoleonic wars, Kennedy, Lee's partner at the Vineyard Nursery, Hammersmith, was allowed a free conduct between England and France with plants for Josephine's gardens at Malmaison. Blaikie himself visited England in 1785 to purchase trees and shrubs for his patrons, and a bill among the accounts relating to Monceau shows that he ordered *Magnolia fraseri* and other plants from Fraser of Chelsea in 1789.[45]

Once Blaikie had established a nursery at Bagatelle, things changed. He became a provider of trees for other gardens on a fairly large scale, often reluctantly, for, to his chagrin, the Count regularly gave his precious trees away in thousands to aristocrats who did not appreciate them.[46] Sometime in 1782, he himself took a stake in a nursery at Sèvres in collaboration with an Englishman, Williams, who had been gardener to the Duc de Bouillon at Navarre, near Évreux.[47]

A close study of Blaikie's diary in conjunction with the records in the French National Archives shows that the work in the garden began slowly. In the last days of 1778 Blaikie began the cutting down of the trees in the wood opposite the pavilion to clear the ground for a lawn but, from the beginning, there were few men at work. 1779 was a bad year as far as Artois' finances were concerned and progress in the garden was erratic. In 1780, the year of the May fete for the Queen, there was a spurt in activity with 120 men employed between 18 May and 3 June.[48] The momentum continued throughout the year with thatchers, vignerons (vineyard workers), basket makers and carpenters as well as gardeners being employed in the gardens. 1781, the

---

43. Diary, 17 February 1780. My thanks to the Museum of Maritime History, Greenwich for information about the *Lady's Adventure*.

44. *The Banks Letters*, ed. Warren R. Dawson, British Museum (Natural History) 1958 records 8 letters from Thouin to Banks.

45. AN., 300 AP (I) 2110. John Fraser had collected plants in America where he obtained the Magnolia named after him.

46. Diary, undated entry, 1783. AN., R1 513 shows that the Count gave away 4990 foreign trees from Blaikie's nursery in 1783 alone.

47. Godefroi Charles-Henri de la Tour d'Auvergne, Duc de Bouillon (1728–1792). He was a Colonel-General during the Seven Years War, Governor of Auvergne, 1776. Butt of much humour and scurrilous verse because of the notorious infidelities of his mistress. Supported Revolution. His wife died in 1788 and he married his mistress's 14-year-old daughter the following year. Navarre was his country estate and Williams told Blaikie that he dined with the Duke most days. Later Navarre was given to the Empress Josephine by Napoleon as part of her divorce settlement in 1810.

48. AN., R1 317.

records show, was the important year for planting, all the construction work in the garden being more or less completed. In 1782 with the visit of the grand Duke Paul of Russia, travelling supposedly incognito as the Comte du Nord, the garden became the focus of attention with many favourable comments from the visitors who flocked to see it. 1783 saw the 'flowering' of the now fairly well established garden and from then onwards it gradually faded from public attention.

CHAPTER 9

A Place Called Bagatelle – Part II

1778/79

Blaikie arrived at Bagatelle in the very last days of 1778 and immediately it became evident that his method of working differed from that of his French colleagues. He describes in his diary how 'M. Briass, Inspector of buildings, and the others present, were surprised 'to see me trace out this garden without line or *toise* [measure]', a technique, he explains, 'which none of them could imagine'.[1] This freer English method of laying out a design had been used by Kent in England some forty years earlier,[2] but it was still, apparently, unknown in France. He began work by cutting the lawns and glades out of the natural woodland of the Bois, leaving as many trees standing as possible until the newly planted trees and shrubs had grown high enough to replace them.[3] His guide to planting the sandy terrain of Bagatelle was probably the *Treatise on Planting, Gardening and the Management of the Hot-House* by J. Kennedy, gardener to Sir Thomas Gascoigne (York, 1776). It contains instructions for 'raising wood on Rocky, Hilly, Waste, and Heath Lands' and was listed in Blaikie's library inventory of 1801.[4] The soil in the Bois was his first challenge. It was composed of thin sand and lacked nutrients. The mature trees that grew there were stunted, but they served as protection for the new planting and gave an air of maturity to the plantations.

There were ominously few men at work in January 1779. Finance dried up completely, and work stopped altogether in February, although Blaikie received a payment of 1000 livres on 14 February, the day on which he signed his contract.[5] The two gangs of workmen employed in February, 27 men in all, downed tools and left when they received no payment at the end of the month and Blaikie, unable to continue the work, took himself off to Manicamp for a few weeks to develop the garden there. Funds were found and more workmen employed at the beginning of May.[6] From May to October Blaikie organised the work of earth moving, always guided by the principle of 'following the nature of the ground'[7] which, in the case of Bagatelle, meant emphasising its slight natural contours, building mounds for the

1. Diary, Wednesday 30 December 1778.
2. See Sir Thomas Robinson's letter of 23 December 1734 to the Earl of Carlisle, Historical Manuscripts Commission Reports, Castle Howard MSS, quoted in John Dixon Hunt, *William Kent Landscape Designer* (London, 1987), p. 46.
3. J. C. Loudon, *Encyclopedia of Gardening* (1835 edn), p. 88. It was also Brown's established practice to overplant or to plant young trees in the midst of existing planting with the intention of removing the nurse trees later.
4. Blaikie Papers.
5. AN., R1 309 for payment, R1 320 for contract.
6. AN., R1 371.
7. Diary, March 1783.

viewpoints and levelling the ground for the lawn. On this task alone approximately twenty men were employed per day from 13 May to 1 October.[8] Many tons of soil were needed and there was insufficient earth at Bagatelle for this purpose, what there was being too thin and poor to make the lawns or to plant the new trees. Permission was later given by the Prince de Conti to take soil from the plain of Bagatelle with the proviso that the ground had to be sown with hay afterwards.[9] The cost incurred in transporting the earth amounted to 11,726 livres. As a way of ensuring that he received regular payment himself, Blaikie tells us that in November 1799, 'Mr St Foix proposed ... to give me the place of *inspecteur* of all the Count's gardens. Finding this was the best way to let them carry on their work by flights, I agreed to their proposition which was 1800 livres'.[10] His salary of 1800 livres (approximately £78) was 300 livres higher than that of the Inspectors of Buildings.[11] Bélanger received 9000 livres (£390)[12] and he, like Blaikie, found difficulty in receiving reimbursement for the money which he paid out on the Comte's behalf.[13] A salary of the equivalent of £78 seems reasonable when we consider that only a tenth of the population of England earned more than £50 per year.[14] Moreover, this payment served only as a retainer, and Blaikie was free to take on other commissions.[15] André Thouin, head gardener at the Jardin du Roi, received a salary of 2300 livres per year in 1777.[16]

On accepting the post of Superintendent of the Count's gardens in November 1779,[17] Blaikie's responsibilities increased. They now included digging out the ground for the river and constructing the rustic buildings at Bagatelle as well as his other duties, plus the supervision of all the gardens belonging to the Count. Soon, he was called to give ideas for a garden in front of the Orangery at Maisons and make a plantation of trees at the chapel of St Fiacre near St Germain. At Maisons, he was, as usual, cutting about Bélanger's work and described his huge new Orangery as 'more like a barn than a greenhouse'.

At Bagatelle, the pace quickened during November 1779. Men worked night and day on alterations to the approach roads in preparation for a visit from the King who was due to dine there on Monday 13 December. Blaikie himself took charge of turfing

---

8. AN., R1 371.
9. AN., R1 371.
10. Diary, undated entry between 1 and 11 November 1779.
11. AN., R1 371 accounts for 1785.
12. AN., R1 379.
13. AN., R1 435.
14. Arthur Young, *Travels during the years 1787, 1788 and 1789 etc.* (Bury St Edmunds, 1792; 2nd edn, 1794; ed. Constantia Maxwell, Cambridge, 1929).
15. The Duke of Burlington's gardener at Chiswick, who was at the top of his profession and had charge of the herds of deer and other animals and the menagerie as well as the gardens, received 300 guineas per year. M. Grosley, *A Tour to London or New Observations on England and its inhabitants*, 2 vols (London, 1772), vol. 2, p. 126.
16. Yvonne Letouzy, *Le Jardin des Plantes à la croisée des chemins avec André Thouin 1747–1824* (Paris, 1989), p. 64.
17. Duchesne, H.-G., p. 132.

and planting the verges with Spanish brooms,[18] alaternus[19] and other shrubs purchased, he tells us, on 8 December from a Parisian nurseryman, called Lecoeur.[20] Unfortunately, rain poured down all day on the 13th and Blaikie's hopes that Artois and the King would visit the garden and see what progress had been made were dashed. He had put his heart into the labour of making this garden but no one seemed interested in it. Sainte Foy, on one of his visits in December, told him that what he was doing was 'folly' since the Count 'took more pleasure in a girl than a garden'.[21]

1780

A heavy frost interrupted the work after Christmas and the ground was not ready to be planted till February 1780 but Blaikie continued working all through January. He records in his diary that he 'made the walk from the pavilion up the left side and a little rock seat'. 'Frost from the 8th to the 15,' he tells us, 'filled the ice house,[22] the Laurus tinus (*Viburnum tinus*, the winter flowering evergreen shrub) and striped alaternus (*Rhamnus alaternus* 'Variegatus') not in the least hurt although uncovered. Continued planting and turfing the banks by the road side, the weather a great part of the later end frosty.'[23]

On Shrove Tuesday (8 February 1780), Blaikie accompanied Briass, the Inspector of Buildings, to see the Mardi Gras celebrations at Longchamps. In despondent mood, he found the celebrations 'foolishness' and was surprised by the contrast between the antics of the day before and the religious devotion of the Ash Wednesday Mass at which a priest anointed the congregation's foreheads with ashes. Although he had adapted extraordinarily well to life in France, the excursion highlighted the temperamental and religious contrasts with his native Scotland. He returned to Bagatelle to find a letter from Scotland, informing him that his elder and only brother, John, had died. Then, on the evening of Ash Wednesday, the Count held a dinner and theatrical entertainment at Bagatelle where the guests crowded on to the lawns and trampled on the shrubs and plants leaving the garden 'in the same state as if an army of barbarians had been there'.[24] For Blaikie this was the lowest ebb of his time in France.

It seemed that the project would die from lack of interest on Artois' part. Desperate to bring the work to a point where it would make some impact, Blaikie determined to complete the area of trees edging the lawn. This involved planting as many of his reserve trees as he could with the aid of Archibald Macmaster who had been working at the *Jardin du Roi*. With Archibald's help, and using men and carts for which he

---

18. *Spartium junceum* L.
19. *Rhamnus alaternus* L.
20. Lecoeur, jardinier-floriste, rue du fossé St Marcel. His bill (AN R1 320) is dated 7 December but amongst the Thuyas, cypresses, phillyreas, laurels and pyracanthas, there is no record of alaternus.
21. Diary, end of December 1779.
22. R1 371. One of his duties as Inspector of the Count's gardens.
23. Diary entry under 1 January 1780.
24. Duchesne, p. 147.

himself had paid, Blaikie finished the planting of the trees in March. André Thouin sent him a cart load of shrubs and herbaceous plants which he added to his own.[25] Then, once he had made paths of raked gravel as in England (French paths were usually of a white chalky sand), his spirits revived and he began to feel pleased with his work. It was a turning point. Sainte Foye, too, approved of what he and Archibald had achieved and so, Blaikie tells us, 'they sent me some more men and on *Jeudi* the 9th had 12 Men and 3 carts from Robert [contractor] and by this the work recommenced. Otherwise they would perhaps never have seen the effects of all the works we had hitherto made'. He was gratified by a visit from the Duke de Chartres,[26] with the Duc de Fitzjames,[27] on 1 April. Starved of favourable comment from Artois, he recorded happily that 'they were exceedingly well pleased with what was done and seemed to have more taste than many who had already come'. Chartres told him that he would employ him to lay out a garden at Neuilly. The Duc de Fitz James was to commission him to plant his town garden at the *rue de la Fermes des Mathurins*.[28]

On 6 April 1780 the Inspectors made their report on the buildings and park of Bagatelle. They confirmed that Bagatelle was almost entirely finished except for the enclosure of the park, a project that would cost 24000 livres but should not be delayed as it was essential for the security of the house and its furnishing and also to keep out fallow deer, rabbits and roe deer which were damaging the young plants. They requested immediate funds for the sowing of a small lawn, arguing that this would make a large improvement at the negligible cost of 4000 livres. The money was forthcoming and on the 19th, Blaikie set 36 *vignerons* (vineyard workers)[29] to break down the soil 'their tools', he tells us, 'being commodious for mixing the soil together'. The seed sown, the lawn soon 'made a beautiful appearance'.[30]

In April, Blaikie records in his diary that the masons had begun the rock opposite the pavilion. Rocks were a feature more common in French gardens than English ones and seemed to appeal more to French than English sensibility.[31] One of the earliest constructed appears to have been at the property of the Duc de Tremouille at Attichy. Here, water was 'distilled' drop by drop from many fissures by means of a hidden siphon. The murmur of the water as it trickled from the rock, which seemed

25. Diary, 27 March 1780. Proves, along with the nursery bills, that planting at Bagatelle was not at all confined to trees and shrubs.
26. Louis Philippe Joseph (1747–1793), Duc de Chartres until the death of his father in 1785 when he became Duke of Orléans.
27. Duc de Fitz-James (1776–1838) descended from James II through his natural son the Marshal Berwick. Another notorious libertine and often blamed for his deleterious influence on Chartres.
28. An earlier name for the *rue des Mathurins* See Hillairet, vol. 2, p. 112. Blaikie kept the list of plants for Fitz-James' garden but he was never paid for them (Blaikie Papers).
29. R1 317. The same source notes that seven pebble pickers were employed on the lawn area, eight labourers and two carters during May.
30. Diary, 19 April 1780.
31. See Monique Mosser, 'Le rocher et la colonne, une thème d'iconographie architecturale au XVIIIe siècle', *Revue de l'art*, 58–9 (1983).

to 'transpire', was considered a masterpiece and this rock became a model for others.[32] It was a fashion that Horace Walpole[33] commented on waspishly in 1775, 'take a mountain break it into pieces with a hammer, number the fragments and observe their antecedent positions: place them in their original order ... plant ivy and grass seeds which will hide the fractures and you may have a cartload of Snowdon or Penmenmaur in the middle of your bowling green'.[34] Blaikie who generally shared his countrymen's views on French gardens, seems, surprisingly, to have taken to the construction of 'mountains' enthusiastically so that a later client, Mme de Coislin,[35] claimed that she had been ruined by the facility of his workmen to raise mountains on her estate at Brimborion, near Sèvres.

Early in June, 120 workers were employed on various tasks in the gardens[36] due no doubt to the Count's awakened enthusiasm after the great moment of 1780 when he gave his long awaited fete for Marie Antoinette and the King.[37] It was a brilliant occasion. Fetes were a familiar court diversion. The Queen held them regularly at the Trianon but this was Artois' first great fete at Bagatelle and, given his competitive nature, he would insist that it be memorable. Bélanger, who had spent his early years at the *Menus Plaisirs* creating just such events, designed it for him with style and inventiveness. The disappearing wall was a feature of fetes at Versailles but the wall in these cases was constructed of greenery. To make a stone wall disappear was an extraordinary feat.[38]

Blaikie had first seen Marie Antoinette at Choisy, the King's hunting lodge, where the gardener, an Englishman called Brown, had taken him with Mr Hairs to see the Royal family, the King, the Queen and the King's sister, Mme Elisabeth,[39] at breakfast with their party before the hunt. His account of that first glimpse of them shows the royal family in a fresh and sympathetic light.

> ... the King was dressed almost like a Country farmer, a good Rough Stout man about 25. The Queen, which is a very handsome beautiful woman, sat opposite with Mme Elizabeth by her, which is young and handsome. The whole *compagnie*

32. Grouchy and Cottin, vol. 3, p. 145, 29 August 1775.

33. Horace Walpole, 4th Earl of Orford (1717–1797). Author of *Castle of Otranto* which set the fashion for gothic novels, his fame rests on his letters which explore with wit the topics of the day from party politics to literature, gardening, the Arts and Society gossip. His correspondence with Mme du Deffand runs to 1600 letters.

34. Walpole to William Mason, 12 June 1775. *Letters*, vol. IX, p. 203.

35. Marie Anne Louise-Adelaide de Mailly, Marquise de Coislin, who employed Blaikie at her garden at Brimborion in 1782. Quotation from the correspondence between Mme de Coislin and the Duc d'Harcourt in Ernest de Ganay, *Manuscript inédit*, Bibliothèque de l'Union Centrale des Arts Decoratifs, p. 203.

36. R1 317.

37. Blaikie gives the date as 20 May, Duchesne as 23 May (p. 142).

38. Described by Blaikie in chapter 1.

39. Madame Elisabeth (1764–1794), youngest child of Louis, Dauphin of France, who died before he could inherit the throne. Sister of Louis XVI, pious and courageous, she stood by her brother and his family and was guillotined in 1794.

seemed exceeding free and gay with an open cheerfulness which is not common to be seen amongst the higher Ranks in England. The King and his suite left the table and got upon horseback without much ceremony leaving the rest at table.[40]

He had thought Marie Antoinette a very beautiful woman then, and now he became devoted to her. The Queen must have been both amused and pleased by the tall, plain speaking young Scot for, within days of the fete at Bagatelle, she and Artois summoned him with Antoine Richard, head gardener at the Trianon, to a fete being held for the Royal family at Ermenonville[41] by the Marquis de Girardin. This proved another golden day. Blaikie tells us, 'the Marquis de Girardin conducted the company. The Queen, Madame Elizabeth and Madame la Comtesse d'Artois rode upon asses and, all their suites following, made a noble procession. Here we were conducted to every part of the grounds by the Marquis and the whole was shown to the best advantage.'[42] Villagers decked out in their local costumes engaged in archery or other sports as a kind of tableau vivant through which the visitors passed. Blaikie returned to Paris well pleased after this 'splendid fete'.

The summer brought many more visitors to Bagatelle where a little garden composed entirely of flowers, foreign trees and shrubs was described as drawing the attention of physicians, botanists and florists. Another area singled out for favourable mention was the grove surrounding the Philosopher's Pavilion planted with lilacs, cherries and viburnum as well as rarities such as bananas, sugar canes, palms and coffee trees.[43]

In June, an existing hydraulic machine[44] was refurbished to pump water to the park. It had a few teething problems and was twice repaired before the end of the year.[45] During the summer, the momentum kept up. He had 93 men under his charge in the second half of June and the first fortnight of July.[46] Sometime during the summer, he made the hermitage, a building constructed from tree trunks thatch and moss. There was still much to do. He describes how he, 'continued the ground work, prepared a place for a nursery and melon ground on the side towards Longchamps, began to stock up the trees, took more ground of Boulogne wood. Upon the north side of this, formed a shade with a mud wall in the manner of the houses of Picardy. This I covered with straw ... began likewise to make the rivers. Made during the summer several seats in a rustic way as I found there must always be something new to please them.'[47] In October his search for trees took him to Orléans to select plants

40. Diary, Thursday 3 October 1777.
41. The garden described in chapter 7. Blaikie gives this fete as having taken place on 1 June but other writers give the date as the 14th. see Mazel, *Ermenonville etc.*, p. 76.
42. Diary, 1 June 1781.
43. Bachaumont, vol. XV, p. 167, 26 May 1780. Bananas and other tender trees and shrubs would be placed outside for the summer months.
44. See Stern, vol. I, p. 66, footnote 2.
45. AN., R1 379.
46. R1 317.
47. Diary, undated between 1 June and 10 November 1780.

at the nursery of one Jacques Bruzeau whose list was extensive.[48] From him Blaikie purchased around 10,000 plants suitable for planting out and some thousands of seedlings for his nursery. One of the astounding things about the plantings both at Bagatelle and Trianon[49] is the many thousands of trees and shrubs ordered for the gardens.[50] However, most of the trees supplied would be small specimens to be brought on perhaps at first in a nursery bed. They would then be planted out close together to allow for losses and later thinned out.

1781

1781 was an even busier year. In January Blaikie asked that all the gardeners on the permanent staff at Maisons, St Germain and Bagatelle should be brought together to work successively in each park under his supervision in order to make an economical use of his time and theirs.[51] Frost hindered the rock work in the latter part of January and only the masons working in the grotto, where they were sheltered from the worst of the weather, were allowed to continue, their work being considered necessary before the rivers were begun in the spring.[52] Blaikie bought a large quantity of plants at the end of 1780 and during the early part of 1781, and 44 workmen were employed in planting them out.[53] He was allocated 45 men for the purpose of planting and sowing lawns.[54] His lawns were naturally a matter of great pride to him. To achieve success, he sowed a special seed mixture, '*Festuca ovina, Avena pratensis* and *flavescens, Poa pratensis angustifolia*, and most of the finer sort'.[55] During the years 1781 and 1782, he ordered two rollers from the Perier brothers, engineers of the famous water pump at Marly.[56] In addition, the daily records of the gardeners employed at Bagatelle show that five or six people, mainly women, were employed regularly to remove small stones from the lawns. This task was necessary to prevent the grass being destroyed when it was rolled. The rollers came in two sizes; the larger would have been about five feet long and about a foot in diameter, weighing around 1500 pounds. The procedure for tending the lawns was probably much the same as that used at Kew.

---

48. R1 318 Blaikie's expenses (264 livres) for his visit to Orléans from 3 to 24 October 1780. Bruzeau's catalogue: Archives départementales, Loiret. BR563. My thanks to the Director M. Philippe Richard for this document. For details of Bruzeaux's list and the plantings at Bagatelle see Patricia Taylor, 'Les plantations du parc', in *Bagatelle dans ses jardins* (Paris, 1997).
49. Requests for plants for the Queen's garden by Mique her architect. O1 1876.
50. In all, 64,747 conifers were ordered for Bagatelle. Amongst them 1500 *Juniperus communis*, 1125 Weymouth Pine (*Pinus strobus*), 1000 *Larix decidua*. Rarer specimens like Cedar of Lebanon, *Juniperus virginiana* and Red cedar (*Thuja plicata*) were purchsed in quantities between 10 and 30.
51. AN., R1 371.
52. AN., R1 371.
53. AN., R1 320.
54. *Ibid.*
55. Loudon, *Gardener's Magazine*, vol. 11 (August 1835), p. 479.
56. AN., R1 317.

The lawns were rolled about sunset. The cylinders flattened the blades of grass and early in the morning of the next day while the dew still prevented the grass from rising again, the lawns were scythed, the grass being cut down in the opposite direction from that taken by the roller so that, according to an eye witness, they appeared to the eye like large pieces of white and green mohair. In the growing period this task would have to be performed every week.[57]

Major work began on the river in March [58] and while engaged on this undertaking, Blaikie found time to make a nursery area to receive the young plants and seeds he had ordered from a number of nurserymen that spring.[59] Archibald Macmaster had left for England in April 1780. In January 1781 he returned to Paris and Blaikie sent him to England on a brief visit to buy trees and shrubs for the gardens and greenhouse, and seeds for propagation. These were the most choice and the rarest to be planted at Bagatelle.[60] Joseph Banks also took the opportunity of the gardener's visit to London to send Blaikie some seeds from Captain Cook's last expedition to Tahiti.

That summer, in spite of the apparent confusion caused by the huge works in progress, the established trees, shrubs and herbaceous plants began to give a hint of the future beauty of the park by the harmony of their foliage and flowers. During 1781, he planted some choice specimen trees; Cedars of Lebanon, Lord Weymouth pines (*Pinus strobus*), junipers from Virginia, spruces, cedars, Scotch and Bordeaux pines as well as thuyas and larches. As Macmaster's invoice shows, Blaikie's rarest plants came for the most part from England.[61] Magnolias were the stars of the Bagatelle gardens as they had been at Dr Fothergill's in Blaikie's days as a gardener there;[62] M. *grandiflora* with shining green leaves, thick, suede-like, cream petals and heady perfume; M. *tripetala*, known as the umbrella tree because of the way its ribbed leaves, pointed at both ends and 46 to 50 cms long, grow in ray-like clusters at the end of their stems so that when looked at from below they give the appearance of an opened umbrella; M. *acuminata* with bluish flowers, known as the cucumber tree, because its three inch long fruits resembled a small cucumber. Only the Kalmia, which he also grew at Bagatelle, was more desirable. All of these required great skill to grow on the poor, dry soil of Bagatelle when their natural habitat was swamp and river bank. As well as these exotics, and rare trees such as halesia, liriodendron, ailanthus and sophora, there were many sweet-smelling Judas trees, almonds, many different sorts of prunus trees, rhododendrons, lilacs, and many herbs and herbaceous plants. The flowers were smaller than today's cultivars, so that more emphasis was placed on their scent.

Today Parisians flock to Bagatelle in spring to enjoy the swathes of tulips that

57. M. Grosley, FRS, *A Tour to London or New Observations on England and its inhabitants*, 2 vols (London, 1772), vol. 2, pp. 118–19.

58. Duchesne p. 132.

59. AN., R1 318, 320, 322. See Patricia Taylor.

60. AN., R1 320.

61. AN, R1 320.

62. B. C. Corner and C. C. Booth, *Chain of Friendship; letters of Dr Fothergill* (Cambridge Mass., 1971), p. 18.

spread across the lawns. A fine display in spring was a feature of the park in Blaikie's day as well. He ordered a large selection of bulbs from a Mr Niewkerke of Harlem in the autumn of 1781.[63] Amongst the latter were 600 single and double hyacinths, 250 of the red, yellow edged tulip, 'Duc Van Toll', 1500 narcissi some of which we still grow today, like the small, double Van Zion, with its pointed ragged-looking petals, the fragrant, bright yellow double *N. x odorus* and *N. x incomparabilis* with pale yellow perianth and deep orange corona. He obtained many bulbs and annuals also from the famous nursery of Vilmorin.[64] The tradition of rose growing, now so closely associated with Bagatelle, began with Blaikie who planted well over 2000 roses in the park. At that time, his choice was limited to centifolias or cabbage roses, of the kind seen in Dutch paintings of the seventeenth and eighteenth centuries, *Rosa gallica* types, damask roses, which included the repeat flowering *Rose des Quatre Saisons*, *Rosa alba* and Scotch roses (*Rosa pimpinellifolia*). It was not till after the French Revolution that a huge advance in the breeding of roses made available the hybrids that we know today. However, there is one rose particularly associated with Blaikie at Bagatelle. It was brought to him from England by Archibald Macmaster and for it he paid the sum of 16 livres français.[65] Named 'Unique', it was a centifolia, red in bud, with creamy, white flowers, the ends of the petals lightly tinged with red, and had been discovered in a garden in Suffolk in 1775 by a nurseryman who managed on that occasion to take a single budding from it. Six years later it was flowering at Bagatelle.[66]

Blaikie records in his diary how the shade from the trees began to have an effect and pleased the French.[67] He was pleased himself with the progress his plantings had made and describes the 'prodigious work' involved in growing them successfully in the 'dry, sandy ground'. More soil was carted from the meadows opposite Bagatelle to improve the ground.[68] One of his techniques was using soot as a fertiliser. In March 1782 he ordered 300–400 boiseaux[69] for Bagatelle and, once people learned his 'secret', their rush to imitate him caused a shortage.[70]

Before the end of 1781, he completed two further rustic buildings fashioned from the roots, trunks and branches of trees; the Hermit's cell and a little hut described as 'like those which Indians make as a shelter from wild animals'.[71] The most ingenious was the Hermit's cell which resembled nothing that had been seen before in that

---

63. AN., R1 320.
64. AN., R1 333. Philippe Vilmorin (1746–1804) married the daughter of the nurseryman, René Andrieux. At the death of Andrieux, Vilmorin renamed the nursery Vilmorin-Andrieux, the ancestor of the famous firm of Vilmorin.
65. AN., R1 320.
66. There is a particularly fine illustration of this rose in Mary Lawrance, *A Collection of Roses from Nature* (London, 1799), pl. 4.
67. Diary, December 1781.
68. AN., R1 371.
69. One boiseau equalled 13 litres in Paris but had a different value in different parts of the country.
70. AN., R1 371.
71. Luc-Vincent Thiery, *Guide des amateurs et des étrangers voyageurs* (Paris, 1787), p. 26.

genre. With its long sloping thatched roof and its porch or entrance supported by what appear to be robust, shingle clad 'legs', a drawing of it shows it has a strongly organic feeling, especially as the trunks of living trees appear to grow through the roof and act as supports for part of it. The hermit's bed was a couch of moss.

The care and skill which Blaikie lavished on his nursery resulted in a phenomenal germination of seeds. Only those from Banks proved disappointing. Already old, therefore less viable, when he received them, he had no hothouses as yet in which to germinate them. But the rest grew at such a pace that, in March 1782, he notified the Inspector of Buildings that he was in urgent need of help in the nurseries where several thousand trees, sown from American seed (both from North and South America) more than a year before, would be lost if they were not transplanted into larger areas of prepared soil. Twenty-five extra nursery staff were allocated to carry out this work.[72]

1782

1782 was marked by a series of visitors. Activity in the garden increased early in the year probably due to the expected arrival of the Comte d'Artois who took up residence for a few days in April with all the attendant fetes and dinners for the royal family. It was during this sojourn of the Count's that Blaikie, taking advantage of his reputation for outspokenness and the licence it gave him, took the opportunity to complain, as he puts it, 'judiciously' about a sore point with him, namely the Count's lack of interest in the gardens. He describes how one morning, before the Count was up, some of the principal ladies of the court arrived. They refused to have Artois wakened and sent for Blaikie to entertain them as they walked in the gardens. No doubt to amuse themselves by encouraging him to indiscretions, they asked him about the Count and whether Blaikie was content with him. Blaikie tells us he answered, 'that I was not, that I never saw a more lazier and a man of less taste and that he had not once come to see the Gardens since he lodged there. This gave no little sport and laughter to those ladies who returned and told the Queen all that I had said. This, with perhaps some additional stories, furnished laughter enough for dinner when the Comte d'Artois arrived, so that their whole discourse was mostly taken up about me.'[73] The dinner table chatter was relayed to Blaikie by the footman who had waited at table during the meal and the man warned him that when the count's party gathered next day for the hunt, the least he could expect was a sharp rebuke. Blaikie, however, knowing that he had not overstepped the mark, was unperturbed. He describes how the next morning when he was in the garden, 'the Comte d'Artois came out and seeing me at some distance called, so that I went directly to him, so he asked me "Well, Blaikie are you not contented with me?" I told him no. "Why so?" "Because," says I, "there is no pleasure in working for you as I hardly know whether or not I please you as

---

72. Report by Briass, Inspector of Buildings on 11 March 1782 AN., Ri 371.
73. Blaikie's diary gives this event as taking place at an unspecified date in 1783, but his dates are unreliable from this stage of the diary on.

you never come to see the works after so much expenses and as I wish to please you and that you should enjoy my works." "What," says he "is it only that? I promise I will come and see you oftener." With that he took hold of my arm and walked all round the Garden.' Artois, however, failed to keep his promise and continued to be an unsatisfactory employer from Blaikie's point of view.

In June 1782[74] the Grand Duke Paul of Russia,[75] the son of Catherine the Great, visited Paris. This was a private visit and the duke and his wife travelled supposedly incognito as Comte and Comtesse du Nord. The grand duke was 28 years old at that time and Blaikie describes him with his usual frankness, 'This Great Duke is very improperly named as he may be called the little Duke as it is hardly possible to find a more little, uglier man than him. However, the Duchess is a fine woman, tall and well made.'[76] He goes on to describe their visit to Bagatelle at which he was in attendance, 'They went all round the Gardens, the Grand Duchess along with the Queen, who seemed exceeding well pleased with the Gardens. The Queen asked me if I liked the French better than I used to do. This surprised the Duchess who asked, 'Why so, and was not I a Frenchman?' The Queen told her that I was English and added, 'One of the best of that country'. After this gratifying commendation from Marie-Antoinette, yet another happy moment was in store for Blaikie. He, with the Queen and the Grand Duchess, had walked on ahead of the party of nobles and he tells us, 'I offered my hand to the Queen and Grand Duchess, going into the Hermitage. This made the Russian Ambassador run to take the hand of his Mistress and in his hurry he tumbled and fell into the River. This gave cause to a deal of laughter ... However, all passed well and the fete ended seemingly with great contentment on all sides.'

These two episodes illustrate rather contradictory aspects of Blaikie's nature. He was very much his own man and social distinctions did not affect his judgment of character. Within the limits of his position, he scorned servility and spoke his mind. Astute enough never to step too far out of line, he used his freedom as a 'character', and a foreigner, to say what he thought. At Versailles one day, he faced up to the formidable Comte de Besenval,[77] who considered himself an authority on horticulture. The Count had been laying down ridiculous rules about the pruning of the tulip tree when Blaikie told him bluntly that his remarks were 'not consistent with common sense' and bet him 100 louis that he was wrong. At first the Count was 'piqued', but the laughter of the Queen and the Comte d'Artois, who offered to put his money on Blaikie, defused the situation and the episode ended in good humour.[78] At the same

---

74. Blaikie erroneously gives this event as taking place in June 1783.
75. Paul I (1756–1801). Emperor 1798. Assassinated 1801, m. 1776, Princess Dorothea of Wurtemburg.
76. The duc de Croy was less kind and described her as '*grosse*', Grouchy and Cottin, vol. IV, p. 256.
77. Pierre-Victoire Baron de Besenval (1721–1794). A roué and a corrupting influence on Artois, he formed part of Marie Antoinette's coterie. Commander in Chief of the Interior in 1781, he was in charge of the troops deployed around Paris in July 1791. Retired and died in his bed.
78. Diary, undated entry, summer 1785.

time, in spite of his hard-headedness, Blaikie was immensely flattered at any mark of distinction from the Queen, to whom he was genuinely devoted. His diary often presents a picture of him as naively pleased by his own successes in minor things like growing the melons which Marie Antoinette insisted on for the royal table.[79] Amongst his possessions was a silver *sucrier* engraved with his initials entwined above a thistle. Its lid was decorated with a cluster of strawberries and tradition has it that he grew a new variety of strawberries of great sweetness especially for the Queen who was so delighted with the flavour that she made him a present of the *sucrier*.[80]

Festivities at Bagatelle did not end that year with the visit of the Comte du Nord. In September, the Comtesse d'Artois took up residence for a few days while her children were inoculated by a famous doctor in Passy. The garden echoed once again to the sound of flutes, hautbois and tambourines from orchestras hidden in the greenery; lanterns gleamed amongst the trees and fireworks exploded in the inky sky.[81] A theatre was erected for the amateur dramatics which were still the rage at court; the guests danced till dawn and strolled languidly around the garden during the day. Blaikie who sometimes was hard put to it to pay the workmen, was disenchanted with these extravagant displays. He grumbled about 'all these expenses for a week' and carried on with the task of assimilating another tranche of woodland from the Bois.[82]

1783

1782 and 83 were the years in which the fame of the garden spread widely. Visitors, both French and foreign, flocked to see them and they were widely praised in the press, especially the *jardin à l'anglaise*, 'Nowadays it is the English garden attached to this delightful spot that merits careful attention … what is particularly worthy of admiration and which one finds nowhere else is the exquisite neatness with which it is maintained and to which end nineteen gardeners are continually employed'.[83] Admission to the park was by entrance ticket.[84] The garden was not yet completed and there were still many men employed there but *the pompe à feu* which had been overhauled to provide water for Bagatelle was working effectively and the river was abundantly supplied. A series of bridges varying in style from the rustic to the Chinese, were now in place, although the Palladian bridge was still in the making. The Baronne

---

79. AN., R1 340, 341, 342 all give details of melons, cucumbers and other fruits being sent to Versailles from Bagatelle. The melons Blaikie grew at Bagatelle were the Rock Canteloup and the Early Romana. See Patrick Neill, *Journal of a Horticultural Tour through some parts of Flanders, Holland and the North of France in the Autumn of 1817* (Edinburgh, 1823), p. 488.

80. Illustrated in Birrell, facing p. 18. A tradition in the Baynham family, the inheritors of some of Blaikie's personal effects. See also R1 340, 23 April 1784.

81. Hénard, 'Les Jardins de Bagatelle', *La Grande Revue*, 10 May 1907.

82. Duchesne, p. 137.

83. Bachaumont XXIII, 2 October 1783.

84. Musée Carnavalet.

d'Oberkirche, who had visited the garden once with the Comte du Nord's party on 1 June 1782 described the park as 'exquisite'.[85]

From his very first day at Bagatelle, Blaikie's sense of the integral relationship between a house and its garden had been offended by the ten foot wall which closed off the pavilion from the *jardin anglais*. All his requests to have it demolished had been turned down and he fulminated in his diary, 'It is remarkable those people have no taste for perspective. Although the pavilion of Bagatelle joins the wood, they have no idea that this is anything ornamental. They look upon a house and a garden as two objects that do not correspond ... and when I spoke of destroying this wall to give an open elegance to the house ... it is surprising what foolish oppositions were made by M. Briass who pretends to be an architect.'[86] His persistence finally won the day, for he relates in an undated entry of 1783/84 that the wall was to come down and that to dispel the fears of the Prince d'Henin that the house would be burgled 'we [presumably himself and Bélanger) agreed to place an iron grille in place therof'. He also succeeded in changing the entry to the park which he describes as 'indeed very badly contrived'. He writes that, 'in this M. Bélanger gave the greatest assistance as he saw the absurdity of what he had done and in this we agreed to say that it was necessary for the river and ... served to make an excellent movement of the ground and some very happy perspectives'.[87] What these changes were we do not know but both alterations give an insight into the collaboration between the architect and the gardener.

1784 *and after*

During 1784 the work began again to suffer from lack of money. Although the park grew daily more beautiful with the maturing of the plantations, interest in it had reached its zenith. The Comte, for all his early enthusiasm for a *jardin anglais*, had rarely made great use of it.[88] Besides, Artois' debts were once again mounting. The Queen's days of innocent pleasure were now clouding over and she came more rarely to the gardens. Blaikie himself was inundated with other commissions although he still lived at Bagatelle, occupying a pavilion in the courtyard reserved for the Inspector of Gardens, and he still supervised the works. He may not have been there often that summer and probably missed the balloon flights made from Bagatelle by the balloonists Alban and Volets that year.[89] However, there was still work to be done. According to a guide published in 1787, the Palladian tower, part of the river and the *Isle des*

85. Baronesse Oberkirch *Mémoires*, vol. 3, p. 297.

86. Diary, 31 December 1778.

87. Diary, undated entry 1783–85.

88. Oberkirch, *Mémoires* vol. 3, p. 297, 'Parisians and foreigners profited more by it than its illustrious proprietors who rarely walked in it'.

89. Bachaumont, vol. xxix, p. 18, quoted in Quellern, *Le château de Bagatelle, étude historique et descriptive* (Paris, *c.* 1910), p. 56 describing how they made a flight from Bagatelle to Longchamps and back to amuse the little Ducs d'Angoulême and du Berry. They dragged a rope behind them so that they could be pulled down if necessary.

Tombeaux were still not completed but that work was to resume with renewed vigour shortly.[90] The estimated cost submitted in July 1783 by Bélanger for the completion of the river was 14,520 livres.[91]

Over the next few years the routine of occasional fetes and visits grew less frequent. Bagatelle ticked over and Blaikie immersed himself in work for the Duke of Orléans and for many private clients. In 1785 he even found time to go on leave to England for three weeks[92] leaving the gardens in the care of the head gardener, Dormier. But the peaceful days were coming to an end and Blaikie's life, along with thousands of others, was soon to be caught up in the turmoil of the Revolution.

Two descriptions of Bagatelle[93] give us a picture of it at its most complete: the gardens in particular were praised in extravagant terms. This was 'the very picture of rustic nature … disordered like a *coquette en négligé* whose dress apparently put together in a haphazard way is really a work of art; but Art so realistically disguised that Nature herself would be taken in by it.'[94] The main entrance, today marked by impressive gilded wrought iron gates, was presided over by the porter in his rustic house, the *maison hollandaise*. This stood at the edge of a half circle in the Bois de Boulogne. The planting was wild and left apparently untended to give the impression of unadorned Nature, the barrier, simple wooden fencing. From this spot, the tour of the garden proceeded via a winding path which led, first of all, to a rustic building, a kind of summer house in wood and thatch, raised on a mound so that from it one could view the village of Puteau in the distance. From here, after passing a temple to the god Pan, the visitor arrived at the rock from which the spring rose. Next to it stood an Egyptian obelisk engraved with hieroglyphics and *'signes mystérieux'*. As the path swung to the left, it crossed a river at two points before passing, first the Hermit's cabin, then a rock bench, and finally a bust of Lucullus, to finish at a little door adjoining the *jardin français*. The rock, from which the spring gushed, overhung a miniature lake fringed with clumps of greenery into which the water poured and fed the river. The latter divided to form a little island before entering a green copse guarded by a marble statue of Diana. In the centre of this woodland stood a rock from which the House of the Philosopher commanded another view out of the garden, the glass of each window being of a different colour; beneath it a vast grotto, its roof and walls studded with minerals. Next, the river flowed under bridges of creepers and mosses towards the Hermitage which opened on to a reservoir from which a cascade thundered. Swans and other birds made their home there and, at the opposite end from the hermitage, the water followed a tortuous route at the foot of narrow ravines, falling in cascades, foaming and crashing against the rocks which obstructed

90. See Luc-Vincent Thiery, *Guide des amateurs et des étrangers voyageurs* (Paris, 1787), vol. 1, p. 30.

91. AN., R1 371.

92. Thiery, p. 30 n. 1.

93. Thiery, vol. 1, pp. 25–30; Dulaure, J-A, *Nouvelle description des environs de Paris contenant les détails historiques et descriptifs des maisons royales, des villes, bourgs, villages châteaux etc.* (Paris, 1786), pp. 15–21.

94. Dulaure.

its passage as it ran under the Chinese bridge on which stood a little pagoda. Next, it passed under the Palladian bridge and flowed around the Island of Tombs with its mausoleum made of porphyry and its scattering of broken columns intended to evoke a gentle melancholy. The final incident, before the river disappeared to water the nurseries, was a Palladian Tower, built at the summit of a mountain in whose depths was concealed the ice house.

During the years 1785 to 1789 Blaikie makes only minimal references to Bagatelle. Artois, unusually for him, spent a month there at the end of 1785 and gave a great dinner for the Queen during his stay. He had, by now, abandoned debauchery for true love in the person of Marie Louise Françoise d'Esparbes de Lussan (1764–1804), wife of the Comte de Polastron and sister-in-law of Marie Antoinette's favourite Yolande de Polastron, Comtesse de Polignac. Bagatelle with its mirrors and voluptuous paintings was no longer his style. In Blaikie's diary we find simply that 'the works continued' or similar expressions of that sort. In April 1789 there is an order for grass seed for Bagatelle. Perhaps this was the time referred to by Blaikie when, writing for the *Gardener's Magazine* in April 1835, he describes how the lawns became infected by the cockchafer grub. He tells us that this, 'entirely destroyed the grass, and together with a flock of birds which came to eat these grubs, rendered this lawn like a newly cultivated field'. The lawn was resown with the mixture he found gave a fine turf at Bagatelle.[95]

In July 1789 while tensions in the city grew, he began repairs to the grotto but he does not mention this work in his diary.[96] As 14 July approached, when the crowds stormed the Bastille, Artois had become so unpopular that it was unwise to wear his green and crimson livery. Artois himself, in constant fear of assassination, was accompanied by a guard of soldiers wherever he went. A dispatch from the British ambassador's office gives an account of his departure on the evening of 16 July and mentions Bagatelle, 'all the furniture of Bagatelle, a beautiful villa belonging to the Count d'Artois in the Bois de Boulogne has been secreted also and none of his servants dare to appear in his livery; the amiable disposition of this prince makes him much regretted by his private friends and those who lived in his society'.[97]

Life at Bagatelle continued for a while unchanged. The post of Superintendent of Gardens was abolished in 1789 and Blaikie refers to this in his diary, writing that Chalgrin, the *Intendant des Bâtiments*, had ordered that work in the garden be limited to keeping it clean and tending the nursery. In September 1790 all the posts of the Building Inspectorate were suppressed except the salary of 1800 livres accorded to Blaikie.[98] He was now the only loyal representative of the Count at Bagatelle but, alone, he could not enforce his authority on the other servants who joined marauders in the park and woods. During his absence on a visit to England in 1789,[99] he left a

95. AN., R1 371. Bill for grass seed, 9 April 1789. Countersigned by Blaikie, 20 April 1789.
96. AN., R1 379.
97. Oscar Browning, *Despatches from Paris, 1784–1790*, 2 vols (London, 1909–10), pp. 245–6.
98. AN., R1 371.
99. Blaikie gives this date as 1790 but, as he had gone there to see the Duke of Orléans who is recorded as having passed the Christmas of 1789 in London, the latter is likely to be the correct date and other events described in the diary seem to confirm this.

young woman called Charlotte in charge of his house. She was afraid, perhaps intimidated, and asked for soldiers to protect the house. On his return, Blaikie moved from his pavilion in the courtyard to a more out of the way spot, the new gardener's cottage near the nursery. His time at Bagatelle was drawing to a close but, before he left, one other poignant event is recorded in his diary. Unfortunately, he gives no date but it is likely to have taken place in June 1790.

He was in the gardens one day when Mme Elizabeth, the King's sister, appeared at his side and engaged him in conversation about the Revolution. He declared his loyalty, and his distrust of the revolutionaries, and she came and rested in his house which he tells us, 'she admired for its cleanliness'. He goes on to describe how 'some days afterwards, the Queen came and enquired of the porter where I was'. The lack of respect that she had now to endure was evident in the porter's reply that Blaikie was somewhere in the Park.

When he heard she was there, Blaikie joined her and, dismissing her retinue, she walked with him in the gardens. By this time Marie Antoinette was sadly changed. Gone was the buxom figure of her mature years. Now she was thin and pale, her hair already turning grey and her beauty faded. Queen and gardener walked together on the lawns where she had performed so light-heartedly in the opéra-comique on the day of the fete no more than a decade ago. Together they made their way under the trees and along the winding paths both silently reliving their memories of happier days. She said to him, 'You had a visit from my sister Elizabeth who told me what you said. I know your way of thinking and shall never forget you. I have known you long.'[100] She went to see his house and then, repeating that she would never forget him, she left. He was never to see her again but he remained attached to her memory and a porcelain bust of her is still among his possessions.[101] He does not tell us of his own feelings that day but he wrote in his diary that 'this expression of her goodness had almost been fatal to me, for some out of jealousy and others out of revenge spread that the Queen came to Bagatelle to form a conspiracy'.[102] Then, one morning, he found a sentinel under his window and soldiers in the park. Two of them came to his house with a warrant to search it but, fortunately, he knew them and they good naturedly sat down with him to breakfast, drank a couple of bottles of his best wine, and left. Blaikie's troubles, however, were only beginning. The porter was a young man called Bressy. Recently appointed as successor to his father, he had none of the old man's affection for Bagatelle. He was the first to join the crowds who invaded the park to hunt the game, and on one of these illicit expeditions lost an eye as a result of a shooting accident. Blaikie, disgusted at his dishonourable behaviour, made a dangerous enemy of him by telling him that it served him right

---

100. Diary, undated entry.
101. Blaikie Collection, Private Archive.
102. A de Lescure, *Correspondence secrète inédite sur Louis XVI, Marie Antoinette, la cour et la ville*, 2 vols (Paris, 1866), 'les aristocrates ont tenu jeudi dernier une assemblée nombreuse et secrète au château de Bagatelle, dans le Bois de Boulogne (vol. II, p. 452, letter of 12 June 1790).

for betraying his duty. From then on Bressy, who was indeed an unsavoury character,[103] took pleasure in making life difficult for Blaikie.

Instead of protecting the park, where 85 panes of glass from the large greenhouse had been broken by the end of 1792,[104] he set up a stall selling refreshments for visitors. Although Blaikie received a personal message from the Comte to stay on, after the abolition of his post of Superintendent of the gardens[105] he could do nothing. His position became more and more difficult until, on 9 February 1792, a decree was passed by the Legislative Assembly announcing the sequestration by the nation of emigré property. Blaikie, who no longer had any right to live there, was obliged to leave and rented a house at the Grille de Chaillot. In May, Bagatelle was closed.

His last words on leaving reflected, rather incoherently, his love of the park: 'this place which I had formed and [where I] was always looked upon as a patron of a Natural Garden, although established in a very bad soil and [where it] was almost thought impossible to form any thing that could attract the fancy, but the movements of the ground varied the perspectives, and formed many beautiful landscapes'.[106]

Bagatelle is the only surviving major garden entirely laid out and planted by Blaikie, and his diary, in conjunction with the detailed records in the French National Archives, and the National Museum of Natural History,[107] give a unique and fascinating picture of the construction and planting of an eighteenth-century garden at a moment when enthusiasm for botany, and a more 'natural' style, was beginning to change such gardens. Carmontelle's Monceau begun in 1773 depended almost entirely for its effects on garden buildings and exotic 'scenes',[108] Bagatelle, through the influence of Blaikie as well as a growing interest in 'exotic' planting, combined artefacts and a 'natural' landscape, while Méréville, the last of the great pre-Revolutionary gardens, but on a much larger scale than the others, would rely to a greater extent on scenery and planting.[109]

The records, much more than the diary, reveal what an enormous task co-ordinating the work on the gardens was, with over 90 men employed each day during its most important phase, and thousands of trees and shrubs purchased for the garden and greenhouses or raised in the nursery. From them, it is evident that the term 'gardener' is completely inadequate for the responsibilities shouldered by the Scot. The diary highlights the sometimes difficult relationship between architect and gardener and it is a pity that Bélanger has left no account of his view of Blaikie. Bélanger adopted a

---

103. In *an 6* of the Revolutionary calendar (1797–98), Bressy was the subject of a complaint by the *agent municipale* of the Commune of Neuilly for abusive and threatening behaviour. Duchesne, p. 173.
104. Bibliothèque du Muséum nationale d'Histoire Naturelle, MS 306.
105. Diary, undated entry *c*. 1790.
106. Diary, February 1792.
107. Bibliothèque du Muséum nationale d'Histoire Naturelle, MS 306, contains an inventory of plants at Bagatelle by order of the Minister of Culture under the direction of André Thouin who was authorised to remove as many of them as he thought fit to the *Jardin des Plantes*.
108. The botanical interest was in his greenhouses.
109. See chapter 12.

number of Blaikie's ideas during the course of the garden's construction, and there were probably other day to day design decisions in which his view prevailed, since he was never reluctant to make suggestions or point out what was wrong with Bélanger's plans.[110] Yet whatever reservations or even disagreements Blaikie may have had with Bélanger about the design of Bagatelle, his personal loyalty to the architect was never in question. When the owner of the neighbouring Folie St James, the financier Baudard de St James, asked him to make changes to Bélanger's scheme for his garden, Blaikie refused on the grounds of his friendship with the architect.[111] That Bélanger probably called on Blaikie to furnish the trees for the great garden, Méréville,[112] showed that the architect recognised Blaikie's genius for planting. Blaikie was certainly a skilled gardener and co-ordinator of work, but he was also committed both emotionally and intellectually to the 'natural' garden. Amongst the books in his small library were some of the most important literary influences on the eighteenth-century English garden; Addison's *Essays*,[113] the poems of Milton, whose description of the Garden of Eden influenced French and English alike [114] and the poems of Pope. In his diary, he quotes from Pope's seminal Epistle to Lord Burlington with the famous admonition to 'Consult the genius of the place'. A true child of his time, he owned a copy of Thomson's *Seasons* and Young's *Night Thoughts*, the popular eighteenth-century poem extolling 'melancholy' which influenced the funerary aspects of the picturesque garden.[115] In addition, it is hard to think of any single landscape gardener who had travelled so extensively over such a long period in the Alps, that source of pre-Romantic emotions about nature; who had observed the sublimely savage scenery of the region so closely and responded to it with such strong feeling.[116] Bélanger, the great architect, utilised Blaikie's unique skills and modified his English conception of the natural garden to suit French tastes. The result was a highly successful synthesis of two cultures.

As far as we know, Bagatelle was only Blaikie's third garden project, the first two being for Lauraguais, at Mont Canisy and Manicamp which he began laying out only

---

110. Woodbridge, p. 13.

111. Diary entry for March 1783.

112. Created by Bélanger for the financier Delaborde and considered the triumph of the picturesque garden in France. See chapter 12.

113. Essay no. 414 in *The Spectator*, 1712, is considered one of the first expressions of a change in taste in gardens.

114. See Bélanger's inaugural address as Professor at the *Athénée des Etrangers*, 30 October 1802 on the Formation of the Modern Garden from which extracts printed in Stern, vol. I, p. 29.

115. He also owned the poems of Robert Fergusson and James Macpherson's *Ossian* but not Burns.

116. Thomas Gray in a letter of 1765 to William Mason, *Correspondence*, ed. P. Toynbee and L. Whibley, 3 vols (Oxford, 1935), vol. II, p. 899, writes of the Scottish mountains (although the same sentiment could apply to the Alps): 'a fig for your Poets, Painters, Gardeners and clergymen that have not been among them: their imagination can be made up of nothing but bowling greens, flowering shrubs, horse-ponds, Fleet ditches, shell grottoes, and Chinese rails'. Quoted in J. Dixon Hunt, *Gardens and the Picturesque. Studies in the History of Landscape Architecture* (MIT, 1992), p. 149.

shortly before Bagatelle.[117] No evidence has yet come to light that he had ever conducted any landscape scheme in England. However, from the way clients flocked to him after they had seen Bagatelle, it is evident that his contemporaries attributed the success of the *jardin anglais* to his talents.

Blaikie's original plan indicates that he would have preferred fewer of the buildings and bridges which were so much a feature of Bélanger's design, and the small concrete bedded streams would not have been to his taste. The German architect Friedrich Gilly who visited Bagatelle in 1797 was also unenthusiastic about these aspects of the English garden at Bagatelle and elsewhere.[118] He did, however, make a distinction between the gardens and the artefacts at Bagatelle and felt that these 'outdated embellishments' were alleviated by, 'the beauties of nature, the charm of the woods and the splendour of the groups of trees which surround the buildings contrasting with the largely open views towards the horizon'. Perhaps the last word on the pre-Revolutionary stage of the garden should go to one Englishman, Simon Weston, who in 1792 was enchanted by it as 'altogether the prettiest garden in the neighbour-hood of Paris'. He describes it as, 'A garden dressed up with altars, gods and great men, and adorned ... with the inequalities of Nature in full beauty'. He goes on, 'The French who reside near Versailles tell you, this garden is nothing in comparison of the Queen's gardens at Trianon & elsewhere, and not to be named on the same day with many others; but then they forget the river, the village of Puteau, and the bridge of Neuilli, which belongs to the comte D'Artois's grounds,[119] and seem to touch every part of them; whereas the gardens of the Queen & Mousseaux are rich parterres in chalky deserts'.[120]

The park of Bagatelle that we see today is the result of a number of interventions. Bélanger and Blaikie together created it as a folie for Artois, a prince of the royal family. At the Revolution, by Decree of the Convention[121] it was handed over to the people as a park for their diversions and they were enjoined to conduct themselves there with propriety or risk arrest. Various licences were granted to caterers for restaurants and cafés within the park. The Directoire, short of funds, sold it to entrepreneurs who turned Bagatelle into pleasure gardens. Once again rockets burst in the night sky and shed showers of starry sparks over the gardens. 'Lamps suspended from the bushes transformed the park into a palace of rubies, emeralds, topazes and

---

117. For a references to these two gardens see chapter 7.
118. See Edgar Wedepohl, 'Description de Bagatelle', in *L'Oeil* 1965 (June), vol. 1. A number of travellers commented on the style of Bagatelle with mixed reactions and it is not possible to quote them all here but some are listed in the Bibliography. For a nineteenth century English critique of Bagatelle see J. C. Loudon's description, *Encyclopedia of Gardening* (1825), p. 78–9.
119. These were picturesque views visible from the park. They did not belong to Artois, but skilful landscaping made them appear to be part of the gardens.
120. S. Weston, *Letters from Paris* (London, 1793), pp. 196–8.
121. *16 floreal an II* (5 May 1793). Former royal châteaux to be maintained for the good of the people by the Republic as establishments useful for agriculture or the arts. Bagatelle was to used as a place for public diversion.

diamonds ... the flutes in the orchestras breathed their sighing notes while lovers played in its mysterious grottoes,' [122] However, although it was a favourite spot for Parisians it failed financially. Bonaparte named it le *Pavillon d'Hollande* and reclaimed it for the State. He did little more that maintain it [123] and for a while the little prince of Rome played in its grounds. Josephine, divorced for her inability to bear an heir, was allowed a meeting there with Napoleon to see the longed for child, the cause of her unhappiness.[124]

At the Restoration, Bagatelle was handed back to Artois. He gave the property to his younger son, the Duc de Berry, who was assassinated in 1820. Berry's children, a daughter born in 1819 and his posthumous son, spent happy childhood days there and their governess, the Comtesse de Gontaut,[125] restocked the gardens.[126] Artois became Charles X, King of France in 1824. His grandson was playing in the grounds of Bagatelle in 1830, when news came of the King's forced abdication in favour of Philippe Egalité's son, Louis Philippe, who in 1835 sold Bagatelle to Lord Richard Seymour, Marquess of Hertford for 313,100 francs. Hertford, a collector of furniture, pictures and *objets d'art*, undertook a huge work of alteration and reconstruction which his heir, Sir Richard Wallace, completed after his death. By an agreement with the *Ville de Paris* in 1852, the town undertook never to destroy the view from the terrace at Bagatelle and to make no changes in the *Champ d'Entrainement* (the low lying fields between the château and the Seine) without Hertford's consent. A large part of the old garden and its buildings were swept away. The *Communs* (staff and service area) were demolished, and new ones built to the right of the courtyard entrance. By raising the building by one storey, enlarging the first-floor windows and enclosing the old dome inside a larger one, the symmetry of the pavilion was, unfortunately, destroyed. The *pompe à feu* was rebuilt. The Orangerie was constructed and in front of it a field, now the rose garden, was adapted as a riding school for Napoleon III's son (Napoleon III and his wife Eugénie were frequent visitors at Bagatelle). A belvedere was built to give a view over the riding school. The garden itself was simplified by the removal of many of the now decaying garden buildings and a rationalisation of the river system was carried out to distance the house, affected by damp, from the water. Hertford, to prevent speculative building impinging on Bagatelle, took the opportunity to enlarge the garden from around 16 to 24 hectares, which remains its present extent.

New and sensitive plantings of exotic trees in wide prairie-like lawns were made under the direction of the landscape gardener, Varé (1802–1883). These respected the spirit of Blaikie's eighteenth-century 'natural' garden. Sir Richard Wallace, who removed a large part of the furnishings of Bagatelle to his house in Manchester Square (now the Wallace Collection), pulled down the *Bâtiment de Pages* and replaced it in 1872 with the Trianon which today overlooks the courtyard and backs on to the

122. Mercier L-S, *Le Nouveau Paris* (1798), vol. IV, p 206.
123. O2 249 Bagatelle named as Pavillon d'Hollande. O2 312 *Mise en état des rivières et bassins de Bagatelle* 1810.
124. Ducrest Mme *Memoires sur l'Impératrice Joséphine* (Paris, 1828), vol. 3, p. 253.
125. Marie Joséphine de Montant-Navailles, Duchesse de Gontaut (1772–1857).
126. AN O3 1237, O3 1238.

gardens. In 1905, some years after the latter's death in 1890, the City of Paris acquired the park from Wallace's heir for a sum of over six million francs. In 1907 the garden was redesigned by J. C. N. Forestier, another gifted landscape gardener who again held to the spirit of the place. The rose garden for which Bagatelle is famed, was established then, and gradually the park took on the aspect that it has today.[127]

---

127. J.-C. Forestier, *Bagatelle et ses Jardins* (Paris, 1910). Victor Perrot, 'Communication sur le château, le domaine et le site de Bagatelle', *Procès verbaux de la Commission du Vieux Paris* (Paris, 1923), pp. 116–24.

CHAPTER 10

The Duc de Chartres and his Gardens at St Leu and Monceau

WITH THE VISIT from the Duc de Chartres to Bagatelle on 1 April 1780, Blaikie found that he had an important new patron. Over the next ten years he was to alter and improve three gardens for the Duke: St Leu, Monceau[1] and Le Raincy.[2] In each case he acted as architect and landscaper. His career had entered a new phase.

Louis Philippe-Joseph, Duc de Chartres (1747–1793), heir to the dukedom of Orléans, has never enjoyed a good press. He was said to have been his cousin Artois' tutor in vice and his instructor in freemasonry. His anglomania, often ridiculed at court, outstripped that of Artois, embracing England's constitution and way of life as well as its fashions. He felt so at home in London that he bought and furnished a house for himself at 35 Portland Square as a *pied à terre* for his numerous visits. His marriage in 1769 to Adelaide de Bourbon-Penthevière,[3] great grand-daughter of Louis XIV, and the richest heiress in France, provided him with an immense fortune, yet he was always short of money. In an effort to improve his finances and against widespread opposition, he transformed the sedate parterres and allées of the Palais-Royal into a sort of Vauxhall so that its gardens became a magnet for amusement and pleasure. He installed shops, cafés, playhouses, clubs, concert halls and taverns in its arcaded galleries and both Parisians and foreign visitors flocked to it. There is scarcely a traveller's diary of the period that does not describe a visit to this brilliant place which epitomised the excitement and dangerous glamour of Paris. As a royal domain it was outside the jurisdiction of the Paris Secret Police and was the haunt of prostitutes and swindlers, while later it served as the main focus for insurrection and revolutionary demagoguery.

Chartres was invested as Grand Master of the French Freemasons in 1773. His support for the Parlements and his popularity with the people aroused the hatred of

---

1. Monceau was variously called Mousseau, Mousseaux and sometimes Montceaux at different periods.
2. The town of Le Raincy stands today in place of the estate of Le Raincy, which was also sometimes called Rinci or Rainsi.
3. Marie Adelaide de Bourbon (1753–1821), descendant of Louis XIV through her father, the Duc de Penthièvre. The early death of her dissipated brother, the Prince de Lamballe, left her sole heir to a vast fortune. Married Chartres in 1769 at age of 16. Pious and timid, she was no match for Mme de Genlis who alienated her children from her when she became their governess. She survived the Revolution which she spent in Spain. Regained the large part of her fortune but the end of her life was saddened by financial disagreements with her children. She died of cancer.

Marie Antoinette who suspected him of plotting the downfall of the royal family to make way for a constitutional monarchy in which the House of Orléans would replace that of the Bourbons. (This it did in 1830 with the accession of Chartres' son, Louis-Philippe, Duc d'Orléans.) At the Revolution, he adopted the name of Philippe Egalité and became a deputy in the National Convention. There, he shocked the world by voting for the death sentence on his cousin Louis XVI. Less than a year later he, in turn, was compromised and betrayed. He was executed by guillotine on 6 November 1793 at the age of 46.

His character has always been something of a mystery. Contemporary pictures of him are mostly unflattering, dwelling on his superficiality as well as his refusal to take the most solemn occasions seriously. His gullibility was well known and he was always interested in and susceptible to innovative ideas or schemes. Blaikie tells an amusing story about one of those 'Schemers', the man who pretended he could walk on water. 'The duke ... came to see this Miraculous performance which was in a Bathing place about 40 feet long by 20 broad and about 6 deep where the Actor with his cork boots, after leaving the borders, soon began to lose his *équilibre* and his light heels soon was uppermost and kept his head in the water so that the Duke and those that were with him went off in such a fit of Laughter that they did not think about the poor fellow who would [have] probably been drowned if I had not called some workmen to pull him out.'[4]

With Madame de Genlis,[5] who was for a time his mistress and remained a major influence in his life, Chartres adopted a progressive system of education for his children, carried out under her supervision. Supposedly, as part of their educational experiment, Philippe sent to England for a six year old orphan girl[6] to be brought up with his daughters and to be adopted by him. Although his letters about the child to his English agent, Nathaniel Forth, appear to indicate that the little girl, Pamela, was genuinely unknown to him, his action caused endless gossip and speculation. Horace Walpole, after seeing Pamela as a young woman in 1785, remarked how Madame de Genlis had educated her pupil to be very like her in the face,[7] and she did bear such a marked resemblance to her governess, that most people, including Pamela herself, thought that she was the Duke's illegitimate child by Mme de Genlis. Others accused him of evil designs on the little girl. Yet others suggested she was his child by another unknown woman. Few would accept that he may have been motivated by philanthropy alone.

The three gardens in which Blaikie was involved trace, in some measure, Chartres' personal as well as artistic development. St Leu, the first in which Blaikie had a hand, fostered in him an appreciation of a more 'natural' garden and made him dissatisfied with Monceau, the work of Blaikie's predecessor, Carmontelle, the creator of contrived 'illusions' at Monceau. This garden, a kind of early theme park, was remodelled by

4. Diary, undated entry.
5. Stephanie Félicité de Crest de Saint-Aubin, Madame de Sillery, Comtesse de Genlis (1746–1830). Mentioned already in connection with her *Mémoires* in chapter 7.
6. Pamela, who later married Lord Edward Fitzgerald (1763–98) the Irish patriot.
7. Walpole, *Letters*, vol. XIII, 23 July 1785, to the Countess of Upper Ossory.

Blaikie when it was enlarged during the building of the famous wall round Paris c. 1785.[8] At Le Raincy, the last of his gardens, the Duke put into practice his liberal conception of an English park run with respect for the needs of its servants as well as its owner and open to visitors, with a café for their relaxation and refreshment. Chartres did not employ Blaikie at his newly acquired property of Neuilly, as he had promised at their first meeting, but wasted no time in summoning him to St Leu on 28 April 1780.

Swallowed up by the town of St Leu la Forêt, St Leu no longer exists. It had been bought by Chartres in his wife's name in 1779, when he had completed the more famous garden of Monceau. The château stood high above a plain on the edge of the forest of Montmorency about twelve miles north-north-west of Paris. It had already undergone extensive renovation and enlargement by a previous owner, the Marquis de Laborde,[9] the King's banker, who lavished 'several millions'[10] upon it, transforming the formal French gardens into a *jardin anglais* under the supervision of an English gardener called Prescott. Blaikie was greatly taken with the place. He praised the situation of the house. The gardens, 'lying pleasantly on the hillside', were laid out in the style that met with his approval; with a shrubbery, a walk and clumps of shrubs and trees round the whole enclosure. The views in every direction were fine. He had only one criticism; Mr Prescott had 'too much imitated England' in planting low shrubs along the walks thus providing inadequate shade for the French climate. Laborde had channelled water from a spring in the woods to the park by means of an aqueduct. The water was then pumped up to the top of a *grand rocher*.[11] Although Blaikie praised the effect of the cascade and rock, he did find some imperfections, commenting that 'If they had made a second cascade and lowered the river before the house it would have made a better effect'. As he was only immediately concerned with alterations to the layout, he does not describe any of the other features of the garden. Outstanding amongst these were the temple which crowned the top of the rock, and a staircase leading to a room beneath the river and accessible from both banks.

After his first visit he drew up plans for the improvements he advised and returned the following spring (10 April 1781) to begin the works at Taverny, the sister estate which was absorbed into St Leu after the Revolution. At the same time he made a model for the *rocher* and the adaptation of the beginning of the river at Saint-Leu. Drawings by Le Rouge[12] showing the cascade flowing strongly suggest that he did

8. This wall was commissioned the Farmers-General (the tax-raisers of the Ancien Régime) to curb the smuggling of taxable goods into Paris. Several gateways with toll houses would be the only entries into the city. The idea was very unpopular and was expressed in the popular saying '*Le mur murant Paris rend Paris murmurant*'.

9. Jean-Joseph, Marquis de Laborde (1724–1793). A man of immense fortune he bought St Leu in 1774 His estate at Méréville was considered the triumph of the picturesque garden in France. He had scarcely completed it when he was condemned to death on the guillotine.

10. Ernest de Ganay, *Les Jardins de France et leur décor* (Paris, 1949), p. 222.

11. H. Gagniard *St Leu la Forêt*, p. 69.

12. G. L. Le Rouge, *Details des nouveaux jardins à la mode* (1776–1785), Cahier XII, Planches 7, 8.

work on a second cascade to improve the rock.[13] On one of his early visits he met the engaging Madame de Genlis. She shared the Duke's radical views (although she was to distance herself from him at the Revolution) and had made herself indispensable to him as governess to his children. Her enlightened approach to education had led to the installation of a large farm in the park where her charges could learn to milk cows, tend the animals and cultivate the earth. Each child also had his or her own garden there and a botanist was employed to give them lessons on plants. She invited Blaikie to have dinner with her one day but, unfortunately, he left no account of their conversation except that she spoke good English. His silence gives the impression that she did not charm him. If so, he was not alone in disliking her. Mme Vigée Le Brun did a sharp demolition job on her character when she wrote, 'I do not think her face would have adapted easily to an expression of kindness, however, it achieved every other with prodigious speed'.[14]

Throughout 1781 Blaikie made many changes. These, he wrote, 'wrought a great effect upon those gardens and upon the mind of the Duke who began to see the difference from the changes I made in following the nature of the ground and drawing *perspectifs* upon the different objects already placed'. This, he explains, he achieved by designing the paths to pass or cross at places where 'the different objects and parts of the gardens are seen to the greatest advantage'. He adds in a remark probably written later, after he had become the leading landscape gardener in France, 'in this I have succeeded as the first in this country'. His success is borne out by a description of the mature park in 1808 when it belonged to Louis Bonaparte and his wife Hortense. The author praises the 'fine views in all directions'. He admires the way in which 'plantations serve as wings ... and prevent the wide views of the plains intruding into solitary areas'. He also draws attention to their variety, pointing our that they 'proceed from the whole circumference of the eminence and carry the eye sometimes on the valley of Montmorency, sometimes on to the environs of Paris and more frequently on the park itself'.[15] So powerful was Blaikie's influence on the Duke's ideas about the beauties of a 'natural' garden that he became discontented with Monceau and began to involve Blaikie first in its management and later in redesigning it.

According to his diary, Blaikie was at Monceau several times during 1781. In February he was already directing the choice of plants there. In March 1781, Archibald Macmaster on Blaikie's orders returned from England with a fine collection of greenhouse plants for Monceau as well as plants for Bagatelle.[16] At that time, the head gardener at Monceau was a German called Ettinghaussen. Ettinghaussen was a protégé of Madame de Genlis (she calls him Etickausen). According to her *Memoirs*[17] she was asked by

13. De Ganay refers to four waterfalls. Three emerged from the false spring and a fourth formed a cascade from the grand rocher.
14. *The Memoirs of Mme Vigée-Le Brun*, trans. Sian Edwards (London, 1989).
15. A. L. J. De Laborde, *Description des nouveaux jardins de la France, et de ses anciens châteaux* (Paris, 1808–15), pp. 113–14. See also Pierre Villiers, *Manuel du voyageur aux environs de Paris* (Paris, n.d.), vol. 2, p. 500.
16. Diary, March 1781.
17. Genlis, vol. 3, pp. 97–8.

Chartres to find a good gardener who would be willing to marry a pretty dairymaid and live at Monceau, a request that might have defeated lesser women and explains her influence over Chartres when she was no longer his lover. She remembered that the milkmaid at Genlis had a pretty, unmarried daughter about 18 years of age. She brought the girl to Paris, had her trained by Madame Adam, the city's leading dairy expert. Then she found 'Etickhausen', a gardener 'renowned for his art', arranged the marriage, paid for the bride's trousseau and set them up, at the Duke's expense, in a charming little house at Monceau. However, on 22 December 1781, in spite of all Madame de Genlis's arrangements, the Duke summoned Blaikie to the Palais-Royal where he asked him to find an English gardener for Monceau as he intended getting rid of Ettinghaussen. Blaikie, who found the German 'a good hearty man', refused but after the gardener's dismissal, gave his approval for the appointment of an Englishman called Scott who had previously worked for Lord Howe.[18] From then on, Blaikie seems to have had complete responsibility for the garden.

Monceau was one of the most extravagantly fanciful of French picturesque gardens. Shortly after his marriage in 1769, Chartres purchased a hectare of land near the village of Monceau on the road to Courcelles and on the edge of the plain of Monceau, a vast stretch of land to the north-west reserved for hunting game. His choice of area was unusual since the fashionable district for building was the west side of the city along the Champs Elysées. (Today the Parc Monceau is well within the city boundaries and lies at the end of the avenue Hoche some half mile from the Arc de Triomphe.) He commissioned the architect, Colignon, who had sold him the land, to build the house and arrange the gardens.[19] Colignon designed an octagonal pavilion and a garden in the formal French style but by the time the project was completed in 1773, Chartres already wanted something new. He was continually acquiring more land to add to his property and turned to Carmontelle, the organiser of his fêtes and spectacles, for an extended garden more in tune with the times.

Blaikie would have scorned the idea that the garden he had 'inherited' in 1781 was an English garden. And so would its creator Louis Carrogis, or Carmontelle.[20]

---

18. Lord Howe was probably Admiral Richard 1st Earl Howe (1726–1799), who distinguished himself in the Seven Years War and relieved the siege of Gibraltar in 1782. He was created Viscount Howe of Langar in 1782 and Earl Howe in 1788. He owned the estate of Langar in Nottinghamshire. See *Burke's Peerage*.

19. See *Grandes et petites heures du parc Monceau. Hommage à Thomas Blaikie (1750–1838) jardinier écossais du duc d'Orléans*. Exhib. catalogue, Musée de Cernuchi, July 1981. This exhibition was mounted through the efforts of Mr George Dickson of the Association Franco-écossaise. I have used its bibliography in studying the history of the park. Carmontelle's views are explained in his book, *Jardin de Monceau, près de Paris, appartenant à son Altesse Serenissime Monseigneur le duc de Chartres* (Paris, 1779). It contains also a number of delightful engravings by Carmontelle of the various scenes described here. Luc-Vincent Thiery, *Guide des amateurs et des strangers voyageurs à Paris* (Paris, 1787), t. 1, pp. 64–6, gives a contemporary description of the park.

20. Louis Carrogis or Carmontelle (1717–1806) was the organiser of the Duke's fetes. An artist and amateur garden designer, he was already well known as a designer of stage sets and the author of light dramas. Famous for his book, *Les Proverbes*.

Carmontelle was already well known as an artist and author when he began the reconstruction of Monceau. He was determined that his garden would not be some pale imitation of the *jardin anglais* which he condemned as 'austere, sombre and savage'. The English, he wrote in his book, *Jardin de Monceau, près de Paris*, loved the country as an escape from society where they retired to 'feed their melancholy'. For the French, it was a place where men and women could enjoy the pleasure of each other's company in pastimes such as conversation, fetes, and spectacle. He paints an amusing picture of the discomforts to be met in the countryside; the damp woods and the persecution by insects. His garden, by contrast, would be a constant source of entertainment and novelty. 'If it were possible to make a picturesque garden a land of illusions why deny oneself that pleasure,' he wrote, and set about creating a garden which would encompass 'all times and all nations', with swiftly changing scenes as dramatic as any at the opera, pastoral one moment and exotic the next. He wanted to realise three dimensionally in the garden the images which the most skilful painters represented on canvas. The French, having freed themselves from the rules of formal French gardening, should not now become slavish imitators of the English when their temperament and climate were so different from that of their phlegmatic neighbours.

The result was an irregular garden with intricately winding paths and a serpentine river. At each turn, the visitor entered a new 'world'. It might be a ruined temple of Mars or a Dutch windmill; a medieval fort or a Turkish tent; an Egyptian pyramid or an Italian vineyard with a statue of Bacchus at its centre. A camel, and turbaned attendants, gave verisimilitude to the minaret which stood on a mound, while a rustically attired shepherd tended his flock on the Island of Sheep. Amongst the most frivolous of these varied objects was a Chinese *Jeu de Bague*, a kind of carousel or merry go round supported on three pillars and furnished with reclining seats supported by Chinese figures for the ladies, while the men rode on dragons. The game involved spearing rings which hung from the 'parasol' that sheltered the riders as they rode round. The whole machine was kept in motion by servants dressed in Chinese robes who worked a kind of treadmill in the centre. The formal French garden set around the pavilion was retained and there were blue, pink and yellow flower beds and a field of wild flowers. The *Bois de Tombeaux*, set in an appropriately shadowy wood, was intended as an exploration of different funerary styles. The most striking of these was the pyramid still to be seen in the park today. Its interior was richly decorated with columns of granite supporting a white marble entablature. Bronze rosettes decorated the vaulted ceiling above two black marble tombs on either side of the entrance. In a niche facing the entrance was the figure of a young Egyptian woman carved in black marble, sitting on her heels and holding her breasts from which water spouted into a basin below. In another part of the park, sloops were anchored on a large oval lake called the Naumachée.[21] A line of columns delineated the borders of the lake. Today, the lake is smaller and, on any fine weekend, dozens of brides in

---

21. A stretch of water for conducting mock sea battles and which might be used in the fetes, illuminations and fireworks to great effect. The columns came from the demolished chapel of Notre Dame de la Rotonde at Saint-Denis.

1. Corstorphine Old Parish Church.

3. James Lee by George Garrard. The large buttons on his coat portray scenes from the garden of Monceau, one of the French gardens in which Blaikie worked. Borough of Hammersmith and Fulham.

4. Dr John Fothergill (1712–1780). Cambridge University Library.

2. Edinburgh, the Physic Garden. Dr John Hope and the Gardener by John Kay. From John Kay, *Original Portraits and Caricature Etchings*, Edinburgh 1837–38.

5. Joshua Reynolds: Dr William Pitcairn (1711–1791). This portrait of 1777 shows him in the robes of President of the Royal College of Physicians. Courtesy of the Royal College of Physicians.

6. Joshua Reynolds: Joseph Banks. Commissioned by Banks in 1772, it shows him as a young, scholarly explorer. Courtesy of the National Portrait Gallery.

The bearer Thomas Blakey, Gardiner by Profession and Botanist, travels into Switserland, in our service, in search of rare and curious plants. Should he by sichness, or any accident stand in need of assistance all reasonable demands on this account will be gratefully paid, by applying either to

D.r William Pitcairne, Fellow of the college of Physicians in London and F.R.S. werwick?

or to D.r John Fothergill, in Harpur Street London.

London ½ April 1775 -

7. The letter of recommendation from Drs Pitcairn and Fothergill which Blaikie took with him on his journey to Switzerland. Blaikie Papers, Private Archive.

NOMENCLATOR

Thomas. EX *Blaikie*

HISTORIA

PLANTARUM INDIGENARUM

HELVETIAE

EXCERPTUS

AUCTORE

ALBERTO V. HALLER.

BERNÆ.

Súmptibus SOCIETATIS TYPOGRAPHICÆ.

8. Blaikie's signature on the title page of his copy of the abridged version of Haller's *Historia Plantarum Indigenarum Helvetiae*. He used it as his field guide and indexed and annotated it. Blaikie Papers, Private Archive.

9. Horace Benedict de Saussure (1740–1799). Alpine Club.

10. Voltaire. Caricature of 1777. Bibliothèque Nationale de France.

11. Dr Michel Gabriel Paccard (1757–1827). From an engraving celebrating his conquest of Mont Blanc. Alpine Club

12. A dried specimen of *Senecio alpinus* collected by Blaikie in Switzerland in 1775. The Board of Trustees of the National Museums and Galleries on Merseyside (Botany Department, Liverpool Museum).

13. The Jardin de Talèvre, where alpine plants flourished in the middle of the Talèvre glacier. Alpine Club.

14. The Jardin du Roi. Water-colour by Jean-Baptiste Hilaire 1794. Bibliothèque Nationale de France.

15. The gardens of Versailles at the moment when the trees were being felled in the winter of 1774–75. View of the grove by the *Bains d'Apollon*, 1775, oil on canvas, by Hubert Robert (1733–1808). Musée de Versailles.

16. Guiscard, seat of the Duc d'Aumont, laid out by J-M Morel (1728–1820), the most 'English' of French designers. From a drawing by C. Bourgeois. Photo P. Taylor.

17. Ermenonville, the park showing the château, the large lake and the Temple of Philosophy from *Nouveau voyage pittoresque de la France*, Paris 1827.

18. Moitte: the Comte d'Artois in hunting dress, in front of the pavilion of Bagatelle which can be seen in the background to the left. Amiens, Musée de Picardie.

19. Courvoisier, The entrance to Bagatelle. Blaikie may have lived in one of the small pavilions in the foreground. To the left behind the wall are the entrance towers. The large building at the back is the *Communs*, the staff and domestic offices. Musée Carnavalet.

20. Bagatelle. View of the *cour d'honneur*, the courtyard directly in front of the pavilion. To the left are the *Communs* or staff and service quarters. The hill in the background is Mont Valerian. Bibliothèque Nationale de France.

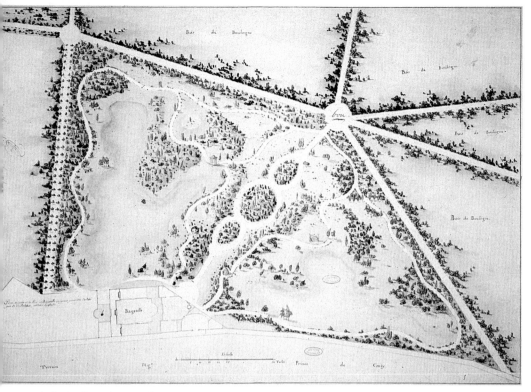

21. Blaikie's plan of Bagatelle, 1778. Archives Nationales, France.

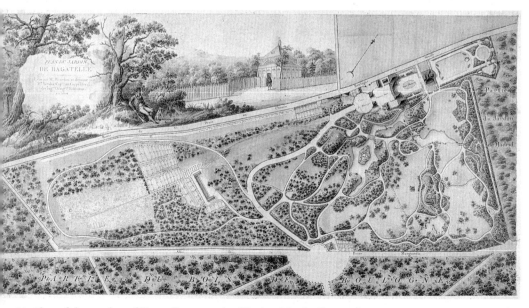

22. Plan of the garden of Bagatelle *c.* 1814 by Nicolas. Musée Carnavalet.

23. A scene in the garden of Bagatelle showing the Philosopher's Pavilion built above the grotto to the right with the house in the background. Bibliothèque Nationale de France.

24. Bagatelle, the *jardin anglais*, a romantic view of the large wooden bridge by Hill after Natte. Musée Carnavalet.

Le Concierge laissera entrer
M.r desvignes et 4.
personnes
Paris, le
C.te Dela ferronnay

PARVA SED APTA

BAGATELLE

25. Entrance ticket to Bagatelle by N-L Rousseau after Bélanger. Musée Carnavalet.

ÉLÉVATION DU TEMPLE ET DU ROCHER

VUE DU ROCHER, TEMPLE ET CASCADE DE S.T LEU. Prix du point E.

26. St Leu. View of the rock, the temple and the cascade on which Blaikie worked, by Le Rouge. Photo P. Taylor.

27. Plan of the
garden of
Monceau by Le
Rouge 1783,
illustrated with
three views of
the garden.
Bibliothèque
Nationale de
France.

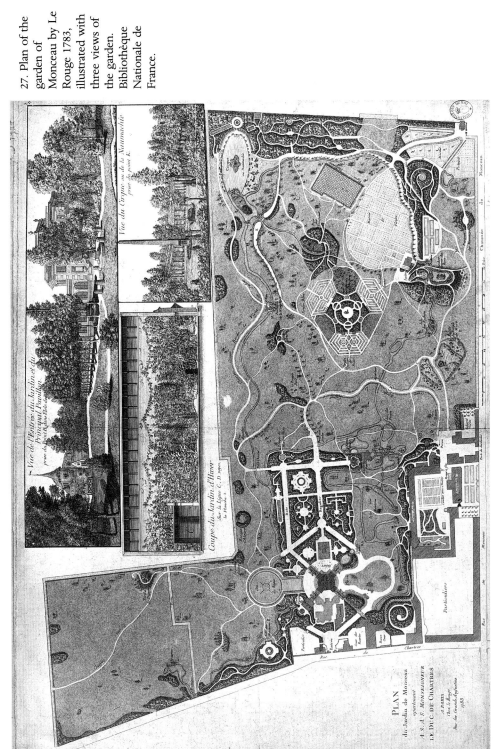

billowing white dresses and floating veils flock with their grooms to pose for photographs by its pillars. A smaller pool, called the Pool of the Bathers, displayed two statues by the great sculptor, Houdon. One portrayed a lady of quality going to bathe and the other a beautiful negress pouring water over her. Near the entrance was a gothic building, a chemistry laboratory for the Duke.

In spite of Carmontelle's insistence that his garden was not an English one,[22] it was certainly influenced by earlier English gardens and was most often compared to Stowe. It was also criticised for the same reasons; too many buildings and artefacts in a small space at too great an expense. These are exactly the criticisms Blaikie made when he visited Monceau for the first time in 1777. Later, in March 1783 when he took over the whole management of the gardens he added, '... the winter garden adjoining to the hothouses was more beautiful than elegant. The whole was a small confusion of many things joined together without any great natural plan, the walks serpenting and turning without reason'.[23]

Over the next few years, Blaikie made a number of changes that he tells us 'were agreeable to his Highness'. He took in further land, remodelled the Italian vineyard and destroyed those walks he thought unnecessary or unnatural. One major work of alteration was the lowering of the ground before the pavilion to improve the view from its windows. 34 men were employed here trenching and hollowing out the ground.[24] It is also said that he installed a new English water pumping system.[25]

A little later, outside events brought a rush of activity to the rarefied world of Monceau. To end the smuggling of taxable goods in and out of the city, the enormously unpopular measure was taken to encircle Paris with a wall. As the wall was to skirt Monceau, Blaikie tells us, 'M. Le Doux[26] who was the Architect, gave a sketch to his highness to pass [i.e. place] the wall and boulevard where his highness should judge'. Blaikie was sent to measure out the line and, if necessary, modify it to suit the layout of the garden. In the end Orléans decided to extend the park as far as the wall and incorporate in it some 58 small parcels of land which he would purchase.[27] The Duke agreed to bear the expense of a large *fosse* (ditch) and Blaikie tells us that the new wall was then constructed in the ditch.[28] A rotunda, in the form

22. He apparently had the words, 'Monceau is not an English garden' written on the wall of the park. See A. F. F. de Frenilly, *Souvenirs du Baron de Frenilly, Peer of France* (London, 1909), p. 5, quoted in Dora Weiberson *The Picturesque Garden in France*, p. 76.
23. Diary entry for March 1783.
24. AN., 300 AP I 185.
25. Philippe Vassal, *Les eaux de Paris en Révolution 1775–1825* (Paris, 1997), p. 41. This seems to contradict Blaikie's own statement in an undated entry of his diary c. 1786 that the Perier brothers built the pump at Monceau.
26. Claude Nicolas Ledoux (1756–1806), the outstanding architect of the late eighteenth century in France. He constructed the toll houses of the *barrières de Paris*. The scheme to wall in the capital was not completed but some of the toll houses still exist, among them the one at the entrance to Monceau.
27. See *Grandes et Petites Heures du parc Monceau*, p. 43.
28. Diary, undated entry c. 1785.

of a temple, housed the customs office and is still there today, although altered. Orléans paid 12000 livres towards its cost and in return was allowed exclusive use of the attic room above the columns with the staircase that led up to it.[29] During September 1787, as well as the men employed in improving the view before the pavilion, thirteen workmen were employed at the walk in the ancient fosse, forty-four were employed at the various walks Blaikie was changing and seventeen were employed trenching the borders and earthing up the ground around the melon beds.[30]

The archives confirm,[31] as Blaikie notes in his diary, that there were so many projects being undertaken at Monceau that four foremen were employed, each in charge of a different undertaking. At the same time Blaikie placed Charles Miller, an English gardener in charge of the men occupied on various smaller projects. However, there was not one amongst them capable of understanding, let alone directing the works. As a result, Blaikie was obliged to supervise the day to day programme of works and to settle the accounts every fortnight.

In his next undated entry Blaikie tells us that, 'Mr Spiring[32] continued the houses at Monceau and at the same time a *galerie* to conduct from the [Duke's private] apartments to the *Serre* [greenhouse] and winter garden'. It is with the designing and supervising of these new galleries and green houses that Blaikie is credited. The winter garden, designed by Carmontelle, was an extraordinary place. Blaikie tells us, that when it was lit at night and the lights were reflected in the numerous mirrors in the buildings it 'had a most beautiful and enchanting appearance'. He adds that, 'there had not been seen anything of that taste neither in England or in France'.[33]

Four plans illustrate the progress of the garden of Monceau before the Revolution.[34] The first by Colignon, dated 1769, shows the original garden with its octagonal pavilion which he designed for Chartres at the time the plot was purchased.[35] A second, dated 1773, the year the pavilion was completed, shows the building and its formal garden plus an area which looks as if it might be the beginnings of an English style garden with a river and either a mound or a maze.[36] The third by Le Rouge, in 1783, presents Carmontelle's garden. The French garden near the pavilion is retained although slightly

29. 'Monceau', *Commission de vieux Paris*, Paris, 25 April 1901, p. 52.
30. AN 300 AP I 185. Also includes an account of the work on the greenhouses and hothouses.
31. AN 300 AP I 185 lists the foremen and workmen employed at Monceau and their hours during parts of 1788.
32. Jean-Baptiste Spiring, joiner at Raincy. 300 AP I 185.
33. Carmontelle does not describe them in his *Jardin de Monceau*, but Georges Poisson 'Un transparent de Carmontelle' in *Bulletin de la Soc. Hist. de l'Art français*, 10 November 1984, describes how for one of the galleries Carmontelle painted ten transparent blinds with a trompe l'oeil design showing the garden beyond. This way it could be summer outside all the time. These galleries were, it is thought connected with the ceremonies of free-masonry. the whole is described in detail in Thiery.
34. These appear with others detailing the lots of small properties acquired by the Duke over the years, in the catalogue of the exhibition, 'Grandes et Petites Heures du Parc Monceau'.
35. AN Minutier central, Etude LIII 1.459 (quoted in *Grandes et petites heures*).
36. BN Estampes, Collection Destailleur.

modified. Three drawings of 'scenes' from the new garden appear above the plan.[37] A fourth, unsigned, reveals the increased size of the park and its transformation by Blaikie.[38] The changes here are fundamental. The extended gallery leading to the larger greenhouses is clearly marked. The formal garden has disappeared and the straight allées have been suppressed. There are fewer paths and those that remain have been made less sinuous. The planting has completely changed in its character with fewer single lines of trees along the paths and dotted about the garden. Instead there are more groups and thicker, less regular, plantations. It confirms Blaikie's undated note in his diary that, 'The plantations in the garden began to make a tolerable appearance and joined with the ancient made a better effect. At the same time, he emphasised how important shade was in the French climate both for walks and at those places designed as spots from which to admire the view.

As time progressed, Blaikie's diary becomes less and less specific. When he indicates a particular date, it is not always clear if he is still referring to the year which was last mentioned in the text. Exact dates can only be checked by his references to historical events. One natural phenomenon which he mentions is well documented and enables us to fix the events around the date of its occurrence on 13 July 1788. This was a hailstorm which caused catastrophic damage and great hardship throughout France. In many areas it flattened whole fields of grain, and destroyed the young fruits throughout the country, from apples in the north to olives and citrus in the south.[39] Monceau and Bagatelle did not suffer, but when he went to Raincy on 15 July to meet the Duke, Blaikie found that, hail, falling as large lumps of ice, had caused much destruction; cutting down branches of trees and killing 'hares, partridges and many other things'. This is also the period which he gives for the completion of the hothouses and new galleries at Monceau.[40] The hothouse or pineapple house was separated from the gallery by sashes which, he tells us, admitted air more moderately than the external cold air, and the collection of plants in both formed a Botanic School where the Duke and sometimes his children came to learn plants. This Blaikie arranged according to the Linnean System.[41]

Blaikie's satisfaction with the new greenhouses and galleries was justified and praise for them and the winter garden to which they were joined was universal. In 1786 they were described by one visitor[42] as 'one of the most beautiful we have seen'. A long passage is devoted to them in Thiery's Guide published in 1787 and shows the ingenuity and imagination as well as the costliness of ornament and the high level of craftsmanship used at Monceau from the beginning. It describes how a gallery leads from the yellow pavilion to the greenhouses at the end of which is a little Chinese pavilion decorated with mirrors painted in arabesques. One of these mirrors is opened

37. Le Rouge, 1783.
38. Bibliothèque d'Art et d'Archaeologie. Fondation Jacques Doucet, Fo I 103.
39. Simon Schama, *Citizens* (Penguin edn, 1989), p. 305.
40. AN., 300 AP I 185 confirms the completion of the greenhouses by the order of Blaikie and Spiring during the course of the year 1788.
41. Muséum National d'Histoire Naturelle MS 1308.
42. Dulaure, *Nouvelle Description des Environs de Paris* (1786), vol. 2, p. 121.

by pressing a button and reveals the winter garden which fills a vast and immense gallery ... Behind the trees placed near this door a statue of a Faun, holding two torches, lights the entrance to a grotto. Thiery describes the rocks and cascades of the interior of the grotto and goes on, 'All this gallery whose floor is covered with a fine red sand, is filled with trees and shrubs in flower all winter, like lilacs, Judas trees, laburnums, Indian nut trees, banana trees, cherries, coffee and tea bushes, sugar trees etc.'. He tells us also that below these galleries was another deeper grotto decorated as a white tent and used as a dining room by the duke to entertain his close friends where music played by unseen musicians in the gallery above filtered down to the guests by means of fissures in the rocks.

The combined complex of galleries, winter garden and hothouses were particularly beautiful at night when the Duke held a fete there and they were lit by 'a thousand lamps' On a winter day when the ground was covered with snow an infinite variety of flowers diffused their delicious fragrance and the air was kept at the temperature of spring. The effect was magical. An English visitor vowed that 'the charms of nature and the embellishment of art are blended together in a manner which I imagined was only to be found in the palaces of sylphs and fairies'.[43]

The Duke of Orléans was for Blaikie in some ways a far more satisfactory master than Artois because he was interested in botany and botanical exploration.[44] The list which Blaikie prepared for the botanical education of the Duke and his children was not confined to the tender plants in the pine house but seems to have included all the plants in the garden. Written carefully in his own hand it includes 482 genera and covers 125 pages, with a brief explanation of each Linnean category for the benefit of his noble pupils.[45] The trees and shrubs are generally the same as those planted at Bagatelle and the Trianon. In addition to the gardens at Monceau, Blaikie had overall control of the Duke's nurseries. Lists of seed sent from America in 1788 were copied to him for planting in the nurseries of the Duke's various estates. These included seeds from America from Bartram's and Marshall's nurseries and some sent by Franklin. They show that he was involved in the general supervision of all the Duke's properties.[46] Large quantities of narcissi and anemones were also regularly ordered on his authority.[47]

As well as private parties, the duke held fetes at Monceau. Blaikie tells us that the Duke of Dorset, the British ambassador, 'was a great acquaintance of the Duke and came frequently to Monceau'. Other accounts of visits to Monceau before the Revolution tend to demonstrate the more debauched side of Orléans life, as this account of an evening spent there by the young Lord Herbert, son of the Earl of

43. Helena Maria Williams, *Letters written in France in the summer of 1790 to a friend in England.* 2 vols (1790), vol. 2, pp. 87–8.
44. His accounts for his house in Portman Square show that in 1785 he purchased an account of Cook's Voyages. AN., 300 AP I 185.
45. Muséum National d'Histoire Naturelle MS 1308.
46. AN., AJ 15 511 for seeds. AN., 300 AP I 185 Blaikie's agreement with Duc d'Orléans, 1 April 1788. Also amongst Blaikie Papers.
47. AN., 300 AP I 2110.

Pembroke, reveals, 'On Thursday ... after the Hunt the Duke of Chartres carried me to his petite Maison at Moussow, where we dined a pretty numerous, noisy Company, there being some Females of the Party. After Dinner we amused ourselves in flinging one another into the Water, at last by stripping naked & hunting the Hare through Wood, Water, etc., etc.'[48]

The works at Monceau appear to have finished by 1788. In the meantime the pace of events leading to the Revolution was increasing. In July 1789 rioting began in Paris. On the very day of the storming of the Bastille (14 July 1789) Dr Rigby, an English medical practitioner was so unaware of the seriousness of events that he took time to visit Monceau, 'the celebrated gardens of the Duke of Orléans' which, he explains, 'happened to lead us to a part of the city very distant from the Bastille'. On his return through the streets from the quiet backwater of Monceau, he heard the news and joined in the general 'joyful shouts of liberty'. However, his rejoicing was cut short when he found himself caught up in a crowd bearing two bloody heads raised on pikes. Shocked and disgusted by this horrible sight, he retreated to his hotel. Two days later Rigby met Smith,[49] the concierge of Monceau, who had shown him around on their visit to the park. Smith's considered opinion, which he told them that he knew from his own situation, was that the danger was by no means at an end and they determined to take his advice to leave Paris.[50]

For a time, while the Duke of Orléans was still the darling of the crowds, the position of his servants was more or less safe. Blaikie continued to work at Monceau but had great difficulty in receiving payment and had to pursue the Duke to England in December 1789[51] in order to gain his authorisation to settle accounts. In 1792 the Duke gave up his estates to his creditors. In 1793 he voted at the National Assembly for the death of his cousin, the king, but his own situation was soon undermined. Among Blaikie's papers is a copy of the *Journal de Paris* announcing the return of his old employer as a prisoner to the city. It reads, 'The ci-devant Duke arrived from Marseilles on 3 November 1793 at five o'clock in the evening; he was taken to the Conciergerie'. His stay in the grim fortress where Marie Antoinette had passed her last, lingering days was short. He was condemned and went bravely to his execution on 6 November 1793. Monceau was confiscated by the State.

After numerous vicissitudes the park became, like Bagatelle, a pleasure garden, the scene of fetes, illuminations and balls, and demonstrations of the new pastimes of

---

48. Lord Herbert (ed.), *Henry, Elizabeth and George. Letters and Diaries of Henry 10th Earl of Pembroke, and his Circle.* From Lord Herbert's diary 19 May 1780, p. 479.

49. Smith is mentioned frequently in Blaikie's diary. At times the two are drinking companions and at others seem locked in a power struggle at Monceau. Smith is an interesting character whose influence seems to have been greater than his title would suggest. He was paid the extraordinarily high salary of £100 sterling per month (AN 300 AP I 2110). He accompanied the Duke to London and apparently made an income by lending money to financially embarrassed noblemen like the Marquis de Tilly who was arrested in London because of his debt to Smith. C. Melchior-Bonnet (ed.), *Mémoires du comte Alexandre de Tilly* (1965).

50. Dr Edward Rigby, *Dr Rigby's Letters from France in 1789*, ed. Lady Eastlake (London, 1880).

51. Blaikie gives this as 1790 in his diary, but it is likely that he is mistaken.

ballooning and parachuting. Gradually with the depredations made by a succession
of entrepreneurs who rented the property and its buildings, the gardens became
neglected and Colignon's pavilion so fallen into disrepair that it was demolished. In
1802 an English visitor wrote in one of his letters, 'I know not how to describe
Mousseaux; it consists of a number of little hillocks, stones heaped on each other,
little defaced walls and puddles which are called here mountains, rocks, ruins and
rivers'.[52] However, another English visitor at the same period writes, 'After dinner
we drove to the beautiful garden of Mousseau formerly the property of the Duc
d'Orléans. It is laid out with great taste, and delights the eye with the most romantic
specimens of improved rural beauty ... Here we rambled till evening. The sun was
setting, the nightingales were singing in great numbers ... In a sequestered part of
this beautiful ground, under embowering shades of an acacia tree, upon the ruins of
a little temple we seated ourselves.'[53]

At the Restoration, Monceau was returned to the Orléans family. Louis Philippe,
son of Blaikie's employer, preferred his property at Neuilly to Monceau and removed
the little white marble temple to an island in the Seine, the *Île du Pont*, near the bridge
at Neuilly where it still stands. But at least he saw to it that the gardens were well
maintained and the buildings restored. In 1852 the ownership of the property was
contested by the State and as a result split between the State and the Orléans family.
The reason for the State's interest was the increasing value of the eighteen hectares
or so of land which the estate comprised and which were now situated in a prime
development area. In 1860 on the pretext of opening up the Boulevard Malesherbes,
Haussmann, the great developer of Paris, was able to claim the whole area of Monceau
for the city of Paris. The park was reduced by half at one blow, and Haussmann
proposed that it should become a public park. This plan was carried out during 1861
under the direction of Alphand, the Chief Engineer of the Department of Promenades
et Plantations.[54]

The new Parc Monceau was bisected by two main allées. The rotunda erected in
1788 by the architect Ledoux was retained but its proportions were destroyed by the
addition of a heavy dome and columns in 1861. The ground in the new park was
mostly given to lawns planted with specimen trees and shrubberies. The old constructions by Carmontelle being made of flimsy materials had not weathered well and
were removed and new features added. Only the pyramid and the colonnade round
the Naumachée remained. The lake itself was greatly reduced in size, as was the
course of the river. Today the latter no longer exists.

The Parc Monceau, as it was now called, became, at the end of the nineteenth
century, the centre of a district favoured by many artists and writers. Guy de
Maupassant described the park in his novel *Fort comme la mort*. Emil Zola was so taken
with it that he used it as the inspiration of one of his novels, *La Curée*, and took many
photographs in its allées. Monet too was inspired in the 1870s to paint six paintings

---

52. Henry Redhead Yorke, *Letters from Paris in 1802*, vol. 2, p. 133.
53. Sir John Carr, *Stranger in France* (1803), p. 173.
54. See A. Alphand, *Les Promenades de Paris* (Paris, 1867–73), vol. II.

of the garden.⁵⁵ Today, it is one of the few green spots in the 8th arrondissement where children can play and office workers stroll at lunch time. Still standing is the largest tree in Paris, an *Acer pseudoplatanus* more than 35 metres high and with a circumference of about 4 metres.⁵⁶ The oldest tree in the district it may even have been planted by Blaikie with the memory of the Corstorphine *Acer* in mind. To the tune of bagpipes played by a Scottish piper, a tree was ceremoniously planted in the park in honour of Blaikie in 1981.

55. *Grand et Petites Heures du Parc Monceau* which also gives the location of two of these paintings as the Metropolitan Museum of New York.
56. Information from *Sentiers-Nature de Paris*, Direction des Parcs, Jardins et Espaces verts. Mairie de Paris.

CHAPTER II

Le Raincy: an English Colony in the Heart of France

W HILE he was still working on the changes at Monceau, Blaikie became involved, in 1786, in his third and most important commission for the Duke and one that was to cost him personally very dear. On the death of his father in November 1785, Chartres became Duke of Orléans and inherited the château of Le Raincy in the forest of Bondy some nine miles to the north east of Paris. Here was no small scale park but a vast estate of 700 arpents (about 800 acres)[1] of which the park, enclosed by a wall, covered approximately 400 acres.[2] Its size gave Orléans the opportunity to create one of those English parks that he had always admired and to put into practice the political and humanitarian ideas he cherished.[3]

The château had been built for Jacques Bordier, the royal *Intendant des finances*, by Le Vau,[4] the architect of Vaux le Vicomte, in 1643 and the park, according to tradition, had been laid out by Le Notre. A plan of 1663 shows a classic French garden with its characteristic geometric allées, statues, parterres, round ponds and fountains, with orchards and vegetable gardens laid out in squares. The two large axes on which the park was constructed crossed each other at right angles in the forecourt of the château. The main avenue led directly to the château while the more commonly used Avenue de Paris extended, also in a straight line, across the *avant cour* (the outer court yard) to the Porte de Chelles on the opposite side of the park.[5] On the Paris side it measured 108 toises (around 200 metres) with a double row of trees on each side for part of the way. The vast stables, large enough to hold two hundred horses, were surrounded by a dry ditch.

The whole estate had remained virtually unchanged until in 1769 it was bought by Louis Philippe, Duke of Orléans, the father of Blaikie's employer. A fire in May 1773 almost destroyed the château[6] and gave him the opportunity to have the magnificent

---

1. Dézallier d'Argenville, *Voyage pittoresque des environs de Paris* (4th edn, Paris, 1779), quoted in J. Bugon and M. Gaulard, 'Le parc de Raincy', *En Aulnoye jadis*, vol. I, no. 3 (1974), pp. 18–40. The dimensions of the park are given as just over 367 arpents in the plan of the park of Le Raincy by Poisson, 1781 (Bibliothèque Nationale, Cartes et Plans).

2. Blaikie's conversion, which makes one arpent equal roughly 1.1 acres. The arpent was not a consistent measurement and varied from place to place. Two of the most common measures were the *arpent de Paris*, which measured 1.1 acres and the *arpent des eaux et forêts* which measured 1.6 acres. In converting d'Argenville's arpents to acres I have used the arpent de Paris.

3. See Patrick Bracco et Elizabeth Lebovici, 'Les vestiges du parc du Raincy', *Monuments historiques, Ile-de-France*, no. 129 (October–November 1983), pp. 47–52.

4. Dulaure, vol. 2, p. 196. Louis Le Vau (1612–1670).

5. Plan of 1663 AN., N II Seine-et-Oise 64.

6. Jean Astruc, *Le Raincy* (Paris, 1969).

but inconvenient building remodelled by his architect, Piètre, who had worked at the Palais-Royal.[7] The old Duke commissioned his estate manager, a Monsieur Pottier, to construct an English garden in a corner of the park and to bring the rest of the garden up to date.

There was one serious obstacle; Le Raincy lacked water, an essential feature in any *jardin anglais*. To remedy this defect two springs were capped by Pottier, and the water led by two aqueducts into the park at the highest point of the new garden. From here it fell in a cascade and then took its serpentine course for about a mile and a half till it flowed into a lake. As well as the introduction of a river, a number of new buildings designed by Piètre were erected, among them an orangery and a mill tower. The parterres were replaced by lawns.[8]

This was the situation when the new Duke, who was later to renounce his title for the name Philippe Egalité, inherited Le Raincy. Monceau had been innovative in its day and the conception of Carmontelle had been in tune with the Duke's own desire for amusement and variety in the early 1770s. He had other plans now. He was committed to political reform and Le Raincy was to be the expression both of his taste and his aristocratic radicalism. It was also an expression of his commitment to an English way of life.

Rousseau had praised agriculture as the earliest and most honourable of arts and put metal work and carpentry next. Madame de Genlis had brought up the Duke's children according to Rousseau's principles[9] both at Saint-Leu and Raincy and, at Raincy, Orléans hoped to live as an enlightened English landowner surrounded by a prosperous and contented peasantry where every building would combine beauty and utility. The farm and dairy (*laiterie d'agrément*), the hamlet or English village (*le hameau*), the Kennels (*Le Chenil*) would all be ornamental in the manner of the *ferme ornée* but they would also be used as workshops and services for the estate and, most importantly, would house its employees, whose comfort and happiness were to be his concern. Previously, as in other great houses, the servants at Le Raincy had been crammed into the attics, separated from their families in the surrounding villages, with no communal social life of their own. Orléans set out to provide dwellings and gardens for every family, where each could cultivate a garden and keep cows and hens. He also furnished their houses and provided them with linen and everything necessary for a home.[10] The appearance of the estate in the 1780s can be seen in nine gouaches, now hanging in the Musée Marmottan, by Carmontelle, the designer of Monceau. In addition at least two sets of buttons show a variety of scenes at Le Raincy before 1793.[11]

7. AN., NIII Seine-et-Oise 574 1–95. Plans of the park of Raincy showing the reorganisation of the Park before 1786 most of which signed by Piètre. Illustrated in Bougon and Gaulard, 'Le parc de Raincy'.

8. Plan of 1781 BN., Gc B 110.

9. Set out in *Emile* (Paris, 1762).

10. A Dejouy, 'L'Etonnant M. Spiring', *En Aulnoye jadis*, vol. I (1972), pp. 23–5.

11. Collection of Baron Nerciat. See chapter 2, p. 17, n. 72.

The work carried out between 1786 and 1792 was to constitute a complete remod-
elling of the park by Blaikie. This time, however, although he planned and directed
the changes to the gardens, he played no part in their maintenance, nor was he
involved in the running of the nursery. As well as laying out the park, it was his
responsibility to find a contractor for the works. Amelot signed a contract in February
1786 [12] for, among other works, the remaking and enlarging of the old entrance road
from the entrance at Bondy to the courtyard of the château and the replanting of 130
lime trees. All the allées were to be changed to gravel and suitable foundations laid.
To ensure that the lawns flourished, Amelot was charged with digging over 46 arpents
of soil to a depth of 2 feet in preparation for the sowing of the lawn area. In 1786,
he also dug out the soil for a projected river as well as clearing out the old water
courses and changing the shape of the lake to make it irregular.[13]

Blaikie's contract [14] was to excavate the large pond or *pièce d'eau*, to transport the
earth therefrom to different parts of the gardens and to use it either to create elevations,
or for plantations. He was also responsible for digging up trees, cutting them into
logs and transporting them from the site. In addition he had to lay out 680 toises
(1 toise equalled just under 2 metres) of allées through the woods and line them with
sand and pebbles.[15] All this work had to be completed by 1 May 1791 at a cost of 12790
livres. He is credited also with the building of the Chenil (Kennels) [16] and according
to his diary, 'at the new Kennel we sunk a well' the 'we' presumably referring to
himself and the contractor Amelot with whom he went into partnership for the
project.[17] Growing lack of funds made this sort of separate agreement with his
employees the Duke's preferred method of carrying out special projects. Whereas he
paid his staff a modest salary for their normal duties, they received an agreed sum
for conducting special works and were then completely responsible for their realisation.
That the Duke would not be able to pay them was inconceivable.

A plan of 1790 [18] shows Blaikie's reworking of the gardens. The two main axes have
been suppressed and the old allées in the outer areas of the park have been replaced
by winding paths. The circular pieces of water have been modified in shape to look
more natural, as has the course of the artificial river which is crossed by two wooden
bridges.[19] The rocky features at its source have also been given a more natural
appearance. The old stables have disappeared along with the recently built *Tour du
Moulin*. Other existing buildings have been modified and there is a host of new ones.

These new constructions are not quite so varied as at Monceau and, of course, are

---

12. 300 AP I 317.
13. In 1787 between 1 January and 1 April Amelot undertook further work for 26873 livres and
    from 1 September to 1 December he contracted for a further 30828 livres. 300 AP I 317.
14. AN., 300 AP I 317.
15. AN., 300 AP I 317.
16. Bougon and Gaulard p. 34. 'Le parc du Raincy'.
17. Diary, mid February 1786. See Dejouy, p. 24, on the same sort of agreement with Spiring.
18. BN., Cartes et Plans. Ge c 3860.
19. The one near the Orangery is described wrongly as an iron bridge in Laborde *Descriptions
    des nouveaux jardins français* (1808). See Bougon and Gaulard, 'Le parc du Raincy', p. 25.

not crowded together as at Monceau either. Nevertheless, they are an eclectic mixture. The groups of buildings and outhouses which form the farm and the English village or hameau with their facings of brick and roofing of slates are, as their name suggests, intended to be vaguely English in feeling. Here was to be a model village of the kind the Duke had seen at great houses in England.[20] The cowhouse is a Swiss chalet with Swiss cows but an English bull. Attached to the cow house is the house of Hudson, the English guard or gamekeeper of the park. Then there is a small group of *maisons russes* that may have existed earlier. These are rustic chalets with plasterwork ornamentation and with galleries running round the first storey which in some cases link two buildings. They were used as cafés for the public during the time of Philip Egalité. When the château grew too dilapidated for repair in the 1830s, the *chalets russes* served as a house for his son, Louis Philippe, who had been declared King at the forced abdication of his father's cousin, Charles X (Artois). Later still they were used as the Mairie and a school for the town of Le Raincy which grew up on the site of the old estate. They were eventually demolished in 1911.

The vogue for Chinoiserie was almost spent by 1786, but there were two buildings which were Chinese in inspiration at Raincy, the Hermitage and the Boucherie. The Hermitage was really a bridge reached by a flight of wooden steps which climbed the sides of a kind of rockery at the edge of the river. At the centre of the bridge was a small pavilion inspired by Chinese temples. The Boucherie which sat on top of the ice house was used for dressing game after the hunt and seems an unlikely choice of design for such a bloody purpose.

Another important building was the Chenil or Kennels which also provided accommodation for the keeper of the hounds. It reflects the late eighteenth-century enthusiasm for Gothic architecture and was built in the form of a fortress with a crenellated parapet and loopholes. There were four towers on the corners of the building, two round and two square and the doors were massive. The towers have been incorporated in a modern restoration as community housing and it is possible to gain an impression of the old building in the much simplified restoration.

The new stables, however, were neo-classical buildings. The only ones on the estate to be constructed entirely in stone, they were decorated with horses' heads and pillars on the side which faced the château. Throughout the park many of the statues and urns which had decorated the first garden also remained to remind the visitor of the classical world.

Blaikie recorded in his diary his own first impressions of Le Raincy when he visited the estate in February 1786. He writes, 'the 15 *fév*. 1786 went to Rainsy to examine the ground. Found M. de la Hay, Concierge, to whom I addressed. He has been a long time here under the Old Duke but as he is Old he sent along with me one Allen who is *Garçon* of the *Appartements* who made all Supplications for me to try to conserve his place and little Garden he had behind the Kitchen and indeed every one solicited me as if I could keep them. The park is extensive and contains nearly 400 acres

20. Lord Egremont built a model farm at Petworth, and Lord Harcourt a model village at Nuneham Courtenay but it is not known if any specific village inspired Orléans.

enclosed with a wall. There is 4 gates and an Avenue of Poplars from the great road across the Park to another gate called the porte d'Echell (Porte de Chelles) and the entry to the Château turns at right angles and opposite an other gate to Livry. The Stables is to the right and left and surrounded in the old way with dry fosses (ditches). The Château is a noble structure with a *terrasse* and lovely green in front. All this requires a great deal of work.' His comments on his predecessor's efforts were scathing, 'The Duke's father has been trying to make some part of it into an English garden but without taste or judgement. He has made a River upon the top of the hill and a Rock with a little piece of water before the Château, and at the lower side of the *Parc* there is a tower where the Marquis de Cray (Ducrest),[21] the Duke's Chancellor who pretends to great Schemes, wanted to Make a Candle Manufactory upon some new plan, but how I can not say. Dined with M. Lahaye who gave me an ancient plan of the park with the dimensions.'[22]

It was clear that Orléans was in a hurry to start the new works. The next day Blaikie saw him 'to *rendre* account of what I had seen and what I proposed'. The Duke, well pleased with his scheme, asked him to make a plan, agreed it and left Blaikie to find a contractor for the work. Blaikie employed a M. Amelot whom he knew. They agreed to go partners in the undertaking, estimates were prepared and accepted by the Duke without delay and the work began on 1 March 1786, eighteen days after Blaikie's first visit.

Blaikie notes in his diary that Spiring,[23] the English carpenter who worked on the greenhouses at Monceau, was contracted for the joinery work. In addition Spiring acted as master of works.[24] It is not clear who designed the buildings but at least a number of them may have been the work of the Marquis Ducrest, brother of Mme de Genlis, a man of great inventiveness whose plan for a candle factory at Raincy, mentioned by Blaikie in his diary, came to nothing. Blaikie records how 'the Marquis ... proposed to make buildings of paper or as he called it *carton*'. He had already made some small boats at Monceau painting them with a strong varnish which kept them watertight for a time. He also, according to Blaikie, 'proposed to build a Cowhouse for the *Suisse* Cows that his highness was to bring from that country. He even proposed to me to go partners with him in this undertaking which I thought so ridiculous that I declined. However as his highness was always the protector of all new schemes he left the Marquis proceed in his undertaking.' In the end he not only designed and constructed buildings for the Swiss cows but also a most elegant dairy and *orangerie* and Blaikie was obliged to include them in his plan. 'This miraculous building,' he adds with heavy irony, 'was framed with thin *dalles* [lathes] upon which

21. Charles-Louis, Marquis Ducrest (1747–1824) was a brother of Madame de Genlis and renowned for his innumerable projects. It was he who suggested to the Duke of Orléans the development of the Palais Royal site, which caused so much controversy. He was an amateur economist and scientist and published several works on these subjects, including an *Essai sur les machines hydrauliques.* (1777).

22. Diary, undated entry 1786.

23. Diary, undated entry 1786.

24. Diary, undated entry 1786.

they pasted paper and even good white writing paper [of] which were sent several loads from Paris and this fabric [was] begun with great glee and a great deal of paper already pasted, when all of a sudden a hurricane of wind and rain happening and all this frail construction was to be found in pieces all over the park ... and so ended this foolish project; but the Marquis still persisted in his carton projects.' [25]

However foolish a project it may have seemed to Blaikie, a development of the marquis' idea was used at Le Raincy as an inexpensive method of construction. The foundations of most of the buildings seem to have been of parpen, stones dressed at both ends and used to build a wall one stone thick. The rest of the structure was of lathe and plaster coated with plaster on which was fixed false brick, wood or stonework made of plaster and suitably coloured.[26] The exteriors of the Russian chalets were decorated with plaster sculpture to represent knotted wood, or garlands of flowers. This kind of construction had been used at Monceau but, at Raincy, careful attention to guttering and the use of slates and tiles for roofing and sometimes for cladding the walls meant that in spite of their apparent fragility, some of them are still in existence today. The barn which was part of the farm complex is now the church of St Louis; Spiring's house, much altered, is still occupied, the little clock tower of the *pavillon de l'horloge* remains as part of a house and the little pavilions on the Paris approach, which feature in one of Carmontelle's drawings, stand in their original positions although in an extremely dilapidated state and surely deserving restoration.

Raincy was primarily a hunting estate because of its situation in the forest of Bondy. And sometime in 1788, Orléans held a hunting party and a great banquet for the Comte d'Artois to further a marriage contract between the Duc d'Angoulême, Artois' son [27], and Orléans' elder daughter, on whom one million livres were to be settled by her grandfather, the Duc de Penthièvres. Blaikie, of course, was on hand to observe events and draw his own conclusions. He tells us that he watched the arrival of Artois and his suite on horseback at the entrance to the chase where his host awaited him. After the initial greetings, Artois looked around and spotted Blaikie. He said to the Scot laughingly that he found him everywhere he went these days, then taking him by the arm, drew him aside and, Blaikie tell us, 'asks what I was doing. I told him it was I that was charged to distribute [lay out] and make the Park for his highness and that I hoped to make something very fine as not being contraried, so he told me in a laughing strain, '*Scavez vous que le Bougre est plus riche que moi? Ne menager pas'.* (You know the b ... is richer than me, don't you? Don't stint on the expense.) [28] Plans

25. Diary, undated entry 1786.
26. Detailed descriptions of the construction of each of the buildings is given in an inventory made by Fontaine the architect of Napoléon dated 17 April 1814 (AN., 02 344 piece IV).
27. A letter from Lord Dorset, the English ambassador to Carmarthen dated 26 February 1789 sets out the contract for the proposed marriage. See Oscar Browning, *Despatches from Paris, 1784–1790.*
28. Diary, undated entry. There is an interesting parallel in the case of the Chevalier St James the rich financier who commissioned Bélanger to build him a garden next door to Bagatelle which he wanted to be bigger and better than the Count's. Artois made almost the same comment to Bélanger. See chapter 12.

for the matrimonial alliance between the two houses were already so advanced that the officers of the new household had been chosen. Its abandonment was a humiliation for the Duke and his daughter. Blaikie attributed its failure to the Queen's hatred of Orléans but the exchange between Artois and Blaikie demonstrates that Artois, too, was to blame. The result, Blaikie tells us, of this debacle was that, 'the court made the Duke of Orléans their enemy, which after [he] went seldom to court'. This passage pinpoints the moment when relations between Orléans and the royal family went seriously wrong. As far as Blaikie is concerned, it shows how much in demand he had become in court circles. Also, his remark to Artois that he hoped to make something fine with out being contraried, suggests that he had resented the rein put upon him by Bélanger at Bagatelle and felt that he would succeed much better on his own, answering only to his employer.

In spite of the mockery of the court, where his ideas were more and more treated with derision, Orléans had decided that in his English park he would hunt in the English fashion[29] and Blaikie relates how, when the Duke returned from a visit to England, he 'brought over an English game keeper, one Hudson, and a great many fancy deer and at the same time a great many monkeys and birds of different sorts which were placed in the rock with a young man named Brooks to take care of them. He likewise brought over a pack of English hounds with a huntsman (Edward Rowley[30]), and in short Raincy was almost an English colony, as there was one Mr Farrer whom he placed as a sort of governor and to conduct the farm *a l'Anglaise'*. There were others as well, a groom called William Shavington whose wife was employed in the laundry, a saddler called John Walker and another man called Roper.[31] Of one of the few Frenchman among them, Blaikie writes that the Duke 'formed an English nursery under the conduct of one Gerard who had been sent to England by M. Barbançon[32] and had worked for some time with Gordon at Milend and pretended to be more an English man than any of the English'.[33]

Blaikie was asked to provide an English gardener and he approached his old friend Mr Hoy[34] but Hoy refused to leave his post with the Duke of Northumberland at Sion House. Mr Lee at Hammersmith eventually recommended someone, but this

---

29. Letting the deer run free throughout the park instead of the French way of confining them to the forest where they were chased and killed.

30. AN., 300 AP 1 317 gives his name. This part of diary is undated but probably covers events between 1786 and 1788.

31. AN., 300 AP 1 317.

32. Comte Duprat de Brabançon (1750–1797). Blaikie describes him as a 'pretended cultivateur' who obtained many seeds from America and formed a nursery on his country estate but who was 'no botanist' However, he was the Duke's head falconer so could not be contradicted even by Blaikie. Diary, undated entry *c.* 1785.

33. Gerard is possibly the French gardener described in Desmond, p. 248, as having come to London at the Revolution. He settled in Marylebone and became a relatively well-known London botanist. He died in 1840.

34. Thomas Hoy, head gardener at the Duke of Northumberland's estate at Syon, was a member of the first council of the Horticultural Society (later the Royal Horticultural Society). He died in 1822.

gardener, 'seemed rather dissatisfied but greedy of gain' and we do not hear how long he lasted. He was probably replaced by Alexander Howatson, one of the Scottish gardeners at Monceau, whom Blaikie describes as 'no great genius' but who kept the lawns at Raincy in 'tolerable order'.[35] Howatson had been born in Leadhills, in Scotland. Where he was trained is unknown. Williams, the ex-gardener of the Duc de Bouillon, was an English gardener who had started the nursery at Sèvres with Blaikie's help, and was working on his own by 1786. He went often to London, Blaikie tells us, and 'furnished several loads of trees' for Monceau and Raincy. Lee also provided plants for Monceau and Raincy.[36] Raincy was indeed an English colony.

The monkeys were intended for the *Rocher* and grotto which Pottier had built and which were modified by Blaikie. There was an aviary there as well for the birds. The monkeys were allowed to play on the rocks where, with the deer roaming the park, they were an attraction for visitors. Before long there were several English boats on the lake as well.[37] The park was taking shape fast but, in spite of the previous duke's actions to increase the flow of water into the estate, lack of water was still a problem. Wells were sunk without success and Flemish workers who had supposedly achieved miracles elsewhere were imported by the Duke who was always impressed by novel schemes. They had no luck either. Meanwhile, the search for water continued and eventually it was decided sometime in 1789 to drill a deep well at the top of the hill. Blaikie's part in this was to 'trace the new piece of water proposed by the new fire engine [*pompe à feu*]'. He goes on, 'This *pompe* was to be executed by M. Perier who was the first in this country and had made those at Monceau and that at Chaillot which brings the water to Paris likewise that at Bagatelle and another at M. St James'.

This is Blaikie's last reference to the building at Raincy except to say that the Duke pressed him to move to the estate after Artois' flight from France in July 1789, and wanted him to become governor there. Blaikie declined, saying with fatalism that he preferred to 'await the *evenement*'. In spite of the Duke's evident regard for him and their close association it seemed that Blaikie felt his true loyalty lay with the royal family.

In late December 1789 he and M. Amelot,[38] his partner in the venture, followed Orléans to London to arrange payment and get instructions for the continuation of the works at Monceau and Raincy. While he was in London, Blaikie signed surety for the debt of several hundred pounds which Orléans still owed the nurseryman, Lee. The money was never paid and the firm of Kennedy and Lee pursued Blaikie for payment for some time after 1815.[39] In 1792 the duke gave up his estates to satisfy

---

35. AN., 300 AP I 317 describes 'Hownstson' as *jardinier en chef* with a salary of 1732 livres in April 1788. AN., 300 AP I 2110 gives 'Howatson' as head gardener in 1788 at a salary of 2,300 livres.
36. The Duke owed Lee £710 in 1790. Blaikie Papers.
37. In the diary (undated entry) Blaikie recounts how 'the Duke had from England several boats or scullers to row upon this lake, with a small sloop. All of which made a very agreeable prospect for several parts of the park'.
38. AN., 300 AP I 317 contains all his accounts.
39. Blaikie's papers contain a number of letters asking for him to honour this payment.

his creditors amongst whom Blaikie is listed[40] and this and other misfortunes left Blaikie penniless.

Contemporary impressions of Raincy just before the Revolution are few. Helen Maria Williams, an English visitor with Revolutionary sympathies, who saw the park in 1790 had nothing but praise for the Duke. She tells us that, 'while the French princes are employing their revenue in training soldiers [referring to the activities of Artois who had fled abroad in 1789] Monsieur d'Orléans is spending a considerable part of his revenue in paying workmen who are making improvements at Raincy'. In her observations on the park, she writes, 'The grounds are laid out in the English taste, are very beautiful and of considerable extent'.[41]

An English nobleman, Henry Temple (2nd Viscount Palmerston), father of the statesman Lord Palmerston, has left a brief and more critical description of Raincy as he saw it, only a year later. He relates in his diary, 'Sat Aug. 21st Dined at Raincy, a seat of the Duke of Orléans about 9 mls from Paris. It is on the whole a fine place, the house is very good with handsome stables and various offices. It is situated at some distance from the road with an avenue of large poplars. There is a forest adjoining to it and an extensive pleasure ground about it, of which a large part is laid out in the English taste. This is the worst part as all the trees are young and do not thrive, the water trifling, and the grass of which there is too much, in such bad order by the heat of the summer, the badness of the soil and the want of rolling and mowing, that it looks like a very rough poor field.'[42] The soil was a mixture of sticky clay and chalk[43] and the problem of inadequate water had obviously gone unsolved.

The duke, who was in dire financial and political straits, had other things on his mind than his gardens when Palmerston made his visit to the newly planted part of the park. Egalité had hunted there in 1791 but as a Deputy at the Convention he was absent all the following year.[44] At Monceau, where Blaikie's alterations had become established, Palmerston's opinion was more favourable, 'Sun. Aug 28 Went to see the Duke of Orléans' house and gardens on the skirts of Paris, called Monceaux, which is well worth the trouble. The house is not good but has many rooms, is fitted up with expense and in a very whimsical manner, and is well adapted to parties and entertainments. The gardens are extremely pretty, in the English taste with much variety and a great number of buildings some of which are in very good taste.'[45]

In 1793 on the execution of the Duke, Raincy was confiscated. Like the Royal

---

40. AN., 300 AP I 24 – 9 January 1792, Concordat between Orléans and Thomas Blaikie 'entre-preneur des jardins'. Blaikie's name also appears in the list of those who were to receive an annuity from Orléans, but very soon the duke went bankrupt and the annuity was not paid. Blaikie then joined the list of creditors of the duke.

41. H. M. Williams, *Letters written in France in the summer of 1790 to a friend in England*, vol. 2, p. 88.

42. Oscar Browning, *Despatches of Lord Gower containing the Paris diary of Henry Temple, second Viscount Palmerston* (1739–1802) for the period 6 July to 31 August 1791, p. 305.

43. AN., 300 AP I 308.

44. G. Poisson, *Evocation du Grand Paris; La Banlieue Nord-Ouest* (Paris, 1961), p. 328.

45. Oscar Browning, *Despatches of Lord Gower*.

domains it was destined either as a place of entertainment for the people or a rural establishment for the development of agriculture. The menagerie and farm animals were sold and then bought back, the park was invaded by the people, the château vandalised, then the property was leased and finally owned by the financier Gabriel Ouvrard who held fetes for the notables of the Directorate. He invited his government friends to use the dwellings in the park as little country retreats.

In 1802, in the short spell of peace before England and France went to war again, an English visitor, Henry Redhead Yorke, joined the Sunday crowds who escaped from Paris to stroll in the park and eat in the restaurants there just as Londoners did at Richmond or at Hampton Court. In one of his letters, he wrote that Raincy 'resembles an English gentleman's park', but he pointed out the depredations it had suffered in the Revolution. 'The château had been demolished,' he tells us, 'and the massy pillars lay broken and dispersed upon the ground.' Many of the statues had already been plundered but he found that the stables were in 'a tolerably good state of preservation' as were the gravel walks, the aqueducts and the lakes in the *jardin anglais*. He was agreeably surprised that the trees and copses had not been cut down. The 'magnificent' dairy was untouched and he also talks of wandering in a labyrinth.

Yorke also visited the Vacherie (the Swiss cow house), which he called 'a pretty cottage'. The English occupant was standing in the doorway and invited his fellow countrymen to rest in his house. It was Hudson, the gamekeeper, who had survived the upheavals of the Revolution. During their conversation, which gave the visitor time to note the neatness and comfort of the interior, Hudson said that he had been imprisoned in the Conciergerie during the Terror and had only just escaped execution.[46] He enquired about the Orléans family, asking whether they were in England, and talked in a fond way of Orléans' son, the young Comte de Beaujolais, whom he had taught to ride. This was in keeping with the tones of 'deep regret' with which, Yorke noted, the poor people on the estate spoke of the Duke. Of all his description, the following would have appealed most to Blaikie. 'From every elevated scite [sic] in these grounds there are beautiful champain prospects, some confined and others ranging over a vast tract of countryside but all agreeably diversified.' This creating of perspectives was what Blaikie had set himself to do and what he regarded as his most useful contribution to French gardens.

Yorke's comment was confirmed by a description of the mature park of Raincy around 1808 when the château had been rebuilt in a different style. The author praises the park as 'this beautiful place ... the first English park in France and the one which most perfectly resembles them'. He agrees that the trees are not fine in themselves but commends 'the art with which they have been laid out' which makes the whole aspect of the park 'most agreeable'.[47]

During the Napoleonic era, Raincy was occupied for a time by General Junot, the military governor of Paris and his wife Laura; then it became the property of Pauline Bonaparte, Napoleon's sister. In April 1812 Napoleon himself was the proprietor and

---

46. No doubt an effort to impress. Other sources give the place of his imprisonment as Ecouen.
47. De Laborde *Description des nouveaux jardins en France*, p. 136.

his architect, Fontaine was commissioned to draw up a detailed report on the state of the Estate. It is preserved at the French National Archives and describes in detail each of Le Raincy's many buildings noting their state of disrepair.[48]

In 1814 when the Comte d'Artois returned to France at the defeat of Napoleon, Raincy was prepared by the authorities to receive him. He declined to use it and it was occupied and sacked by Prussian and Russian troops.[49] At the Restoration, the estate was returned to the Orléans family. Louis Philippe, Philippe Egalité's son, converted the *Maisons russes* into accommodation for himself, as the château, rebuilt on a less grand scale after the Revolution, was now too dilapidated to be lived in without a great deal of expenditure. After the 1848 Revolution, the park was again devastated. An inventory of the state of the park taken in 1848, no doubt in preparation for its sale by the State, reveals that in the *jardin anglais* there were still a considerable number of fine trees of different species both foreign and indigenous, giving a picturesque effect. Amongst them are listed fine oaks, pines, firs and evergreen trees, limes and poplars.[50]

No single buyer could be found for Le Raincy; instead, it was divided into 23 lots and sold in 1852 to developers who divided it further. A number of the existing buildings were adapted and altered but the layout of some of the roads and pathways of the estate were preserved. The arrival of the railways transformed the little village. In 1858 the barn of the old farm became the village church. and Le Raincy, now a commune, prospered and changed. But even today one may still walk along streets whose names reveal their situation in the old park; the Allée du Rocher or the Allée de l'Hermitage bordered by nineteenth-century houses set in leafy gardens whose trees may even be seedlings from Blaikie's *jardin anglais*. What remains of the lake, now no more than a pond, can be seen in the grounds of the lycée. The town of Le Raincy still harbours the vestiges of the eighteenth-century park in which it has its roots.

48. AN., O2 344. Many of the buildings are illustrated in Bougon and Gaulard, *op. cit.*

49. G. Poisson, *Evocation du Grand Paris; La Banlieue Nord-Ouest* (Paris, 1960), p. 332.

50. AN., 300 AP I 308.

CHAPTER 12

The Years of Success

THE POPULARITY of Bagatelle and the unabating enthusiasm for English gardens together with the patronage of both Artois and Chartres assured Blaikie a highly successful career from 1781 until the spring of 1792.

His clients, like those of Bélanger, with whom he occasionally collaborated, were fashionable, rich and famous; members of the court, farmers-general, wealthy government officials, and the actresses and demi-mondains on the edge of these inter-related worlds. Many were in favour of political reform while others, like Artois and his coterie were die-hard conservatives.

Town houses and country retreats
(Courtesans, blue-stockings and great ladies)

His first private garden in Paris was one he made during his early days at Bagatelle for the singer, Sophie Arnould. Sophie had rented a house near the *pompe publique* in the *Chaussée d'Antin*, a newly fashionable development in what had been countryside to the north of the Boulevard de la Madeleine[1] but was parcelled up in the early 70s and sold by speculators for building. Nearby, Ledoux[2] had designed a neo-classical villa, a small masterpiece, for Mademoiselle Guimard, principal *danseuse* at the Opéra. A sculptural group in the niche above the entrance represented the crowning of Terpsichore, the muse of dancing, and the building became known as the temple of Terpsichore.[3] It was the talk of Paris and the jealous Sophie asked Bélanger to draw up plans for her, on a site next door to La Guimard's. But, at the age of thirty-nine, with her career finished,[4] she was no longer in the same financial league as la Guimard and the plans were never carried out. Sophie had to content herself with her existing, simpler house, renovated under Bélanger's supervision, with a garden laid out by Blaikie who describes in his diary how he made a plan for her garden in December 1779. Then, in a lull in the activities at Bagatelle the following February, he returned to lay it out.

It was through Bélanger that he met his next client in April 1780 when, on Bélanger's orders, he delivered some trees from Bagatelle, to Anne Catherine de Ligneville (1719–1800), the widow of the philosopher Helvétius,[5] who had been living in retirement in a

---

1. Rodolphe Trouilleux, *N'oubliez pas Iphigénie*, p. 160.
2. Claude Nicolas Ledoux (1735–1806). See p. 188, n. 26.
3. Allan Braham (1986 edn), pp. 173–6. There is a painting of Mlle Guimard as Terpsichore by Fragonard in the Louvre. In financial difficulties on the bankruptcy of her lover, the Prince de Guéménée, she sold her house by raffle ticket in 1786.
4. Sophie's voice, always fragile was no longer able to cope with major roles.
5. Claude Adrien Helvétius (1715–1771), financier, *fermier general*. Retired from public life to devote himself to philosophy.

small house at Auteuil since shortly after the death of her husband in 1771. This little hamlet adjoining Passy was the chosen retreat of painters and writers and Mme Helvétius had purchased her house from the painter, De La Tour. Passy itself was at that time a picturesque village of vineyards and green terraces sloping down to the Seine.

The members of the famous Nine Sisters Masonic Lodge, founded at the suggestion of her husband, often gathered at her house, number 24 La Grande Rue (the site of 59 rue d'Autueil today). Diderot and the Encyclopedists frequented her salon. Turgot[6] and Benjamin Franklin, the American representative at the French court between 1776 and 1785, vied unsuccessfully for her affections. Foreign visitors of note called on her, Garrick amongst them. Only women were not welcome.[7] Napoleon, recognising her influence on the intellectual world, called on her during the Consulate. The visit was not a success. He remarked on the smallness of her garden and she told him that if he had any idea of the contentment to be found in two acres he would not have attempted his conquests. Franklin who first met her in 1777 when he was 69 and she was 56, christened her 'Notre Dame d'Auteuil' because of the way she used her fortune to succour the poor. Her fresh complexion, fine blue eyes and magnificent blonde hair had brought her many admirers in the past and she still possessed the remnants of great beauty. Franklin proposed marriage to her but she refused his offer,[8] preferring her independence and the company of her 18 cats, and her numerous ducks and hens. Blaikie also fell under her spell. He returned the day after his first visit to suggest changes to her garden and while he was carrying them out, he met Franklin there and stayed to dine with this 'very plain man'. Madame Helvétius, pleased by the improvements he had made, presented Blaikie with two priceless volumes of botanical drawings, a present from the king to her husband. What happened to her gift is not known.[9]

Blaikie was to have one more famous female client at Auteuil, the Comtesse de Bouffleurs[10] for whom he worked in 1785. She lived opposite Madame Helvétius in a much larger garden of 25 acres.[11] The Comtesse, who had visited England in 1763, was one of the earliest to possess a *jardin anglais*, 'begotten on her,' according to Horace Walpole, 'by an English gardener'. Blaikie tells us the gardener's name was

---

6. Anne Robert Jacques Turgot (1715–1781), Baron de l'Aune. *Contrôleur Général de Finances*, August 1774. He was dismissed in 1776 when he divulged his plans to abolish pensions and other useless offices. For his relationship with Mme de Helvetius see Bernard Fay, *Franklin the Apostle of Modern Times* (USA, 1929).

7. Guy de la Prade, *L'Illustre société d'Auteuil 1772–1830; ou la fascination de la liberté* (Paris, 1990).

8. A. Guillois, *Le Salon de Mme Helvétius* (Paris, 1894).

9. The only valuable botanical book listed amongst Blaikie's possessions appears to be Jacob Cornuti, *Canadensis Plantarum aliarumque nondum editarum Historia* (Paris, 1636).

10. Marie-Charlotte-Hippolyte de Campet de Saujon (1725–1800) married Edouard, marquis, later Comte de Bouffleurs-Rouverel, in February 1746. Their son was born in December of the same year but the couple separated and the Countess became the mistress of the Prince de Conti.

11. Walpole erred when he described her garden as double this size. See A Guillois, 'Les Bouffleurs à Auteuil', in *Bulletin de la Société Historique d'Auteuil et de Passy*, no. 1 (1892), pp. 238–47.

Prescott,[12] the man who had laid out St Leu. Nothing is known of this Englishman except that the garden he made for Mme de Bouffleurs was considered the most authentically English garden in France.[13] Highly frivolous and vain, Mme de Bouffleurs was also charming and intelligent and had a large circle of friends. She conducted a long and indiscreet relationship with the Prince de Conti and was devastated when, on the death of his wife, he would not marry her. Her salon was an intellectual one frequented by Rousseau and the Scottish philosopher, David Hume. Rousseau quarrelled with Hume and broke off relations with him but she managed to remain friends with both of them.[14]

Horace Walpole came to visit her and, although he admired the wonderful views from the terrace, her garden did not escape his sharp tongue. He decided that it lacked nothing but 'greenery and water'.[15] Others describe the vast lawn in front of her house as magnificent.[16] Towards the Bois de Boulogne which bounded her property lay a wilder, natural garden with winding paths and flowering shrubs and trees, ending in a little copse of scented 'exotics'. In 1783 she had sought permission from the king to take in a small portion of the Bois [17] and in 1785 she asked Blaikie to suggest some improvements. He found her garden 'tolerably well made' but the changes he effected pleased her so much she sent him a 'silver plate and soup dish' as a present.

On the outskirts of Auteuil, Blaikie designed a garden and a hothouse of 'considerable size' for the financier, Micault d'Harveley, friend of the Finance Minister, Calonne [18] and brother-in-law of the banker, De Laborde. This commission highlights the main problem posed by clients generally, namely the client's desire for a complete transformation of the garden via a few minor changes. In the Harveleys' case, 'there was a straight avenue of limes, this they would not change although they wanted a crooked walk in this straight which', he added ironically, 'was rather difficult'.[19]

12. Diary entry for 1785. See H. Walpole, *Letters*, ed. Paget Toynbee (1935), vol. 5 (1760–64). Letter to Rev. William Mason, 6 September 1775, p. 243.
13. Grouchy and Cottin, vol. 4, p. 258, le 28 mai 1782. Also de Ligne, *Coup d'oeil sur Beloeil*, ed. E. de Ganay (Paris, 1922), p. 177.
14. Five days before his death on 25 August 1776, Hume sent her a note commiserating with her on the death of Conti and ending with the words, 'I salute you with great affection and regard for the last time'. Quoted in Peter Jones 'David Hume' in Daiches, Jones and Jones, *The Scottish Enlightenment 1730–1790. A Hotbed of Genius* (University of Edinburgh, 1986; 1996 edn), p. 49.
15. Walpole to William Mason 10 September 1775. For another English view see Sidney Charles Herbert 16th Earl of Pembroke, *Pembroke Papers*, 19 May 1780, 'On Tuesday I dined with Madame Bouflers & after dinner she carried me to Auteuil, her villa truly in the English Gusto & very pretty and well understood'.
16. Thiery, p. 20.
17. AN., O1 1581.
18. Charles Alexandre de Calonne (1734–1802). Appointed Controller-General of Finance in 1783. Responsible for calling the Assembly of Notables in February 1787 with the intention of using them as a rubber stamp for a new single tax on all goods. His enemies accused him of profiteering and double dealing. He was dismissed in disgrace in April 1787 and departed for England.
19. Diary, undated entry 1786.

Blaikie's solution was to convince his clients with one alteration at a time and so 'bring them on by degrees'. In the discussions, it was generally the wife who had to be convinced, as was the case here. Archibald Macmaster, Blaikie's old friend and protégé had recently returned to Paris from Chanteloup on the death of his employer, the Comte de Choiseul,[20] and Blaikie offered him to the Harveleys, to plant the garden and supervise the work. They took him on as *jardinier anglais* at a yearly salary of 2400 livres. Williams, the English nurseryman from Sèvres, provided several loads of trees. Blaikie worked fast with a large team of 40 men 'which,' he wrote, 'soon made an appearance and seemed much to please the *propriétaires*'. This ability to show quick results is evident from a contemporary account of the Harveleys' house at Auteuil dated 5 July 1786 which describes it as having vast *jardins à la française* when they bought it but that very soon, as if by magic, they had changed these into an English garden, a perfect example of the type.[21] Harveley whom Blaikie describes as a plain man and 'garde de la Tresorie' (*garde du trésor royal*), did not have long to enjoy his English garden. He died during 1786 and his wife followed the disgraced Calonne to England, where they married in the Catholic chapel, Corn Street, Bath on 2 June 1788.[22] The ex-minister put their joint wealth at the disposal of the emigré royal princes. As neither Artois nor the future Louis XVIII could honour their debts, the princes' creditors turned on Calonne and ruined him. His health broken, he returned to France in 1802 and died shortly after.

Most of Blaikie's clients had no real interest in plants but Comte Charles Hector D'Estaing,[23] as Blaikie confides in his diary, 'delights in his gardens'. Estaing's choice of an 'English' gardener confirms that gardening transcends national prejudice since the Count was a sworn enemy of Albion. Vice-admiral of the French fleet, he had harried the English both at sea off the Indian coast and during the American War of Independence, in which the French navy had been such a decisive factor. Estaing was also a poet and playwright. The description of Alcinus's orchard in the *Odyssey* probably inspired his wish that every tree in the garden of his country retreat[24] should be a

---

20. Etienne François de Choiseul (1719–1785). The favoured minister of Mme de Pompadour and Louis XV, he became an object of hatred to Mme Du Barry. After a campaign against him she succeeded in having him dismissed in 1770 whereupon he retired to his property of Chanteloup. He died in May 1785.

21. Marquis de Bombelles, *Journal*, 3 vols (Paris, 1977), vol. II, p. 151. The site of the garden is 11 bis rue d'Auteuil (Lycée J. B. Say).

22. I am grateful to Father M. Davies, parish priest of St John's Church, Bath for confirmation of their marriage.

23. Charles Hector, Comte d'Estaing (1729–1794).

24. Unless d'Estaing owned two country retreats on the outskirts of Paris, there are conflicting accounts as to its locality. Batcave, 'Le Seizième arrondissement' *Société Historique d'Auteuil et Passy* SHAP XIV, No. 4 (pp. 7–14), gives it as no 70 rue de Passy (today rue Guichard). Blaikie also tells us it was in Passy (Diary, undated entry *c.* 1786), but M Calmon-Maison, *L'Amiral D'Estaing (1729–1794)* (Paris, 1910), p. 411, writes that Estaing had rented a house in the Roule (Champs Elysées) called Les Chaumières, whose vast garden stretched to the edge of Monceau and was planted with three hundred fruit trees.

fruit tree.[25] He asked Blaikie's advice on the varieties to choose and by 1792, he had over three hundred trees growing there. However, like Harvelay, his pleasure in his garden was also short-lived. He was sent to the guillotine on 18 August 1794.

The charming Duchesse de Rohan-Chabot[26] wound the susceptible Blaikie round her little finger. She told Blaikie she had already consulted Gabriel Thouin (brother of Blaikie's friend, André Thouin)[27] over her small country house garden at St Mandé, a village adjoining the woods of Vincennes to the east of Paris. But he 'could give her no ideas of beauty or simplicity'. Blaikie, already laden with commissions, rose to the challenge and allowed himself to be persuaded to complete her garden in three months using one of her servants as his clerk of works. She and the Duke showered him with compliments on the success of their garden and asked him to find them a gardener, preferably a Catholic. Blaikie's patronage apparently extended to German as well as English and Scottish gardeners and he offered them a young German Protestant instead, who stayed with them till they left for Nice at the Revolution. She took Blaikie to advise her cousin,[28] the Spanish ambassador, on altering the garden at his hotel in the *rue de L'Université*, but he was another of those clients who 'wished to change the whole without changing any thing'. Blaikie wasted no time on the ambassador but in good humour from the Duchess's praises, parted amicably from him assuring him that he 'found his garden well' and advising him to change nothing.

There were other commissions like the one at St Cyr for the Princesse d'Hénin,[29] wife of the Captain of Artois' Guards, but no traces remain and few descriptions survive of these small, ephemeral gardens. However, through extracts from the letters of its owner, the Marquise de Coislin[30] and her friend, the garden authority, the Duc d'Harcourt,[31] we are afforded a glimpse of Blaikie at work in one of them.

'*Blaquey est insaissisable*' (It is impossible to get hold of Blaikie), complained the

---

25. *The Odyssey*, bk VII. See A Bartlett Giamatti, *The Earthly Paradise and the Renaissance Epic* (Princeton, 1966).

26. Born Rosalie de Chatillon, wife of the 5th Duc de Rohan, Louis Bretagne de Rohan Chabot. She and her husband died at Nice at the beginning of the Revolution. I am grateful to the Duc de Rohan for this information and that concerning the Spanish ambassador. See note below.

27. J. C. Loudon described Gabriel Thouin, author of *Plans Raisonnés de Toutes les Espèces de Jardins* (Paris, 1819), and Blaikie as the foremost landscape gardeners in France in the 1820s. *Encyclopaedia of Gardening* (1830 edn), p. 42.

28. Actually her husband's nephew, the Comte de Fernan-Nunez, whose house was the Hotel de Soyecourt, 50 rue de l'Université.

29. Adelaide-Félicité Henriette Guinot de Monconseil (1750–1825). Married Prince d'Hénin in 1765.

30. Marie-Anne-Louise de Mailly (d. 1817) married 1775 Charles-Georges-René du Chambout, Marquis de Coislin. Tall, beautiful, 'incomparable freshness', witty, good figure. See Fleury, *Louis XV intime et les petites maitresses* (Paris, 1899), p. 145.

31. E. de Ganay, *Les Jardins à l'anglaise en France au XVIIIeme siècle* (unpublished manuscript deposited at the Bibliothèque des Arts Décoratifs). Stern vol. I, p. 149. This correspondence does not seem to have survived the Second World War.

Marquise to the Duc d'Harcourt in July 1782.[32] She added that he was so busy that he did not even reply to letters. Her house and garden on the *butte de Chatillon*,[33] commanded a superb view. It overlooked the bridge across the Seine at Sèvres on the road to Versailles and from here the vista extended across the river to the abbey of Longchamps and took in the distant towers, spires and domes of Paris as far as Montmartre. To the left in the verdant countryside, stood the château of St Cloud, and beyond were the slopes of Mont Valérian and the vineyards of Suresnes. Above here, the aptly named château of Bellevue dominated the slope. Owned by Louis XVI's spinster aunts, Madame Adelaide and Madame Victoire, it had been built in 1748 for Madame de Pompadour whom the young Marquise de Coislin had briefly challenged for Louis XV's affections. However, by 1778, the Marquise's thoughts had turned to gardening and we find her writing to the *Pépinières du Roi* (King's nurseries), requesting 50 Italian poplars and the same number of plane trees.[34] The project for her garden was an absurdly costly one, partly because, as Blaikie put it, her ideas were 'unsettled and changing'. He was particularly scathing about the erection of what he describes as a costly 'bridge' designed by an architect he calls 'Tripesall'[35] to divert the eye from the rooftops of the houses below.

As well as the Duc d'Harcourt, Mme de Coislin consulted the Marquis de Girardin, the owner of Ermenonville, and other luminaries like Hubert Robert, the landscape painter of romantic ruins, who is credited with the design of the courtyard. As a result she was often torn by conflicting advice. Harcourt recommended his own architect to her but, in the end, after some expensive building and roadwork by Trepsat she called on Bélanger, '*le grand faiseur*' a sure way of guaranteeing even higher expenditure. Blaikie was appointed to conduct the landscaping while André Thouin supplied many of the plants and set up a nursery on the site to grow plants for the garden. She watched with trepidation as Blaikie's workmen showed such a facility for building mountains that she feared they would ruin her, and the Scot's plan to create gentle grassy slopes instead of terraces sent her scurrying to various 'artists' for advice. In

32. François Henri d'Harcourt, 5th Duke of Harcourt (1726–1802). Distinguished himself as a soldier, becoming *Maréchal de camp* in 1758 and *Lieut. géneral* in 1762. Replaced his father as governor of Normandy on the latter's death in 1783. Louis XVI entrusted the education of the dauphin to him till the death of the child. He was a member of the *Académie française* and famed as an authority on gardens. *His Traité de la décoration des dehors des jardins et parcs* written *c*. 1774 was published in Paris, 1919 (ed. E. de Ganay). During the Terror escaped to England and was well received at Court, becoming the most respected of the émigrés. He died at Staines, Middlesex in 1802.

33. Also called the *Butte de Belleville*. In the nineteenth century it was known as Brimborion after a pavilion, belonging to the estate of Bellevue nearby.

34. AN O1 2111.

35. J. Barrier and M. Mosser, p. 219, identify the architect as Guillaume Trepsat, pupil of Blondel. Director of Les Invalides during the Consulate and later architect to Napoleon during the Empire. The 'bridge' was in imitation of Ledoux's gateway to the Hotel de Thélusson, a monumental Doric triumphal arch built to set off the view of the house. See Braham, pp. 186–9. For further details of Trepsat (1740–1813) see Michel Gallet, *Architectes parisiens du XVIIIe siècle. Dictionnaire biographique et critique* (Paris, 1995).

the end, reluctantly, she gave Blaikie his head and was well pleased with the results.[36] Enthroned on her 'butte', she held court there until the Revolution forced her to flee to Rouen disguised as a servant. Surprisingly, she managed to sustain this role undetected throughout the Terror. Bellevue was sacked and so, probably, was her house [37] but the marquise eventually returned. After her death in 1817 the property changed hands several times until ceded by its last owner, the Comte de Saint-Cène, to a government body, the *Caisse des depots et consignations*. Since then those who cared about the site have struggled to preserve it from various types of development. Its current owner is the commune of Sèvres.[38]

Grands châteaux

Guiscard

The first important garden in which Blaikie worked, apart from those belonging to Artois and Chartres, was one he had visited with the Comte de Lauraguais in April 1779 during a stay at Manicamp. Guiscard, some 14 kilometres from Manicamp and ten from Noyon, belonged to the Duc d'Aumont.[39] Its park extended to over 1000 arpents (1100 acres) and had been designed by the landscape architect, Morel,[40] for whom Blaikie had the greatest admiration. However, he did find one or two imperfections: 'where there was formerly a quincunx of limes they have left them too regular and the head of the river is not hid enough'. Lauraguais and Blaikie stayed three days with the Duke and Blaikie returned in 1780 to carry out alterations to the gardens, presumably to remedy the imperfections he had noted.[41] The Duc d'Aumont was an eccentric man. Blaikie describes him as 'curious' in the eighteenth-century sense, meaning interested in the sciences. He survived the Revolution without imprisonment but lost Guiscard. The park, previously considered too English, came into its own in the Empire when the fashion for large sweeping park lands at last became

36. De Ganay, *Manuscrit inédit*.

37. It came to be known as Brimborion. See *Commission du vieux Paris*, Procès verbale, 1929, 'Domaine de la butte Coislin', p. 5, letter dated 23.1.29 from André Morizet. Contains a plea that the site be classified. This was done in 1934.

38. For varying accounts of the previous owners of the property and the date of Mme Coislin's purchase, see *Bulletin de la Soc. des amis de Meudon*, no. 82 (July/September 1958); *Le Figaro*, 18 May 1965; *Le Monde*, 26 May 1965; *Toutes le Nouvelles de Versailles*, 28 December 1964 and 14 July 1965; *Sèvres: Sites et Monuments*, no. 114 (3e Trimestre 1986). I am grateful to Madame Marianne de Meyenbourg, Librarian, the Musée de l'Ile de France for drawing my attention to these publications.

39. Louis Marie Augustin Duc d'Aumont (1709–1782). After a successful military career became governor of the port of Boulogne. In favour at the court of Louis XV he became Premier gentilhomme de la Chambre. He was also responsible for the department of *Menus Plaisirs*. His interests were architecture, furniture and precious stones. Unpopular, even hated by the artists employed by him.

40. See chapter 7.

41. J. C. Loudon, *Encyclopaedia of Gardening* (1835 edn).

admired in France.[42] It was bought, in 1822 by Baron Émile Oberkampf, the son of one of Blaikie's later clients.

Gennevilliers

The Comte de Vaudreuil,[43] Grand Falconer of France, was a key figures in the close circle of courtiers surrounding the queen and Artois. In 1783 he invited Blaikie to make some changes at Gennevilliers and much to Blaikie's gratification, came to Bagatelle in the Queen's coach with six horses to collect him.[44] At Gennevilliers, he found Mme Elisabeth Vigée-Le Brun, esteemed, Blaikie tells us, 'as one of the first painters in France' and 'the Mistress of the Comte de Vaudreuil'. Blaikie was delighted to explain to 'so knowing a person' his ideas for the garden. No doubt he was also taken by her looks. A number of narcissistic self portraits bear witness to her beauty as a young woman. The most famous shows her in her youth with flowing unpowdered curls, wearing a white muslin dress and a flower-decked, straw hat.[45] In her memoirs, she describes Vaudreuil as 'one of the most amiable of men' who 'added to his refined gallantry a politeness that was the more flattering since it came from the heart'.[46] Very critical of the work of the architect Labrière [47] who had already laid out the garden, she listened approvingly as Blaikie described the changes that he would make. Any criticism of an architect was manna to the Scot who constantly complains of their arrogance and he praises her in his diary as possessing 'a great taste' and 'one of the first painters in France'. Together, Blaikie tells us they, 'examined the gardens explaining all the different landscapes which I showed might be done'. What he proposed involved a minimum of alteration, 'the whole consisted only in changing the walks and making them pass through the different places where the *vues* are most agreeable and to cut out a few trees so that those *vues* might appear'.[48] He agreed to do the work within a fortnight and, as Mme Le Brun had endorsed his ideas, the count was pleased.

Blaikie had already seen the garden before his visit there with the count. It was a hunting estate and Vaudreuil acquired it in 1783 to please the Comte d'Artois by giving

---

42. Laborde, *Description des nouveaux jardins* (Paris, 1808).
43. Joseph Hyacinthe François Paul de Rigaud, Comte de Vaudreuil (1740–1817) owed his immense fortune to his estates in the Caribbean and his position at court to his mistress, Yolande, Duchesse de Polignac who obtained lucrative posts for him at Versailles. He amassed a large collection of paintings and furniture, and was Mme Vigée-Le Brun's most important patron in the years leading up to the Revolution, finding positions for her family at court. He left Paris speedily with Artois and the Duchess after the storming of the Bastille and remained with the prince in exile until 1801. On his return to France, he was appointed to the *Chambre des Pairs* and became governor of the Tuileries. For an estimation of her portrait of him, see Joseph Baillio, *Elisabeth Louise Vigée LeBrun 1755–1842*. Exhibition catalogue (Fort Worth, 1982).
44. Diary, undated entry 1783/84.
45. National Gallery, London.
46. *Memoirs of Madame Vigée Lebrun*, trans. Lionel Strachey (New York, 1903), pp. 47, 49.
47. Alexandre-Louis Labrière (fl. 1770s), Vaudreuil's architect.
48. Diary, 1783/84.

him yet another venue for the hunt. Seventeen years older than Artois, he was the prince's closest friend, and his mentor, advising him on his collections of furniture and paintings. Although Blaikie's visit took place in 1783 his contact with the garden was to continue until the Revolution. In 1787 Chartres, now the Duke of Orléans, bought it from Vaudreuil, and Blaikie, as superintendent of Orléans' gardens, took on responsibility for it.

The name of Gennevilliers came to be associated with the Impressionist painters, particularly Manet and Caillebotte who painted there at a time when the commune of the same name was a centre for pleasure parties on the river. The château has also one other unlikely claim on our interest as a cradle of the Revolution. It was here, on 23 September 1783, that the first performance of Beaumarchais' play, *The Marriage of Figaro* took place. Louis XVI had banned any showing of the play but relented, on the pleas of his brother, to its presentation as part of an evening of festivities at the château. So it happened that the courtiers applauded while the servant Figaro berated them for having done nothing to merit the rank and fortunes they had inherited. For the first time, the revolutionary idea was promulgated that an aristocrat was no better than his servant for he had done nothing to merit his wealth.

After the proscription of Orléans, Gennevilliers was confiscated and its decline commenced. In 1914 the château, the orangerie and a number of garden features, such as a belvedere with a maze and underground passages and a few little bridges, survived in a dilapidated state.[49] By the end of the First World War, most of the garden features had disappeared. The château became a school, and housing replaced the gardens. Today Gennevilliers is a heavily industrialised port for Paris.

Liancourt

Another great aristocrat who came himself to conduct Blaikie to his garden was the Duc de la Rochefoucauld-Liancourt.[50] Sometime in 1784 he asked the gardener to design a *jardin anglais* for him at his château about 38 miles from Paris where he had already built an English farm managed by an English farmer and had started a nursery for plants.

Rochefoucauld-Liancourt was a liberal in politics, a philanthropist on his estates and keenly interested in agricultural reform.[51] He had set up a cotton factory and a school where the young girls of the area were taught reading and writing as well as the skills of spinning and weaving. Orphan boys were educated for a career in the army in a military school which he built and maintained. Arthur Young, the English agriculturalist and writer, who was his guest for several weeks in 1787, would have preferred that the boys learnt improved methods of agriculture instead, but, generally, he was full of praise for the Duke and his ideas.

49. 'Communication relative au château de Gennevilliers (Seine)', *Procès verbaux de la Commission du Vieux Paris* (Paris, 1914–15), pp. 72–3.
50. François, Duc de la Rochefoucault-Liancourt (1747–1827).
51. He was a friend of Arthur Young, the English agriculturalist, author of many works and articles on agricultural matters. Young describes Liancourt in *Travels in France during the Years 1787, 1788, 1789*, ed. M. Bethan-Edwards (1913), pp. 82–4.

Blaikie spent three days at Liancourt tracing out an area at a little distance from the magnificent formal gardens. He was happy with the site although at first appearance it was not promising, 'the part of the garden the Duke wants made is all along the side of a hill where it is full of bushes and unequal grounds,' but it had one great advantage as far as the Scot was concerned, 'the hand of regular art has not destroyed it'. He continues, 'here I traced the walks and marked the best objects for *vues* and left the rest to be executed afterwards by the Duke's people as he seems not inclined to make great expenses'.[52]

From Arthur Young we learn how the new area of garden looked in 1787. 'At about half a mile from the château is a range of hill [sic] that was chiefly a neglected waste: the duke of Liancourt has lately converted this into a plantation, with winding walks, benches, and covered seats, in the English style of gardening. The situation is very fortunate. These ornamental paths follow the edge of the declivity to the extent of three or four miles. The views they command are every where pleasing, and in some places great'.[53] Young's account, although it gives the duke himself the credit for the garden, confirms Blaikie's own claim that his outstanding skill was his ability to recognise the natural advantages of a piece of ground and to make the most of any external or internal views. As was often the case with owners, the duke preferred to let his visitor think that he had designed the garden himself, since there is no mention of Blaikie. In spite of his support for reform of the Constitution, and his good works, the duke felt it wise to emigrate in 1793. He was able to return to France during the Consulate and lived quietly on his estate until his death in 1827.

Mauperthuis

In 1789, Young visited Mauperthuis in Brie (Seine et Marne), which he described as 'an extensive English garden, made by the Count d'Artois' gardener'.[54] Mauperthuis belonged to Anne-Pierre Fezenac, Marquis de Montesquiou (1741–1798), Gentleman in Waiting to the Royal Children and *Premier Equyer* to the Comte de Provence (Artois' older brother and later Louis XVIII). He was also a soldier and commanded the *Armée du Midi* in 1793. An order was made for his arrest after his failure to capture Geneva and he emigrated for a while but returned to France at the early date of 1795 once the Terror was over.

Mauperthuis was one of the most original of the late eighteenth-century gardens. Its château, destroyed at the Revolution, had been built by the architect Ledoux (1736–1806). Completed sometime around 1767, it was probably the great architect's first important commission. The formal park surrounding it was laid out in a series of circles featuring round ponds with parterres radiating from them. An extraordinary, spherical sheepcote, that might be at home in a science fiction city, was also part of the architect's design for the park but this was never realised. By the early 1770s the marquis had set his heart on a second more natural garden. It may have been the

52. Diary, undated entry *c.* 1784.
53. Young, *Travels in France*, ed. M. Betham-Edwards (1913 edn), p. 191.
54. Young, 2 July 1789, p. 191.

lengthy description of Stowe in Whately's *Observations on Modern Gardening*[55] translated into French in 1771 that gave him the idea for his own Elysée. The grotto that served as its entrance was of almost titanic proportions. It was reinforced by iron bars, its central retaining pillar hewn from massive blocks of stone, and was symbolic of the dark mineral world of primeval nature. It gave on to an underground room of elliptical shape, at one end of which was a doorway framed by four Doric pillars and a classic pediment. In passing through this doorway the visitor entered a new world of sunshine and greenery, an elysium. Only in looking back did he realise he had emerged from a pyramid. He had left behind the darkness of the tomb to enter the world of light. One of the recurring themes of these gardens, the descent into darkness and rebirth in light, has led them to be associated with the rites of freemasonry. Monceau was always thought to have been used for masonic ceremonies since its owner, the Duc d'Orléans, was Grand Master of French freemasonry. The Désert de Retz and the Folie of Sainte-James described later have also been connected with these rites.[56] Blaikie recounts in his diary that the marquis accompanied him to view Mauperthuis. He found the château 'remarkably fine and elegant', and continues, 'Here he has laid out a great deal with some tolerable taste. He has by means of a very extensive arch of rocks in form of a grotto formed a passage under the great road to join his gardens together. Although this grotto is not very artfully done to imitate nature, yet it has the advantage to join together his grounds and what he calls the Elysee at the entrance of which he has built a tomb dedicated to the famous Colinet (Coligny) the great Admiral of France massacred the day of St Bartholomew when the Protestants were massacred in Paris under Charles the 9'.[57]

In a letter to J. C. Loudon, author of *The Encyclopaedia of Gardening*, Blaikie gives the date of his visit to Mauperthuis as 1785[58] but no documentary evidence of his involvement there has been found, apart from Young's account of his visit. There is no reference to him in the estate accounts held at the National Archives in Paris. Hubert Robert, who painted representations of this and many other gardens of the period, is believed to have designed some of the romantic buildings in the park, although no archival reference exists for his involvement either. Blaikie has been credited with planting the estate of Coteaux, on the opposite side of the main road from the château, acquired by the Marquis in 1781 and added to his garden[59] and it may have been this that Blaikie was called to lay out and plant in 1785. Blaikie also laid out Montesquiou's town garden[60] and in 1819 he received payment from the Vicomte de Montesquiou (later Marquis) for unspecified work done in his

---

55. Thomas Whately, *Observations on Modern Gardening* (London, 1770).
56. Magnus Olausson, 'Freemasonry Occultism and the Picturesque Garden towards the end of the 18th Century', *Art History*, vol. 8, no. 4 (December 1985).
57. Diary undated entry *c.* 1785. Plan, Lerouge, Cahier 12, pl. 15.
58. J. C. Loudon, *Encylopaedia of Gardening* (1835 edn).
59. Pierre Dosque and Yves Richard, *Au coeur de la Brie; Mauperthuis*, 1982; a more recent work of research on Mauperthuis is J. P. Denef 'Le parc de Mauperthuis. Ledoux, Brogniart, Hubert Robert', in *Le Temps des Jardins* (Paris, 1992), pp. 103–9.
60. Diary undated entry 1785/86, around the time he laid out the Harvelay garden.

gardens.[61] In a letter dated 22 August 1829, Blaikie's wife writes that her husband has received a letter from the Marquis de Montesquiou and 'has gone to his seat [Mauperthuis][62] where he is likely to stay for at least another week'.[63] So it seems that Blaikie's connection with this garden was ongoing. Of his first visit Blaikie writes, 'Here I stopt three days and marked some changes to be done which did not agree with the Architect[64] but the Marquis approved of it ... This part of the country is very pleasant although rather flat; there is a small river which runs through the grounds and in some places there are some fine springs; ... their *pottage* which would not be much admired in England nor reasonably anywhere else as a *pottage* should be for convenience and placed as near the stables as possible as such a garden can never be clean but it is very difficult to change people['s] ideas'.

Young, too, admired the springs and shared Blaikie's opinion about the potager. By 1835, the trees in the park had grown to an extraordinary height,[65] their knotted trunks shooting upwards and their branches spreading out at the top like huge umbrellas or tapering in plumes. Water lilies floated in the lake in front of the château and the branches of the weeping willows that overhung the banks were reflected in the waters. Today almost nothing remains of one of the most outstanding gardens of the Enlightenment.

Four other major gardens of the period visited by Blaikie

In his diary,[66] Blaikie described his first visit to the Trianon at Versailles in October 1777 when Louis XV's botanic garden was being destroyed to make way for Marie Antoinette's 'English' garden. But although he must have visited it, and the famous Hameau constructed between 1776 and 1789,[67] many times, he does not mention it again his diary.

Only at her private refuge, the Petit Trianon and its gardens was Marie Antoinette free from the ceremonies of the court and from unwelcome intrusion. The public was excluded and none but her closest friends were invited to share this haven with her. In its idyllic village (the *Hameau*), they could enjoy the gentle pleasures of country life amidst a bucolic stage-set of picturesque farm buildings and little gardens planted

61. Blaikie's account book. Private Archive.

62. In the eighteenth century the ornamental mill had become the château. De Laborde, p. 155.

63. Letter from Mrs Blaikie to Earl of Lismore. Blaikie Papers, private archive.

64. Theodore Brogniart (1739–1813) succeeded Ledoux as architect at Mauperthuis. See Denef, 'Le parc de Mauperthuis'. Morel also played a part as a letter outlining his plans show (AN., 349 AP 8 fol. 325). Bélanger, too, was briefly connected with this garden organising a fete there in honour of the Comte D'Artois in July 1780 (AN., 349 AP 1). R. Middleton in 'The Château and Gardens of Mauperthuis; The Formal and Informal', *Garden History Issues, Approaches, Methods*, ed. J. Dixon Hunt (Dumbarton Oaks, 1992), gives a bibliography of works on this garden. Further archival sources are given in Denef.

65. Théophile Gautier, *Mademoiselle de Maupin* (Paris, 1835–36; ed. GF-Flammarion, 1966), p. 136.

66. Diary, 4 October 1777.

67. See Annick Heitzmann, *Trianon La Ferme du Hameau* (Paris, 1991), pp. 8–22.

with strawberries and gooseberries where vines tumbled over trellises. A working dairy and farm completed the scene and gave it vitality and authenticity. The cows and goats were imported from Switzerland, home of all that was best in nature. Here the simple life eulogised by Rousseau, so conducive to peace of mind and nobleness of spirit, was reproduced in exquisite surroundings, and at enormous expense. However, it would be a mistake to think that the Queen's *hameau* was an eccentric fancy of her own. Rather, it was part of a particularly French expression of interest in rustic life and was probably derived from the earlier hameau at Chantilly.[68] No documentary record exists of Blaikie's having had any part in the construction of this garden [69] but, given his reputation, and Marie Antoinette's liking for him, it would be surprising if he had not been asked to give advice, however informally. J. C. Loudon writing in 1830 records that, 'Blaikey also formed some scenes in the Petit Trianon, especially in the lower part of the grounds now occupied by ruins, water and a cottage and in their kind very picturesque'.[70] This was probably the last part of the garden to be completed before the fateful day of 10 October 1789 when the King and Queen were forcibly returned to Paris and took up residence in the Tuileries. Among Blaikie's personal effects are a set of small measuring instruments in a shagreen covered case, which tradition holds were the ones he used in designing some part of the Trianon garden.[71] Among them, also, is a clock [72] with a label attached describing it as a gift from Louis XVI. If true, such a gift from the monarch is most likely to be a reward for unpaid work done at the Trianon.

Le Désert de Retz

One garden which particularly influenced the taste of the Queen was the Désert de Retz, the most singular of all the fanciful paradises of the last years of the Ancien Régime. A *désert* (desert) was a wilderness to which a philosopher might retire to enjoy solitude while Monville,[73] the owner of this desert, was a highly sociable man, a courtier who excelled in dancing and the harp and was an outstanding archer. He had many mistresses (a girl every night of his life, it was said), and relished the fashionable life of the court. Fashion was no doubt at the heart of his desire to create

68. David Watkin, p. 168.
69. I am indebted for this information to Mme Annick Heitzmann.
70. J. C. Loudon, *Encyclopaedia of Gardening* (London, 1830 edn), p. 37, para. 169.
71. Private Collection. They were made by the firm of Dollond whose premises were situated at no. 59 St Pauls Churchyard, London during the latter part of the eighteenth century (information provided by Mr B. D. Keefe of Dollond and Aitchison).
72. Private Collection. See chapter 14.
73. François Nicolas Henri Racine de Monville (1734–1798). His grandfather, the son of a wealthy draper's merchant established the family fortune and became a *fermier général*. His father was *Receveur général* of taxes in Alençon. At the age of 23, he obtained the less than onerous post of *Grand Maître des Eaux et Forêts* of Normandy. He married in 1775 but his wife died in 1780. About the same time his grandfather also died and left him a large income so that he was able to devote himself to the pleasures of life. In 1774, he bought some land at Retz near Chambourcy and thereafter acquired some 38 hectares on which he built his Désert.

a natural garden according to Rousseau's principles, where the owner could roam in solitude or entertain a group of his friends. In his own very personal development of the fashion already set by Monceau for a landscape which would combine all times and all places, he embellished his park with buildings from different cultures and ages and planted Lombardy poplars, Indian chestnuts, Judas trees, cornuses and pine trees[74] in his leafy paradise.

His greenhouses were filled with tender plants, a knowledge of botany being another essential accomplishment of the fashionable. 'Experts' such as he were a thorn in Blaikie's flesh. One of them, the Marquis de Barbançon (1750–97), Blaikie writes, 'sometimes showed me a berry of a *Vaccinum* and said it was an *Andromeda* but as he was Grand Commander of the *Chasse* to the Duke so that was enough'. He goes on to grumble that, 'The Duke had many of those pretended connoisseurs about him; he had frequently M. de Monville who was frequently one of his party and', he adds disparagingly, 'a pretended connoisseur in every thing'.[75]

Monville's Désert near Chambourcy, some dozen miles from Paris was a small estate of about 100 acres. He described his creation as 'an English garden known as the Désert situated in the forest of Marly', a misleading description intended to give the impression that he had been allowed the privilege of creating his Désert in the royal forest. In fact it adjoined the forest and borrowed its leafy background to great effect. By making the entrance to the park face the forest, he created the impression of a secret place accessible only to the privileged.[76] Marie Antoinette loved to visit it with members of the court and came to it on foot through the woods but anyone who wished to enjoy its walks could apply to Monville for an entry ticket. Beyond the gates, the visitor found himself before a grotto made of a dark, rough hewn stone. Two statues of satyrs holding torches stood on rocky outcrops at either side and lit the way into the arch of the dark grotto from which, on emerging, one caught a glimpse of the Désert's most remarkable feature, a colossal shattered column. Its apparently ruined top, overgrown with ivy and colonised by shrubs and mosses, looked as if it had been blasted by lightning in some ancient cataclysm. Once through the grotto and in the green shelter of the garden, a path wound to the left towards another important feature, a temple dedicated to Pan. Below it, streams gushed from the earth. Beyond it stood a pyramid based, like other pyramids in these eighteenth-century gardens, on the mausoleum of Caius Cestius on the Appian way. At the base of the pyramid was the entrance to the ice-house. Further on, on a rise, stood a gothic ruin; not some fake assemblage of medieval architectural features but the remains of the old parish church of the commune. To the other side of the column, a green lawn was the site of an open air theatre, and on an island in the lake, stood a Turkish

---

74. These are listed amongst the trees and shrubs Monville ordered from the Royal Nurseries. AN., O1 2110.

75. Diary, undated entry. Blaikie follows it with an account of the Diamond Necklace scandal of 1785, so he probably visited the Désert in 1784/85.

76. Olivier Chopin de Janvry, 'A much visited Solitude', in Rosemary Verey and Katherine Lambert, *Secret Gardens Revealed by their Owners* (London, 1994).

28. Larivière (after A. Kauffman): the Duc de Chartres (detail). Musée de Versailles.

29. Attributed to Carmontelle: the Duc de Chartres, on the right, receiving the keys of Monceau from Carmontelle. Musée Carnavalet.

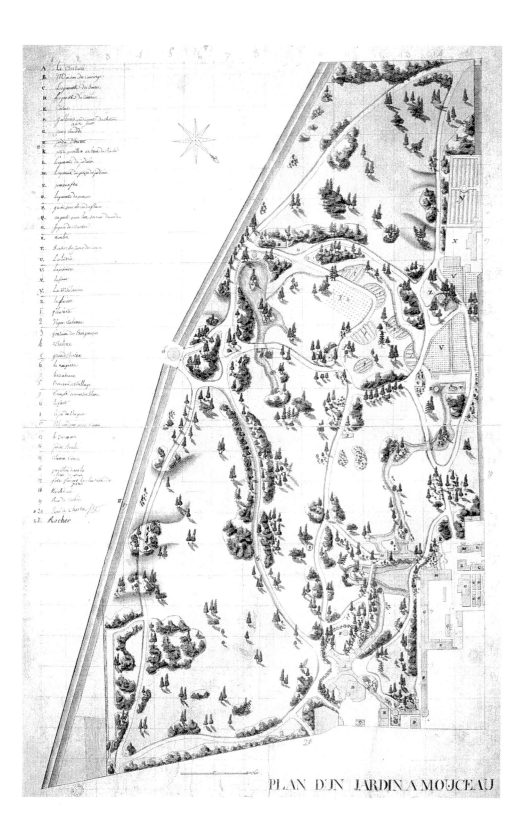

PLAN D'UN JARDIN A MOUCEAU

Opposite 30. Plan of the garden at Monceau showing the alterations made by Blaikie. Bibliothèque d'Art et d'Archéologie, Fondation Jacques Doucet.

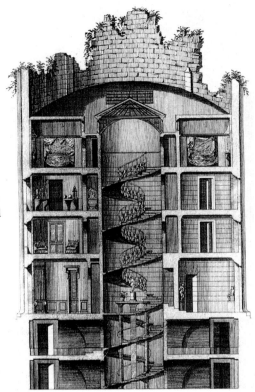

Coupe du Levant au Couchant avec construction pour les Caves.

31. The Désert de Retz. A cross-section by Le Rouge of the broken column which concealed living accommodation. Courtesy of M. Pierre Renard.

32. Another view of the Broken Column. From a drawing by C. Bourgeois. Photo P. Taylor.

a. The main avenue of Le Raincy
with its two pavilions

b. A view of the château

33. Six buttons from a series of fourteen by Carmontelle depicting the gardens of Le Raincy. This particular series was first published in *En Aulnoye Jadis*, the journal of the Société Historique du Raincy et du Pays d'Aulnoye. Le Raincy, Seine, Saint Denis France (Bulletin No 13, 1984). Private Collection.

c. The English Village at Le Raincy

d. The Orangery

e. The Hermitage

f. The Kennels

34. The immense rock construction designed by Bélanger, the architect of Bagatelle, for the Folie Saint James. Le Rouge. Photo P. Taylor.

35. Méréville, the last of the great picturesque gardens in France before the Revolution. From a drawing by C. Bourgeois.

36. Louis Léon-Félicité de Lauraguais, Duc de Brancas (1722–1824), in his old age. Bibliothèque Nationale de France. Photo Giraudon.

37. Malmaison, a view of the gardens looking towards the house. From a drawing by
C. Bourgeois. Photo P. Taylor.

38. Montcel. The grounds were laid out by Blaikie for Madame Oberkampf, wife of
Christophe-Philippe Oberkampf, cotton manufacturer at Jouy-en-Josas. From a drawing by C.
Bourgeois. Photo P. Taylor.

39. Marshal Ney (1769–1815). One of a series of mosaic panels set in a round table at Malmaison portraying Napoleon's marshals. Château de Malmaison. Photo P. Taylor.

40. Agläe-Louise Auguié (1782–1853) (left), later wife of Marshal Ney, with Hortense de Beauharnais, Josephine's daughter, c. 1800. Château de Malmaison.

41. Les Coudreaux, the country house bought by Ney in 1808 at Marboué near Châteaudun in the Eure et Loire. From a drawing by C. Bourgeois. Photo P. Taylor.

42. A view of the façade of the château of Raray (1996). Note the unusual stone 'hunting' screen to both sides. Photo J. Mazel.

43. The château of Raray from the garden side (1996). Photo J. Mazel.

44. Caulaincourt, Duc de Vicence (1722–1827). Bibliothèque Nationale de France.

45. The château of Caulaincourt near Saint-Quentin belonging to the Duc de Vicence. Engraving published in 1822. The château was reduced to rubble by the Germans in 1917 and later rebuilt. Bibliothèque Nationale de France.

46. The Prince and Princess of Salm Dyck.
Bibliothèque Nationale de France.

47 The château of Manicamp already showing signs of
decay. It was demolished *c*. 1835. Société Historique
de Compiègne.

48. The château of Mont l'Evêque near Senlis. Photo Gabrielle Joudiou.

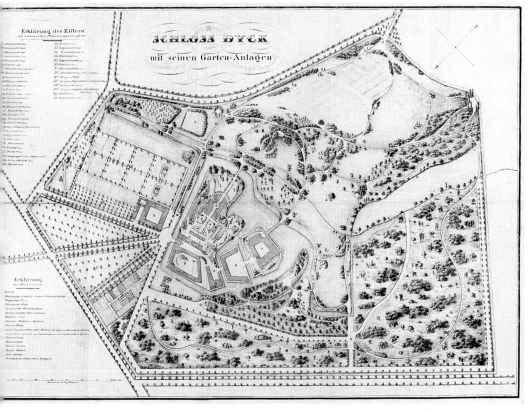

49. Undated plan of the estate of Schloss Dyck showing the English garden laid out by Blaikie. The key in the top left-hand corner lists the families of plants grown in the garden. Archiv Schloss Dyck: Rheinisches Amt für Denkmalpflege.

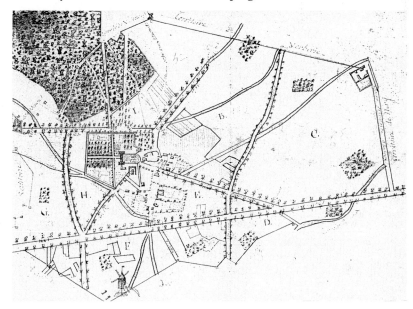

50. Plan of Raray at the end of the eighteenth century showing the château of Raray before the transformations effected by Blaikie. Raray, Private Archive.

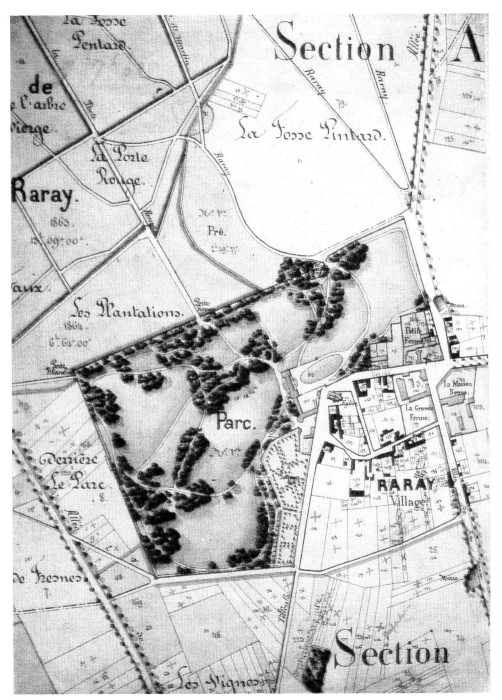

51. Plan of Raray 1861 showing the English garden laid out by Blaikie. Photo Jean Mazel. Raray, Private Archive.

52. Henry-Noël-François de La Bédoyère (1782–1861). Painting by Alexandre Caminade in 1821. Photo Jean Mazel. Raray, Private Archive.

53. Ambroisine Henriette d'Estampes (1791–1847). Painting by Alexandre Caminade in 1821. Photo Jean Mazel. Raray, Private Archive.

54. *Sibbaldia procumbens*, the insignificant little plant that Blaikie recognized as a fellow countryman near Chamonix. It is also the logo of the Edinburgh Royal Botanic Gardens. From Reichenbach L. and Reichenbach H. G. *Icones flora Germanicae et Helveticae*. Vol. 25. Gera, Reuss, *Friedrich von Zezschwitz*. 1909–1912. Plate 5. Edinburgh Royal Botanic Gardens Library.

55. A clock belonging to Blaikie with a label describing it as a gift from Louis XVI to Thomas Blaikie and stating that it was buried during the Terror at Malmaison. Private Collection.

tent. There was also a Chinese pavilion furnished as a private lodging for Monville. In addition the park contained a picturesque farm, a dairy, and orangery, a thatched cottage, and numerous other buildings; in all twenty *fabriques*.

The tower standing on a low mound still dominates the garden. Its colossal scale created a sense of unease in the spectator and altogether the garden has, even today, the slightly mysterious, even sinister atmosphere intended by its owner. The tower's crevices and cracks concealed the windows of an interestingly designed house with a spiral staircase which wound right to the top of the four storey building. Pots of flowers and garlands of sweet smelling leaves and blossoms decorated the treads and banisters and daylight entered by a glass dome concealed in the apparently ruined top storey whose fissures concealed its windows.

Blaikie visited the Désert in around 1785 and his description is perhaps a little tinged by professional jealousy. He tells us that 'Monville ... had formed a garden and path according to his own designs adjacent to the forest de Marly where he had made his château in form of an old round tower with a stair in the middle surrounded with flower pots which made a tolerable agreeable effect. The *Appartements* were small all around the tower from the staircase. The top of the tower seemed to have been ruined – I cannot think but he meant to imitate the tower of Babel. He had some good hot houses and by them he had a little Chinese building where he generally lodged. The whole of the park was a labyrinth of rather narrow crooked walks without forming many agreeable Landscapes. The Entry was rather an Arch of Triumph of Gothic building and to the left upon the rising ground stood a Small temple in the Doric taste, the tower formed another but too confined.'

Before the Revolution Monville sold the Désert to an Englishman, Lewis Disney Fytche. Between the Revolution and Waterloo the French government confiscated and returned the house to Fytche according to the state of peace or war with England. Then, a year after the Treaty with France in 1815, Fytche reclaimed his property on payment of the debts of Monville. Because of his friendship with Orléans and his scandalous way of life Monville had been called before the Revolutionary Tribunal but had failed to attend on a plea of sickness. He succeeded in avoiding the fate of his friend, the Duc d'Orléans, and died in his own bed in 1798. The Désert was sold in 1827 and after that had a succession of owners until the 1930s when its proprietors abandoned it to nature. At that period, a group of writers, fascinated by its Sleeping Beauty atmosphere, took to visiting it. The *fabriques* were now collapsing and the tower crumbling and choked by vegetation. But, just before the garden's final disintegration, Colette, who was one of the writers intrigued by the place, succeeded with others in having the garden declared a national monument. The work of publicising and saving it was carried out from the sixties by Olivier Chopin de Janvry, now the joint owner of the core part of the park. Once more, as in the eighteenth century, thanks to an enlightened owner, visitors may wander round the garden and speculate on the meaning of the tower. Was it indeed the Tower of Babel as Blaikie suggests? Or was the broken tower part of the iconography of freemasonry? Did it symbolise man's punishment by a wrathful God for his attempt to create perfection? Or was it the triumph of the primeval powers of nature over the work of man? To the imaginative visitor the atmosphere still seems haunted by ghosts of its eighteenth-century past; a certain agreeable *frisson* of the strange and awful still hovers over de Monville's Désert. It and Ermenonville are the two gardens in which one senses the very different spirit of their owners, Girardin, champion of Rousseau and his ideas, and Monville, the brilliant, imaginative courtier. Yet both reflect the preoccupation of the time with natural science, history, architecture and love of nature.

Folie Saint-James

Another garden, part of which still exists today (it may be visited when the Lycée which has occupied part of the site since 1922 is *en vacances*) is the Folie of Saint-James at Neuilly. It belonged to another kind of eighteenth-century figure, the immensely rich and extravagant financier and business man. Baudard de Vaudésir, Baron de Saint-James (1736–1787) was Treasurer General of the Navy, from which post he was said to draw an income of 500,000 livres a year. He was also one of the founders of the company that became the Banque de France. With the intention of building a *folie* he had bought around sixty acres of ground at Neuilly, on a slope overlooking the Seine next to the estate of Bagatelle, two years before Artois bought his property. In 1777, Bélanger's success at Bagatelle fired St James to give the architect carte blanche to design a *jardin anglais* at Neuilly, the only proviso being, it is said, that it should '*coute cher*'. Bélanger found no difficulty in carrying out such instructions but according to Blaikie, 'all this extravagance was the desire of the Comte D'Artois who I heard say to Mr Bélanger, "I hope you will ruin St James"'.[77] St James was to pay a severe price for flaunting his wealth and reminding Artois of his own relative poverty.

The château, now the administrative centre for the Lycée, still fronts the Avenue St James, with its interior decoration largely intact. In a side street, rue Henri Berthier, stands the little pavilion which served as Saint-James' *cabinet des curiosités*, housing his collection of stones and minerals. It is free-standing now but originally abutted the greenhouse designed by the architect J. B. Chaussard, a friend of Bélanger's.

Of the fourteen bridges which spanned the man-made river, only one, *le pont palladien* remains. There were numerous building, and statues echoing those at Bagatelle but St James' garden contained one unique feature still *in situ* today. It was an immense *rocher*, modelled by Bélanger on the rocks of Dovedale in Derbyshire,[78] the huge stones used in its construction being dragged from the forest of Fontainebleau. One immense rock, it is said, required a train of forty horses to bring it to Neuilly and earned St James the title of *l'homme du rocher* from the King, who saw it being transported as he returned from hunting in the forest.[79] Water was conducted from a pump on the edge of the Seine to a reservoir of 50 cubic metres housed above the rock and reached by two staircases on either side of a Doric temple embedded

---

77. Diary, 1783.
78. See Gabrielle Joudiou, 'Saint-James', in *Cent jardins à Paris et en Ile de France* (Paris, 1992), pp. 237, 240.
79. G. C. Leroux-Cesbron 'Le Baron de Sainte-James et sa folie de Neuilly', *La Revue de Paris* (1 fév. 1925).

under an arch of the rock. The temple itself was inspired by the temple of Paestum. Behind its columns gushed two cascades which tumbled into the water of a small lake below. Just above the water, were the entrances to two grottoes which passed under the rock. Blaikie's view of the structure is down to earth. He sees in it none of the preoccupation of the time with the primitive, colossal power of nature symbolised by rugged stone.[80] He writes, 'There is a rock formed before the house or rather an arch of prodigious large stones where the water seems to arrive, but this, although at a great expense, has nothing of nature or natural beauty being intermixed with hewn stone, and a little temple in the middle in the Corinthian order, and every thing equally ridiculous as there is neither elevation nor mountain to form this huge pile of rocks'. Blaikie, although invited by Saint-James to make improvements to the gardens, refused. Instead he went one day and planted the lawn from the house towards the hothouses which, he writes, 'pleased very much Mr Bélanger and Mr St James'. He goes on, 'This garden is certainly an example of extravagance more than of taste as Mr Bélanger has carried every thing to the greatest pitch of extravagance'. Blaikie's view was shared by that connoisseur of gardens and friend of Bélanger's, the Duc de Ligne who declared that the garden suffered from a surfeit of money.

The collapse of one of his companies, caused by the loss of a government contract, obliged Saint James to ask the Treasury for five million livres owing to him. Calonne as Controller-General, delayed the payment. Saint-James was declared bankrupt and taken to the Bastille. He spent only two months in the fortress before receiving an advance on some of the money due to him but it was too late. His property had been liquidated at ridiculous prices. Worst of all, on 12 June 1787, his cherished *folie* was sold for 200,000 livres. The rocher alone, it was estimated, had cost 1,700,000.[81] Broken hearted, he died at his brother-in-law's house three weeks later on 3 July 1787 aged 51. Like Fouquet at Vaux Le Vicomte, he had been foolish enough to flaunt his wealth before a royal prince.

Méréville

Dissatisfaction with Bélanger's work, rather than his extravagances, persuaded the royal banker Laborde[82] to dismiss the architect before the completion of his commission to design what was probably the most expensive of all the pre-Revolutionary gardens, at Méréville in the valley of the river Juine some ten miles south of Étampes in Essonne.[83] Laborde, who took possession of the property in 1784, spent vast sums in the creation of his garden of over 900 acres. His first expense was the stabilisation of the marshy valley by the removal of a whole layer of its soil and its replacement with that of a nearby mountain. The course of the River Juine was completely altered

80. Monique Mosser, 'Le Rocher et la colonne: Un Thème d'iconographie architecturale au 18e siècle', *Revue de l'Art* 58/59 (1983), pp. 53–74.

81. Leroux-Cesbron.

82. See chapter 10 for biographical details.

83. J. E. Lefevre, 'Le parc de Méréville', *Gazette des Amateurs de Jardins* (Paris, 1921). See also Stern Papers BHVP MS 2832. Oswald Sirèn, pp. 153–7.

and various tributaries conducted through the park to create impressive water features. Constructed between 1785 and 1793, Méréville was the culmination of the garden art of the period and reckoned the most beautiful, and most expensive, of all. It depended for its grand effects on the carefully contrived 'wild' landscape of rocks, waterfalls and rushing streams where precarious bridges spanned deep ravines. Alexandre de Laborde, writing in 1808, described it as representing the whole Alpine experience without the travelling, and its creation marked the beginning of a movement towards a new Romantic style. Its realisation was the work first of Bélanger and afterwards of the painter, Hubert Robert, who designed the garden monuments.[84]

According to J. C. Loudon,[85] Blaikie, too, although not generally associated with this garden, played a part by providing and planting the fine and rare trees. These were 'of an incomparable diversity and rarity and constituted one of the most interesting curiosities of the place'.[86]

An inventory of the foreign trees growing in the park accompanied by a report on the condition of the gardens of Méréville was drawn up in 1792 by André Thouin at the request of the Revolutionary government. In it he describes the area laid out as a *jardin anglais* as planted in '*massifs et bosquets*'. Tree clad slopes rose swiftly from the river valley and afforded protection from strong winds, but he notes that the soil there was particularly bad, dry and full of chalky stones, so that the plants suffered from dryness and strong winds. On the other hand, he found the foreign trees flourishing in the swampy areas in the valley, especially the *Liriodendron tulipifera* which stood out amongst the other American trees. Almost all of them, he found, were too strongly established to be pulled up and replanted successfully in the *Jardin des Plantes*. Thouin regretted that, for quick effect, the trees and shrubs had been planted too close together to allow them to attain their full beauty of form.[87] Close planting, as well as being a method of giving protection to young trees, drew them up towards the light so that they achieved height quickly to create an immediate effect. No doubt, had the Revolution not intervened, the saplings would have been thinned out later. As it was, the trees survived well. In the 1830s, in response to Loudon's request to his correspondents for a description of the largest specimens of trees in their region, for his monumental *Arboretum et Fruticetum*, of 1838, Blaikie sent in the information that at Méréville there were many fine American trees planted some forty years earlier by him, particularly 'the ailanthus which grows there to a large size, many specimens having attained the height of 80 feet in 40 years'. He also

84. J. Sabattier, 'Méréville', *100 Jardins à Paris et en Ile-de-France* (Paris, 1992), pp. 190–1. These monuments consisted of a classical dairy, a monument to Cook, two obelisks, one dedicated to Laborde's two sons who died on board the ship La Pérouse during a botanical expedition, a temple of filial piety whose goddess was modelled on Laborde's daughter. Only an immense Trajan column remains on site. The four finest buildings of the park were purchased by a collector at the end of the nineteenth century and today can be seen in the park of Jeurre near Etampes.

85. J. C. Loudon, *Arboretum et Fruticetum* (1844), vol. I, pp. 138, 291, 371.

86. J. E. Lefevre, pp. 1–9.

87. Bibliothèque du Muséum National d'Histoire Naturelle, MS 315.

notes a Liriodendron which by 1835 had reached 60 ft and a *Tilia europaea microphylla* of which the trunk, measured at one foot from the ground was five feet in diameter and the spread of the branches 40ft.

Like many of Blaikie's clients, including De La Haye at Saint-Firmin near Chantilly, Laborde, as one of the hated *fermiers-géneral*, was guillotined in 1794. The estate was eventually restored to his family but was sold in 1822. Much neglected for generations, it has, in part, survived. Its construction marked the end of the age of the French picturesque garden. Blaikie's major years of success were over.

CHAPTER 13

Private Life, Public Events, 1777–1792

IF IT IS POSSIBLE to judge a man by his friends, Blaikie's friendship with André Thouin, head gardener at the *Jardin du Roi*, does him credit. Thouin, 'the greatest horticulturist of the day', was known for his integrity and his humanity. He showed Blaikie the King's Garden with 'great civility' on the Scot's initial visit in December 1775, and Blaikie spent his first New Year's day in Paris at Thouin's house in the *Jardin du Roi*. They remained friends until Thouin's death in 1824.[1] On that first visit in 1776, Blaikie noted that the school of botany was laid out according to the French system of the botanist, Bernard de Jussieu,[2] rather than the Linnean one. Measured against Kew and Upton, the plants in the hothouses were in an 'indifferent' state and the scarce ones 'stunted'. Nevertheless, the garden became part of Blaikie's life and he returned to it many times, making his own Linnaen catalogue of the plants in 1777 and cataloguing the fruit trees when he was an old man. His friendship embraced other members of the Thouin family. Thouin's younger brother Jean, 'no botanist' but good company, was Blaikie's companion on at least one outing to Versailles and another brother, Gabriel, was a respected fellow landscape artist.

The other major botanist gardener of the day was Antoine Richard, Marie Antoinette's gardener at the Trianon, but although Blaikie acknowledged him as a first class botanist, Richard was not a kindred spirit. Blaikie found his conceit or *'orgueil'*, and his 'presumption' objectionable and judged him a bit of a charlatan in the way he pretended that he could recognise from the appearance of any seed, not only the genus to which it belonged, but also its species.[3] However, Blaikie confined his opinion to his diary and remained on good terms with Richard. They exchanged plants and seeds and Blaikie always found the whole Richard family courteous towards him.

Certainly, in his pre-Revolutionary years in France, he felt most at home in the company of his compatriots. He was particularly fond of the fatherly Brown, the king's gardener at Choisy, later *Intendant* of the king's gardens at Versailles. Williams, gardener to the Duc de Bouillon at Navarre, was one of a satellite group surrounding Blaikie as was his fellow Scot, John Murray, who came from Stowe to be head gardener at Ermenonville, and was a bit 'bragadoccio' about his lawns. Amongst these men were a number of gardeners for whom Blaikie found posts. He brought Archibald Macmaster over from England to work for the Comte de Lauraguais, then found him

---

1. For Thouin's life see Yvonne Letouzy, *Le Jardin des Plantes à la croisée des chemins avec André Thouin 1747–1824* (Muséum National d'Histoire Naturelle, Paris, 1989).
2. Bernard de Jussieu (1699–1777), developed a method of classification that took account of the most stable characteristics of plants and, with Thouin, used it in laying out the school of botany. See Marguerite Duval, *The King's Garden* (University of Virginia, 1982).
3. Diary, undated entry *c.* 1785.

employment at the *Jardin du Roi* and generally forwarded his career. Another Scot, Alexander Howatson, benefited from his patronage as well, but his part in this story comes later.

Blaikie's time for relaxation was limited. In the autumn of 1777, accompanied by the English nurseryman, James Hairs, he paid a visit to the recently completed Vauxhall pleasure gardens in the Champs Elysées. These were modelled on the English ones of the same name but never achieved the same popularity. Fine weather had brought out the crowds that particular day and he writes, 'there is little to be seen but the people and Building which is newly finished and fine, the middle is a large circular place for dancing supported all round with columns. In the gardens there is some pieces of water upon which they exercise different games and in the Evening, fire works. In the garden there is a high pole upon the top of which is a dragon fixed full of fire works which is to be set on fire by sky rockets. Many tried but none succeeded so it was left so finished'.[4]

English racing and gambling were popular pastimes that held little appeal for him. With Mr Briass, the inspector of buildings at Bagatelle, he spent an occasional day at the Vincennes races where Chartres and Artois pitted their expensive English horses against one another and bet huge sums on them. Artois alone was accustomed to win or lose two or three thousand louis[5] a day in bets of one kind or another. The 'half-starved', insolent and foul-mouthed English jockeys irritated the Scot as did Orléans' arrogant English stable manager, Singleton. This man, nicknamed the 'bull' kept house like a lord and was a notorious tyrant in his domain.[6]

Abstemious in his early days in France, Blaikie, the mature bachelor, enjoyed drinking socially. He describes three drinking sessions in his diary each to illustrate some aspect of French life; the easy living of the monks with whom he got merry one night at the monastery of Saint-Germain; the corrupt army recruiting system which made young men drunk and then signed them up for military service;[7] and the humanity of French workmen in sending home in a cab a drunken English gardener who had been carousing with Blaikie the night before (Diary, undated entry 1781). With the luck of the catatonically inebriated, he ended up on their building site at dawn having wandered all night in Paris, even entering the pump house at Marly and crossing an unfinished bridge over the Seine without mishap.

An incident described in the later part of his diary, probably around 1785, recalls

---

4. Diary, Sunday 5 October 1777.
5. A louis was approximately one pound sterling in 1789. January–May 1778, Artois' gaming bill shows he lost 158,720 livres. (R1 310).
6. Henry, *10th Earl of Pembroke*, p. 473.
7. Blaikie, angered at the recruitment this way of a young gardener in his charge, pretended with a friend to be raw countrymen. They were plied with drinks by a recruiting officer but insisted that the officers drink glass for glass with them while they themselves offered passers-by drinks at the expense of the officers whom they made drunk. They were recognised by a senior officer who, as was common at the time, had held back the young man's papers in the hope of payment from his family to free their son. On this occasion, Blaikie was too late, the papers had been registered.

the cool-headed courage and caution of his Swiss days. In the early hours of Boxing day, after supper at Monceau he was returning to Bagatelle by a short cut over the fields and through the Bois de Boulogne. Near the Porte de Maillot, he heard voices coming from a building called the Remise on the edge of the Bois. He stopped to see what was happening. As he stood there, a man came out of the Remise only a few yards from him. Startled to find himself face to face with an observer, he froze for a moment then began to circle warily around Blaikie who, leaning on his stick, stood his ground and turned to face the man, keeping eye contact with him as he moved round. Another man materialised out of the darkness and after standing still for a minute, the two robbers, for that was what Blaikie had guessed they were, turned to go back into the wood to summon their comrades. Taking advantage of the blackness of the night, Blaikie, knowing he would soon be outnumbered, writes, 'I presented my stick as if it had been a gun and told them to stop or I should blow out their brains. Upon this they called out, *"O mon dieu, c'est Mr Blaikie!"* and all ran away and I made the best of my way back to Porte Maillot'.[8] There he summoned help to return to the scene where a cache of stolen jewellery and other valuables was discovered. It turned out that one of the robbers was a gardener at Bagatelle.

Blaikie's sole reference in the diary to a member of his own family occurs on the 8 February 1780, when he records that he received a letter from Scotland informing him of the death of his brother. John Blaikie died on 15 January 1780 at the age of 35 and Blaikie succeeded him as the owner of Corstorphine Hill. John's grave stone near the entrance to Corstorphine kirk bears the initials TB and AB and carries the following epitaph:

> Here lies the best of brothers, here the Friend
> Loving and beloved by all mankind. To him the noble virtues all were given
> To fit him to enjoy his native Heaven
> Henceforth be every tender Tear supprest
> Or let us weep for joy that he is blest.

The TB is Thomas and the AB his sister Agnes Blaikie, the elder of Thomas's two sisters and unmarried at the time of her brother's death. The saccharine religious sentiment suggests Agnes rather than Blaikie. It was she who broke the news to her younger brother. She wrote in an illiterate hand but the surviving part of a letter, probably her second letter to him after their brother's death,[9] is shrewd. In it she asks him to assert his right to the property as soon as possible otherwise one William Blaikie (either a cousin or an uncle) might lay claim to it as the heir.[10] She also puts in a plea that she should be allowed to remain at Corstorphine Hill since, loving the place as she does, she would be the best custodian of it until her brother's return. She

---

8. Diary, undated entry *c.* 1782–83.
9. Blaikie Papers.
10. There may have been something in this as William's branch of the family claimed the family grave of John Blaikie and their burials later took place there. I am indebted for this information to Miss A. S. Cowper the author of *Corstorphine and Roundabout.*

asks Blaikie in another letter, dated 26 February 1780, to make this clear to their sister, Isabel, or there might be trouble with the latter's husband. Isabel, she fears, has made an unfortunate marriage to a man much given to drink who, if given any part of the property, 'would soon dispose of it'. She signs herself 'Nannie'. Blaikie must have agreed to her proposal since there is no further letter from Agnes amongst his papers.

Between 1779 and 1781, his accounts [11] show that Blaikie lived frugally. There are no bills for wine until June 1781, when the purchase of cooking pots, goblets, an iron and other domestic utensils show that he has set up house. It was probably at this time that he moved to the gardener's pavilion in the courtyard of Bagatelle [12] of which he writes, 'although small was rather more convenient',[13] a tongue in cheek play on the motto, *Parva sed Apta* engraved by Bélanger above the entrance to the Communs, the building which separated the château of Bagatelle and its *cour d'honneur* from the outer courtyard. The purchase of cherries and artichokes, capers and anchovies marks a culinary refinement absent from his previous accounts which list mainly bread, meat, eggs and bacon and suggests a female housekeeper or companion. Brandy appears for the first time in his accounts in September of the same year. His expenditure on clothing is slight; a chemise here, a pair of gloves there, his trousers mended and a modest bill from a shoemaker and the hairdresser. It is not until 1782 that he appears to pay more attention to his appearance with a payment to the hairdresser for powder, pomade and a ribbon. That same year, he purchases a pair of silk breeches and two hats.

1781 seems to have been a turning point in other ways as well. Bagatelle, with its atmosphere of luxury and sensuality and its constantly changing cast of young women servants, must have offered many opportunities for sexual encounters, yet Blaikie makes no allusion to his sexual life until the end of April that year. Then, on 30 April, he includes the first of two concealed references in the diary to sexual involvements with the words 'Thérèse began'. Thérèse was a servant at Bagatelle and she left less than six weeks after the beginning of her affair with Blaikie, while Blaikie himself was absent carrying out work at one of the Comte d'Artois' other gardens. However, that was not the last Blaikie had to do with her. His involvement with Thérèse was brief but, from his accounts, it appears there may have been a child from their liaison. He notes that on the 10 July 1781 he agreed to pay her 40 écus per year from the beginning of May. Later on, he writes, 'Sent the boy to Chatelin the 25 Mai 1783'. And underneath, he itemises two unspecified payments for the months of June and July. There are no further bills for Thérèse or 'the boy', so that it is possible the child may have died. His next affair began on 1 July, soon after Thérèse left Bagatelle. Again he uses an almost identical formula. He writes, 'B.T. came to Bagatelle and began'. The reference would remain a mystery were it not for a legal document, a *quittance*, amongst Blaikie's

---

11. His pre-Revolutionary accounts are written at the back of the Diary. Blaikie Papers.
12. In his diary he gives the date as 1783, but his dates are becoming unreliable. He gives the date of the grand duke of Russia's visit to Bagatelle in 1782 as 1783. Before he moved to the gardener's pavilion, he lodged with the porter and would have had no need of cooking utensils.
13. Diary entry about the time of the visit of the Grand Duke Paul of Russia.

papers, which reveals that a young woman called Barbe Thuillaux bore him a daughter. The child is named as Constance Blaikie, so he recognised his paternity and may even have intended marriage to her mother. It is evident from his account book that he had written compromising letters to Barbe which were returned to him by the lawyer who drew up the *quittance*.[14] Dated 1803, the document is translated in full below. How long this relationship lasted we don't know. Confirmation that someone of the name of Thuillaux worked at Bagatelle appears in a list of names in Artois' accounts as having received a tip from him while in attendance *'a l'entrée'* of the château on 10 April 1782.[15] Below is a translation of the document signed by Barbe Thuillaux:

> *I the undersigned Barbe Thuillaux, spinster living in Paris rue du haut Moulin no. 22 'Division de la Cité' recognise that I have received from Thomas Blaikie by the hands of Citizen Rose, the sum of two hundred and fifty pounds* [i.e. French livres] *and before that six hundred and fifty pounds on several occasions by the hand of M Gellé making in total a sum of nine hundred pounds for the receipt of which I quit and discharge the said M Blaikie of all claims, obligations and demands whatever until this day, in particular for that which concerns the nourishment and upkeep of his daughter Constance Blaikie; agreeing that in this regard, all the commitments, promises or obligations which he might have made to me be regarded as null and void.*
>
> *1st Germinal, year eleven* [22 March 1803]
> *approved and signed by the above*
> *thuillaux* [sic]

Why did he seek these assurances from her at such a late date? Had their daughter come of age? Married? Died? What is certain is that, apart from one payment, not dated, of 100 livres in his account book for the *'fille* Th.' and another of 300 to *'la Citoyenne* Th.' for 29 January 1800, there is no other reference to Constance Blaikie among his papers, nor has it been possible to trace her.

The third and last woman whose name appears in the diary is 'Charlotte' who became his wife. Francis Birrell, the editor of *The Diary of a Scotch Gardener at the French Court*, surmised that 'Charlotte was probably an English housekeeper' and writes that, according to Blaikie's papers, his wife was a Miss Tarbut of Edinburgh.[16] It is puzzling to understand how Birrell came to this conclusion, since other legal documents amongst the Blaikie papers confirm that Charlotte, named as Charlotte Letitia Lockier was Blaikie's wife. There is, however, no marriage certificate amongst Blaikie's papers, nor has it been possible to trace a marriage in Paris.[17] A study of the Edinburgh parish records reveals no Letitia Tarbut (nor variations on this surname) as having been born there around 1770. Some letters to Blaikie are signed by an Elizabeth Torbet. Torbet is the married name of Blaikie's sister, Isabella (Isabel), and Elizabeth Torbet is her daughter-in-law. She addresses Blaikie as 'my dear uncle' and signs herself as

---

14. Blaikie Papers.
15. AN., R1 339.
16. Birrell, Introduction p. 9.
17. This is not surprising, There are no British consular records for the period and a large number of French records were burned in 1870.

'your affectionate niece'.[18] When Blaikie married Charlotte is not clear. In April 1792, he made an official complaint to a local court, about the vandalisation of his house at Chaillot. Charlotte was living in the house with him and in his complaint, he writes that his spouse and domestics had been thrown out of the house by the *huissiers*.[19] Among Blaikie's papers is a *laisser-passer* issued on 19 January 1812 to 'Charlotte Letichet (Letitia) *épouse de M. Thomas Blaikie*'. Her death certificate[20] made out in the name of Letitia Lockier, widow of Thomas Blaikie, shows that she was born in Ringwood in Hampshire and was in her 80th year when she died on 20 May 1850, making her twenty years Blaikie's junior. But there is a mystery here. No Charlotte or Letitia Lockier was born in Ringwood in the year of her birth,[21] although Lockier (with its variants Lockyer or Lockyier) is a common name in the area. The names Charlotte and Letitia do not feature in any of the Parish registers of the various Hampshire districts in the eighteenth century. However, there was a Betty, born to George and Mary Lockyier in Ringwood on 22 May 1771. Had Blaikie's wife, whom we know changed her name from Charlotte Letitia to Letitia, decided to discard the unromantic and humble 'Betty' when she came to France? It seems possible. In two letters from Blaikie to his wife, written from Edinburgh in September 1822[22] he addresses her as Letitia and confirms their married state in his valediction. We know nothing else about her except a passport summary of her appearance which describes her at the age of 42 as one metre 59 cm tall, with brown hair and eyebrows, a high forehead and grey eyes. Her nose is '*ordinaire*', her mouth of medium size, her chin pointed, her face oval and her complexion '*coloré*'.[23] To Blaikie, writing from Edinburgh in 1822, she is his 'Dear and Lovely Letitia'.

Political events rarely feature in the Diary in Blaikie's early days at Bagatelle. But, little by little, they begin to penetrate the enclosed world of the garden. France and England were at war over the American colonies from 10 July 1778 until 3 September 1783 yet there are only a few hints of this conflict in the diary. He remarks, in passing, on the 'great preparations' for the departure of Artois to the siege of Gibraltar[24] in the summer of 1782 and how, 'they were much disappointed and came back rather ashamed of their adventures exclaiming against the lashity [*lacheté* or cowardice] of the Spaniards as the cause of their disgrace'.[25]

---

18. A series of letters from the Torbet family to Blaikie is preserved amongst the Blaikie papers. They mention Mrs Blaikie but make no claim to any family connection with her.
19. Charlotte is described as Blaikie's 'young companion' in *Histoire de Neuilly* Pierre Coulomb et Maurice Gonon, Neuilly 1966, p. 104.
20. *Acte de décès*, A de P, Document no. 13296.
21. I am grateful to the Hampshire archivist for this information.
22. Birrell, Introduction, pp. 12–14.
23. Blaikie Papers.
24. Artois spent two months at the siege of Gibraltar by French and Spanish forces from 1779 to 782 as a result of an agreement between France and Spain that Spain would regain the rock. The siege was lifted in 1782.
25. Diary, undated entry 1782. Artois is said to have joked that the only *batterie* that did any damage to the Spaniards was his own *batterie de cuisine* since, unused to the rich food he served at his table, his Spanish guests often suffered from indigestion, Bachaumont XXI, 65.

The first sign in the Diary that the *beaux jours* of the French monarchy were beginning to cloud over appears during the course of a visit by Blaikie to Versailles where his old friend Brown was now *Intendant* of the King's Gardens. Blaikie gives no date but recalls that on that day[26] 'the Cardinal Rohan was stopped and sent to prison which much alarmed and astonished all the people of Versailles'. He continues, 'All this began to work upon the minds of the people as some of them began to blame the Queen ... many of the people were very dissatisfied with the court'.

He was alluding to the sensational scandal known as the Affair of the Diamond Necklace in which there were three main protagonists; Cardinal Rohan, a shallow and foolish courtier, cold-shouldered by the Queen; an adventuress, Jeanne de la Motte, who persuaded Rohan that he would win the Queen's favour by acting as her go-between in the purchase of a diamond necklace; and the notorious 'Sicilian jailbird' Cagliostro, a charlatan who had gained a strong influence over the mind of Rohan. There was also a young milliner, a Marie-Antoinette look-alike, whom Motte employed to impersonate the Queen.

La Motte had ingratiated herself with Mme Elizabeth as an impoverished descendant of the French king, Philippe de Valois, and gained a foothold at Versailles. Pretending that she had influence with the Queen, she obtained a great deal of money from Rohan supposedly to plead his case. As proof of her success on his behalf, she arranged for him to meet 'Marie Antoinette' (the beautiful milliner) at eleven o'clock one night in the garden of Versailles. Dressed in a gown of white muslin, the Queen's habitual dress, the figure glided up to him and, her head averted, handed him a single rose with the words, 'You know what this means'. Rohan, overjoyed at first, was downcast when no signs of the Queen's change of heart followed, but Caliogstro convinced him that she did indeed look upon him with kindness. Next, La Motte prevailed on him, by means of a forged letter from the Queen, to obtain for her from the court jewellers an immense diamond necklace. This cumbersome and old fashioned piece of jewellery, a *'rivière'* of 647 brilliants, many of them the size of thrushes eggs, and with a total of 2,800 carats[27] was originally intended as a gift for Mme du Barry from Louis XV. The court jewellers, Bohmer and Bassange, had repeatedly offered it to the Queen as the only person likely to take it off their hands at its price of 1600,000 francs[28] but, apart from its association with the hated royal mistress, this sort of vulgar ostentation was not to the Queen's taste. Rohan arranged for the necklace to be handed over to La Motte to give to Marie Antoinette, whereupon La Motte's husband broke it up and took it to sell in England. In the forged letter, Marie Antoinette had promised to pay for the necklace in instalments but months passed and nothing happened. The jewellers pressed Rohan for their money and eventually he went to the King. Louis, enraged, immediately ordered his arrest and removal to the Bastille, where he managed to live in some style and comfort. Unwisely, the King decided to

26. The night of 16/17 August 1785 was the date of the Cardinal's arrest.
27. Simon Schama, *Citizens* (London, 1989 pbk edn), pp. 203–4.
28. Ritter von Arneth (ed.), *Marie-Antoinette Joseph II und Leopold II, der Brief Wechsel* (Leipzig, 1868), p. 91.

put the conspirators on trial. The eloquence of their lawyers (Rohan's described him as held in 'irons') and the unpopularity of the Queen, a totally innocent victim of the whole scam, led to Rohan's acquittal and that of the milliner whose beauty and poverty, together with the birth of her child during her imprisonment, turned opinion in her favour. Cagliostro was deported. Only La Motte was convicted. Her sentence was harsh. Condemned to life imprisonment she was ordered to be publicly flogged and her shoulder branded with the letter 'V' for *voleur* (thief). Public indignation at this cruel punishment turned to revulsion when the branding iron slipped and seared her breast. Public anger was directed at the Queen for what they saw as an act of malice motivated by Marie Antoinette's vindictiveness. Rumours circulated that she had had an affair with Rohan or at least had encouraged him. Others suggested that the dreadful punishment was retaliation against La Motte for refusing her lesbian advances. A third school of thought held that the Queen had wanted the diamonds and that the letters were not forgeries. As Rohan had not bothered to keep them, this accusation could not be completely disproved. Marie Antoinette's reputation was ruined. A stream of scurrilous pamphlets labelled her 'The Austrian Whore' and imputed every vice imaginable to her. For the Queen, the glad confident morning of light hearted fetes and tranquil days was over.

One of the interesting and sometimes amusing aspects of Blaikie's diaries is the way in which by strange coincidence he seemed to find himself in the midst of important events, and a later undated entry in his diary describes one of these. 'About this time,' he writes, 'the people began to speak very disrespectfully of the Court and the judgement of Mme La Motte &c. At this time, the Duke d'Orléans proposed to change the hothouses at Monceau, for which I made a plan and estimation of the work, which was to be done by Mr Spiring the joiner at Raincy.' Blaikie and Spiring went to select the wood for the greenhouses at a wood merchant's near the Salt-pêtrière, where Mme La Motte was prisoner. While they were settling the accounts, Blaikie relates, 'one of the men of the yard entered and told us that there was a woman had come over the wall and was coming across the yard. The *marchand* told his man to be quiet and say nothing, so she came to the gate where a coach was waiting and so went off. Some time after we were informed this was Mme La Motte who had escaped from prison and gone off for England, so that she did not escape in the night but in broad daylight, so it was clear she was favoured and the orders of government little respected.'[29]

On Monday 4 May 1789 Blaikie was invited to dinner by Mr and Mrs Brown at Versailles. From the top of the potager wall, they watched the newly summoned Estates General process, in all its brilliance, to the Chapel of St Louis as a part of its opening ceremony. First came the King and the royal princes, heralded by fanfares of trumpets, and the Swiss Guards in a flash of scarlet and gold. On their heels followed the King's falconers each carrying a hooded hawk strapped to his arm. Behind them came the nobles, the white plumes of their hats nodding in unison, all dressed

29. The escape took place on 5 June 1787 and she went to London where she fell out of a window in mysterious circumstances some time later.

alike in their ceremonial robes, black silk coats and gleaming gold or silver waistcoats. The clergy were almost as splendid in their lace-encrusted surplices, the rich folds of their capes swirling round them. Both contrasted sharply with the Third Estate which brought up the rear of the procession in the sombre black frock coats ordained as their uniform for the proceedings. Blaikie noticed that the Duke of Orléans headed the third estate and comments, 'this seemed to be the first open opposition to the court which was criticised by some and admired by others,' He declared his own support firmly for the King who wanted 'to render what good he could to his people'. A few pages further on, he describes how, 'the Assembly, not agreeing with the King retired[30] and made some laws and one Mirabeau became the head orator of the *tiers état* so that this step which was to bring down the crown was looked upon as a great step towards the *bonheur* and liberty of the people'. Orléans was banished to his estate at Villers-Cotterets once again and Blaikie was obliged to follow him there for his instructions.

Only at this stage of the diary do accounts of gardens give way to the urgency of events. Joseph Necker, the Swiss financier, had been Director-General of Finance from June 1777 until May 1781. After the breakdown of his successor Calonne's tax reforms and the impending bankruptcy of the government under Calonne's successor, Brienne, there was popular clamour for Necker's recall. Blaikie writes ironically that, 'Mr Necker was the only *personne* talked of as to be the redeemer of France'. Recalled in August 1788, Necker agreed the calling of the Estates General. His dismissal by the king on 11 July 1789 sparked off the riots of that day. Artois, the arch conservative and opponent of Necker as Director-General of Finance, was hissed and hooted at by the people of Paris, relying on his guards to protect him from the crowds. Blaikie does not tell us about the series of riots and disturbances in the city during June 1789 but records the measures taken by the crown. The company of *Allemands* under its commander, the Prince de Lambesc, was brought first to La Muette, the king's hunting lodge near Paris, and then into the city because of increasing unrest. Swiss regiments were camped in the Champs de Mars but far from calming the situation, their presence spread alarm, especially when the French guards, whose loyalty to the crown was uncertain, were confined to barracks. On the 11 July, a Saturday, news of rioting in the streets reached Monceau where Blaikie was paying the workmen. At once he postponed the payments and returned to Bagatelle fearing it would be invaded but all was quiet there. The next day, 12 July, he returned to pay the workman and to dine at La Muette with his friend the contractor for Raincy, Monsieur Amelot. A company of Swiss guards had manned the Chaillot *barrière*, the entrance to the city by the Champs Elysées and even the normally cool Blaikie found 'such preparations for hostility alarming'. The German Guard, mostly composed of 'fine and stout' men from Alsace were at La Muette when he arrived at the château but, during the course of the evening, were ordered to join the rest of the regiment in Paris where the people were gathering in the Champs Elysées and the Place Louis XV (Concorde). At first, the

---

30. To the *Jeu de Paume* or Real Tennis Court at Versailles, an event that took place on 20 June 1789.

demonstration was confined to abusing the soldiers and their Commander but, when an old man was struck to the ground, Lambesc, to avoid confrontation, took refuge with his troops in the gardens of the Tuileries from where he escaped with difficulty. Rumours of attack flew round the city. People started arming themselves with pick axes, anything that came to hand. They were reinforced by the French Guard which had broken out of its barracks and a night of tumult began. Blaikie again rushed back to Bagatelle. Hatred of Artois was so intense by now that he was certain the park and château would be a prime target. He spent the day of the 13th at Bagatelle and decided to take Charlotte to Paris since he dared not leave her alone and unprotected at Bagatelle. The next day, the 14 July, the day of the storming of the Bastille, they took the cabriolet to the city. The barriers were deserted and thrown open and, as he drove along the boulevard, he was advised to wear a cockade, a green leaf if he had nothing else but, further on, the sight of his green cockade, the colour of Artois' livery, drew unwelcome attention to them and shouts of '*a bas le livrée*'. He procured a cockade of another colour. Then, after driving through streets full of people carrying rusty arms and calling on each other to attack the Bastille, he deposited Charlotte safely in the city and returned to Monceau where he left his cabriolet. Blockades were being erected everywhere and cannons drawn up. Back in the centre of Paris he met up with a Mr Gordon, and the two men took refuge in a restaurant to watch what was happening in safety. From the windows, they saw the 'bleeding heads of some which the mob had murdered' being carried past on poles or picks. 'This horrid scene' he tells us, 'soon decided us to leave our place and we parted'. Blaikie returned to Monceau for his horse. 'At every step,' he writes, 'there was the continuation and preparations for defending Paris.' Orléans had been at Monceau all day but Blaikie describes him as uneasy and reports that, 'in the evening he set off for Versailles'. Blaikie decided to try for Bagatelle leaving Paris by the barrier of the Roule. 'Hundreds, perhaps thousands' of people were assembled there 'some crying out to go to Bagatelle to burn it.' The next moments were terrifying ones for him, but he kept his head. 'Here I was stopped in the midst of this mob some holding my horse by the bridle others holding me by the legs so that I remained for some time in this situation, several demanding who I was, others where I was going, some saying I was an aristocrat [31] etc. At last one came and whispered me in the ear, "*Mr Blaikie sauvez-vous*". I then told them that I believed there were soldiers patrolling in the Bois de Boulogne.' Pretending to put himself under the mob's command, he offered to ride forward into the Bois, then return and tell them if the soldiers were there. His friends among the crowd backed his proposal and he escaped, making his way by Neuilly to Bagatelle. The place was deserted except for his old servant, Lafrance, who had hidden among the trees awaiting his return. Keeping the horse saddled, they kept up their courage by drinking a bottle of wine together. They agreed that Blaikie would sleep while the old man kept watch on the road to warn of any approaching crowd in time for

---

31. Aristocrat was a term used for anyone suspected of right wing sympathies. the opposite was Democrat.

them to slip away by another route. Nothing happened and, little by little, 'the people of Bagatelle crept back'.

Meanwhile, the King was at Versailles, locked in dispute with the National Assembly. The shocking events of the 14th unnerved him so much that, although only a few days earlier he had declared that the troops were essential for the protection of the Assembly itself, he arrived alone and on foot before the Assembly and agreed, in order to prevent further bloodshed, to remove his troops from Paris. The news travelled back to the city and eased the tension but it was not till the 16th that he agreed to all the demands of the Assembly and recalled the hero of the crowds, Necker. Blaikie heard the news almost immediately from a Swiss guard who came in disguise to Bagatelle to let them know what had happened. He was dining with Edward Rowley,[32] the Duke of Orléans' huntsman/coachman from Le Raincy, and they decided to leave at once for Paris, but on finding that no one entering the city would be allowed out again that night, Blaikie left his guest to go on to Monceau alone. Later he heard that 'Rolly', on being stopped and questioned, told his questioners that the King had given in to all the people's demands. Apparently, the news had not yet reached Paris and the Englishman was carried off to the *Palais Royal* where he was enthroned as the bringer of such welcome tidings. Blaikie's comment on all this was that 'it did honour to the English to show a lusty roast Beef Englishman instead of some of those half Starved Jockeys which is often seen at the races'.

That same night, recognising the King's cause was lost, Artois, the Prince de Condé, and the Duke and Duchess of Polignac, departed for Chantilly and from there fled to Turin where they intended to raise a foreign invasion to restore the power of the Bourbons. Their departure set off a chain of emigrations and their intrigues abroad succeeded only in weakening further the King's position at home.

In the city, fear and suspicion had taken hold. One night Blaikie and two friends went into the Café de Foy[33] for a liqueur and the waiter was so afraid at the sight of them that he left a bottle of brandy on the table and told them to help themselves! At Bagatelle, Blaikie's situation was deteriorating. One feature of the Ancien Régime was its punitive game laws. Severe penalties were inflicted on starving peasants who shot a rabbit for the pot or killed a pheasant for scratching up the newly sown grain in his fields, but in 1789 the peasants started invading the game preserves. There were so many of them that they intimidated the gamekeepers who were forced to turn a blind eye to their depredations. These game incursions spread to the estates bordering Paris, the massacre of pheasants reaching such a level that they were sold in the markets at the equivalent of a penny each.[34] Bagatelle was one of the hunters' targets. Blaikie's lack of sympathy for those employees of Artois who joined in the invasion of the park earned him the spite and enmity of people already jealous of his favoured position at Bagatelle.

---

32. This is how his name appears in the Accounts for Raincy where he receives 492 livres for 2 month's wages and board in 1790. AN., 300 AP I 2110.
33. Café de Foy one of the most famous cafés of the Palais Royal.
34. H. Walpole, *Letters*, vol. XIV, p. 213.

The 5th of October 1789 was a milestone on the road to Revolution. Early that morning the tocsin sounded its call to arms. Crowds of *poissardes*, the market women of Paris, surrounded the Town Hall. Angered by the shortage of bread, and incensed by tales of a supposed orgy at Versailles on 1 October when, at a reception attended by the King and Queen, the Royal Guards were said to have trampled the national cockade underfoot, they set out for Versailles to confront the King and the National Assembly. Heavy rain failed to discourage them and the crowd swelled to around 6000. This huge caravan, dragging cannon from the Hôtel de Ville and armed with a collection of 'broomsticks, lances, pitchforks, swords, pistols and muskets,' [35] attracted others to join them so that the mob had swelled to around seven thousand when it reached Versailles. Two hours behind it, held up by the crowds in the city centre, came 20,000 National Guards reluctantly headed by Lafayette who was virtually the prisoner of his own men. Another host of civilians with pikes and whatever weapons they could find brought up the rear. When this fearsome procession reached Versailles late in the evening, they swept aside the reception committee gathered to meet them and invaded the Assembly. Their leader presented their case before the deputies; then the King received a small group of the woman to whom he gave his assurance that he had already ordered the provisioning of the city. These palliative steps, plus their fatigue, quietened them and they bedded down where they could for the night. The palace itself was heavily guarded but, early on the morning of the 6th, some of the crowd broke into it by a distant door, opened for them, it was said, by the connivance of the Duke of Orléans. Spreading through the palace, they surged towards the Queen's apartments. One guard was shot on the stairway and Marie Antoinette's bodyguard was killed defending her door. His resistance alerted her and gave her time to escape by a secret passage to the King's apartments. It seemed as if battle was about to begin between the King's bodyguard and National Guards who wanted to bring the King back to Paris, but the crisis was averted. The King and Queen appeared on the balcony and the King agreed to go back to Paris. A few hours later the procession set out on its six hour journey to the city.

It is not clear from Blaikie's diary whether he was at Versailles that morning or whether he joined the procession as it reached the city. One account affirms that he rode at one side of the Queen's coach the whole way, while the oldest of the royal bodyguards kept one hand on the door at the other, and that these two loyal retainers were the only people outside the coach to whom the queen spoke during the six hour journey.[36] Blaikie wrote, 'The Scene was most shocking to see, the *poissardes*

---

35. *Procédure criminelle instruite au Chatelet de Paris*, 2 vols (Paris, 1790), pp. 117–32, quoted in George Rudé, *The French Revolution* (London, 1988), p. 57. See also Chateaubriand, *Mémoires de l'outre-tombe*, trans. A. A. Teixeira de Matos (London, 1902), vol. I, p. 164.
36. Joan Haslip, *Marie Antoinette* (London, 1987; pbk edn, 1989), pp. 213–14. I have been unable to retrieve the sources for this statement. The Duchess de Tourzel, *Memoirs* (London, 1886), pp. 38–43, describes herself as holding the dauphin on her knees and writes, 'The King and the Queen spoke with their customary kindness to those who surrounded their carriage'. Joan Haslip also writes that Blaikie was at this time in the queen's employ, presumably referring to his unrecorded work at the hameau.

mounted up on the Cannon, some with one of the guards coats or hats, and the poor guards obliged to be conducted along with them in this manner, and the heads of their comrades that was killed at Versailles brought along with them. The King and Queen and Dauphin was likewise conducted in this humiliating condition.' To cries of *'Voilà le Boulanger et la Boulangère et le Petit Mitron'* (the baker, the baker's wife and the baker's boy), the procession continued. Blaikie goes on to describe the frightened Queen and his own efforts to assist her, 'The Queen sat at the bottom of the Coach with the Dauphin on her Knees in this condition while some of the Blackguards in the rabble was firing their guns over her head. As I stood by the coach, one Man fired and loaded his gun four times and fired it over the Queen's head. I told him to desist but he said he would continue but, when I told him I should try by force to stop him and not have people hurt by his imprudence, some cried it was right and so he Slugged off very quietly, and after, the court went on and they lodged the King and his family in the Tuileries.'

At Bagatelle, maintenance was reduced to a minimum and 'everyone was at variance'. The improvements at Le Raincy came to a temporary halt with the Duke's departure for England on 14 October 1789, a visit which lasted until July the following year.[37] As the accounts could not be settled or new work undertaken without his permission, Blaikie went to London with M. Amelot, the contractor at Le Raincy, to see the Duke and obtain his authorisation. He gives the date of this visit to London as December 1790 but it was more likely to have been the previous year. They spent three weeks in the capital. As well as showing Amelot the Tower and other sights, Blaikie took the opportunity to meet old friends again and visited Southgate to call on his uncle whom he had not seen for many years.

The evening of his return to Paris, a number of his friends gathered to see him off. Amongst them was Mr Hoy, now head gardener at Sion, and Mr Fairbairn, probably the Fairbairn who replaced Miller at the Chelsea Physic Garden. The atmosphere was one of foreboding, all aware that they were perhaps meeting for the last time. Blaikie himself was eager to return to Paris where he had left Charlotte in charge of his house, and feared that the people at Bagatelle had made trouble for her. It turned out she had felt threatened and had called in two Swiss guards to protect her. For greater security, Blaikie and Charlotte moved from the courtyard to a newly completed cottage in the *potager*. Shortly afterwards, he records in his diary the visit from the Queen and the difficulties it made for him.

At this point Blaikie's chronology becomes confusing. If his visit to London took place in December 1789, this would date the Queen's visit to Bagatelle as June 1790, while she was still free to drive out from the Tuileries without constraint, a situation that did not last beyond Easter 1991 when the royal family were prevented from leaving Paris for St Cloud. From then on they were prisoners, except for the brief period of their escape to Varennes in June 1791. A summer 1790 visit would also tie

---

37. Browning, *Despatches from Paris before the Revolution*, 2 vols, vol. II, p. 266. Letter dated 15 October 1789 from Fitzgerald to the Duke of Leeds, 'The Duke of Orléans to the astonishment of everybody quitted Paris yesterday morning early for England'.

in with the reports of a conspiracy at Bagatelle in June 1790.[38] Blaikie's next diary entry concerns the Princesse de Lamballe, Marie Antoinette's faithful lady-in-waiting. He tells us that he went to her house in Passy[39] to deliver a plan for her garden one week and returned a week later to find the Swiss porter at her door in tears because 'the Princess *est enlevée cette Nuit et elle est perdue'*. The princess was sent to the prison of La Force in August 1792,[40] yet he next describes making a little garden for the banker Legrand at Passy and meeting Benjamin Franklin there. Franklin left Paris in 1785 and died in America in 1792. Subsequently, Blaikie describes the preparation for the celebrations commemorating the first anniversary of the storming of the Bastille; of how the whole of Paris went to work to prepare the ground at the Champs de Mars, 'Ladies wheeling the barrow and loading along with shoe blacks'. This much documented event took place on the 14 July 1790. It seems that as Blaikie comes to the end of his diary, he is recalling incidents at random as they occur to him much later in life.

By 1790, apart from his work at Le Raincy for the Duke, Blaikie had apparently only one major client left, the Farmer-General, De la Haye (1757–1794), who had called on Blaikie in 1789 to improve his property at St Firmin, overlooking the gardens of Chantilly. The Prince de Condé, owner of Chantilly, had already left France when Blaikie began the work but expected to return and had plans for the refurbishment of the gardens at Chantilly. He gave his permission for Blaikie to take some of the land at the fringe of the Chantilly estate into De la Haye's garden and to clear a view from there to the Isle d'Amour so that the two gardens might enhance each other. It was while he was working here early in 1792, that Blaikie saw the people from Senlis swarm over the gardens below, carrying off the statues and the lead from the roof, smashing up what they could not take away, even, to Blaikie's amazement, 'selling the fish, some of them they said was very old and almost white with age'.

On 6 February 1792, on the sequestration of emigré estates, Blaikie was forced to leave Bagatelle and rented a substantial, three storey house to the south west of the Grille de Chaillot[41] with courtyards, a garden, and a pavilion, where the gardener and his wife lodged. It had an entrance on the rue des Bouchers. A detailed inventory, amongst Blaikie's papers, of its furniture and fittings including the numbers and types of the trees in each of the gardens shows he was obviously a prosperous man at this time. He had his shirts and linen monogrammed and sent from England, his cellar was full of good wines. He had prudent investments and no financial worries. Yet within a few short months he would be almost penniless.

Unmoved by the worsening situation for foreigners, he had continued to work at St Firmin for De La Haye. While he was there on 5 April 1792, a messenger arrived

---

38. See Chapter 9, note 89.

39. Her house still exists. See R. Avezon and M. Dumolin, 'La Maison de Madame de Lamballe à Passy', *Bulletin de la Société Historique d'Auteuil et Passy*, vol. XL, pp. 93–101.

40. Tourzel, *Memoirs*, p. 243, gives Saturday 18 August as the date of her arrest.

41. In 1788, when the wall was built around Paris, the Grille de Chaillot was moved from an earlier position to one just to the east of the Arc de Triomphe which, of course, did not exist at that time.

for him from Paris, with the disturbing news that his house had been seized by *huissiers* (bailiffs) who, after stealing his money had piled his furniture on to a cart and taken it away. He hurried home from St Firmin to find 'everything in the greatest disorder'. He writes, 'What a scene! All my people had been turned out and every thing seized and the house occupied by *huissiers* and Soldiers' Rather than approach the house, he set off for the neighbouring district of Boulogne to bring a judge to the scene but the judge, he was told, had gone to church. The judge's clerk advised Blaikie to go to Passy to the district judge there. Instead Blaikie returned to Chaillot. He learned, probably from John Murray, the Ermenonville gardener, who had called at the house and had managed to remove some of Blaikie's possessions while the *huissiers* were drinking,[42] that his house had been emptied, that the guards had occupied the building since 2 April and had stolen or destroyed most of his possessions. They had left shortly before his return. Furious, he set off in pursuit of them and caught up with the cart carrying his belongings and guarded by a group of soldiers in the rue J.J. Rousseau. He immediately stopped them, and the scuffle that followed brought the National Guard to see what had happened. The officer in charge, whom Blaikie happened to know, ordered everything to be taken into a court and Blaikie and his robbers conducted to the Palais de Justice. Here he met with no better luck than before. He was told that his property had been seized by order of the district Tribunal. Determined to see some justice, he took hold of one of the *huissiers* and swore he would not let him go. As a result of this action he was taken before a Tribunal Judge who ordered Blaikie's belongings to be returned to him the next day on surety of 1800 francs. The next morning the judge from Passy arrived with a lawyer to examine the damage. The doors had been locked and a locksmith was called to open up the house. He confirmed, 'that he had been ordered by the *huissiers* to break open the secretaire and drawers and had seen those rascals take out pieces of gold but he could not positively declare how much'. An inventory of the damage[43] shows that around 3000 livres in cash, two dozen initialled shirts and much of the household linen had been stolen. The wine cellar had been emptied. A large cheese and a ham from England had been eaten but, more seriously, Blaikie's plans had been used to light the fire during the *huissiers'* occupation. They had torn pages from his account book and, he tells us, 'it was clearly seen by some of the fragments that what I had lost exceeded 50,000 francs'.[44] The justification for this devastating attack on his house and possessions was the doubtful charge that, at some stage in the past, before the house had been rented to Blaikie, a tenant had absconded without paying his rent and that Blaikie, as the present occupant, was liable for the debt which he did not even know

---

42. Pierre Coulomb et Maurice Gonon, p. 104. The authors confirm that the whole thing was an excuse to rob Blaikie and that even the document allowing the seizure of Blaikie's property was in the name of someone called Sarrey not Blaikie.

43. Among Blaikie's papers is an inventory, taken by the Justice of the Peace, of the goods and money he had lost.

44. The term 'franc' was, at this time, interchangeable with 'livre' There were between 22 and 23 livres to the pound sterling at that date, which means that Blaikie lost around £2000 in 1792 terms.

existed.⁴⁵ It was a case that could never have stood up in normal times. In the climate of xenophobia existing at the period, with France about to declare war on Austria, and Blaikie the servant of the hated emigré, Artois, there was no redress available. Gamely, he brought his case before the National Assembly on 18 September 1792.⁴⁶ His petition was referred to the Minister for Justice, the notorious Danton. The Assembly asked for a report within eight days but nothing seems to have been done. In the meantime, his financial problems grew. He was owed large sums of money by the Duke of Orléans who arranged in August 1792 to pay his debts to Blaikie by means of a *rente viagère* (an annuity for life) but before long Orléans was bankrupt and Blaikie became his creditor for 120,250 francs⁴⁷ His only income was now a small annuity from an investment of 12000 livres. This was intended to bring him an income of 1000 livres a year and it was paid in rapidly diminishing amounts until it ceased in 1796 when 100 livres invested in 1792 had a cash value of 0.5 livres.

After the events of April at Chaillot, he rented a small house with a garden in the rue de l'Oratoire situated off the rue de Neuilly and not far from his previous house.⁴⁸ It was from here that he would witness, on 10 August 1792, the aftermath of one of the most horrifying events of the Revolution.

Meanwhile, the campaign against the King intensified with each day. On the 20 June, the anniversary of the Flight to Varennes in 1791 and of the Tennis Court Oath in 1789, crowds gathered at the Tuileries led by the brewer, Santerre, a familiar figure at gatherings and riots. The guards, instead of holding them back, stood by while they invaded the palace. Blaikie witnessed the scene and, contemptuous of this 'ragged regiment' carrying sticks with blades of knives or scissors tied to them, told the National Guards beside him that '20 good fellows with sticks could have drove back Santerre'. He reports, 'they told me they had no orders to interfere, so that the tumult went on and seemed to please the people to see the royal family humbled'. Once inside the building, the mob cornered the King in his private apartments where, his back to the window, he sat composedly facing them and responded calmly to their insults. He drank a toast to the nation and accepted the red bonnet or Phrygian cap, the head gear of the *sans culottes* and symbol of freedom from tyranny. After two long hours a member of the Assembly came to deliver him and he was able to return to the Queen and his children.

It was now only a question of time before the monarchy would be overthrown. On 30 July, 500 Marseillais soldiers arrived in the city, one deputy described this

---

45. The inventory shows that the property had been rented to a Dr Daignon by its owner a M. Thibaul, who states in the inventory that the property belongs to him and has previously been occupied by a Mr Gillerond. Dr Daignon sub-let it to Blaikie.

46. Hand-written extract from *Le Moniteur*, 20 September 1792, submitted as part of Blaikie's claim to the Commissioners of Liquidation, Arbitration and Award appointed in 1815 to examine and settle the claims of British citizens against the French State. Blaikie Papers.

47. Blaikie also took on the debt owed by Orléans to Amelot, the contractor whom he had asked to be his partner in the undertaking.

48. Not the current rue de l'Oratoire but a street that later disappeared or was renamed. See BHVP, *Plan routier de la ville et faubourgs de Paris, 1836*; and Hillairet, p. 298, vol. 1.

'fearsome' band as '500 madmen, mostly drunk' wearing the red bonnets of the *sans culottes*. It was known that they had been summoned for some sort of insurrection. On the 6 August, Dr John Moore travelling to Paris met carriages of Parisians fleeing from the city. Those he spoke to could not believe that he thought of going there and all seemed to think that a conspiracy would break out on the 9th of the month, but he could not take seriously the idea of a conspiracy known to the whole population and continued on his way.[49] On 9 August the city was in a state of expectancy. Blaikie heard shots about nine in the evening then at around 11 o'clock the dreaded tocsin sounded. At the Tuileries, the King and Queen waited, surrounded by about a thousand Swiss guards and two battalions of National Guards. Around two in the morning the crowds from St Antoine, St Marceau and other sections of the city, marched towards the Tuileries with the men from Marseilles and regiments of National Guards who supported them. Shooting broke out in the courtyard where the Swiss guards and loyal forces of the National Guards defended the king. At 6 a.m., Louis reviewed the guard, then decided that, to spare further bloodshed, he would take his family to the Assembly for protection. Between lines of soldiers, Louis and the red eyed and weeping Queen, with their two children made their way to the Assembly, the seven year old Dauphin scuffling the fallen leaves as he walked. They reached the building safely but the ineffectual King had forgotten to order the Swiss to lay down their arms and they refused to give way without his orders. They fought bravely killing some 300 of the attackers but when the King eventually sent word for them to cease fighting, the mob rushed upon them determined on revenge. They were pursued up the great staircase of the palace, chased through the apartments, dragged from hiding places in corners and cupboards, thrown alive from the windows, impaled upon pikes and torn to pieces, their bodies stripped and mutilated. The crowd rampaged through the Royal apartments, killing any aristocrats they could find. They broke into the wine cellars and kitchens, murdered the servants and contested their trophies with each other. A group of about 60 Swiss Guards managed to march in good order to the Hotel de Ville to surrender their arms. An impromptu court was held on their arrival and they were condemned to death there and then. Atrocity followed atrocity as the fleeing Swiss sought refuge in the streets. Blaikie, immobile as a result of an accident to his leg, sat on his terrace hearing the tumult and watching the figures running around in the Champs Elysées. 'By good fortune or providence', he records, 'some were saved. One poor fellow who knew not where to run was met by chance at our door and conducted by Bob Roberts. We soon took him in and so saved his life. We changed his clothes in case of search. I told him to remain quiet as they could not come into the house without first applying to me who Sat upon the *terrasse* and saw this horrible Scene.' Five unarmed Swiss guards, who had arrived from their barracks at Courbevoye to see their comrades, were massacred a little way from Blaikie's door. Their groans and the shouts of the rabble so affected the poor man Blaikie and his wife had concealed, that he begged Blaikie to let him out to perish with his comrades.

49. John Moore M.D., *A Journal during a Residence in France from the beginning of August to the middle of December 1992*, 2 vols (London, 1793), vol. 1, p. 1.

But Blaikie, determined to save one life at least, refused. Filled with revulsion for the crowd, he writes, 'Many of those anthrophages passed in the Street and stopt to show us parts of the Suisses they had massacred'. What was worse he knew some of these assassins and would never have imagined them capable of anything like this. 'Every one,' he observes, 'seemed to glory in what he had done and to Show even their fury upon the dead body by cutting them or even tearing their clothes as monuments of triumph, so that this seemed as if the people were struck with a sort of Madness'. Scarcely a single Swiss survived.

Blaikie describes the aftermath, 'Those poor wretches that was thus massacred was put in heaps in the Champs Elysées and then taken by cart loads and buried in a field opposite the Church at the Roulle'. He and his wife got their fugitive away safely without danger to themselves through the help of two French friends who had already saved two Swiss. However, before he could get the man safely away, the news of his action spread and the poor fugitive's wife came to his door with her four children crying and begging to see her husband. Blaikie continues, 'Although it touched our heart, we were forced to deny that we had done any such thing as it might both expose him and us who were Strangers. Next day we had the pleasure by the help of M. Vaudemond to have him enrolled in the Parisian *gardes*'. It seemed that the crowd was ready to vent its fury on anyone of Swiss nationality. The Swiss porter at the British Embassy, a man with four small children was seized. Blaikie describes how, 'His children upon their knees begged their father's life. He asked that they would murder his children before him and then he would die contented at not leaving them to perish. However this Scene softened the hearts of those cannibals and they left him'. 'But,' Blaikie finishes, 'it was impossible to describe all the acts of wanton horror that happened this day and the Mortification that the King met with from those he had put his trust in. They condemned him and his family to the prison of the Temple'.

The diary ends here. Blaikie's action in saving the Swiss was a noble one for, as a foreigner, had he been caught, both he and his wife would have undoubtedly been killed. Further horrors were to come. Feelings of hatred and distrust against the 'enemies' of the state were fomented during the following weeks and culminated in the September massacres, in which the priests imprisoned in the Abbaye were murdered by the mob. The fury spread to other prisons. Many of the courtiers and servants of the crown, who had narrowly escaped death on the 10 August, were confined in the prison of La Force where they met a cruel end on that terrible day. Amongst them was his client, the soft-hearted Princesse de Lamballe. She refused to swear an oath of loyalty to the régime and one of hatred of the king. Pushed into an alley, she was stripped and hacked to death, her mutilated body dragged through the streets and her head paraded on a pike before the Queen's windows.

Blaikie's world and those of countless others had collapsed and before long Paris would become too dangerous a place for him to live.[50]

---

50. To protect himself Blaikie enrolled in the National Guard at Neuilly in February 1790. Lauraguais papers, private collection, Château d'Arlay.

CHAPTER 14

Manicamp Revisited

U NREST AND LAWLESSNESS prevailed in Paris for a time after the September massacres.[1] Patriotic fervour mingled with trepidation greeted the news that the Prussians had crossed the borders and might soon be at the barriers of the city.[2] However, the successful stand of the French forces at Valmy on 20 September against the Prussian army sent the enemy back not just to their own borders but across the Rhine and opened a new phase of the Revolution. On 25 September the monarchy was finally overthrown and a republic declared. The 22nd of September was the date chosen to mark year one of the Republic and in October the debate began on the fate of the King. The Prussian retreat left the way open for a French advance to 'liberate' the peoples on the Rhine's left bank and by the end of 1792 war with England and Holland seemed inevitable. In December that year, the King was put on trial for his life, condemned to death on 16 January 1793, and executed on the 21st.

The declaration of war on Britain by the National Convention on 1 February 1793 probably decided the Blaikies to quit Paris for the estates of Lauraguais in Picardy.[3] On their way, they stopped briefly at Malmaison, the property that would be associated with the Empress Joséphine. Here, they hid their most treasured possessions, amongst them the clock given to Blaikie by Louis XVI.[4] In happier days Blaikie had laid out the gardens of Manicamp near Chauny for Lauraguais. Now, Lauraguais, like many another aristocrat, had decided that the safest option was to retire to the country and cultivate the land. Doing nothing by halves, he immediately became a committed agriculturalist, an occupation smiled upon by the Revolutionary government. Besides, as it was no longer possible to collect his rents with impunity, farming had become his only source of income. The loyal Blaikie was a godsend. He and his wife settled down to blend as best they could into the community where, after the Law of Suspects of September 1793, as foreigners, they were prisoners subject to the authority of the *maire* and forbidden to leave the commune.

André Thouin, at the *Jardin du Roi*, now *the Jardin national des Plantes*, was occupied

---

1. Oscar Browning, *Despatches of Lord Gower*, p. 246.
2. Brunswick Manifesto of 25 July threatened death to National Guardsmen and citizens who opposed the Allied advance into France together with exemplary measures against Paris if the royal family was harmed. August 1792, invasion by Allies. Verdun, the last fortress between the enemy and Paris surrendered to Prussians, 1 September.
3. They went first to Mont Canisy but did not stay. Blaikie Papers.
4. The hand-written ticket on the back of the Blaikie clock reads exactly as follows: 'Presented to T. Blaikie by Louis XVI buried at Malmaison in the reign Terror'. What connection Blaikie had with the family of Le Coulteux du Moley, the owners of Malmaison is unknown. Their garden was laid out *à l'anglaise* and Blaikie or one of his protégés may have been employed by them at some time.

on many fronts. His major concern was to secure finances for the gardens since its expenses were no longer paid for by the royal treasury and, with the professors of the botanical school, to lobby the National Assembly for the establishment of a Museum of Natural History with its own library. Their representations were successful and Thouin himself was *appointed Professeur de la Culture*. He wrote to Blaikie at Manicamp on 22 November 1793 suggesting an exchange of plants and seeds and hinting that Blaikie was being considered for a post in one of the agricultural colleges which the Revolutionary government intended to set up in the provinces. There was no definite information as yet but he urged his friend not to worry. At the same time he reassured him that he would not be harmed, since, he wrote, 'the Scots have always been friends to France'.[5]

Blaikie's interest in agriculture was not new. His quotation from Pope's Epistle IV to Lord Burlington on seeing the park of Guiscard[6] shows that, in the tradition of English landscape gardeners, he saw the cultivation of the land and the needs of agriculture as an essential ingredient of a fine landscape.[7] He had acted as Lauraguais' farm manager at Mont Canisy, and during his travels, the observations he made in his diary on the condition of crops and of the soil reflect his interest in the land. Now, he applied himself diligently to agricultural improvement. He produced a system by which a smallholder could cultivate 100 acres of land on his own with only two horses. His plan was approved by the Agricultural Committee of the Revolutionary Government, and he set himself to work on trying out different strains of potatoes to be used as an alternative to wheat. High bread prices with their concomitant riots persuaded the Revolutionary government of the value of this 'new' crop. It decided to promote the potato, and make a political point at the same time, by converting the parterres and lawns of royal palaces to the production of the tuber. The palace gardeners had received no wages since the departure of their royal masters, consequently they brought scant enthusiasm to this backbreaking task. The cost of digging up beds and lawns, preparing and manuring the ground, and throwing up barriers to protect the crops from theft, far outweighed any but the symbolic benefits of the project. Blaikie provided the seed potatoes for the Tuileries and Thouin wrote to him on 31 March 1794 thanking him for a present of several varieties of potatoes and promising to let him know if he succeeded with them. Lauraguais, too, threw himself into disseminating the virtues of the potato. As an aristocrat, he was imprisoned in April 1794 at Chauny but his incarceration lasted only a few days and during it, he arranged for trucks of potatoes to be brought to the prison so that he could sell them to the people from behind his cell bars.[8] No doubt these potatoes, too, were furnished

---

5. Blaikie Papers, quoted in Birrell, Introduction, pp. 10–11.
6. Diary, between 10 and 19 April 1779,
    Whose ample lawns are not afraid to feed
    the milky heifer and deserving steed.
7. See John Dixon Hunt, *The Figure in the Landscape* (1976), p. 99.
8. See Alfred Pontieux et Jules Bouzard, *Notice historique sur Manicamp (Aisne) d'après les notes de Monsieur l'Abbé Carlet* (Chauny, 1937).

by Blaikie. The Scot was never paid for the seed potatoes he provided for the Tuileries but a fulsome letter of praise from the Committee dated 7 July 1794, survives among his papers, assuring him that, 'We are very pleased to receive this testimony of your fraternity and can only applaud you. We see in your letter a new mark of your interest in your brothers in the way you are improving your lands to increase their cereal richness. The example you give to cultivators is a blessing which merits their esteem and their affection. Continue, dear citizen, your gentle and useful occupation, let us know of your researches to increase public prosperity.' [9]

Blaikie's reward was the offer of the post of director of a national botanical school at Versailles in 1793. He turned it down. Why, he does not say but he was not the sort of man to submit to the restraints of the life of a public servant. He wrote to a member of the council of Versailles asking him to convey his thanks and regrets that he could not accept their offer. [10]

Lauraguais emerged from his imprisonment without any evidence against him, the faithful Blaikie having destroyed or hidden a number of incriminating documents at the château. However, some time later the count came to the attention of St Just, Robespierre's dreaded henchman, and his arrest was ordered on 16 July 1794 by the Committee of Public Safety, the instrument of the Terror; the pretext for his arrest, that he had brought an action against the people for cutting down trees in his woods and had himself cut down the one that they had chosen as their 'Tree of Liberty'. The document arrived at Chauny on 20 July and Lauraguais was despatched under guard for Paris. At Senlis he was taken ill with a fever and had to spend the night there. He reached Paris and was imprisoned in the Conciergerie on the 9 thermidor (27 July), the very day of the fall of Robespierre and the end of the Terror. A month later he was released. His wife did not share his good fortune. She had taken refuge on her estate in the Pas de Calais, was denounced, brought to Paris, condemned to death on the 18 pluviôse an 2 (6 February 1794) and executed the same day.

In Paris, during 1793, Bélanger, in spite of all the proofs he had given of public spirit and a genuine enthusiasm for political reform, found himself in danger. In the middle of the night of October 1793, he was called before the Revolutionary Committee of his district and told that his house in the rue des Capucins had been commandeered as a prison for foreigners (it became known as *la maison d'arrêt des Anglais*). The architect objected but was informed that it was either acceptance or prison. His compliance did not in the end save him. On 3 February, he and his mistress, the actress Mlle de Dervieux, were arrested on trumped up charges and taken first to the prison of Saint Lazare and subsequently to that of Saint-Pélagie where the regime was more severe. They, like Lauraguais, were saved from the guillotine only by the

---

9. It is not clear whether the letter, headed simply 'Dear Citizen' was intended for him or Lauraguais but Blaikie makes it clear that he was the one who furnished the seed potatoes. Blaikie Papers.

10. Blaikie Papers. A declaration by Lauraguais to the Municipality of Chauny (18 October 1793) confirms as proof of Blaikie's loyalty his appointment as a commissioner for the Seine et Oise. Private archive, Château d'Arlay.

fall of Robespierre. Once out of prison, they married and Bélanger wrote to tell Sophie Arnould the news. Sophie had bought an ancient monastery at Luzarches where she lived in retirement. In her reply, she told Bélanger that the members of the local Committee had respected her person but had fallen upon her fortune. Although she made light of it, her situation was dire. Once the centre of a brilliant world of artists, she now lived penniless, in total solitude, in a ruinous dwelling, tending her potager like an old peasant countrywoman. Her courtesans, she tells Bélanger, are numerous; cocks, hens, turkeys, sheep and rabbits. She lives like a savage and has almost forgotten the language of humans.[11] He and Sophie continued to correspond to the end. She died in great pain and in poverty in Paris on 22 October 1802. Among the few mourners at her graveside were both Lauraguais and Bélanger.

On his release from prison, Bélanger found himself in grave financial difficulty. He energetically lobbied the Minister of the Interior, who was responsible for the administration and conservation of public monuments and, in 1796, was briefly put in charge of the upkeep of the Conservatoire and the Bibliothèque Nationale but his projects for these buildings and others proved too grandiose for the members of the Directorate; his only success, the replacement of the cupola of the Halle au Blé[12] (Corn Market) by an iron one in 1807. His career limped on. He made some money out of private commissions but lucrative government appointments eluded him.[13] It was only with the return of the Bourbons in 1814 that his position was restored. In 1815 he became once more the official architect of Artois, now heir to the throne with the title of Monsieur. The King, Louis XVIII, had already nominated Bélanger in 1814 as *Architecte des Menus Plaisirs et dessinateur du Cabinet de Sa Majesté*, responsible for the staging of all court events, but his tenure of these posts was brief. He died on 22 May 1818 and was buried in the cemetery of Père-Lachaise. In spite of his distinguished career, he had been unable to pay off his debts and his wife was forced to sell all his drawings, his library and other possessions at auction.[14]

Blaikie, although erstwhile superintendent of the hated Artois, had successfully reinvented himself as a noble cultivator of the soil but he, too, was still in a precarious position financially. On 24 August 1793 all joint stock companies had been suppressed and replaced by a consolidated national debt, the *Grand Livre de la Dette Publique*. The livre steadily declined in worth. In 1794, 100 livres were worth only 40 percent

---

11. Stern II, pp. 84–7.
12. Built by the architect Nicolas Le Camus de Mézières, it was begun in 1763 on the site of the residence of Catherine de Medici and finished in 1767. Situated between Saint-Eustache, the Louvre and the Palais Royale it was built as a huge rotunda with a central court open to the sky. This was later covered over by a wooden dome which burnt down in 1802. In spite of great hostility to the idea of a dome of iron, Bélanger's iron cupola replaced it. In 1889, the Halle au Blé was transformed by the architect Paul Blondel and became the Bourse. Michel Gallet, *Les architectes parisiens du XVIIIe siècle* (Paris, 1995); Stern, vol. II, p. 202.
13. See Martine Constans, 'L'architecte-décorateur François-Joseph Bélanger. L'énigme d'une carriére brizée', *Les cahiers de Maisons* No. 23, été 1994, pp. 6–19.
14. Stern, vol. II, pp. 350–3.

of their 1789 value in assignats, the paper currency of the Revolution, and by 1796 the original hundred was worth only 0.5 of one livre[15] so that the savings of a lifetime were wiped out. In response to an Act of 2 floréal an 3 (20 April 1795), Blaikie was obliged to put forward his claim as a creditor of Philippe Egalité who had been guillotined in November 1793. To satisfy the authorities he had to obtain a certificate from the local mayor and in it he is described as Thomas Blaikie, living at Chauny (i.e. in the commune of Chauny) *'sans profession'*. At first he refused the offer made to him on the grounds that it was incorrectly calculated, and not in his favour but, eventually, he was ordered to accept a bond equivalent to an annuity of 6000 francs. That he sold it for just 5900 francs the very day he received it, is proof that he was in desperate straits financially.

However, in September 1796, although he could not reside outside the district of Chauny, he secured permission to travel outside it, thus virtually ending his imprisonment and, at the beginning of 1797, a contract he made with Lauraguais to manage his farms and gardens shows that he either possessed or had borrowed enough cash to invest 3956 livres in the improvement of the farms in return for an annual payment of '2400 livres metalliques'. He described the farm buildings and houses as being in a ruinous condition and he and his wife provided furniture, linen and china to make them habitable.[16] The venture was doomed but Lauraguais was later to confirm in a letter to Blaikie how much he regretted that he had been unable to realise his ambition to set up a fine agricultural establishment with the Scot. What Blaikie did not realise was that Lauraguais was without the means to accomplish this aim and was beset by creditors, that his impecuniousness was not a temporary state, arising from the losses he had suffered during the Revolution, but a result of his massive debts over many years. He appeared to be solvent. In 1797 he purchased the church of Manicamp from the Revolutionary authorities who, in 1789, had begun the sale of church property in an unsuccessful attempt to transfer wealth to the people. Lauraguais' action caused riots in the village. He and previous châtelains of Manicamp had complained that the church was so close to the château that it disturbed their privacy. The disestablishment of the church offered him the perfect opportunity to demolish the building in the guise of supporter of the new secularism. The villagers were incensed and, after violent disturbances, succeeded in being granted an injunction against him.[17]

Initially work on the farm went well. The weather in 1797 was fine but the excellent harvest brought Lauraguais' creditors down on his farms. Blaikie, kept unaware by Lauraguais of the true situation, regarded this as a temporary setback and worked on, selling the wood and crops, paying the servants and labourers, building a hut for a guard in the woods and rendering his accounts regularly to his employer who wrote

15. Colin Jones, *The Longman Companion to the French Revolution* (London, 1988), p. 237.
16. Blaikie Papers.
17. *Lettres du Cn B. Lauraguais à l'occasion du contrat de vente que le Deptnt de l'Aisne lui a passé du Presbytère et de l'Eglise à Manicamp; et de surcis que le Ministre des Finances a mis à l'exécuter de ce contract* (Paris, 1797); letter to Cn Desmajeaux landowner in Manicamp, dated 10 pluviôse, Year 5 (1797).

to him frequently about his affairs. The tone of the letters was friendly, even affectionate with expressions such as 'my dear Blaikie' and 'we must dine together'. He reminisced about the walks they had taken together and it seems that Lauraguais was engaged in writing some kind of paper on the potato, assuring Blaikie, 'I have decided to talk about you a great deal, and honourably, for you deserve it'.[18]

Lauraguais tried various ploys to evade his creditors during 1798 and 1799 but in November 1800 he wrote to Blaikie to tell him that he had sold his woods; his reason, he assured Blaikie, was to save his daughter from some sort of financial embarrassment. Blaikie asked to leave his service at this time but Lauraguais persuaded him to stay with the prospects that they would be able to harvest the land and carry on farming. A fortnight later, he sold his estate and farms to his nephew Bufile de Brancas in return, he said to Blaikie, for an 18 year usufruct of the land. He assured Blaikie that this step would free him from the demands of his creditors since Bufile had engaged to pay his debts, including that to Blaikie. Blaikie would be compensated for what was owing to him and he would be able to secure some money for the farm workers and servants who had received no wages. As Lauraguais had supposedly received 80,000 livres for his estate from Bufile, and had at the same time apparently sold his property of Lassay for 400,000, Blaikie felt it was worthwhile continuing. His hopes were destroyed when, on 24 May 1801, Fouquet the bailiff of Chauny, acting for one of Lauraguais' creditors, and Bureau the bailiff of Laon, acting for the Préfect to secure arrears in taxes, both descended on the farm and seized the harvest. According to the irate Blaikie, Lauraguais, feckless as ever, instead of paying his creditors, had dissipated the money on women without thinking of the plight of his servants or the debts he owed. More probably his affairs were now so complicated that he could not extricate himself from his difficulties. He wrote to Blaikie telling him he planned to go to America (22 November 1801).

His actions, carried out in bad faith and amounting as they did to a betrayal of their joint venture, left Blaikie bitter and beside himself with anger, as his letters to Lauraguais show. He tried to salvage what he could to pay the servants but his efforts were frustrated by the creditors. His health began to suffer as he tried to make sense of Lauraguais' byzantine moves to confuse and mislead both him and the other creditors. On 17 brumaire an X (7 November 1801) Lauraguais returned to Manicamp but left a few days later promising to come back in a month's time, leaving a sick Blaikie to deal with his affairs. A month later he had still not returned. In January Blaikie wrote to Lauraguais urging him to sell as much as possible before the bailiffs arrived but in February 1802, Blaikie received a further blow when Fouquet seized the farm horses and ploughs and set guards on the estate to make sure Blaikie sold nothing. To make things worse, Lauraguais castigated him bitterly for allowing the farm horses to be sold, since, by law, a man's implements of toil, his means of livelihood, could not be taken from him by creditors. He urged Blaikie to take the

---

18. Letter of 24 May 1799. Transcripts/extracts of some of these letters can be found at the BHVP in the papers of J. Stern the biographer of Bélanger. (MS2826) The originals are among the Blaikie Papers.

bailiffs to court and in his letters railed against Bufile who was now claiming any surplus funds as his own. Blaikie struggled on until the summer when in desperation he went to Paris to face Lauraguais and demand how he could extricate himself from this 'labyrinth'. The Peace of Amiens had been signed between France and her enemies on 25 March 1802. The war that had brought about the death of a million French citizens was over and Blaikie, overwhelmed by his experiences of the last few years, wanted to return to England with his wife.

It was obvious now that the farm the Blaikies lived in was to be sold. He had tried in May 1802 to take out an injunction against the sale of Lauraguais' land on behalf of the employees who had not been paid but the Judge of the Peace, a relation of Fouquet's, refused to accept the Scot's submission. Lauraguais approved of his action writing in an undated letter around this time, 'I know that for as long as you stay at Chauny you will voluntarily take on the task of helping these people'.

Blaikie returned from Paris to the farm of La Chapelle on 21 August 1802 and the following day the sale of cows, sheep and furnishings was begun by Fouquet and Bureau, the *huissiers* or bailiffs of Chauny and Laon. Blaikie sent the details of the proceedings, the *procès verbaux*, to Lauraguais who accused him of taking money for some horses he had asked the Scot to remove from the estate in advance of the sale. Blaikie asked him what else he could do, having nothing left with which to feed them. Lauraguais complained bitterly, also, that his belongings had been sold too cheaply, and this may well have been the case, but Blaikie had no influence with the bailiffs. He himself was to apply to the courts in July 1805 to receive any surplus from the sales as a privileged creditor and was awarded 5800 francs by the justices. However, in the end he received nothing, Fouquet claiming that he had already paid all the monies to other creditors. No longer able to live on the farm, Blaikie went to Paris in December 1802 and presented his accounts from the beginning of his stewardship. The count accepted them as an exact statement of his affairs and promised that although he could not pay Blaikie he would always care for him, and Mme St Luce, his daughter, would honour the debt he owed the Scot.

With nothing left to keep him in France, except Lauraguais' debt, Blaikie prepared to leave. On 11 April 1803 he received funds realised on stocks that he held in England to finance his journey. He packed up his books and selected the pictures he cherished as mementoes of his past. Amongst them, there was a view of the valley of Chamonix, and one of Professor Saussure reaching its summit. Of his two coloured engravings of Paris scenes, he chose one of the bridge at Neuilly, which he had crossed so many times on his way to and from Bagatelle. Of Bagatelle itself he had amassed six pictures; one of the 'grand pont', views of the greenhouse and two pavilions in the garden and one of the temple which was to crown the mountain which concealed the ice house. As a memorial of Raincy he chose a view of its 'grand pont' with the river and the orangerie in the background, another of the Kennels, and two of the château itself. He made an index of that precious record of his days as a botanist, his two volume herbarium. Then, having completed his packing, he bought his wife two lengths of cloth for dresses plus a necklace and pair of earrings so that she could appear well when she meet her family again. But events defeated his plans. First his wife fell ill, delaying their departure. On 15 January 1803 Lauraguais acknowledged his debt to Blaikie, now amounting to 12697 francs agreeing to pay him the whole within two years. In May he wrote to Blaikie, urging him to leave before the precarious peace collapsed. 'You say you will stay here if there is a war … at least take your wife to England … I am telling you what I think, counting on your attachment of thirty years, you ought to count on my friendship and take what I say as a sign of it.' It finishes, 'With all my heart'.

On 18 May 1803 George III declared war on France. Shortly afterwards, Napoleon, incensed at the capture at sea of a vessel carrying relatives of Mme Bonaparte, gave an order for the arrest of all British subjects who had applied for passports to leave France.[19] The Blaikies were stranded as prisoners in Chauny where they had found lodgings and once more had to take up the struggle to make a living. In a letter of 29 August 1803 Lauraguais told Blaikie that he had ceded everything to his daughter, Mme St Luce. Blaikie, to whom he agreed he owed 12697 livres, would have to take his place with the other creditors.

There was a touch of his old charm in his reply to an eloquent letter from Mrs Blaikie revealing the depth of her unhappiness and poverty. She wrote to him early in 1804, without her husband's knowledge, to tell him of their 'distressed situation' and of how her illness during the past year has caused them great expense. She begged him to open his mind and heart not only to the situation of their affairs but 'the position of my mind being obliged to remain in this miserable situation deprived of seeing my kindred and friends'. Having being obliged for a time to the kindness of a M. Dochez for allowing them a roof over their heads, they are now forced to seek other lodgings for which they will have to find the rent and she asks him to have the goodness to pay 500 francs on account.[20] Lauraguais was touched. In his reply he assured her that he would do what she asked and that he would write to Blaikie that day, declaring, 'I am sorry that you are so far from your friends and relations but be sure I will be happy if in this situation I can give you some relief and comfort … Believe me forever your friend'. Blaikie and his wife did receive the 500f. but in two payments and they had to make further representations to get it.

At the Restoration, Louis XVIII made Lauraguais a peer of the realm. Blaikie, still deeply angry about his treatment, approached Lauraguais again in the vain hope that, as Duc de Brancas and a member of the House of Peers, he might have more funds at his disposal. Lauraguais eventually (5 April 1816) signed a document promising to pay Blaikie 3000 francs at the rate of 500 francs per month. This was payment of interest, not a waiver of capital, but he declared it to be in full and final settlement of his debts to Blaikie. Complain as he might, Blaikie could get no more out of him. Lauraguais, to get rid of him once and for all, issued a statement, patently false, that it was Blaikie himself who was liable for the failure of his agriculture since he was

---

19. Avrillon Mademoiselle de, *Mémoires de Mademoiselle Avrillon*, ed. Maurice Dernelle (Paris, 1969), p. 53.

20. Blaikie Papers.

responsible as farm manager for the exploitation of his employer's farms. There was nothing Blaikie could do.

Lauraguais, the man who had let millions slip through his fingers, who could charm and entertain but whose character had another much less likeable side, spent the last part of his life with scarcely a sou to his name. Undaunted, right to the end he continued to demonstrate the gaiety and wit that had first captivated Sophie Arnould, Sir Joseph Banks and Blaikie. He became the focus of a group of younger men and women who gathered around him in a room set aside for him in the Bibliothèque Nationale to listen, fascinated, to his engaging stories of the personalities and events of the distant world of the court before the Revolution. He died of gout in his ninety-first year on 9 October 1824 and was buried in the Church of St Roch in the rue St Honoré.

Blaikie, 51 in 1802, had devoted himself to a failed experiment for 12 years. He obtained a permit to travel throughout France in March 1804 but he and his wife would not be free to leave the country again until peace was restored in 1815. With his fortunes and his spirits at their lowest ebb ever, he turned again to his old career to make a living.

CHAPTER 15

The Survivor, 1802–1815

I N TRUTH, Blaikie had never really abandoned gardening completely and this new phase of his career would establish him again as one of the leading gardeners in France. He would design and lay out gardens not only for the aristocrats who had survived the Revolution but for the new manufacturing class and the Napoleonic aristocracy of generals and administrators. He would also become involved in industrial and civic planting and burial gardens.

As early as 1795, he had set out to establish himself in the community, designing gardens for the more important local citizens, the lawyers, civil servants and other notables around Chauny and Laon, the chief towns of the district. The end of the Terror in July 1794 and the repeal of the Law against Suspects in April 1795 left him free to resume his former career both within and outside the district of Chauny.

Beaumont

The first fee for a garden recorded in his account book[1] was in the name of M. Desmarquette, a former mayor of Chauny,[2] at his estate at nearby Beaumont. In March 1795, Blaikie drew up a plan for the park and began planting. The following year he was back, beginning alterations to the course of the rivers and widening them. He started work on a newly acquired part of the park and, in the area in front of the château, he planted a lawn. Between 1796 and 1801, he returned in the spring and autumn each year to plant trees and shrubs. He constructed rivers, a grotto, a Chinese bridge and a *rocher*. A note in his account book describes how he had designed and laid out the garden 'to create a picturesque effect' and 'with the greatest care and expense'. At first he did not charge by the hour. Payment was slow and he was desperately short of money, but he was in no position to insist. It was 1801 before M. Desmarquette paid him a first instalment of 300 francs and in all he was paid 550 francs[3] for seven years' work. He returned to this garden for a total of twenty days

---

1. Blaikie's account book is a notebook of approximately the same size as the diary and, like it, bound in cream vellum. It covers the years 1792 to 1820 and contains 219 pages of which 70 have been torn out randomly throughout the book. Every so often there is a page containing a 'Recapitulation' of the year's accounts with page references making it possible to discover references to clients whose detailed accounts were contained in the missing pages.
2. Pierre-Momble Desmarquette, *équyer* (squire), mayor of Chauny from 1791–93. Except during the Terror, the mayor of any locality was usually a member of the nobility or the prosperous legal class – Lauraguais was more than once mayor of Chauny.
3. In the 1780s the pound sterling was worth about 24 livres although Blaikie gives more exact exchange rates in his accounts for that period. After 1814, there were 24 francs to the £. The period in between was highly inflationary.

between 1810 and 1812 to carry out repairs to the rock work of the grotto and to the terrace. For these visits he seems to have accepted payment in wood and wine. Clearly, he intended this garden to be a showcase for his work and did not press for payment, even in later years.

Malmaison

He now called himself *'architecte des jardins'* and his local commissions as a landscape architect gradually brought new and more prestigious clients. Between 1795 and 1820 his account book records the names of more than 70. He had concealed some of his possessions at Malmaison before his flight to Picardy in 1793. Now, in 1802, he was involved indirectly in the laying out and planting of the gardens for the Empress Joséphine.[4] Joséphine spent the happiest hours of her life in her country retreat of Malmaison and was to die there in May 1814 shortly after Napoléon's exile to Elba. The park she acquired from M. Coulteux du Moley was already beautiful, with woods and lawns and an abundance of streams, but the simple, seventeenth-century manor house, surrounded by farms, lacked importance and convenience as far as Napoléon was concerned.[5] He began to buy adjacent property to add to the domain of 200 hectares and engaged two young architects, Percier and Fontaine,[6] to adapt the château to his way of life and to design the gardens. Their task initially appeared quite small but turned out to be extremely difficult and highly expensive,[7] particularly the park, for which Josephine had very strong ideas of her own. She insisted on a menagerie, and hot houses filled with tropical plants to remind her of her childhood on the island of Martinique. Above all she was determined to have a *jardin anglais*, a Petit Trianon of her own. The straight lines and regularity of planting recommended by Fontaine whose style was classical and masculine, were anathema to her, and the architect could scarcely persuade her to retain the formal avenues leading up to the château.

4. Marie Josèphe Rose Tascher de la Pagerie (1763–1814). By her first marriage to Vicomte Alexandre de Beauharnais she had two children, Hortense and Eugène. Beauharnais from whom she had been estranged was guillotined in 1794 and in 1796 she married Napoleon Bonaparte. In 1804 she became Empress of France and was divorced by Napoleon in 1809 because of her inability to give him a son.
5. G. Poisson, *Evocation du Grand Paris; La Banlieue Nord-Ouest* (Paris, 1960), pp. 15–57.
6. Charles Percier (1764–1838), architect, won the prestigious *Prix de Rome* at the age of 22. His visit to Rome opened his eyes to classical architecture and formed his architectural style. Malmaison was his first imperial enterprise but many joint works with Fontaine were to follow.

   Pierre-François-Léonard Fontaine (1762–1853), restorer, decorator, architect and designer. The man most identified with the 'Empire' style. He spent some time in Rome as a young man with Percier and they collaborated until Percier's death. Napoleon's favourite architects, they were also responsible for ceremonials such as the Coronation of Napoleon and his marriage to Marie-Louise of Austria. They continued their careers during the reign of Louis XVIII but were particularly favoured by the Duke of Orléans, later Louis Philippe. Fontaine was responsible for the *Arc de Triomphe du Carousel*. Percier and Fontaine collaborated in numerous publications and Fontaine also wrote his memoirs.
7. Percier and Fontaine, *Residences de Souverains* (Paris, 1833).

She insisted on appointing an English gardener and the man chosen, Alexander Howatson, was another thorn in Fontaine's side. Fontaine regarded all gardeners of the English school as charlatans, and labelled them mere 'dendrologists'. He confided in his diary on 14 February 1801, 'Madame Bonaparte has taken an English gardener who like all the artists of this sort find fault with whatever plantings we make.[8]

Howatson, a Scot from Leadhills in Lanarkshire,[9] had close associations with Blaikie. He had probably worked at Monceau before the Revolution[10] and no doubt on Blaikie's recommendation had been appointed head gardener at Raincy in 1788.[11] Fate had been kinder to him at the Revolution than to Blaikie. In spite of probably being questioned at Raincy,[12] he escaped imprisonment or detention, returning to Monceau in 1792[13] where he was employed to maintain the rare plants in the green houses after the confiscation of the property of the Duc d'Orléans. He appears never to have been harassed during those years and with four other British subjects, felt secure enough to add his name to a petition to the Convention for the release of English prisoners in 1794.[14] He looked after Blaikie's affairs during the latter's enforced residence at Chauny acting as his proxy in Paris.[15]

Howatson was appointed head gardener at Malmaison at the beginning of 1801 at an annual salary of 2,400 francs.[16] He was at first entrusted with the laying out and planting of the *jardin anglais* under the supervision of the various architects who succeeded each other on the site.[17] Blaikie told J. C. Loudon that he, Blaikie, had laid

---

8. Pierre François Leonard Fontaine, *Journal 1799–1853* (Paris, 1987 edn), 2 vols, vol. 1, p. 20.

9. I am grateful to M. Pierre Renard, for this information from Howatson's death certificate. There is no surviving parish record for Leadhills at the time of Howatson's birth.

10. Patrick Neill, in a note p. 359 of his *Journal of a Horticultural Tour through some parts of Holland, and the North of France in the autumn of 1817*, Edinburgh, 1823 says that one 'Houtson' was sent by the Earl of Egremont to Monceau to look after the Duke's pineapple house. (Howatson's name does not appear in the lists of gardeners at Petworth but I understand from Mrs Alison McCann, Keeper of the Petworth archives that the list is not complete for this period.)

11. AN., 300 AP I 317 gives HOWNSON as *jardinier en chef* at Raincy with a salary of 1732 livres. Later the name appears in the same archive correctly spelled. Howatson's name seems to have caused a great deal of difficulty all round. Neill himself, although he visits Blaikie at Howatson's house, erroneously calls him Hudson.

12. Jean Astruc, 'Les Anglais au Raincy', *Bulletin de la S.H.R.P.A.*, No. 31 (January 1964), pp. 19–22. Describes one 'Uxson' as being among the English servants questioned during the Revolution according to the archives of the district of Livry (the 22 of the 1st month of year 2 of the Republic). As no one of that name is mentioned in Blaikie's diary or in the Raincy accounts at the Archives Nationales, this is probably yet another misspelling of Howatson's name.

13. Bernard Chevallier, *Malmaison Château et domaine des origines à 1904* (Paris, 1989).

14. John G. Alger, *Paris in 1789–94. Farewell Letters of Victims of the Guillotine* (London, 1902), p. 170 n. 1.

15. AN., ET XVIII 951.

16. AP DQ[10] 797 quoted in Bernard Chevallier, *Malmaison château et domaine etc*.

17. Percier and Fontaine were appointed architects at St Cloud in 1802 and were replaced by one of their colleagues who after a few months was ousted by Morel. Morel was succeeded

out the gardens during the Consulate, with a rich stock of trees and shrubs,[18] so it is likely that Blaikie was the driving force behind Howatson between 1801 and 1803, since no reference to Blaikie exists in the archives which relate to Malmaison.[19]

Joséphine's love of flowers and her passionate acquisitiveness (she thought nothing of paying 3000 francs. for a bulb[20]) made her the nurseryman's dream client. It may even have been as a result of Blaikie's recommendation that she made contact with the firm of Lee and Kennedy.[21] James Lee, who had recommended Blaikie to the Comte de Lauraguais, had died in 1795 but the firm kept in occasional contact with Blaikie in an effort to secure the repayment, through him, of the money the Duke of Orléans still owed them.[22] They supplied Josephine with plants throughout the period of the Continental System when Napoleon prohibited all European ports to British ships, John Kennedy being given a special pass to travel between London and Malmaison until the cessation of hostilities in 1814. Josephine obtained from them, in particular, an important collection of rare trees and shrubs.[23] With them also, she shared the expenses of sending a collector, Joseph Niven, to South Africa and received part of his collection of heathers, ixias and pelargoniums in return. Her account with the firm amounted to £2,600 in 1803 and in 1811 her expenditure with the firm was £700.[24] It was said that the only books in the Empress's apartments were botanical ones.[25] She could name every plant in the greenhouse in Latin and give its country of origin; a botanical erudition that her courtiers found deeply tedious.

Howatson's career as head gardener was brief. His name ceased to appear in the accounts after 19 July 1803[26] dismissed, it was said, by the new Intendant of the estate,

---

in 1805 by two more architects, Thibault and Vignon who again lasted only a few months before the arrival of Berthault. See Bernard Chevallier and Christophe Pincemaille, *L'Impératrice Joséphine* (Paris, 1988).

18. J. C. Loudon, *Encyclopaedia of Gardening* (1835 edn), p. 35. S. Weston in *Two Sketches of France Belgium and Spain* (London, 1817), p. 120, writes that Malmaison 'had been laid out by an English gardener ... and dressed with all the charms which wood, water and exotic botany could adorn it'.

19. Information received from M Bernard Chevallier, Conservateur en Chef of the Château of Malmaison.

20. *Mémoires de Mademoiselle Avrillon*, ed. Maurice Dernelle (Paris, 1969), p. 104.

21. Alice M. Coats 'The Empress Josephine', *Garden History*, vol. 5, no. 3 (1977), pp. 40–6.

22. Kennedy & Lee wrote to Blaikie as late as 1821 for payment of the bill for which Blaikie had signed in 1790. It amounted to just over £700 plus interest owed to them by the Duke. The firm finally abandoned its efforts when it became clear that Blaikie's claim for recompense had been turned down by the Commission set up to reimburse British citizens who had suffered losses during the Revolution.

23. Mary Berry, *The Journal and Correspondence of Miss Berry*, ed. Lady Theresa Lewis, 3 vols (1865), vol. 2, p. 172. Audience with Mme Bonaparte. 'We talked of the taste of her apartment, of Mal-maison [sic] of her garden there, of the plants she was getting from England from Lee and Kennedy: of those she wished to have'. See also vol. 3, pp. 96–7.

24. Alice Coats, *op. cit.*

25. Bertie Greatheed, *An Englishman in Paris, 1803: the journal of B. Greatheed* ed. J. T. B. Bury and J. C. Bury (London, 1953).

26. Bernard Chevallier, *Malmaison Château et domaine des origines à 1904* (Paris, 1989).

Brisseau de Mirbel, who accused him of having lost a valuable delivery of trees in transport from Bellevue to Malmaison.[27] Shortly afterwards, Mirbel's own extravagances led to his dismissal and by 1805 there was also a new head gardener but this time at a salary of only 1200 francs per year. We next come across Howatson at Hennemont near Saint-Germain-en-Laye in 1817, but of his career between 1803 and 1817 no record has so far been found. A number of letters sent to Blaikie by his family in Edinburgh are addressed to 'Mr Blaikie at Hennemont',[28] confirming a close and continuing connection between the two men. Howatson died in Saint-Germain in 1851 at the age of 84.[29]

Dissatisfied with her architects' interpretation of her ideas, Josephine called in the doyen of designers of the English garden, the distinguished old architect of the Ancien Régime, Morel, whose achievement at Guiscard had so impressed Blaikie. Much to Fontaine's chagrin, since it was he who had mentioned the aged practitioner as the best of the 'English' landscape designers, Morel, a robust and irascible septuagenarian, was whisked out of retirement at Lyon to transform the garden. He would retain nothing of what had already been done, not even the half completed green houses, and ordered all to be pulled down.[30] His restrained style was too austere for Josephine and he was either dismissed or resigned, tired of her caprices. It is at this stage, sometime in 1805 according to Patrick Neill,[31] Secretary of the Royal Society of Edinburgh, who visited Paris in 1817 and met Blaikie and Howatson, that the grounds originally laid out by Morel, 'were greatly altered, or recast, and brought into their present character, by Blaikie and Hudson [Howatson]'.[32] His statement although apparently at odds with that of Blaikie to Loudon (since Napoleon was proclaimed Emperor on 18 May 1804) may have some substance. The architect, Berthault,[33] who managed to please Josephine at last, and remained her architect till the end, was

---

27. *Ibid*. Bellevue was the château built for Mme de Pompadour on the hill overlooking the Seine and subsequently owned by Louis XVI's aunts. In the early years of the nineteenth century it was owned by a M Testu de Balincourt.

28. Blaikie papers. Hennemont had been part of a monastery purchased by Howatson in 1817. (Information supplied by Mr Pierre Renard.) It may have been this property that J. C. Loudon was referring to when he described Blaikie as having, in 1822, 'one of the best kept villa gardens' in France of about 40 acres. *Encyclopedia of Gardening*, pp. 35, 39. Quoted in Birrell, p. 15.

29. I am indebted to Mr Pierre Renard also for this information from Howatson's death certificate.

30. Ménéval, *L'Impératrice Josephine* (Paris, n.d.), pp. 100–1.

31. Patrick Neill (1776–1851), Printer and contributor to early editions of the *Encyclopaedia Britannica*, He was a founder member of the Royal Caledonian Horticultural Society. He was responsible for the laying out of Princes Street gardens after the draining of the North Loch about 1820.

32. Neill, p. 397. See also p. 361.

33. Berthault (*c*. 1771–1823), architect particularly well known for his designs for parks and gardens; Malmaison for Joséphine; château of Jouy-en-Josas and Montcel for Oberkampf; St Leu for Hortense. He was named architect for the château of Compiegne during the Empire and kept his post at the Restoration.

responsible for the final layout of the garden and it is possible that he continued to use Blaikie and Howatson to assist with the plantations. Blaikie certainly later laid out and planted at least two properties for which Berthault was architect.

Neill with his Scottish companions visited Malmaison, 'this charming place', in 1817. He found the grounds somewhat neglected but still very fine, the situation admirable and the climate delightful, warm enough for the Indian Sage (*Salvia indica*) to naturalise itself among the shrubberies and spring up in the hedgebank. The *jardin anglais* described by him as 'brought to their present character by Blaikie and Howatson,' he found only 'a near approach to the English style'. Neill was impressed by the fine, large specimen trees on the lawn near the house; *Magnolia grandiflora, Pinus palustris, Ligustrum lucidum* and *Melia azedarach* as well as several other exotic trees and shrubs. He describes how these were protected from frost in winter by having wooden huts erected over them with the interstices filled with straw. 'These,' he explains, 'are only removed in the middle of April when the buds, protected from frost, are swelliing and ready to expand.'[34] While Neill was admiring the trees, his friend Hay measured and sketched the magnificent greenhouses. The spacious glasshouse still contained a rich collection of exotics, amongst them the original bulb of a spectacular Cape plant, *Brunsvigia josephinae*, a gift to the Empress from a Dutch collector. The gardener, delighted with Neill's interest in this plant with its great umbel of flame coloured trumpets, gave him three or four of the ripe seeds. One of these germinated in the hothouses of the Palace of Dalkeith.

Arrancy

In 1804, Blaikie was commissioned to lay out the gardens of the château of Arrancy near Laon. Blaikie laid out the gardens of many châteaux or country houses in Picardy but Arrancy is one of the rare survivors. Although severely damaged in the 1914–18 war, it is still owned by the Tour du Pin family, descendants of the M. Maussion who first employed Blaikie there.[35] Blaikie gives little detail in his account book of the work he carried out here between 1804 and 1809 except that in 1805 he constructed the entrance to the grotto and spent the autumn of 1806 laying out the ground in front of the château. Photographs of the building before 1914 show a large expanse of grassland or meadow gently sloping from the house and bordered by trees laid out in irregular clumps. Four enormous plane trees, a species rarely seen in the region, stand out in the landscape as remnants of Blaikie's planting. One of them now bears the scars of a mortar shell from the time of the First World War attack that destroyed part of the château. Four ancient yews of immense age must have been preserved by Blaikie when he laid out the garden and, until recently, a fine sophora was another relic of Blaikie's presence at Arrancy. An extract from a letter to him dated 3 July 1833 from Mme Maussion, Vicomtesse de la Tour du Pin, recalls the days he spent at

34. Neill, p. 403.
35. It is also one of only two gardens for which correspondence survives amongst the Blaikie Papers.

Arrancy. 'You have left behind you many good friends here, and both young and old would all be very pleased to see you again. Arrancy would gain much from a visit from its originator and, as for me, I would be very happy to have a talk with you and ask your advice since I know there is so much to learn from your conversation.'[36]

The Industrialists of Picardy

1804 also marked the year he began to work for a new sort of client, wealthy manufacturers who had established factories in Picardy and elsewhere in the years before the Revolution. Through the patronage of these industrialists, he was to extend his practice to include urban and commercial landscaping. His first client in this group was a M. Piplet de Montizeau, a glass manufacturer and owner of The Royal Glass-works at Folembrai. Possibly through him, Blaikie began an association with a close-knit group of textile manufacturers, Protestants and freemasons often bound by marriage, in the region around Saint-Quentin. The first of these was a M. Samuel Joly de Bammeville.[37] Samuel Joly's grandfather, also Samuel Joly, was a Protestant who in 1705 had fled from persecution in his native Poitou to settle at Saint-Quentin where he established himself and his family as leading figures in the community. In 1786, his younger son Pierre and his grandson, Samuel, bought jointly the estate of Pommery outside Saint-Quentin. At that time, the property consisted of a park of five hectares and some farmland but Pierre built a new château and acquired more land. During the Revolution, young Samuel was imprisoned in l'Abbaye in Paris having been denounced by his commercial rivals,[38] and it was only in 1804, seven years after his father's death, that he was able to carry out renovations to the gardens of Pommery. He invited Blaikie to conduct the works and these lasted until 1807. The château of Pommery is now an Old Peoples' Home and no trace remains of the gardens. Around the same time, Blaikie worked also for Samuel's cousin Jean Joly (*l'aîné*) at his château of Remaucourt, and Bélanger, too, may have been involved in the Joly works at either Pommery or Remaucourt. A much quoted letter survives from the architect to a Mme Joly explaining his plan to construct a bridge in her park at a point where there was no stream to cross. He reminded her that one cannot make one's garden without a little poetry, that a bridge does not need to straddle a stream or a river but may cross a road or a ravine as in the Alps or Chinese gardens.[39]

In 1810 Samuel Joly, now mayor of Saint-Quentin commissioned Blaikie to plant the promenades and boulevards of the town as part of a far-sighted urban plan. No record exists of the trees Blaikie planted but he according to his account book he was paid the sum of 198 francs. The following year, Samuel employed him to lay out the

---

36. Blaikie Papers. I am indebted to Gabrielle Joudiou and the Comtesse de la Tour du Pin for information on Arrancy.
37. Others were the families Houel and Hoult according to Blaikie's account book.
38. Monique Severin, 'La famille Joly de Bammeville', *Fédération des Sociétés d'Histoire et d'Archéologie de l'Aisne*, Mémoires 1984.
39. Quoted in Stern, vol. I, p. 29 and dated 28 ventôse but without the year.

grounds around the entrance to his factory at Porte de Lisle, on the opposite side of the river from St Quentin, now a faubourg of the city. This energetic and civic-minded business man died suddenly in 1811 at the age of 52 and was buried at Pommery near the graves of his parents. His son, Aimé, asked Blaikie to plant trees and shrubs around the sepulchre. Blaikie had already accepted a similar commission for a M. Palmide de Janson in 1811 accompanying him to a *'calvaire'* where, according to Blaikie, 'he proposed disposing a burial place and placing several monuments'.[40] During 1812 and 1813, Blaikie completed the project for the Joly family, marking out the spots for the monuments and utilising the skills he had acquired in creating, with poplars and willows, the peaceful setting and melancholy mood necessary for the Île des Tombeaux at Bagatelle. This aspect of the eighteenth-century 'natural' garden, of which Rousseau's tomb surrounded by poplars on its island in the middle of a lake at Ermenonville was the defining example, had a strong influence on attitudes to death and burial in the first half of the nineteenth century. It became the custom, for those who could afford it, to erect an urn or other funerary monument in some peaceful spot surrounded by a group of trees; a custom that culminated in the idea of the nineteenth-century garden cemetery.

Montcel

Joly de Bammeville had amicable relations with another important Protestant textile manufacturer at Jouy-en-Josas (Yvelines), Christophe Philippe Oberkampf (1738–1815). Their sons shared a tutor and, in April 1813, Joly's daughter married Oberkampf's son, Emile. Oberkampf was a Swiss whose factory at Jouy-en-Josas as well as printing 'indiennes', named after the floral prints originally imported from India, perfected the copper-plate monochrome designs printed on calico known as *Toile de Jouy*. The name became a generic word for cotton printed with idealised rustic scenes, and the designs are still popular today. Drawings of romanticised male and female gardeners embowered in garlands of vegetables and flowers might be scattered across the cloth; similarly, shepherds and shepherdesses, or episodes from the fables of La Fontaine.[41] The designs were created by first rate artists,[42] and these fabrics with their bucolic scenes found favour with Marie Antoinette, so thoroughly were they in the spirit of her hameau at the Trianon. As a result, Oberkampf was awarded a Royal Appointment. His success outlasted the Ancien Régime, and the Revolution, and his designs changed to meet the times; villagers planting a Tree of Liberty during the Revolution, medallions and lozenges depicting classical themes during the Directoire and the Empire.

---

40. Blaikie's account book, Private Archive.
41. Other designs were; the four quarters of the world, the farm, the village fete, the works of the toile factory showing the process of manufacture, the Montgolfiers making their balloon ascent and the Federation, consisting of idealised pictures of the Revolution. Many of his *Toile de Jouy* designs and those of his other fabrics are still used in furnishing fabrics today.
42. The most famous was Jean-Baptiste Huet (1745–1811).

Napoleon visited his factory on two occasions, first with Josephine and then with his second wife Marie Louise of Austria. On the first visit he rewarded Oberkampf with the Legion of Honour and on the second created him a baron. In 1795 Oberkampf bought the château of Montcel at Jouy for the mother of his second wife, Anne-Michelle Elisabeth Massieu.[43] Around 1806, Madame Oberkampf undertook a complete programme of renovation at Montcel lasting five or six years, extending the building to give the country house the appearance of a château with stables, a *basse-cour* and other buildings appropriate for such a dwelling.[44] She had already demonstrated her love of gardens by improving those at her house near the factory[45] in the earlier years of her marriage. When her first child Alphonse died in 1802 at the age of six she consoled herself as best she could by creating an Elysée at Montcel as a burial place for her son and other members of her family. Her husband would be buried there in 1815 and she was interred there on her death in 1816. The *Mémorial*, the account of the family's history in the archives at the Musée de la Toile de Jouy, written by Oberkampf's nephew, Gottlieb Widmer, tells us that Madame Oberkampf called upon Blaikie as one of 'proved talent and in vogue as a landscape architect at that time' to carry out the work on the garden at Montcel and, the writer adds, 'these exterior works were executed without any other plans than the inspiration of Mme Oberkampf and the advice of the Scotsman Blaikie'.[46] Fashion had finally caught up with Blaikie's style of gardening some 30 years after he had first expressed it in his plan for Bagatelle and he was now in demand as one of the leading interpreters of this 'new' style of gardening. He arrived from Chauny on 11 March 1807, stayed for a month and returned in June when he spent 41 days at Montcel. The following spring he was back, this time for 84 days and his accounts show that he was there again in 1809. Mme Oberkampf loved her garden and threw herself with '*ardeur*' into the transformations. She had set her heart on the construction of a *rocher*, the realisation of which was to involve a great deal of expense. The cost of extraction of large blocks of stone, their transportation from a distance plus the manoeuvring required to put them in place, amounted to almost 8000 francs. Blaikie was charged with transporting the rocks, a journey that took him two days. He does not say from where he obtained them but the forest of Fontainebleau was the usual source of huge blocks of stone. It then took a further nine days and, no doubt, a large number of workmen to manoeuvre them into position. At the same time he put a bridge in place – presumably close to the rocher – and planted the area. He charged 12 francs a day and, from his account book, his bill for his work over four years amounted to 2892 francs.

---

43. Anne-Michelle Elisabeth Massieu (1757–1836), daughter of a prominent industrialist in Caen. The marriage took place on 17 March 1785. See Serge Chassagne, Oberkampf, *Un entrepreneur capitaliste au Siècle des Lumières* (Paris, 1980). Oberkampf's first wife died of smallpox in 1782.

44. The architect was a Mr Barthélemy Vignon. *Etat d'honoraires pour direction de travaux pour la Maison Oberkampf dit harivelle (sic) à Jouy. Depuis l'an 1805 jusqu'à la fin de 1812.* MMTJ.

45. Part of it is now the Mairie of Jouy-en-Josas.

46. MMTJ, Gottlieb Widmer, *Mémorial* para. 298.

Montcel is one of the few gardens in which Blaikie worked that have survived and where traces of the *jardin anglais* remain. Originally a hunting lodge given by Louis XV to his doctor, the building was replaced by a country villa at the end of the eighteenth century and it was this which was extended by Madame Oberkampf in 1806. The estate subsequently belonged to the Mallet brothers, directors of the Bank Mallet and sons-in-law of Oberkampf. In 1923, the house became a school. At this time, an additional floor was inserted in the château spoiling the slope of the roof, and sundry other buildings were added for the use of the pupils. In 1968 the estate extended to approximately 68 hectares and the entrance and main allées of the plan of the grounds in the school brochure are recognisable as those in an undated plan of the gardens marked 'chez Berthau' [Berthault], with the heading '*Plan d'un terrain à Monsieur Oberkampf à Jouy*' [47] among the Oberkampf archives. The similarities between the two plans make it likely that Berthault's plan was at least Mme Oberkampf's starting point in making the garden. While the property was a school, the lake was turned into a swimming pool but the grounds still had the feel of a *jardin anglais*, with its winding river, lawns and large trees, amongst them a fine cedar of Lebanon, as well as magnificent rhododendrons. In spite of the lawns being used as playing fields the perspectives of the garden were retained along with their allées of conifers and poplars. In 1984, the jeweller Cartier acquired the property and established a foundation dedicated to contemporary art so that the grounds became a showplace for modern artefacts and were opened to the public. In the mid 1990s the Cartier Foundation moved to Paris and the house and gardens reverted to private ownership. Now [48] it stands unoccupied, its survival uncertain.

Blaikie's connection with the Oberkampfs was a long one. He worked not only for Oberkampf and the Joly family but also at the château of Faurès near Rambouillet for the Petineau brothers, Oberkampf's brothers-in-law by his first marriage, one of whom, James, was Oberkampf's right hand man at the factory. Oberkampf as well as being Protestant and drawing his employees and friends from amongst his co-religionists, had a liking for Scots. He employed a Scotsman called Robert Hendry at Jouy as a designer, engraver, colourist and chemist at his factory. Hendry proved himself very skilled and became a close friend of the family. Samuel and Gottlieb Widmer, Oberkampf's nephews, crossed secretly to England from Ostend in 1810, during the Napoleonic blockade, and visited him in Glasgow in October of that year. He showed them round the textile and dye works in Glasgow and Paisley. [49]

In 1810 the need for further capital obliged the Oberkampf manufacture to admit new investors. [50] Blaikie took this opportunity to invest his fees in the factory and he added a further sum belonging to his wife, so that by 1818 he had a stake of 12000

---

47. MMTJ.

48. 1999.

49. MMTJ, Memorial, paras 308–12. I have tried without success to trace Robert Hendry, whose brother was a minister in Glasgow, and would be grateful for any information about him.

50. Serge Chassagne, p. 293.

francs in the company. Oberkampf died in 1815 and the business continued under the direction of his son until 1821 when the firm was sold. That year, when the accounts were closed, Blaikie received the sum of 13,843 francs in final settlement of his account.[51]

Raray and Nogent L'Artaud

The stunningly beautiful seventeenth-century château and park of Raray near Senlis (Oise) and that of Nogent l'Artaud (Aisne), both owned by the same family, occupied Blaikie at various periods throughout his life. He was involved in the development of both from before the Revolution until he was in his eighties. In 1789, Comte Charles-Marie-Philippe de La Bédoyère built the existing château at Nogent l'Artaud and commissioned Blaikie to lay out the gardens *à l'anglaise*.[52] A late eighteenth-century plan[53] of the main family property, Raray, shows the gardens laid out in the classic French style with straight allées and parterres. However, its owner, the Comte's mother-in-law the Marquise Des Barres,[54] had, with her husband,[55] undertaken a programme of restoration and building at the seventeenth-century château, reserving work on the garden till last. Living so near Ermenonville it is not surprising that she set her heart on an English garden and she, too, invited Blaikie to design and plant her English garden.[56] The Revolution put an end to the project and it was not until 1806 that Blaikie was recalled by Madame Des Barres' daughter, the Comtesse de La Bédoyère,[57] wife of Charles-Marie-Philippe, to recommence the English garden at Raray. The garden designed by Blaikie can be seen in an 1861 plan of the estate.[58] When he succeeded to the family properties, after his mother's death, Comte Henry-François-Noël de La Bédoyère (1782–1861), the grandson of Blaikie's first employer, Madame Des Barres, recalled Blaikie once more. He kept a diary, and his wife, Ambroisine,[59] a 'Journal des Champs', a large, leather bound notebook chronicling

---

51. Archives of the Fondation de la Haute Banque, Paris. 41AQ 7. The same sum is recorded in Blaikie's account book. See also Chassagne, p. 293, where he describes Blaikie as a 'manufacturer of chemical products, Thomas Blaikie of Chauny'. I have been unable to find any evidence of Blaikie's involvement in the chemical industry.

52. Raray, Private Archive. See Genevieve Mazel 'Raray et son château', *Groupe d'Etude des Monuments et Oeuvres d'art de l'Oise et du Beauvaisis*, Bulletin no. 90–1 (1999), pp. 5–83, which gives a detailed history of Raray, the château and its owners until the present day. Also J. B. Molin, 'Nogent l'Artaud pendant la Révolution', *Mémoires de la Fédération des sociétés d'histoire et d'archéologie de l'Aisne*, vol. XXXVIII, pp. 28–34, in which he also credits Blaikie with planting the gardens of the Prefecture of Laon around the same time.

53. Raray, Private Archive.

54. Agnès-Henriette-Félicité Testu de Balincourt (1732–1793).

55. Antoine-Henri-Claude des Barres (1721–1767), Baron de Cussigny, a brigadier in the 1st Scottish company of the King's bodyguard.

56. Geneviève Mazel, *Raray et son château*, p. 31.

57. Judith Félicité des Barres (1757–1817).

58. Raray, Private Archive.

59. Ambroisine d'Estampes (1791–1847).

the domestic works, repairs and family sojourns at Raray and Nogent l'Artaud.[60] Both are invaluable documents[61] which confirm the entries in Blaikie's account book, but they are much more. They give us not only a picture of the man at work but are a tribute to his character and his long and happy relationship with his clients, the de La Bédoyères, designing and laying out the gardens for three generations of the family, an association culminating in his friendship with the young couple, Henry and Ambroisine. Unfortunately, the pages of Blaikie's account book detailing his work for Mme de La Bédoyère in 1806 are missing but his recapitulation of accounts for that year reveals that in September he was paid 24 francs, two days work at his current rate. His accounts for 1811 and 1812 confirm his continuing presence at Nogent l'Artaud[62] and a letter from Raray dated 1811 from the Countess's younger son, Charles[63], to his older brother, Henry,[64] at Nogent l'Artaud, enquiring whether Blaikie has arrived safely from Raray, reveals that Blaikie was working on both estates. Henry's diary gives us a unique picture of the Scot's professional and personal qualities. At Nogent l'Artaud, Henry noted on 18 June 1811, 'Blaikie arrived to begin our *jardin anglais*'. Blaikie's account book reveals that he stayed there until 6 July at 'different works' especially the river and the walks. His fee was now 18 francs per day and Ambroisine complained that he was expensive. He returned each autumn until 1814, for periods varying between 12 and 51 days. The information he gives about the work is slight. In September 1814 he was 'tracing and arranging the meadow by the tower and the entrance on the village square' at other times he was planting trees or 'carrying out works'. His professional relationship with the scholarly bibliophile, Henry, and his wife, Ambroisine, developed during this time into a genuine friendship, in spite of differences of class, outlook and age, and Blaikie educated their taste in garden making. On the 22 June, Henry notes that he and Ambroisine took several long walks with Blaikie in the neighbourhood. They chose foreign trees together at a nursery at Chézy, where they had gone to look at an ancient Abbaye nearby and together they selected forest trees in a wood. The following autumn, he records that Blaikie returned with 30 men to continue the work. Henry's diary describes Blaikie as 'always first on the site and last to leave it, ready to turn his own hand to the work when a labourer did not understand what he had to do, or did it badly'. Ambroisine, he tells us, 'liked Blaikie very much and became his pupil, learning the names of rare and precious shrubs, the art of laying out an allée, creating a view point and all the science of English gardens which Blaikie possessed to perfection'. Henry follows this description of Blaikie at work with an account of his character, 'He was an excellent man, with

60. Raray, Private Archive. My thanks to Madame Geneviève Mazel for communicating these documents to me while she was preparing her own work on Raray.
61. Raray, Private Archive.
62. Blaikie's account book. Private Archive.
63. Charles Houchet de La Bédoyère (1786–1815), aide de camp to Napoleon. For the life of Charles de La Bédoyère see Marcel Doher, *Charles de La Bédoyère. 1786–1815. Aide de Camp de l'Empéreur* (Paris, 1963).
64. Henry Huchet de La Bédoyère (1782–1861).

an original mind, his character was open, completely honest but,' the Catholic Count adds sorrowfully, 'he was imbued with Voltairean ideas and carried scepticism to more and more deplorable limits'.

At the end of May 1814, Henry and Ambroisine with Charles and his bride, Georgina, whom he married in September 1813, made an excursion to the *Jardin des Plantes* in Paris with Blaikie. In October that year, Henry, at his mother's request, accompanied Blaikie to Raray to supervise the Scot's work there and later, they travelled to Nogent from Paris together to continue the programme of planting early in February. While they were on the return journey to Paris on 8 March 1815, they heard what Henry described with prescience as 'the fatal news' of Napoleon's escape from Elba and on their arrival they found the city in a state of 'great agitation'.[65] Although he was devoted to the Emperor, Charles de La Bédoyère had allowed himself, after Napoleon's defeat in 1814, to be persuaded by his young wife's staunchly Monarchist family, the Chastellux, to accept an army post, procured for him through their influence. At the call to arms from his Emperor, Charles' deeper loyalty prevailed. He rallied the regiment he commanded at Grenoble to Napoleon's cause during the Hundred Days, thus ceding the city to the Emperor. After Waterloo, he ignored the urgings of his friends to leave the country secretly, returning instead to Paris to see his wife and infant son. He was arrested and tried as a traitor. Justice would have been satisfied by a condemnation followed by banishment, or a pardon from the king, but Louis XVIII was obdurate in his refusal to spare the young man's life. Georgina and her loyal, royalist family, begged in vain for mercy. Even Louis' own friend of many years, Charles de Damas, related by marriage to the La Bédoyères, failed to move him. Charles de La Bédoyère was shot by firing squad on 9 August 1815 at the age of 29. He refused a blindfold and died bravely, directing the firing squad himself. Georgina died in September 1871 at her château of Harfleur. Her son Georges predeceased her.[66] This tragedy halted the work on the gardens but Blaikie was to return there again after Henry inherited both estates in 1817.[67]

Fourdrain

1810 had been a busy year for Blaikie. As well as his ongoing commissions for the Jolys and the Oberkampf family, he worked for a number of aristocrats and prominent people in the department of the Aisne.[68] Lauraguais' half brother, Albert de Brancas, Napoleon's Chamberlain, employed him during 1811 and again in 1812 and 1813 at his château of Fourdrain in the canton of La Fère not far from Laon, and it seems that Blaikie was now a favourite designer amongst the Napoleonic elite.

---

65. From the diary of Henry de La Bédoyère. Raray, Private Archive.
66. Geneviève Mazel. *Raray*, p. 44.
67. See chapter 16.
68. Amongst them the Comte d'Héricourt at his châteaux at Plessis du Roye and St Amand, and the Comte de la Motte at Davenscourt.

Les Coudreaux

One of his more important undertakings was the garden of Les Coudreaux in the Eure et Loir, seat of Marshal Ney (1769–1815), Napoleon's great general. Ney's wife was a lady-in-waiting to Josephine and a member of the Empress's inner circle. It was she who took an interest in the gardens at this estate purchased in 1808.[69] The 'lovely and amiable' Aglaë-Louise Auguier, was the daughter of the former *Receveur-général* of Lorraine. Her mother, a lady-in-waiting to Marie Antoinette, died when she threw herself from an upper window of the Tuileries during the events of 10 August 1792.[70] Her mother's sister, Mme de Campan, also a former lady in waiting to Marie Antoinette, established a fashionable school for young ladies at Saint-Germain. Hortense, Josephine's daughter, and Aglaë were educated there together and became close friends. Napoleon encouraged Hortense and his own sisters, who also attended the school, to invite their friends to Malmaison. He liked to rule every aspect of the lives of his court, and from this band of young women, he selected brides for his generals. Hortense, in her memoirs, describes her friend as '*rempli de bonté de sensibilité et d'agréments*' (kind, tender-hearted and agreeable to the utmost degree), and goes on, 'we married her to General Ney and I have always remained attached to her'.[71] Ney, born on 10 November 1769, the same day as his great antagonist, Wellington, was the son of a cooper from Sarrelouis and a simple hussar before the Revolution. Although he was a national hero, his rough appearance and outmoded pigtail were death to romance and after their first meeting Aglaë refused to consider him, but Josephine worked assiduously for the match, saw to it that Ney was given a 'makeover' and pleaded his cause with both Aglaë and her father. The couple married in 1802. Napoleon rewarded Ney's outstanding valour and success at the battle of Ulm against the Austrians with the title of Duc d'Elchingen. Unofficially, he named the marshal his *brave des braves* and showered him with riches. Nevertheless, after the fall of Paris, it was Ney who told Napoleon that the army could support him no longer and he and most of Napoleon's marshals, swore allegiance to Louis XVIII. In the end, however, like Charles de La Bédoyère he could not turn his back on his old chief. With Soult, he rallied to his Emperor during the 100 days and almost wrested victory from the Allies at Waterloo.

Ney had bought the estate of Les Coudreaux in the district of Marboué, near Chateaudun (Eure-et-Loir) in June 1808.[72] Cartloads overflowing with the rich spoils of his Peninsular campaign rattled over the cobblestones in the courtyard of his newly acquired house earning for it the alternative name of 'Little Spain'. Berthault, Josephine's architect, drew up designs for the park and gardens,[73] while Blaikie was engaged to lay them out. He paid his first visit there in 1810, from 15 September to 3 October.

---

69. AN., 137 AP 17.

70. Madame Vigée Le Brun, *Memoirs*, trans. Sian Evans (London, 1989), p. 68.

71. La Reine Hortense, *Mémoires de la Reine Hortense, publiés par le prince Napoléon* (Paris, 1927), vol. 1, p. 122.

72. AN., 137 AP 17.

73. Henri Lizier, *Marboué, cité historique, site touristique* (Marboué, 1979) p. 169.

The park was a fine one with beautiful woods[74] and although he does not describe it himself Blaikie must have enjoyed working there. During this stay, he drew up his own plan for the garden and traced it out on the spot. Then, on 20 October he returned and remained 16 days until 4 November.[75] He charged 20 francs per day and his dealings were mainly with the Duchess[76] whose love of flowers dated from her school days, for Madame Campan believed that her pupils, 'in the flower of their youth' should discover the 'gifts of Flora',[77] a sentiment that Josephine endorsed. Blaikie's plan for the garden has not been found but a list of trees, ericaceous shrubs, perennials and seeds to be delivered to 'Madame la Marechalle [sic] Ney en Mars 1811' survives, as does his bill. The list[78] contained a number of foreign trees and shrubs, amongst them, liriodendrons, catalpas, sophoras, diospyros, kalmias and calycanthus. There was also a flower garden planned, with an order for simple old fashioned flowers; lychnis, campanulas, primroses, hollyhocks, pinks and periwinkles as well as fifty white lilies.[79] 'Madame la Marechalle' was obviously a romantic and, like Josephine, roses must have been her favourites. She ordered over 900 of them in 1811, 400 centifolias, and 300 of the long flowering 'Rose des Quatres Saisons' as well as *gallicas* and other unnamed varieties. Fruit trees were ordered as well, and lawn and vegetable seeds were purchased from a list sent to her by the firm of Vilmorin-Andrieux in March 1811. Of Berthault's design, little is known. Coudreaux's next owner, Marshal Reille, is said to have replaced Ney's garden by one 'in the picturesque style' in which 'the walls surrounding the park and the moat were removed and the park extended as far as the river Loir'.[80]

On the defeat of the emperor and the return of the Bourbons, Ney was imprisoned and sentenced to death by firing squad. The pleas of his wife and children were rejected by the resolutely unforgiving king. Ney's sentence, which could so easily have been commuted to banishment, was an act of vindictiveness. His army pension was cancelled and his widow was obliged to sell her properties and retire to Italy with her three sons.

In 1815 the château of Coudreaux was completely sacked. The allied soldiers brought the furniture to the market square and tried to sell it but, such was the popularity of the Neys, they could find no buyers. On their departure, the villagers carried everything back to the château.[81] The château still exists and is currently[82] offered for sale.

---

74. AN., 279 AP 14 Description of the grounds by Nancy Macdonald, daughter of the general, quoted in Eric Perrin, *Le Maréchal Ney* (Paris, 1993), p. 123.

75. Blaikie Accounts. Private Archive.

76. AN., 137 AP 17. In a hand written note at the foot of Blaikie's bill, dated 27 November 1810, she asks her estate manager to pay Mr Blaikie the sum of 1100 francs.

77. Letter from Mme Campan to Thouin who supplied the gardens with plants. Quoted in item 8 of sale Catalogue of Autographes, Livres, etc. 13 February 1995, by Laurin Gouilloux, Bouffetaud, Tailleur.

78. AN., 137 AP 17.

79. AN., 137 AP 17.

80. Ernest de Ganay, *Les Jardins de France* (Paris, 1949), p. 268.

81. Comte de la Bédoyère, *Le Maréchal Ney*, 2nd edn (Paris, n.d.).

82. Spring 1999.

Caulaincourt

In 1813 Blaikie's most famous client was Armand Augustin Louis de Caulaincourt (1733–1827), General and *Grand Ecuyer* de France. Caulaincourt was appointed ambassador to Moscow by Napoleon, first in 1801 and a second time from 1807 to 1811. He was created Duc de Vicence in 1808. His friendship with Alexander I irritated Napoleon, as did his efforts to dissuade the Emperor from his disastrous Russian campaign. His family seat in the Vermandois region of Picardy, the château of Caulaincourt, was situated a few miles from Saint-Quentin on the River Ormignon. The building Blaikie knew dated back to the sixteenth century but was remodelled during the reign of Louis XV so that the château, destroyed in the First World War, appears, from drawings of the time, to have an eighteenth-century façade.[83]

Vicence did not marry until 1814 at the end of his diplomatic career. His bride was Adrienne de Canisy, a former lady-in-waiting to Josephine. Possessed of dazzling good looks, she had been married at the age of thirteen to an uncle many years older than herself, and had borne him two sons. The marriage was not happy and she tried unsuccessfully to have it annulled on the grounds of her extreme youth at the time of the ceremony. She failed but eventually, in 1813, she secured a divorce. Caulaincourt wanted to marry her but Napoleon refused him permission since, in spite of his own divorce from Josephine, he would not tolerate divorced people at his court. In 1813, as the end of Napoleon's reign grew more and more likely, Caulaincourt prepared for his marriage by embarking on a programme of refurbishment of the château under the architect De Lestailleur.[84] However, one of Napoleon's last acts as Emperor was to give his approval for the marriage which took place in 1814.

Blaikie records in his account book that on 25 August 1813 he received a message from M. Gronnier, estate manager at Caulaincourt, summoning him to the château. The next day he presented himself at Caulaincourt to examine the terrain and sketch out a plan. He returned on 19 November to examine the ground again and to present his plan. From 21 to 24 December 1813 he traced the allées and the course of the river and gave an estimate of the work required on the terrace and elsewhere. He worked all day on Christmas Eve and returned to Chauny late that night. But thereafter all gardening activity came to a halt in the unsettled and dangerous first months of 1814 when France was invaded by the Allies. Later the region around Chauny, Laon, Soissons and Compiègne became the battleground of Napoleon's brilliant but, in the end, unsuccessful campaign to prevent the capture of Paris.

In June 1814 after the hostilities had ended, Blaikie was back at Caulaincourt, working out 'the different levels in the park'. He records in his account book that the Duke arrived on the 16th. He was back on 1 and 2 August working on the 'embankments of the river'. In January 1815 he spent a few days at Caulaincourt 'on different works'. While Blaikie was planting trees in the park on 3 and 4 April 1815, Napoleon was

---

83. Pinguet et Braveur, *Monumens, établissemens et sites les plus remarquables de l'Aisne* (Paris, 1921).

84. AN., 95 AP 72.

making a declaration claiming he had been restored to the throne by the unanimous
wish of his countrymen. Blaikie was to return once more, according to his account
book in June 1819. The Caulaincourt accounts for his work are incomplete, but
payments to him are recorded in August 1814 and January 1815 and there is a reference
to the 'rivière anglaise' among the garden archives.[85] It was sometime during the period
before 1815 when Blaikie was engaged in work at Caulaincourt that the lake which is
still a feature of the park was constructed, probably under the Scot's direction. General
Cavalié Mercer, commander of a troop of English horse artillery at Waterloo gives
a picture of the château as he saw it when he advanced with his troop on Paris in
the days following the battle. As he descended from the monotonous plain into a
wooded valley, he saw what he described as 'a most respectable looking country
house,' constructed of brick with stone angles and window-cases. It stood upon a
terrace, with an old fashioned garden divided into rectangular beds, with stone vases
etc., sheltered in the rear by the woods. To the south, it overlooked a fine sheet of
artificial water which Mercer surmises was probably formed by damming up the
stream which they had crossed in the bottom. He goes on, 'The hanging woods and
shady winding paths of this ravine appeared to us heavenly when contrasted with the
dreary exposed plain above'.[86]

Caulaincourt represented France at the peace negotiations before and after Waterloo
then retired to his country property. The château was bombarded by the Prussians
in 1870 and restored in the years preceding 1914 only to be reduced to a pile of rubble
by the German army during the First World War. All that now remains of the
eighteenth-century château is the entrance to the domain. The lake, modified in the
1930s, is the only memento of the Blaikie era at Caulaincourt. In 1930–33 a new château
was built a little way from the site of the old one by a Russian architect, André
Belorodoff, thus underlining the links between the nineteenth-century Duc de Vicence
and Russia. The new château was built on an elevated plateau overlooking the lake
so that the latter became a focal point in the view from the house.[87] Caulaincourt's
descendants still live there.

Fromont

The year 1813 had been busy for Blaikie. As well as attending to the tomb of M. Joly,
and beginning his commission for the Duke de Vicence, he took on five new commissions, continuing at the same time his work at Raray, Nogent l'Artaud and
Fourdrain. The château of Fromont at Fromont-à-Ris, 30 km south of Paris on the
road to Lyons via Fontainebleau was one of his new undertakings that year. Fromont,

85. AN., 95AP 70.
86. Mercer Cavalié (General), *Journal of the Waterloo Campaign*, 2 vols (Edinburgh, 1870), vol. 2,
pp. 25–6.
87. M. A. Beloborodoff, 'Le Nouveau Château de Caulaincourt (Aisne)', *La Construction Moderne*,
30 December 1934, pp. 294–305. I am grateful to M. J. C. Cappronnier for this and other
information on Caulaincourt.

on the west bank of the Seine, was, in the seventeenth century, a singularly beautiful estate. The château, originally the property of the Knights Templar, had been rebuilt and the park laid out by André Le Nôtre. During the mid 1600s the estate belonged to a M. Hierosme de Nouveau, Louis XIV's Counsellor, and the king stayed for a night at Fromont on one of his journeys to Fontainebleau.[88] John Evelyn was so impressed by the gardens in 1657 that he included them in a list he drew up in preparation for a book that was never realised on the history of gardens.[89] Two engravings by Israel Sylvestre (1621–1691) show the château in its heyday; the fine *parterres en broderie* near the house; and the view from the cascade, half way down the gardens, towards the river and the rising ground beyond. Another water colour, by an unknown artist of the same period, depicts the view from the parterres below the terrace up towards the château.[90] Blaikie visited Fromont in June 1812 in the company of its owners, M and Mme Calmelet, and had 'marked out some works', returning that year and the next to carry them out. Calmelet, who bought Fromont in 1804 had been *Intendant* to Prince Eugène, Josephine's son and Napoleon's faithful general. Calmelet's son-in-law, Étienne Soulange Bodin, had been First secretary to Prince Eugène in 1807 when the Prince was Viceroy of Italy. Soulange Bodin's main interest in life was horticulture and for a brief period following the death of Joséphine he was appointed superintendent of Malmaison. After his marriage, he took over the running of the gardens of Fromont where he founded a Horticultural Institute in 1820 dedicated to providing a professional training for gardeners. In 1822 he added a nursery. A visit to London in 1824 when he was elected a corresponding member of the Horticultural Society (now the RHS), inspired him to found the *Société Nationale d'Horticulture*. The Comte d'Artois as Charles X gave *the Institut Horticole de Fromont* his seal of approval when he visited the establishment in October 1829. Soulange Bodin became a friend of J. C. Loudon who tells us that the Frenchman 'commenced laying out the garden in the English manner in 1814 so as to combine the picturesque scenery of the park with the profitable culture of the nursery'.[91] Loudon described the grounds of Fromont as covering 'more than a hundred acres of a surface gently varied and sloping to the Seine. They are surrounded by a walk or drive which displays various views of the interior, the main feature of which is the château; and of the Seine with some rising ground beyond the boundary.' Although this description is characteristic of Blaikie's work with its gentle slopes and interior and exterior views, there is no mention of his having designed the garden which is described elsewhere as having been 'so well conceived that when Soulange Bodin installed his nursery there the harmony of the whole was scarcely disturbed'.[92]

88. Henri Collet, *Notes pour servir à l'histoire de Ris-Orangis* (n.d.), vol. I, pp. 18–22. He suggests that Le Nôtre laid out the gardens in 1691.

89. See William Howard Adams, *The French Garden 1500–1800* (London, 1979; pbk edn 1982), p. 76. Further information communicated to me by Mme Marianne de Meyenbourg, Librarian, Musée de l'Ile de France.

90. First engraving BN, 2nd engraving and water colour, Musée de l'Ile de France.

91. J. C. Loudon, *Encyclopaedia of Gardening* (1835 edn), part I, p. 96. Also G.M., vol. 9, pp. 141–2.

92. Le Texnier, *Jardiniers célèbres et amateurs de jardins* (Paris, 1907), p. 2.

However, in a letter to Blaikie dated the 29 August 1823, enclosing a catalogue of the nursery he has newly established at Fromont, Soulange Bodin concedes, a little ungenerously, that Blaikie had 'contributed to the embellishment of the gardens of Fromont'.[93] He goes on to explain to Blaikie that his many travels have denied him the opportunity of making the landscape gardener's acquaintance or of taking lessons from him in an art that Blaikie exercises with such 'distinguished success'. The letter lacks any warmth. Blaikie was essentially an eighteenth-century man while Soulange Bodin personified the rather buttoned-up nineteenth-century bourgeois. The two were unlikely to find themselves in tune. Blaikie enjoyed more friendly relations with Soulange Bodin's wife from whose house in Paris he addressed a letter to André Thouin in 1822.[94] Soulange Bodin became the owner of Fromont in 1846. He died in 1848. Today the château of Fromont, minus its two wings and its terrace, is the Mairie of Fromont-à-Ris.

Ivors and the Campaign of 1814

Among Blaikie's clients in 1813 was Comte Raymond de Nicolay[95] at his château of Ivors near Villers-Cotterets in the department of the Oise. This commission involved the planting of a hunting estate which relied also on an income from wood, rather than the planting of an ornamental park like Les Coudreaux. The correspondence of the estate manager, Joseph Charpentier, with his employer, gives an account of the works undertaken at Ivors between 1813 and 1815 but is particularly interesting for the way it reveals that, even in the middle of the campaign of 1814 with armies locked in combat around the estate, some kind of normal routine prevails as Charpentier struggles to continue the work of the plantations while waiting all the time for Blaikie to appear.[96]

Unfortunately, the very letter which might have given an account of Blaikie's arrival at Ivors is missing and it is from Blaikie's account book that we learn of his first visit there in July 1813. Charpentier provided thirteen workmen for the digging over of the stony ground for the plantations during October. He hopes that 'M. Blaket' will be able to come during the month of November or, at the latest, the beginning of December. He frequently mentions a M. Lemoine in connection with Blaikie and Blaikie himself writes in his account book that he accompanied M. Lemoine to Ivors so that it is likely that Lemoine (or Lemoyne[97]) was Nicolay's architect. Charpentier's source of the deciduous and evergreen trees recommended by Blaikie was a nursery,

93. Blaikie Papers.
94. Bibliothèque du Muséum d'Histoire Naturelle, MS 1984, No. 126.
95. Aymard-Jean-Tanneguy, Raymond de Nicolay (1781–1842), Baron of the Empire 1812, Member of the Electoral College of the Aisne. He married in 1806, Marie-Charlotte de Mural de l'Estang.
96. AN., 3 AP 134 and 341.
97. Possibly Pierre-Hippolyte Le Moyne architect at Saint-Germain-en-Laye during the Empire and the Restoration. Michel Gallet, p. 331.

owned by a M. Pottier, at Bargny, a few miles from Ivors, which supplied other clients of Blaikie. The order for Ivors consisted mainly of native trees, poplars, birches, chestnuts and unspecified evergreens. As well as new plantings and allées in the woods and along the roadsides, once again there was to be a *rocher* or large mound which would be planted with trees. Much of the time Charpentier is lamenting the non-arrival of Blaikie or begging his employer to use his influence to persuade 'M. Blaket' to return.

Raymond de Nicolay was taking a brave step at Ivors in replacing the straight allées in the woods of this hunting estate by winding paths and new 'massifs' *à l'anglaise*, to say nothing of the rocher. His nerve weakened momentarily and he wrote to Charpentier in October 1813 asking him if he was doing the right thing. The agent's reply is amusing. He assures his employer that it is never a mistake to use one's money in improving one's land, especially since the sandy terrain of Ivors was particularly favourable for woodland. Opponents of anglomania might, he ventures, think the Count was wrong but, after the trees were grown sufficiently to make an impression in a year or two, there would be nothing more beautiful, nor, he added, more profitable. He writes that he has not yet received any news of Blaikie who is due to plan the location of the clumps or groups of evergreens. Blaikie did not appear at Ivors at the end of 1813 as expected but sent, instead, a plan to M. de Nicolay on 2 January 1814.[98] By February, Charpentier is resigned to his absence and feels he cannot now expect M. Blaikie till the frosts are over and they can begin planting.

For once, it was not pressure of work that kept Blaikie from returning to Ivors. In the early months of 1814, the Emperor, forced back across the Rhine with the remnants of his defeated army was constrained for the first time to conduct a war on French soil. The region around the Seine, the Marne and the Aisne was to be the main field in his struggle against overwhelming odds to beat off three invading armies and retain his Empire. The veteran Field-Marshal Blücher was in overall command of the Allied contingents, three forces numbering a total of 340,000 men, which would make Picardy their battlefield as they converged on Paris.

Early success at the battle of la Rothière gave Blücher a misplaced confidence in his own strength, and he split his own and the Austrian armies, sending the Austrians under Schwartzenberg along both banks of the Seine towards Paris while he followed the course of the Marne. With Blücher's forces now spread out, and vulnerable, Napoleon seized his opportunity. In a series of rapid marches and brilliant manoeuvres, he attacked the divided army on three successive days and drove Blücher back on Châlons. The Prussians lost 30,000 men and, by 18 February, the astonished citizens of Paris, saw, instead of the invading army they had feared, 2000 Allied prisoners marched through their streets on one of the few sunny days in that cold and wet month. The tide appeared to have turned.

An undated letter from Charpentier to Nicolay gives a picture of the events of 6–18 February in the countryside within a few miles of Ivors during one of Napoléon's

---

98. Blaikie's Account Book. The plan is not among the archive documents of the Nicolay family at the Archives Nationales.

attacks; heavy fighting around Château-Thierry, with cannonades and fusillades all day; the town taken and re-taken more than once and the road covered with the dead. On the night of the 15th and 16th (February) a force of six or seven thousand combined French artillery and cavalry arrived at Villers-Cotterets commanded, he writes, by the Duc de Rovigo (General Savary). The emperor was expected there with 10,000 men and, he adds, 18000 were moving on Soissons by the Compiègne road. Yet, although Ivors is within sound of the combat, a strange normality persists. He does not now expect 'M. Blakie' till the frosts are over. The weather has been terrible, frost for two days at the beginning of the month then, on 3 February, the greatest quantity of snow. The workers have been unable to work on the plantations for 20 days. It was in these wintry conditions that the armies were locked together in the adjoining countryside.

Blaikie at that moment was at home at Chauny (near Laon) where, like every other citizen, he nervously awaited the arrival of the two corps from the Army of the North under Bulow and Winzingerode as they advanced towards Paris via Avesnes and Laon to meet up with part of Blucher's force near the River Aisne. On 26 February, Bulow occupied Laon. The same day 800 Saxon, Prussian and Cossack soldiers commanded by Baron de Gueismar appeared outside Chauny. While he was at the Mairie to receive the surrender of the town from the mayor, M. Mory de Neflieux (one of Blaikie's clients), a detachment of Gueismar's escort riding down one of the streets was met by a group of armed workers who opened fire on the soldiers. The Baron, at that very moment emerging from the Town Hall, heard the shots and noise and bellowed out the word *trahison*. His troops drawn up on the outskirts of the town, hearing the shots and the shouts of the general, rode at the gallop through the streets, sabres drawn, attacking anyone in their path. The people watching the ceremony at the Town Hall were mown down; 12 died and many were injured. The general at once ordered the destruction of the town by fire but, on the pleas of the mayor, he agreed instead to the levy of a fine of a hundred thousand francs to be paid within 24 hours. The mayor also succeeded in saving six prisoners threatened with immediate execution, offering himself and his two deputies as hostages.[99] From the receipt for Blaikie's payment, dated 26 February 1814, Blaikie was required to pay 100 francs towards this ransom but, by the next morning, only half the levy had been raised. The mayor's deputies were released but the mayor remained a prisoner until the full sum was forthcoming. The town was then thoroughly pillaged.

On 27 February the war had reached Mr Charpentier at Ivors. The French army has requisitioned Nicolay's best linen, silver, bed and window curtains, wines and porcelain. As to the plantations, he reports, he will do everything in his power to continue the work but the frost has been so severe that the men have not been able to continue with the digging for the last fortnight.[100] On 28 February the war had

99. For an account of this incident and others in the region during the 1814 campaign see Y. Fleury, *Le département de l'Aisne en 1814* (Laon, 1858).
100. The severe frost and snow during February and March 1814 for once aided Napoleon with his small mobile forces fighting on their own familiar land against a large Allied force.

come even closer. A force of 90,000 Prussians and Russians engaged the French so fiercely between the villages of Rozoy and Rouvres, not far from Ivors, that the people living in the district could not hear themselves speak for the noise of cannon pounding from morning to night. After inflicting heavy injuries on the French, the invaders retreated leaving a trail of burnt houses and dead farm animals behind them.

By 25 March, events were moving rapidly in the Allies' favour. Charpentier had heard that the beaten French general, General Grouvel,[101] had retreated on Soissons. All communications were cut. Nevertheless, even in the midst of these shattering events, he writes, 'I must now say a word to you about your plantations'. He reports that he has sent to Mr Pottier, the nurseryman recommended by Blaikie, and has received plants of sycamore from him with an offer of superb larches at thirty francs the hundred. He has planted almost four arpents with birches, oaks and chestnuts and, since it was now impossible for 'Mr Blaikaie' to reach Ivors, they would wait till the following year for the massing of evergreen trees. He added that the local people were hiding their animals in the woods.

What both Blaikie and Charpentier had witnessed in those last days of March was the final retreat and collapse of the French army in the drive towards Paris. The city fell on 30 March. On 6 April Napoleon abdicated. A troop of Cossacks arrived at the gates of Ivors on 10 April. They departed after consuming a few bottles of brandy but the same day, 3 Prussian hussars terrorised Charpentier and his household, drank five bottles of brandy, pillaged his house, threatened him with a sabre and put a pistol to his throat. Yet, in spite of these harrowing experiences, he assured the Count that he had finished the plantations, and feared that they would not now be able to have a visit from 'Mr Blaikait'.

The plantations continued throughout the summer and autumn of 1814 and began to take shape. Blaikie made his last visit to Ivors on 8 April 1815 and stayed two days tracing out the terrain for the groups of evergreens and the allées on the mountain (rocher). Hailstorms and frosts that spring killed the majority of the larches and the cedars of Lebanon and the thujas fared almost as badly. Then, a month after Waterloo, a regiment of Russians under one Colonel Orgenski took possession of the estate with five or six thousand men and a large amount of artillery. They remained until 31 August and, for the rest of the year, poor Charpentier reported a sequence of visits from Prussian soldiers who terrorised him and his family and behaved '*en vrais brigands*'. A rumour circulated that the English were also expected, and this, he feared, would be the worst fate of all. For once the plantations were forgotten. A new era was about to begin.

---

101. François Grouvel (1771–1836). Enlisted in the Orleans-Aragons in 1791. Aide-de-camp of General Chabot 1795–1799, he participated in campaigns with the Army of the West and the Army of Italy. He was in the Grande Armée in 1807, Promoted Colonel 1809. General of Brigade May 1813. Led a brigade of light cavalry in 1814. April 1815 served in Army of the Rhine. Lieut-general 1825. Grand officer of the Legion of Honour 1835.

CHAPTER 16

Paradise Regained?

THE PAINFUL EVENTS of the spring of 1814 heralded the return of the Bourbons to France. On the 12 April, flanked by the Allies, the Comte d'Artois rode into Paris ahead of his brother, Louis XVIII. Immediately, Bélanger boldly asserted himself as chief architect to Artois and head of the department of Menus Plaisirs,[1] and at once submitted designs for the decoration of the route the King would follow on his ceremonial entry to Paris.[2] This event, which took place on the 3 May, was a triumph of organisation. The slights the architect had endured at the court of Napoléon were wiped out by the success of the moment and his award of the Légion d'Honneur on the 30 December 1814 was assured.

Blaikie may not have travelled to Paris from Chauny to stand among the cheering crowds that welcomed the return of Louis XVIII to the city but, wherever he was, he probably drank a toast to better days ahead and fell asleep contemplating the prospect of new works for the members of the Old Régime, returned from exile to regain their place at court. They and the thousands of faithful servants of the royal family of all ranks, looked to the restored monarchy to compensate them for the long years of suffering they had endured. Blaikie, as one of their number, had hopes of a pension. Louis XVIII and his brother Artois, or Monsieur, as the only brother of the king was known, were to recognise the claims of a large number of their higher ranking retainers. In 1819 Louis XVIII paid pensions worth 2,080,326 francs to 3,327 people 'ruined as a result of political events'. 1,361,000 francs a year were paid in pensions to 1,813 former servants and court officials of the royal family. The awards ranged from 6000 francs a year for a former lady-in-waiting to a few hundred for a servant.[3] Blaikie, apparently by an oversight, received nothing until 1822 when he was awarded an ex gratia payment of 500 francs which Monsieur would consider turning into an annual pension on completion of a few formalities.[4] However, he did have other expectations.

Preserved amongst his papers is his copy of Le Moniteur Universel of Sunday 26 November 1815. The editorial expressed relief for the end of eight months of 'disorder, alarums and calamities' and carried the announcement and full details of the treaty

---

1. The dept of Menus Plaisirs in the Old Regime was responsible for the staging of court events.
2. Stern, vol. II, pp. 261–2.
3. AN 03 539 quoted in Philip Mansel, The Court of France 1789–1830 (Cambridge, 1988), pp. 180–1.
4. Blaikie Papers. Letter dated 13 September 1822 from M. de Belleville, Surintendant de la maison de Monsieur. In it, he explained that his predecessor in the post had inexplicably 'adjourned Blaikie's request for a pension from year to year and had never spoken to Monsieur about it'. Blaikie did in the end receive a pension. Birrell gives the date of the award as 1826 and writes that it was eventually awarded by the Duc d'Orléans but the letter awarding it is not now among the papers.

of 1815 between France and the Allies. Blaikie marked the part that dealt with the handing over of most of the Pays de Gex to the Federation of Swiss Republics for the enlargement of the canton of Geneva. A large inky spot highlights the section which concerned him more directly, namely the setting up of a Royal Commission, empowered by an act of Parliament, for the examination and liquidation of claims by British subjects on the government of France, allowing for them and their descendants to be indemnified and paid once their claims had been recognised as legitimate. In this section there was also a clause regulating the loss of property belonging to British subjects, which had been sequestrated, confiscated and sold. Creditors, it announced, were to receive their capital back with interest. It seemed as if, after the years of poverty and suffering, justice was to be done.

Blaikie set out his case to the Commission in a long document covering all the evils which had befallen him since April 1791, when he had lost almost everything he possessed as a result of the seizure and wanton destruction of his property, with the theft of his money and valuables at the house he rented at Chaillot.[5] He also claimed the full sum plus interest of his claim as a creditor of Philippe Egalité.[6] As a creditor of Egalité, he had already received compensation in the form of an annual rent of 6184 francs This had been offered to him on 22 March 1798 on the basis of a debt calculated to be approximately 124,000 francs Blaikie had at first refused the settlement, claiming that his calculations showed he was owed 155,477 francs. In the end, he was forced to accept the offer under protest for, by his own careful calculations he was still owed 31,477 francs plus interest from the date of the offer.

Yet in spite of his real losses, Blaikie's claim was rejected. Firstly, the Commission disallowed part of it as having been submitted a day late by his representative. The other representations were also turned down as not falling into the categories laid down in the Commission's terms of reference, namely to deal with those who had lost their property by 'sequestration or confiscation'. In their judgment against him, the Commissioners ruled that he had not lost his property as a result of either of these categories but through a legal action in a French court[7] and that with regard to the debts owed to him by the Duke of Orléans, he had received the same terms as all the other creditors of the Duke and had not been treated differently from them because of his nationality.[8] He appealed against the decision. In the first instance, he pointed out that he had carried his case against the court that allowed the seizure of his property and the vandalism at his house to the National Assembly[9] but he had

---

5. Blaikie Papers.

6. 300 AP I 24.

7. Pierre Coulomb et Maurice Gonon, p. 104. See chapter 13.

8. Houtteau, the administrator or liquidator of the Orléans claims, sent a statement to the Commission categorically denying Blaikie's claim. Blaikie's papers are full of sheets of figures calculating the sum he was owed and rebutting Hutteau.

9. He quotes the *Monitor* of June 1792 which carried his appeal, and there is a copy of a document among his papers from the *Depot des Lois, Etabli à Paris, Place du Carousel*. It contains an extract from the *Procès Verbal* of the National Assembly and reads, 'Petition of an Englishman, Thomas Blaikie who complains 1) of armed robbery and thefts carried

been unable to pursue the affair to its conclusion as a result of the law against foreigners of 1793, which obliged him to leave Paris in fear of his life. As for the allocation of money awarded to him as a creditor of Orléans, which he still maintained was miscalculated, he had been compelled, the day after he received the certificate of his annual rent for 6184 francs to sell it at a nominal price of 5,771 francs to his 'jailers' who had provided food and drink while he was under their care and on whose good will he and his wife depended for their survival.

His appeal was disallowed. It was pointed out to him that part of his appeal had arrived late and also that the Commission would not consider losses that had taken place before September 1793. He was not the only one to have been denied compensation because of the terms of reference of the Commission. The English language newspaper in Paris, *Galignani's Messenger*, of Monday 3 May 1819 drew attention to a speech in the Commons by a Mr C. Hutchinson concerning the case of commercial wine merchants in Bordeaux whose goods were taken possession of and sold for 1/20th of their value and who were threatened with imprisonment if they did not agree to the sale. However, as their claims did not fall under the heading of 'sequestration and confiscation' they were disallowed. Castlereagh, who had agreed to the terms of the convention of 1815, replied that it was now too late to remedy any defect in wording and so those, like Blaikie, whose situation was not the result of sequestration and who had been 'legally' victimised received nothing. Blaikie applied a second time when claimants were invited to apply for the residue of the fund but his claim was rejected. He was once again obliged to put the losses of the past behind him and, at the age of 64, continue his career for as long as it was physically possible for him to do so, if he was to provide for himself and his 44 year old wife, while they both lived.

The aristocrats returning in 1814 were eager to put their past behind them, after 26 years in exile. For most of them, the relief of returning was allied to a desire to settle down quietly. 'Country life,' wrote Alexandre de Laborde, 'acquires a new charm after great revolutions, when men wearied by events like to rest for a while in the calm of some retreat.'[10] But the dream of a return to the tranquil countryside was not easy to achieve. Many had difficulty in reclaiming their estates. Some of these had been destroyed or pillaged. Others, according to the law against emigrés, had been sold either entire or in lots.[11] The Napoleonic aristocracy, many of whom now

---

out at his house at Chaillot by two bailiffs and their assistants. 2) of the negligence of the Tribunal of the 2nd District of Paris in rendering him justice and particularly of the refusal which the leader of the Jury to receive his act of accusation made in accordance with the information supplied by the Justice of the Peace of Passy of the 6th and 7th April last.' The National Assembly has referred this petition to the Minister of Justice with the injunction to inform himself of the circumstances of it within 8 days. The Minister was Danton and nothing more was heard of Blaikie's petition – very small beer in view of events at the time.

10. A De Laborde, *Description des nouveaux jardins* (Paris, 1808), p. 1.
11. By a law of 17 July 1792, emigré land to be sold off as national land. By another, of 24 October 1792 their movable property to be sequestrated and sold. By a third, of 3 June 1793, emigré land to be sold off in small lots to benefit poorer peasants.

owned these estates, were not hounded but kept their positions and their property. Many of these were Blaikie's clients but the region to the north and east of Paris, where a number of them owned land, had been the scene of battles and reprisals, the countryside a panorama of sacked châteaux and ruined farms. A period of recovery would precede any new programme of landscape design.

Fifteen consecutive pages of Blaikie's account book, covering the years 1814 to 1817, are missing, torn out. Consequently, it is impossible to know who his new clients were during those years or, in most cases, which of his former employers recalled him. However, sometimes a client's accounts for several years are grouped together on the same page, so that it is occasionally possible to follow a commission as far as 1815. None of these recapitulation pages record commissions during 1816 and 1817. The upheavals following 1815 would account for the absence of clients in 1816. The following year, Blaikie's health was bad and he was ill for most of the year.[12] He was unemployed, possibly until 1817, a circumstance that may have induced him to agree to lend £500 at 5% to John Vaughan, Earl of Lisburne, on 5 June 1817 in order to provide himself with an income. How Blaikie came to meet Lisburne is a mystery. Mrs Blaikie purchased bonnets and lengths of cloth in Paris for Lady Lucy Vaughan, the Earl's daughter, then had the cloth made up by a fashionable dressmaker and sent to her in London.[13] Such a degree of familiarity with the lady's taste in clothes suggests Mrs Blaikie may have worked for the family as a ladies' maid in her youth. The £500 Blaikie lent the Earl was a large sum for a man in his circumstances (13,000 francs according to the rate of exchange of 1817 and a round £15,000 in today's terms).[14] Interest was paid on the money at irregular intervals until April 1829 but Blaikie received neither the full amount of the interest nor the capital.[15]

The end of hostilities in 1815 left him free to go where he pleased and he could have returned to claim his Scottish inheritance, the small, family property of Corstorphine Hill outside Edinburgh. In the summer of 1814, after the first Restoration, he had written to both his sisters expressing his desire to return home and it was undoubtedly in connection with his affairs at Corstorphine Hill that he received a visit towards the end of 1814 from his nephew and namesake, Thomas Mackie, the son of his elder sister Agnes.[16] Agnes had married James Mackie, a gardener some sixteen years her junior, and, in 1789 at the age of 43, she had borne him a son, whom she named Thomas, after her father and her brother. James Mackie had built up and managed the nursery at Corstorphine Hill during Blaikie's absence and was no doubt worried that he might lose it; hence the appearance of his son in Chauny in the

---

12. A letter from his nephew-in-law, James Young from Edinburgh dated 25 July 1816 confirms that he had not been well 'for some time'.
13. Blaikie papers.
14. My thanks to the Librarian, The Bank of England Library, for this information.
15. The complete details of this debt is contained in letters between Lisburne and the Blaikies amongst the Blaikie papers. The note signed by Lisburne, stamped and witnessed, is there also. Lisburne died in 1833 and his family denied all responsibility for his debt.
16. Letter of 16 January 1816 from James Young, Isabella's son-in-law mentions this visit and complains that Isabel Blaikie's other sister had not been told Thomas was going to France.

closing months of 1814. Since Thomas was full of his uncle's 'great kindness' to him, when he returned to Edinburgh,[17] he must have received Blaikie's assurances that the Mackies could remain at Corstorphine Hill, although Blaikie continued to own the property.

Blaikie now knew the sometimes doubtful joys of having rediscovered his family.[18] Isabel had two children; Agnes married to James Young, and Robert married to Elizabeth Baxter. James Young and Elizabeth Baxter wrote to Blaikie fairly regularly on behalf of their mother-in-law. James was first to offer congratulations to his uncle on the return of peace and send him the good wishes of his old friend, the surgeon, Mr Fyfe.[19] From Young also we hear about 'the perils and dangers' Blaikie and his wife had endured during the Prussian occupation of Picardy in 1815. A traveller in the region during the summer of 1815 noted that, 'Every village was full of Prussians on their march, and indeed very few of the inhabitants were to be seen, their houses being shut up, and having generally the appearance of being gutted and pillaged'.[20] As in 1814, Chauny was once again subject to levies.

Young, in another letter of 18 January 1816, describes the downturn in both the agricultural and industrial economies in Scotland after the war. He asks Blaikie, without success, for £500 to buy a partnership in the Edinburgh Chemical Company. He also gives his uncle-in-law an account of his seven children. The youngest, only three months old, they have christened Thomas. Isabel adds a note expressing pleasure that her brother has sent her a lock of his hair.

James Mackie, Agnes Blaikie's husband had prospered and was on the way to becoming a gentleman. A small mausoleum he built during his lifetime stands among the simple gravestones in the kirkyard of Corstorphine, a monument to his pretentions, and his prosperity. The Torbet letters chronicle a bitter family feud at whose root was the growing prosperity of the Mackies and the failing health and fortunes of the Torbet family. In the crowded tenements of the West Bow where the poor lived crammed together, child mortality was high. Little Thomas Young lived only a few months, and an older girl died a short time later. Poor Agnes, the mother, became ill with grief, putting paid to the idea that the high mortality rate somehow made the pain of losing a child less severe. As for the Mackies, the Torbets complained, James and Thomas would not be seen on foot in that part of the town.

With the peace of 1815, the British once again flocked to Europe. In 1817 three Scottish visitors called upon Blaikie. Their leader was Patrick Neill, secretary of the Caledonian Horticultural Society and one of its founder members. After 13 years without contact between botanists and nursery owners abroad, there were many new

---

17. Letter from James Young 18 January 1816. Blaikie papers.
18. Blaikie Papers. Blaikie made a list of the letters he wrote and received from his family. Those he received from Thomas Mackie are no longer amongst them. The correspondence with the Torbets lasted till 1835.
19. Letters of 6 April and 28 July 1814. See chapter 2.
20. Elisabeth Duchess of Rutland, *Journal of a Short Trip during the Summer of 1815* (London, 1814–1815), p. 42.

varieties of plants that were unknown in the British Isles. Neill, in response to a
resolution of the Society, had undertaken to travel with two other members to the
north of France and the Netherlands to 'take notice of any new or uncommon varieties
of fruits and culinary vegetables which might be desirable to introduce into Scotland'.
His aim was also to make useful horticultural contacts for the future. Neill's companions were James Mackay, head gardener to the Duke of Buccleuch at Dalkeith, and
John Hay, a garden designer particularly skilled in the construction of green houses.[21]
They arrived in Paris via the Netherlands on 19 June and, two days later, took a chaise
and made their way to St Germain-en-Laye where Blaikie had moved in 1816.
Saint-Germain, within easy reach of Paris was, and still is a pleasant place to live and
popular with foreigners. There was a fairly large English speaking colony there,
amongst them Alexander Howatson. It was at Howatson's that Blaikie chose to receive
the three Scots rather than at his own lodgings, where, presumably, he felt he could
not offer them proper hospitality.[22]

'The lively conversation of this venerable Scoto-Gallican gardener,'[23] with his
recollections of pre-Revolutionary personalities and gardens in whose making he had
actually played a part, enthralled Neill and he became convinced that Blaikie had not
received the recognition he deserved in his career.[24] To try to redress the balance, he
went out of his way to list the major gardens in which Blaikie had worked, adding
in a note that 'we have not observed that sufficient justice is done to him by French
authors who take occasion to mention the state of gardening'.[25] He quotes examples
of praise for the gardens of Bagatelle, and those parts of Monceau and Raincy for
which Blaikie was particularly responsible, yet he notes, these are always attributed
to Bélanger, Carmontelle and Pottier, respectively. He is at pains to tell his readers
that, 'we notice these things without the slightest communication with Mr Blaikie,'
and adds that Blaikie, 'never wasted a thought about his own fame as a garden-
architect'. Neill returned for another tour in 1821 and, on both occasions, Blaikie
accompanied him on visits to gardens and nurseries around Paris, drawing Neill's
attention to vegetables and fruit crops particularly appropriate for culture in Scotland.[26]
He described French methods of grafting and culture and introduced Neill to influential
nursery owners. One of these was Hardy at the Luxembourg gardens, renowned for
his roses, particularly *Rosa* 'Madame Hardy' (1832), still the most beautiful of white

---

21. John Hay (1758–1836). For details of Hay's career see *Gardener's Magazine* (1837), p. 96,
    quoted in A. A. Tait, *The Landscape Garden in Scotland* (Edinburgh, 1980), pp. 143, 144.
22. Blaikie must have been short of money at this time. The house he lived in has so many
    different and changing occupants that it was probably a rooming house, I am indebted to
    M. Pierre Renard for this information.
23. Neill, p. 358.
24. Amongst Neill's contacts were the Thouin brothers, André and Jean. He spent an evening
    with them at their house in the *Jardin des Plantes* and would almost certainly have confided
    his feeling about Blaikie to them and asked their opinion.
25. Neill, p. 361. Among them he lists Malmaison as mentioned in the previous chapter.
26. Such as a late-flowering walnut that produced its fruit at the same time as those that
    blossomed earlier.

roses with its distinctive green eye. Blaikie confided in Neill that it was 'his earnest wish to revisit his native country after so long an absence'.[27] The two kept in touch and Neill sprinkled Blaikie's recommendations and views throughout his account of his two visits. He also published Blaikie's catalogue of fruit trees at the *Jardin des Plantes* as an appendix to his own book.[28]

In the remaining pages of Blaikie's accounts, only four clients are recorded for 1818.[29] However, in 1819 he was once again greatly in demand for a mixture of old and new commissions. Among his regular clients was the Duc de Vicence (Caulaincourt). Another was the Vicomte de Montesquiou, son of his pre-Revolutionary client, the Marquis de Montesquiou-Fezenac at Mauperthuis, and his young friend, Henry de La Bédoyère. Among his new clients were the Baron de Pontalba and the prince of Salm-Dyck.

Joseph-Xavier Delfau (1754–1834),[30] the first Baron de Pontalba, was born in New Orleans but brought up in France. He took part in the siege of Savannah during the American War of Independence[31] then retired to France and gave up his army career at the end of that war. In 1783 he returned for a time to New Orleans to look after his family's indigo plantation. He married the niece of the governor, and his son, Celestin, was born there in 1791. In 1805, he bought Mont l'Evêque, situated in the valley of the River Nonette about 50 miles from Paris and at one time the summer residence of the bishops of Senlis. At the same time, he succeeded in obtaining a place for his son as a page to Napoleon who created him Baron de Pontalba in 1810, possibly through the influence of Agläe Ney to whom he was related.[32] At the Restoration, letters discovered on Marshal Ney's person after his arrest, showed that Pontalba had arranged for Ney, after the marshal's intended escape from France, to take refuge with the Pontalba family in Louisiana. Surprisingly this action does not appear to have caused Pontalba any problems with the government of Louis XVIII. In

---

27. *Ibid*, p. 361.
28. Neill, Appendix No. VIII, p. 542.
29. The Comtesse de Sade at Condé, the Comte de Vaulx at Villers-Agron, the Comte d'Ourches at Grange aux Ormes near Metz and a M. Waubert at Varenne near Noyon.
30. The information on Delfau is taken mainly from Christina Vella, *Intimate Enemies ; The Two Worlds of the Baroness de Pontalba* (Louisiana State University Press, Baton Rouge and London, 1997). See also 'Réunion du 10 janvier 1946' in *Societe d'Histoire et d'Archaeologie de Senlis*, comptes rendus, 8eme série (Anne 1946–1947), pp. 2, 3, which gives a slightly different account of his life.
31. At the request of the American Congress for aid from France, a fleet under Admiral d'Estaing reached the mouth of the Savannah River on 2 September 1779 from the West Indies and disembarked its troops just below Savannah, setting siege to the town. After four days of shelling, D'Estaing made an unsuccessful assault on the town suffering heavy losses. He sailed back to France with part of his force after the battle, despatching the remainder to the West Indies.
32. They were cousins. On his return to France, Pontalba had submitted a report on Louisiana to the Minister of the Navy in the vain hopes of securing a commission in the French army. He was made a baron in the generous honours list following the birth of Napoleon's son.

the years following the Restoration, his business affairs prospered. His son married a New Orleans heiress and his income was bolstered by his daughter-in-law's fortune.[33]

Blaikie went straight from nearby Raray where he had been working since 2 November to meet M. and Madame de Pontalba at Mont l'Evêque on 24 October 1819. The château, situated off the main street of the village of Mont l'Evêque, sits on a slope below its ancillary buildings with a moat lapping its walls. Of the original fifteenth-century building only two sturdy towers survive with a portcullis over the narrowest part of the moat. The rest of what we see today was built in the nineteenth-century in what is called the troubadour style. Nowadays, the park is dedicated to hunting and there appears no trace of any garden laid out by Blaikie. An ancient and gnarled, multi-stemmed, weeping willow still hangs over the water by the path alongside the moat near the château, and ancient limes, beeches and sycamores grow in the woods but it is impossible to say if any of them date from Blaikie's time. The château itself is in the process of restoration by the Pontalbas who still live at Mont l'Evêque in the Little Château behind and to one side of the main building. In his account book Blaikie comments that there is a 'great deal of water in the park', and it is true today that streams and marshy areas abound. He also writes that he 'continues' to trace the river and alter its course in the ancient potager which suggests that, although no record remains of his visits, he has been there before within the past year or so. During this period of employment which lasted 20 days and brought him 360 livres, he also constructed a waterfall.

In September 1819 Blaikie received a most pleasing commission. He was invited by the Prince of Salm-Dyck to landscape his park near Neuss not far from Dusseldorf. Joseph Maria Franz Anton Hubert Ignaz zu Salm-Reifferscheid-Dyck (1773–1861)[34] spent much of his life in Paris, where he met his second wife, Constance de Théis (1767–1845). The princess, beautiful and talented was a literary star of her day, a poet, dramatist, novelist and letter writer. She published her first collection of poetry when she was 18 and she was known as '*la Muse de la raison et le Boileau des femmes*'. She first married a M. Pipelet, and one of the pleasures of her second marriage in 1803 must have been the abandonment of such a banal surname. She held a literary and aristocratic salon

---

33. Pontalba would become notorious in 1834 for the attempted murder of his son Celestin's wife. Although he wounded her four times in the breast, he failed to kill her and committed suicide immediately afterwards with the same pair of duelling pistols he had used to attack her. The reason for his action? He had become obsessed with securing his daughter-in-law's considerable fortune after being bitterly disappointed in her dowry arrangements. She signed over much of her property to her husband but, after her attempts to live separately from Celestin and reclaim part of her fortune, his obsession turned to hatred.

34. His first marriage at the age of 18 ended in divorce in 1801. During the French Revolution he did not take an active part against the French and retained his estates. Apart from his botanical interests he had a distinguished career in the Landwehr Regiment and King Frederick William made him a prince in 1816. He wrote a number of monographs, in particular *Aloe and Mesembrianthemum*, illustrated with nearly four hundred plates, published in parts between 1836 and 1863.

at her house, the Hotel de Salm-Dyck in the rue du Bac,[35] where, together with her circle, many of the friends and acquaintances of the prince used to meet, amongst them the famous botanists of the day, A. P. de Candolle, A. L. de Jussieu and A. V. Humbolt. Salm-Dyck was also a friend of the painter Redouté who, besides his volumes on the roses at Malmaison, and *Les Liliacées*, illustrated a book of succulents, *Plantarum Succulentarum Historia* by the Swiss botanist De Candolle. This work so impressed the prince that he took drawing and painting lessons from Redouté and decided to devote his life to the study of succulent plants, spending the winters in Paris and the summers at Salm-Dyck attending his collection of some 5000 cacti and receiving visits from the important botanists of his day. In 1819 he decided to make an arboretum at Salm-Dyck in the form of an English garden and in his introduction to *Hortus Dyckensis*, the catalogue of his garden, published in 1834, he described what his intentions were in making his garden. As well as a botanical garden for his cacti and other succulent leafed plants, he intended to plant the complete range of trees and shrubs that could tolerate the climate of his region, and to turn his botanic garden into a landscape garden in which the trees and shrubs – planted according to families and genera – would be grown in the place most suitable for them, yet, at the same time, form a picturesque unity. He writes, 'I entrusted Mr Blakey, one of the most eminent gardeners of the old English school, to carry out this design, and a study of the above mentioned topographical plan [36] as well as other vistas viewed from various points of the garden will show how expertly he has taken advantage of the location'.

The previous site of the English garden seems to have been a largely wooded one and Prince Joseph goes on to describe Blaikie's method of planting particular families of trees and shrubs in the shelter of large wooded areas of oaks and beeches, mixed with bosquets or groves, in which the shrubs – planted in no particular order – are defined through their distinctive forms and various hues to offer a pleasing diversion to the eye. This is reminiscent of Blaikie's project at Bagatelle where he also had to cut a garden out of woodland but this time the soil was good loam which produced fine trees. Amongst those planted in the garden, and still there today, were tulip trees, swamp-cypresses, copper beeches, *Ginkgo biloba*, set off by magnificent beech and chestnut avenues dating from an earlier time.[37] Many 'exotic' trees were acquired by the Prince over a number of years before Blaikie began the garden, but the Scot had developed a method of transplanting quite mature trees at any season. 'As soon as they are taken up, I dip their roots in a puddle of cow dung and loam which preserves their fibres from the influence of the air. Where this practice is adopted in the winter season, the plants may be sent to any distance, or kept out of the ground for weeks without the slightest injury; and I have frequently transplanted trees in the heat of the summer by this precaution, and with perfect success.' [38]

---

35. 'Hotel de Ségur puis Salm-Dyck, 97 rue de Bac', Bruno Pons and Anne Forray-Carlier, *Le faubourg Saint-Germain La rue du Bac* (Paris, 1990), pp. 44–54.

36. *Hortus Dyckensis*, p. xx.

37. For information about the garden as it is today, see Countess Ursula Dohna, *Private Gardens of Germany* (London, 1986).

38. *Gardener's Magazine*, vol. 2 (January 1827), p. 83.

An undated plan (40 × 83cm) in the Schloss Dyck archive shows the English garden as Blaikie designed it with a list of the genera planted.[39] Page 209 of Blaikie's account book records the timetable of his work at Dyck. The page is headed in large copper-plate script, *'Le Prince de Salm à Son Château de Dyck par Neuss'*, and is dated 1819. Blaikie arrived at Dyck on 6 September 1819 from Saint-Germain and began to draw up his plan at once. In his usual fashion, he traced the outlines of paths and masses on the ground and marked out the different works to be done. This took him 51 days including his travelling time of six days each way. He was paid 18 francs per day and his visits are recorded in two letters from the Princess of Salm to a M. Prous at Liedberg.[40] The first, dated the 23 September 1819, informs him that Mr 'Blacquie' is at Salm Dyck and she asks her correspondent if M. Kopp would like to take the opportunity of Blaikie's presence there to 'Anglicise' his garden.[41] The second, written sometime during Blaikie's second sojourn at Dyck from 25 May 1820 until Monday 24 July, is dated simply May 1820. It describes Blaikie as 'such an interesting man' and captures the essence of Blaikie's artistry and technical expertise. '... he is making us hundreds of natural beauty spots in our gardens, which you won't notice. That is the art of it. The eye should glide pleasurably over it all and one should feel the perfection only in thinking of the imperfections that one finds elsewhere'.[42] She also recommended Blaikie to her brother, the Baron de Théis, for his property in Picardy.[43]

Blaikie returned to Dyck on 25 May 1820 to finish the work and left on Monday 24 July. He was paid 918 francs for the first visit and 1000 for the second, plus expenses for the journey.

The success of the gardens of Schloss Dyck is the result of a happy combination of patron and gardener. The Prince with a botanist's understanding of the needs of the plants allowed Blaikie to display his specimens or groups of trees and shrubs on broad lawns backed by wooded areas planted or modified to draw the eye to distant or intimate scenes. In Blaikie, the Prince had a botanist-designer with an unsurpassed knowledge of trees and shrubs. He could visualise at a glance how a pencil thin sapling would look in maturity. His eye was tuned to the subtlest gradations of colour in foliage and bark throughout the seasons, not just amongst different families or genera but within each genus also. As a landscape artist, he was particularly skilled in the

---

39. No plan for the gardens seems to have existed prior to this one and Prince Joseph in *Hortus Dyckensis* credits Blaikie with the design, but it is possible that the Düsseldorf architect Max Friedrich Weyhe (1775–1846) was involved in the general planning of the layout of the gardens of Dyck in 1816. See two letters (CoJ18) in the Salm-Dyck archive from Weyhe to Prince Joseph. My thanks to Herr Dr Weber of the Landschaftsverband Rheinland for copies of these letters and for the plan of the English garden at Dyck.

40. Countess Ursula Dohna, p. 71. It has not been possible to identify Mr Prous or Mr Kopp.

41. That he did have other German clients is confirmed by Loudon, *Encyclopedia of Gardening* (1830 edn), p. 171.

42. Countess Ursula Dohna, p. 71.

43. Note, headed '87 rue du Bac' and dated 13 April but without the year, she asks him to call on her as she has something to propose to him on behalf of her brother, the Baron de Théis. Blaikie Papers.

use of sunlight and shade and the massing of plants to frame a view. In addition, he was a gardener renowned for his skills.[44] The result is that, in spite of the vicissitudes of time, those who see the park today feel the 'aesthetically satisfying sense of space' that Blaikie created in what was essentially a classical eighteenth-century park[45] and it has been described as 'one of the best large arboreta to be created in the nineteenth century in all Europe'.[46] There is a contemporary description of the park in J. C. Loudon's *Gardener's Magazine* of 1836[47] where 'this noble garden' is described as situated on a gently undulating plain on the left bank of the Rhine on the road which leads from Düsseldorf to Aix-la-Chapelle. The author, although primarily concerned with the collection of succulent plants 'the most magnificent ... in Europe', also bears witness to the recognition Blaikie now received among horticulturists in England when he attributes the success of the garden to 'the assiduity and skill of a scientific English landscape gardener [our esteemed friend and correspondent Mr Blaikie]'. The gardens at Schloss Dyck suffered from war and neglect for many years and it was only in 1960 that the Duchess Cecilie zu Salm-Reifferscheidt took on the task of restoring the garden. She commissioned an eminent landscape architect, Professor Hermann Mattern (d. 1972) to restore the park in the spirit of the old garden as well as to make new paths and plantings. The rejuvenation of the garden continues in the same spirit today.

The only published recognition in France of Blaikie's stature as a landscape gardener, during his lifetime, came in 1819 from another professional landscape gardener, Gabriel Thouin, in his *Plans raisonnés de toutes les espèces de jardins*. Thouin was the brother of André, and the Scot's main competitor as a landscaper during the Empire and Restoration period.[48] His book of plans was a mixture of the eccentric, the fantastic and the practical, the fruit of 50 years as a practising landscape gardener.[49] In his introduction, he divides pleasure gardens into three types; the first symmetric, the second anglo-chinois and the third landscape gardens or gardens of nature. The character of the third series, he writes is 'to unite the most beautiful natural scenes while making the art that served to establish them disappear; a description almost echoing that of the Princess of Salm in her letter praising Blaikie's management of the park at Schloss Dyck. Among examples of gardens of nature, Thouin cites Ermenonville, Guiscard, and Méréville and he includes Blaikie with Girardin, Morel, and Bélanger among the leading exponents of the style.

---

44. Soulange-Bodin in his *Annales Horticoles de Fromont*, extols Blaikie's methods of growing Camellias, while the *greffe Blaikie* was a remarkably successful way of grafting.
45. Countess Ursula Dohna, p. 73.
46. Christopher Thacker, *The History of Gardening* (London, 1979), p. 234.
47. M. F. Ranch, 'Gardening Tour in Germany made in the spring of 1836', *Gardener's Magazine*, vol. 12, p. 393.
48. J. C. Loudon, *Encyclopaedia of Gardening* (London, 1830 edn), p. 42. names them as the two best landscape designers in France.
49. One of these theoretical plans was for an immense jardin anglais at Versailles, another for the enlargement of the *Jardin des Plantes* but his book also included plans for small suburban gardens and rural dwellings.

One landowner who needed no convincing of Blaikie's pre-eminence in his profession was Henry de La Bédoyère. He now owned Raray, near Senlis, inherited on
the death of his parents, as well as Nogent l'Artaud where he had first employed the
Scot in 1811. In 1819, he recalled his old friend to continue work at both properties
and this commission was to occupy Blaikie continuously over the next nine or ten
years. Raray is today a Golf-hôtel and was the setting for Jean Cocteau's classic film
of 1945, *La belle et la bête*. A most beautiful château built by an unidentified architect,
it is remarkable for the rare seventeenth century arcaded galleries of stone on either
side of the cour d'honneur. Statues showing gods and goddesses and other figures
from antiquity fill the niches between the arcades, and sculptures associated with
hunting are placed on top of the walls; 38 hounds in all, life size and in various
attitudes, with a stag surmounting the main arcade that forms an entrance on the
south side and a boar in the same position on the north. Bas reliefs of the two hunted
animals decorate the pediments of the pavilions to the right and left of the château
and at the entrance to the wood adjoining the château stands a magnificent stone
gateway, its vast doors painted red, the pediment decorated with a sculpture of Diana
seated between two hounds while atop the pediment at its apex, a seated unicorn is
portrayed between two baying dogs. Nogent L'Artaud, a much more conventional
eighteenth-century building, is now a nursing home for the elderly.

Blaikie's visits to Raray between 1819 and 1829 are well documented in Henry's
diary and Ambroisine's *Journal des Champs*. Husband and wife both note Blaikie's
return to Raray at the end of 1819. Henry gives the date as 2 November and announces
that 'we have had Blaikie return to take up again the works he began at different
occasions during my parents' time here and which remain uncompleted. A great
number of workmen, the designing of new walks, the plantation of many evergreens,
foreign shrubs held up on several occasions by rain, the limes in the forecourt pruned
as well as those along the chases [unenclosed game preserves]'.

Under the marginal heading, *First journey of Blaikie since I have come to live at Raray*,
Ambroisine fills in the details. 'In October we had Mr Blaikie, English engineer here,
and fifty workmen under his direction have worked in the park. They have widened
all the serpentine allées and traced others through the woods, The soil of the park
has been dug over the length of the potager, where we have planted forest and
ornamental trees; about 20,000 birches, 204 evergreens and 500 ornamental trees and
shrubs. We have planted about 200 trees to replace those missing from the allées of
cherry and apple trees, and 74 fruit trees in the potager, replacing the poor soil at
their feet with good soil'. A plan of Raray showing the English garden survives and
Blaikie's list of plants to be purchased is preserved at Raray.[50] Among the evergreen
trees he chooses are cedars of Lebanon (8), Scots pines (104), Lord Weymouth pines
(40), Bordeaux pines (1), Corsican or laricio pines (4), along with unspecified firs, Picea,
larches and a dozen yews. To the limes, elms and poplars he added a few exotics,
liriodendron and *Vernis du japon* (*Toxidendron vernicifluum*). Lilacs and acacias predomi-
nate amongst the varied list of shrubs and there are 200 rose bushes. He orders 6000

---

50. Raray. Private Archive.

birches from Pottier and 9500 elsewhere as well as selecting four or five thousand plants of different trees from the woods of Raray. His first period of work at Raray was completed in 24 days. His fee amounted to 432 francs at 18 francs per day.

Blaikie had been employed almost non stop throughout 1819. Since the beginning of February that year, only the month of May was without clients. From the latter part of August, when he had spent a few days working for the Vicomte de Montes-quiou,[51] almost every day is accounted for by his visits to Schloss Dyck, Raray and Mont l'Evêque. The detailed note by the La Bédoyères of the changes he made at Raray shows the scope of Blaikie's work there and was probably typical of his larger commissions. The last records in his account book show that the following year, 1820, he was employed by at least five clients. Amongst them was the Baron Pontalba, the owner of Mont l'Evêque. Blaikie visited him at another property, Ormesson, near Versailles in September and November.[52] He spent 33 days there but the only detail he mentions is that he stayed to trace out the courtyard and 'arrange' it. His fee of 596 francs suggests a considerable undertaking. Another client was a M. Neret at Cannes near Montereau in the Seine et Marne where he 'traced and planted in the place called La Garenne' and for which he was paid 234 for 13 days. He spent eight days, as his account book informs us, with the Marquis de Saint Simon, 'Peer of France', at Billy, the Marquis's small country house near Arpajon. But his major client that year was the countess of Hinnisdal at her property at Ferfay near Lillers in the Pas de Calais. His commission there lasted from 10 October to 13 November. His fee was 637 francs considerably more than at Ormesson, or even Raray where he had required a team of 50 men to carry out the work. The page devoted to these clients in 1820, is numbered 217 and his account book finishes at page 219, so that any further information about his work as a landscape gardener after these entries has to come from other sources.

We learn from Ambroisine de La Bédoyère's journal that he was at Raray during March 1821 at work on the *Bois joli*, or exterior park of Raray, so-called in memory of a wood at her girlhood home, Leseau in Normandy. Ambroisine was now an enthusiastic gardener and it is no longer Blaikie alone but 'we' who begin the work and she notes, 'our work with Blaikie lasted three weeks'. To make way for this new wooded area, an alley of limes was cut down and a few elms were removed from another avenue, to make the whole merge in with the planting of the *jardin anglais* yet still leave a straight avenue of elms when viewed from the house. Again there was a heavy programme of planting as in 1819. 126 evergreens, 500 ornamental trees and shrubs and 5000 young plants of birch and Swiss poplars were planted. These were mixed with the leftover plants from the La Bédoyère's nursery. They now

---

51. Only his fee for the Vicomte is recorded in the recapitulation of accounts for 1819, not the name of the estate, so it is not possible to be sure it was Mauperthuis at this time. The detailed account sheet is missing but as the fee amounted to 72f. it is likely that he was only there for 4 days at that time.

52. I can find no reference to Pontalba's owning Ormesson. He bought a property called Migneaux (arr. Versailles) in 1823 (AN. Minutier central LVIII 806).

employed a nurseryman growing a wide range of seeds of evergreen trees and other ornamental trees. Ambroisine notes with satisfaction that in this nursery, situated in the grounds of the former boys' school adjoining the main road, they have also planted about 500 buddings of Swiss and Canadian poplars.

But life, even for a landscape gardener, is not all gardening. Blaikie had long hankered to revisit Scotland. There were practical as well as emotional reasons to urge him on. He was 71 years old, a ripe old age in the first quarter of the nineteenth century, and he had never registered his ownership of Corstorphine Hill. This would have to be done, even if he intended to dispose of it to his family. In 1821, as well as enjoying a healthy income from his commmissions, he had received the return of his capital plus interest on the winding up of the Oberkampf family business. He was in a good position, financially, to take a holiday.

CHAPTER 17

The Last Years

I N September 1822 Blaikie made his first visit to Edinburgh for fifty years. He travelled
alone, and two letters written to his wife from Corstorphine Hill describe his visit.[1]
Mr Hay, the garden designer who accompanied Patrick Neill to Paris in 1817, had
presented him on that visit with a plan of the city, 'including the recent additions
and improvements'. Blaikie, Neill tells us, 'felt much interest in tracing the astonishing
progress of the Caledonian capital'.[2] However, no plan could have quite prepared
him for the transformation Edinburgh had undergone during his absence. The city
of his memory still existed, strung out along the Royal Mile, its ancient tenements
clinging to the top and down the slopes of the ridge. The North Bridge connecting
the High Street to Princes Street was already built when he left England for France
but he had never seen the South Bridge at the street's opposite end. On the lower
hill to the north of the Old Town, the Georgian New Town was complete; its broad
streets and uniform dwellings contrasting strikingly with the medieval labyrinths and
gothic tenements of the High Street. Terraces and squares had begun their ordered
downhill progress from Queen Street towards Leith. And outwards, towards both
east and west, streets, squares, churches and public edifices had risen in rapid succession.[3] Adam's Register House faced the North Bridge. The Mound, formed from
the earth dug from the foundations of buildings in the New Town, bridged the valley
between the High Street and Princes Street and, to the west of the Mound, the Nor
Loch had recently been enclosed, drained, laid out with walks and planted with trees
and shrubs, thanks to Blaikie's friend, Patrick Neill.

He returned to Edinburgh at an auspicious moment when the city was spruced
up, its citizens in ebullient mood after the highly successful visit of George IV. In
preparation for the king's arrival new roads had been made. The merchants in the
town had plied a steady trade in silk and worsted tartan shawls and plaids.[4] Illuminations and fireworks had added to the festive spirit of his stay and, at night, Princes
Street was bright with the gas lighting installed earlier in the year. The king had been
charmed by the incomparable drama of the city's setting, the romantic appearance
of the Highlanders and the colourful ceremonial devised and directed by Sir Walter

---

1. Blaikie Papers. The first is dated 12 September 1822 and the second 24 September. Both
   are reproduced, with omissions, in Birrell, *The Diary of a Scotch Gardener*, introduction,
   pp. 12–15. Both letters are addressed to himself at 'rue neuve de l'Eglise N. 16, St Germain-
   en-Laye, Seine et Oise'.
2. Neill, p. 361.
3. J. Wood, *Scotland – Town Plans 1818 to 1823* (Edinburgh, 1823), p. 121.
4. Messrs. Willis and Co. of Princes Street (Tailors to the King, the Duke of York and the
   Royal family) even offered coats with 'welcome' buttons for wear during His Majesty's
   visit. *Edinburgh Advertiser*, 9 August.

Scott. With his innate theatricality, he had responded to the splendid spectacle by acting his part with both aplomb and sensitivity as the first British monarch to make a State Visit to his northern kingdom.

Blaikie missed the monarch's departure from Leith on 29 August by two or three days. The earlier of his two letters, dated 12 September, describes his first two weeks in the capital.

Corstorphenhill near Edinburgh the 12 Sep^t 1822

My Dear and Loving Letitia

I received your very kind and affectionate letter last Sunday as I went to the Church, so you see I am got godly since I arrived here. I was, as you said, at church when you wrote your letter, and [al]so the next Sunday, and perhaps I may be next, as they are all very religious in this country. I have been always rambling from place to place since I arrived. I saw Mr Neil which inquired after you, Mr Hay and Mr Macdonald. The King lodged at that Palace^5 when he was in Scotland and all the People here is ravished with having seen the King. I went to see Mr Macdonald and the fine Palais and Gardens of Dalkeith. But this was a great day as this was a great procession and the Lodge of free Gardeners^6 and a great Dinner of about 160, so that I was obliged to join my brethren and the Whisky flowed in Plenty and many capital toasts were drank.

Since that, the superb horticultural feast was [held] where there was a splendid diner of nearly 200 gentlemen sat down to Diner. Since that, I have hardly had time to do anything but admire the beauties of the Country and everywhere the friendly and whisky bottle is produced &c &c. I hope one day you may be able to see and enjoy all those comforts which was always my desire and wish to render you happy. I hope you are happy with little Betzy^7 who will chatter and make you forget time ... As for the letter I sent you from Dieppe, it must have been that rascal of a waiter whom I trusted to put in the post as I was going to the Custom house to have my trunk examined ... I gave him ten sous for his trouble and was almost sure that you would receive it. However, you will have received my last letter I wrote to you from this place on my arrival in Scotland and that I was safe and sound. We have had but indifferent weather for some time in this part of the country, and high winds and rain which has retarded the Harvest but it is at present fine and unless towards Pentland hills which is opposite the windows where I sit. Next week I hope to take a trip towards Glasgow to see the great improvements there, then I shall think of returning to you, which is the only object of my care, and then I can tell you more fully many things relative to all my adventures. All I can say [is that] I am well in health and hopes ... As soon as I return from my western expedition I shall write to you and let you know when I think I shall have the pleasure of setting out to join you and indeed the weather is not very good for travelling but the high winds

---

5. George IV was in Edinburgh from 15 August until the 29th. He stayed not at Holyrood House but at the Palace of Dalkeith where James Macdonald was head gardener.

6. 'The Lodge of Free Gardeners' may refer to a friendly Society called The British Order of Free Gardeners.

7. 'Little Betzy' is mentioned only in the two letters from Edinburgh and cannot be identified.

will blow us on at a great rate.

I expect another letter from you before I leave this part of the country but, however, I shall not fail to write to you and, wherever I am, I shall always remain your sincere and affectionate friend and Husband.

Thomas Blaikie
PS My best respects to all friends especially little Betzy to which I send kisses without counting.

At Neill's instigation, Blaikie had been elected a foreign member of the Caledonian Horticultural Society on the 10 March 1818 [8] and Neill, Macdonald and Hay saw to it that he was lionised during his stay. Dalkeith Palace, six miles south of Edinburgh where Macdonald was head gardener was the seat of the dukes of Buccleuch. There does not seem to be any record extant of the feast of the League of Free Gardeners held at Dalkeith where the whisky flowed and the conversation was no doubt conducted in the broad Scots of Blaikie's youth. However, the second event, a notch above the first in the social scale, a dinner of the Caledonian Horticultural Society, was reported in the Edinburgh papers. The *Edinburgh Evening Courant* of 14 September recorded the general meeting of the Society in the Hall of the Royal College of Physicians, George Street on 5 September and continued:

> In the afternoon the Thirteenth Anniversary Dinner was held in Oman's large room, when about 150 members and a select number of visitors assembled. Mr Henderson, acting Chief Magistrate, was in the chair. The dinner and wines gave universal satisfaction and the dessert was most abundant and excellent. Among the visitors was Mr Thomas Blaikie of Corstorphine Hill, who had just come to Scotland after an absence of nearly half a century, which he had spent in France as an *Ingeneur des Jardins Paysages* or *Anglais*. [sic]

Blaikie's second letter, written on 24 September 1822 from Corstorphine Hill, is disappointing from the point of view of anyone seeking a contemporary picture of Edinburgh or Glasgow. Concerned with his wife's feelings and the business of his pension from the French royal family, it does not describe the 'celebrated places' he tells her he has seen on his visit to Glasgow and the west of Scotland and adds scarcely anything of his impressions of Edinburgh. He goes on to assure her, 'your prayers has preserved me so far and you see I have been regularly every Sunday at Church since I came to this country, as they are all good Presbyterians in this country'. [9]

Certainly, the tone of both his letters is extremely, even exaggeratedly, uxorious. For want of material relating to his wife among the papers, and the absence of any firm information about her birth or family, Mrs Blaikie is a shadowy figure. [10] There

---

8. Letter from Neill dated 11 March 1818, Blaikie Papers.
9. Another proof that Blaikie's wife was not Scottish.
10. Apart from the information in her death certificate that she was born in Ringwood and was 80 years old at the time of her death, there is a mention in one of Lauraguais' letters to Blaikie that suggests she had business interests through her grandfather in England.

are no letters from her to Blaikie among the surviving Blaikie papers and scarcely any
of her other correspondence survives; two letters to Lauraguais, two to Lady Lucy
Vaughan, daughter of the earl of Lisburne seeking payment for her father's debt to
Blaikie, and two to her friends the Burnetts, after her husband's death. She was
obviously deeply religious, Anglican or Catholic. Blaikie finds churchgoing tedious,
and his reference to being 'obliged' to drink whisky and his, 'you see I am got godly'
are evidently written tongue in cheek, yet he is careful not to mock her beliefs. His
letter is full of reassurances that he appreciates, admires and loves her, expressing the
hope that 'we will both be happy' that, 'it is always my desire and wish to render
you happy'. Had he, one wonders, rendered her unhappy in the past? They had no
children together and this may have been a cause of unhappiness for her, especially
as she probably knew that Blaikie had fathered one illegitimate child before he met
her.[11] The presence of 'little Betzy' to console her for Blaikie's absence, makes such
a hypothesis likely.

Blaikie returned to Scotland with his wife to visit his family in 1825.[12] His sister,
Agnes, had died in 1822 and was buried in the Mackie mausoleum. Thomas Mackie,
according to his aunt, Isabel, spent lavishly on Agnes's funeral, as much as £50. He
failed to inform his aunt of his mother's illness until after her death, so that relations
between the Edinburgh branches of the family remained cool with Blaikie receiving
complaints from the Torbets of the unkindnesses shown to them by Thomas and his
father. Blaikie's correspondence with his family continued fairly regularly and he kept
a record of the letters he received from them but as none of the Mackie letters remains
amongst them, we can follow only the Youngs' lives. Agnes Young, the daughter of
Isabel, had three sons who survived childhood in the West Bow. Typically, one left
for Glasgow, another went to London and the third stayed to become a bookbinder
in Edinburgh which was the centre of a flourishing printing trade. The one who
worked in Glasgow, James Young junior, tells Blaikie in a letter of 9 May 1827 of
Mr Neill's regret at the death of André Thouin and how he 'wishes much to hear
from you'.[13] He reports to Blaikie about 'the incursions' that new building is making
on the limited walks of the city and goes on to describe them. 'Beside a monument
to the south east corner of the Observatory to the memory of Professor Playfair, the
National Monument was begun last year, and on the south side of the hill, near the
Great Road, the new High School has been carrying on these six months. They are
very busy McAdamising Princess Street. I don't recollect whether the Foundling
Hospital was begun when you was here or not. It is situated at the end of the road
which bears exactly East from the foot of Corstorphine Hill, having Ravelston and
Blinkbonny on the left'. The Leith Dock Bill and the Improvement Bill for the repairing
of St Giles and the opening of several new streets were, he informed his uncle, still

11. His account book and his papers mention Constance Blaikie, so presumably Mrs Blaikie
    knew about her, but she may not have known about his relationship with 'Thérèse'.
12. The only record of this visit comes from references in letters from the family to their safe
    arrival in Paris in January 1826 and occasional references in the letters to the pleasure of
    having met their aunt.
13. André Thouin died on 27 October 1824.

before Parliament. A letter of 12 September 1828 tells of a new ornamental steeple for the Tron Church 'that would even look well in Paris'. There were plans 'for two grand new streets to be opened up from the High Street leading south to the Meadows and coming out at the top of West Bow straight to Corstorphine passing close by the castle rocks on the south'. Blaikie did not give up his idea of living in Scotland. In 1834 he appealed to Louis Philippe to have his pension paid in Scotland through the banker Mallet, but either his request was refused or he was now too old to make the effort of uprooting himself from Paris.

However, the years between his return to France late in 1822 and his death in 1838 were fruitful ones. Sometime in 1825 he left Saint-Germain and settled in Paris in number 5 rue des Vignes, a country lane off the Champs Elysées. (Part of it survives today as rue Vernet). His career continued with little abatement.[14] His visits to Raray are the only documented ones but we know he was at Mauperthuis in 1829[15] and another somewhat sketchy source of information about his commissions can be found in J. C. Loudon's *Gardener's Magazine* and his *Encyclopaedia of Gardening*.[16] Both Henry and Ambroisine de La Bédoyère note in their respective diaries that he returned in March 1826 to Raray in the company of Henry. This time he was to begin replanning the entrance to the château from the village and transplanting many trees and shrubs in full leaf and flower. Ambroisine, again participating fully in the activity, writes about transplanting trees, 'we watered them thoroughly and soaked their roots in a mortar made of cow's faeces mixed to a paste with water'.[17] Henry was ill in Paris that October and Ambroisine spent a few weeks on her own at Raray with Blaikie. Under his guidance, she traced out a serpentine path in the wood from the guard's door to where there was a group of fine beeches, thus shortening the road from Raray to Villeneuve and uniting those which existed inside and outside the enclosure of the park. She writes proudly that she made an entrance to the park near the tower on the Brasseuse side and planted a little copse outside the gates. They went from Raray to Nogent together and at Nogent she planted a few clumps of trees under Henry's window, altered one of the main allées and cut down those alongside the School. Blaikie was back again in July 1827 and Ambroisine felt sufficiently confident to question his judgment on the height of a terrace wall being constructed by a local builder. She writes, 'I find it to be a foot too low, and I attribute this to Mr Blaikie's obstinacy in insisting on this height for fear of hiding the view'. However, Blaikie's stubbornness did not prevent her from recalling him in 1828, the year the Dauphine visited Raray,[18] and again in

14. See extract from *The Gardener's Magazine* which follows.
15. From letter of Mrs Blaikie to Lisburne already noted. In 1824 Montesquiou had requested a large number of trees from the King's Nurseries (*Pépinères du Roi*) AN., O3 1238.
16. For *Gardeners' Magazine*, see extracts which follow. *Encyclopaedia of Gardening* (1835 edn), p. 88.
17. Blaikie's technique.
18. Title given to the wife of the heir to the throne. She was the Duchesse d'Angoulême, daughter of Marie Antoinette, daughter-in-law of Artois, now Charles X. See Geneviève Mazel, 'Raray et son château', p. 51, for a description of the visit.

March 1829 when she noted in her journal the planting of cedars, rhododendron, roses and other pretty plants at Nogent l'Artaud.

Before he left Scotland in November 1822,[19] Blaikie was presented with a bound copy of the *Memoirs of the Caledonian Society*. In an unsigned draft of a letter, he asked Neill to thank the honourable members for their labours with the hope that, 'I may have the happiness to add my mite'. Andrew Duncan, the president of the Society, had written to Neill on 30 September asking him if his friend, Mr Blaikie, would 'draw up a memoir giving some account of different fruits & culinary vegetables which he thinks might be introduced to Britain'[20] but Blaikie declined for the moment. In the laborious draft of his letter, he described a number of unusual vegetables, such as chicory and asparagus that it might be possible to grow in Scotland. His expertise in garden matters was incontestable, but his style gave no promise of any sort of journalistic future. Yet, in 1825 he did write an article which combined an impressive knowledge of trees with personal reminiscences of the great gardens and botanists of pre-Revolutionary France. It took the form of a letter from Saint-Germain-en-Laye and was published in the *Memoirs of the Caledonian Horticultural Society*.[21] It was read at the meeting of the Society on 10 November that year as 'Remarks on the Locust-tree recommended by Mr Cobbett, with Notices of other more desirable Forest and Ornamental trees'. In 1825, William Cobbett (1763–1835), the fiery political writer and champion of rural England, published a book entitled *Woodlands*. In it he offered to the public seeds of the *Robinia pseudacacia*, which he called the Locust Tree. To create a market for his seed, which he imported from America, he made extravagant claims for the Locust as the 'tree of trees'. As for himself, he added, 'I believe I know as much on this subject and perhaps more, than any man in the world';[22] a contention that constituted a sure-fire irritant to Blaikie. Part of Blaikie's long letter to the Caledonian Horticultural Society refuting Cobbett's claims for the tree was reproduced in 1828 in *The Gardener's Magazine*,[23] a periodical published between 1826 and 1844 by John Claudius Loudon (1783–1843). A Scottish landscape gardener, Loudon was the outstanding horticulturist of his day, with deeply held social and aesthetic convictions and an impressive output on a wide range of subjects. The *Gardener's Magazine* featured articles on the design and management of gardens, agriculture, and a host of other subjects of an environmental and social nature, such as housing, town planning, and better conditions and training for gardeners. Loudon visited Paris four times between 1814 and 1829. He met Blaikie when he was there in 1828[24] but must have contacted him before then, perhaps through Neill, and invited him to become a foreign correspondent of the *Magazine*. Blaikie began writing for the magazine in January 1827

---

19. The Sasine testifying his inheritance of Corstorphine Hill was signed on 15 November 1822. (SRO, RS 27\959 ff. 155r–159v. It is likely that although he does not sign it he was present.
20. Blaikie Papers.
21. *Memoirs of the Caledonian Horticultural Society* (1829), vol. IV, pp. 212–19.
22. William Cobbett, *Woodlands* (London, 1825), p. 323.
23. G.M., vol. 3, (January 1828), pp. 308–9.
24. Loudon's *Encyclopaedia of Gardening* (1835 edn), p. 88.

at the age of 76, and was to contribute to it eight times over the next nine years until 1836.[25] His name is also mentioned in other connections at least five times. His first article, 'Scheme of a Succession of Crops for one Hundred Acres of Arable Land in Picardy By Thomas Blaikie, Esq. C.M.H.S.'[26] reproduced the scheme he had prepared for the Committee of Agriculture of the Revolutionary government. His second, as a foreign correspondent, expresses his appreciation of the magazine, 'which is well known here, and read by M. Soulange Bodin, M. Cels, M. Boursault and other eminent cultivators and amateurs. I shall be most happy to contribute to a work so truly devoted to our art, in every way in my power'. In the same letter he comments on the popularity of 'gardening improvements' in France, writing, 'I could go to twenty places at once and I could hardly answer all the demands that are made on my time. Every proprietor here, whether he does anything or not, is anxious to know what his place is capable of being made, by planting, and new arrangements of roads, fences, and buildings.'[27]

His contributions to the *Gardener's Magazine* are generally undistinguished, but to Loudon, who sought an international forum for his magazine and considered Blaikie one of the two best designers in France (Gabriel Thouin was the other), his participation in the new magazine was important.[28] In September of the same year,[29] Blaikie wrote a notice of a visit to the Jardin de Fromont (Soulange Bodin's garden), on 13 June by the *Royal and Central Agricultural Society of Paris*. He also gives an account of one of his favourite trees, *Sophora japonica*.[30] This 'exotic' tree had been planted in many of the important gardens around Paris in the 1770s, and Blaikie was so fond of it that it became almost a signature planting with him. The nurseryman, Gordon, is credited with its introduction to England in 1753,[31] but Blaikie disputes this, convinced that he had taken the first plants to England and given them to Sir Joseph Banks, along with *Ailanthus glandulosa* (*A. altissima*), another Chinese introduction that he often planted. In a letter to Banks dated 6 April 1780,[32] he referred to the sophora as *Sophora chinensis* and encloses a drawing of the tree, writing that it was known in England under the name of Chinese Acacia, so he may have sent a specimen to Banks via Archibald Macmaster in 1781. His claim, although incorrect, implies that these trees must have been planted infrequently in England before 1780. In Volume 4, in a letter from M. Oscar Leclerc of the *Jardin des Plantes* he is named as the originator of

25. G.M., vols 2, 3, 5, 9, 11, 12. Some contain more than one contribution.
26. G.M., vol. 2, p. 13 refers to Blaikie as CMHS. It is unlikely that Blaikie was a Council Member or a Corresponding Member of the Horticultural Society and this should probably read MCHS (Member of the Caledonian Horticultural Society).
27. G.M., vol. 2, p. 83.
28. See Melanie Louise Simo, *Loudon and the Landscape. From Country Seat to Metropolis* (Yale University Press, 1988), p. 10.
29. G.M., vol. 3, p. 207.
30. Based on a description in the *Journal de Paris*, 14 October 1779 by a member of the Richard family.
31. William Aiton, Hortus Kewensis, vol. 2, p. 45.
32. Kew BC 128.

a particularly successful mode of grafting, called the *greffe* Blaikie.[33] In the Foreign
notices of February 1829[34] he writes about the severity of the previous winter in Paris
and its devastating effect on evergreens, particularly at Sceau in the gardens of the
Admiral Tschitchigoff (sic), the Russian envoy to Paris. This garden was described by
Loudon as, 'laid out with extraordinary care by the proprietor, aided by the constant
advice of Mr Blaikie'.[35] It was well known for the number of its *Magnolia grandiflora*,
another of Blaikie's favourite plantings.

Loudon's report of his foreign visits, *Reflections of a tour*, were a regular feature of
the magazine. In one instalment,[36] criticising the alterations, supposedly in the English
style, being carried out at a residence called 'Franqueville' in the north of France not
far from Rouen, he deplores the fact 'that the proprietor had not called in Mr Blaikie,
who, two years before (1827), was in the neighbourhood laying out the grounds of
the Marquis d'Estampes near Laboulle. The Marquis d'Estampes was the father of
Ambroisine de La Bédoyère.

In the April 1835 issue,[37] Blaikie remarks on the aptness of the Loudon's new word
'gardenesque' rather than 'picturesque' for the current fashion in gardening. He also
takes up his pen again for an article based on one he wrote for a French magazine
earlier in the year.[38] This gives an insight into his preferences and priorities as a
landscape gardener and confirms his continuing popularity as a landscape artist since
he is still designing gardens at the age of 85. (The French article gives the date of his
employment at the châteaux mentioned below as autumn 1834.)

He starts with a picture of the difficulties all landscape gardeners face; the house
already built and probably badly placed; financial constraints; proprietors reluctant to
cut down already planted common trees so that the landscaper is deprived 'of the
advantages his art might derive from exotic planting'. He discusses Loudon's criticisms
of French gardens published in the *Gardener's Magazine*,[39] namely 'that the art of
landscape gardening is neither generally understood nor duly appreciated in France';
the slovenly way in which most French gardens of the landscape type were maintained
and 'the want of close, green turf'. Blaikie recalls that, at Bagatelle, he tried to produce
a green lawn by careful selection of grass seeds but then had to contend with bird
and insect attack of a sort unknown in England, 'where turf can be rolled up and cut
like a piece of cloth'. French proprietors, he tells the reader, look for a return of hay

33. G.M., vol. 4, 1828, p. 7. Written in response to an article in vol. 2, p. 33 describing it as a
    new method of grafting. This article appeared in the *Annales d'Horticulture*, the journal of
    the Société d'Horticulture de Paris, 1829/30. My thanks to Mme Barbara Tchertoff for
    drawing my attention to this source.
34. G.M., vol. 5 (1829), p. 456.
35. 'Notes and Reflections made during a Tour through Part of France and Germany, in the
    Autumn of the year 1828,' by the Conductor (i.e. Loudon), G.M., vol. 9, p. 142. Blaikie is
    also mentioned in the same volume p. 133, in connection with Bagatelle.
36. G.M., vol. 9, p. 42.
37. G.M., vol. 11, pp. 478–80.
38. Thomas Blaikie, 'Excursion Horticole' par un Anglais. 1835.
39. G.M., vol. 9, pp. 156–7.

from their parks rather than fine turf.[40] Too wise to comment on Loudon's contention that the French do not understand the art of landscape gardening, he concedes that Loudon is right when he talks of the slovenly manner in which the generality of French gardens are kept, as he is also right about the lack of evergreens in France. However, Blaikie blames this on severe continental winters, where frost kills young plants before they can become established. In the French version, he admits that evergreens are too rarely planted, in spite of their beauty in both summer and winter. When his own evergreens failed in a harsh winter, he replaced them with *Viburnum lantana*, *Cornus mas* and *Salix caprea*, planted together. Box he reveals is his favourite planting for underwood. He advises the reader to observe which plants already grow well in a locality and to consider using them. He has been in Champagne, on a commission for the Duke of Laval-Montmorency at his châteaux of Beauvoir and Montigny on the Loire and at another of his châteaux called Courtelaine where the late flowering Ailanthus and Sophora ('not so fine as those in the garden where I now live, and which are coming into leaf'),[41] 'produce an agreeable effect in the landscape scenery' when little else is in flower. In the French version, he describes himself as one of those people who love exotics in a garden but, in both versions, he affirms that fine landscapes can be composed with trees less expensive than those Loudon recommends. One of his favourites is the common horse chestnut as producing 'a most beautiful effect when left to nature, particularly in blossom'. He also recommends *Populus alba* and *Salix alba* 'seen in a distant view joined with Eleagnus'. His own inclination is to group together trees of nearly the same colour of foliage that 'the lightness of their shade may prolong the perspective which should be varied from as many different parts as possible. This I look upon as the greatest art in landscape-gardening and I think it ought to be a standing principle'. To his French readers, he reveals that he admires all trees when they are well grown, well grouped and form part of a picture. 'The art,' he writes, 'is to group them well, to mix their forms and their colours to produce happy contrasts and above all to divide these groups so that their shadows add to their effect'.[42]

Richard Anthony Salisbury FRS after whom the *Ginkgo biloba* was formerly named (*Salisburia adiantifolia*), was the subject of a letter from Blaikie dated 6 March 1836.[43]

---

40. In the French version Blaikie points out that in general in France the trees are not sufficiently linked by large areas of lawn. 'This green carpet of lawn, that harmonises so well with great trees and allows them to make large pools of shadow and light, is too little appreciated.'

41. 5 rue des Vignes was at Chaillot, in what had been the estate of the Chevalier Janssen, the pioneer of exotics in France.

42. In the same volume of the magazine, a reader remarks on the beauty of horse chestnut trees near the ornamental pond or basin in the garden of the Tuileries and Loudon adds that Blaikie has described a variety of *Aesculus hippocastanum* in the Tuileries gardens that is always a fortnight earlier in flower than any others. He intended it for his book *Arboretum et Fruticetum Britannicum; or The Trees and Shrubs of Britain, native and foreign etc.*, 8 vols (London, 1838), in which he lists exceptional trees described by his correspondents in different countries.

43. G.M., vol. 12, (May 1836), p. 266.

It was written in response to a piece by Loudon published in the July 1835 edition of the magazine suggesting that all the female Salisburias in Europe had been propagated from one tree growing in a garden at Bourdigny, near Geneva. He had reached this conclusion from information he had received from the Swiss botanist, De Candolle, whose father had discovered the tree some fifteen or eighteen years earlier. Loudon surmised that this female tree must have been raised from seed. Bourdigny was the garden of Blaikie's old friend Mr Gaussen and Blaikie was able to solve the mystery of the tree's origin. He had regularly sent M. Gaussen packets of all the new plants he grew at Monceau. The last packet he sent was in 1790 and amongst the plants it contained was one of *Gingko biloba* grown from a cutting taken in the garden of Monceau.[44] Blaikie reckoned that the tree, observed by Mr de Candolle's father, had been grown from this small plant and would have been about 29 years old when the botanist's father had seen it. Many of the trees at Monceau had been cut down, and so he could not say whether the trees at Monceau were masculine or feminine. The Monceau ginkgo was raised from a cutting taken in the Chevalier Janssen's garden where Blaikie was living and, to his distress, 'the garden is cut up for building all round and many fine trees that were in it have been destroyed'. Blaikie's Paris is fast disappearing. Bagatelle, he informs the readers of the *Gardener's Magazine*, has been sold to Lord Yarmouth.[45]

His letter evoked a request from Loudon for more information and Blaikie responded on 8 May 1836.[46] The ginkgo raised in the Chevalier Janssen's garden, was known as the tree of *quarante écus*,[47] the price Janssen had paid for the original. Other sources of this plant were the Abbé Nolin, director of the King's Nurseries and Richard, the gardener at the Trianon.[48] Nolin received seeds from the French missionaries in China and grew the ginkgo[49] and other tender plants from them in another garden he owned near Marseilles or Toulon. Young plants of ginkgo growing at the *Jardin des Plantes* in 1836 came from Toulon. This story revived another memory of Blaikie's Swiss days, his meeting with Mr Garcin, the botanist described in his diary. He concludes with an account of the superstitions surrounding the rowan tree or sorbus in Scotland.

This was Blaikie's last contribution to the magazine. The next mention of him is his obituary in October 1838.[50] However, he included, at the end of his letter of 6 March, an interesting throwaway line. He wrote, 'I have been executing some works

---

44. Gaussen's acknowledgement of this last gift is among the Blaikie papers.
45. See chapter 9 on Bagatelle.
46. G.M., vol. 12, pp. 690–1.
47. An écu or louis d'argent varied in worth from around six livres before the Revolution to three francs after it.
48. See chapter 9 on Bagatelle.
49. The Ginkgo is a hardy tree but many trees and shrubs were at first thought to be tender and grown in greenhouses or in areas where the climate was milder.
50. G.M., vol. 13, p. 448. It mistakenly calls him Francis Blaikie. Although it expresses the hope that some of Blaikie's friends would give a memorial of his life, this is the last article concerned with Blaikie in the magazine.

lately at Mortefontaine for the Baronne de Feuchères'. What he does not say is that the Baronne was one of the most scandalous figures of the day. He goes on, 'This place I daresay you saw when you went to Ermenonville, a great part of it was laid out when it belonged to Joseph Bonaparte, when there were many things badly placed, which cannot now be changed. There was a long and narrow dark passage from one park to another which I proposed to enlarge so that the two parks might join. This the lady saw the propriety of; but former arrangements rendered it impracticable'.

Mortefontaine was one of the more famous of the pre-Revolutionary gardens and was often visited in conjunction with Ermenonville. Blaikie himself had first seen it this way on 22 April 1779 and had found it 'hardly worth looking at after Ermenonville'. He wrote in his diary, 'This Garden has the same fault as most of those I have seen elsewhere; a great number of narrow serpentine walks without reason or meaning. Here is a rock made of Sea stone almost in form of an old dead tree. But, as the gardener said they were going to change most of their Garden, which I think has much need, we spent the evening at the Publick house'.[51]

This vast property,[52] divided in two by the road from Paris to Senlis was owned, at the time Blaikie first saw it, by Louis Le Pelletier, *Intendant de Soissons*. It was he who transformed part of the park near the house around 1776. In contrast to the more natural and larger part (*le grand parc*) on the other side of the main road, this part (*le petit parc*) contained the whole repertoire of the *jardin anglais*, obelisks, a Chinese bridge, a belvedere, an artificial hill, an antique temple, statues and urns and a maze of twisting paths and winding rivers. Arthur Young on his visit there in 1787 found it as remote from English taste as the formal gardens of the age of Le Nôtre.[53] However, he discovered a pleasing 'gaiety and cheerfulness' in the *grand parc*, and noted that 'much has been done here; and it wants but few additions to be as perfect as the ground admits'. The improvements begun by Le Pelletier were carried on by Joseph Bonaparte, who planted many fine trees and shrubs and modified the *jardin anglais* so that it came to resemble Malmaison. The subterranean passage described by Blaikie was built by Joseph to give easy access below the main road to the *grand parc*. It was in the *petit parc* on 1 October 1800 that the Treaty of Mortefontaine was signed between France and America, a commercial treaty to cement the friendship between the two countries. In 1814 the château was pillaged. In 1826 the Prince de Condé, owner of Chantilly, bought it. As it was his intention to hunt over it and not to live in it, the château was left empty and the park neglected. Condé died in 1830 and the property was inherited by Madame de Feuchères but her right to inherit was contested since the elderly and infirm Prince had died in suspicious circumstances. He had been found hanging by a window cord at his château of St Leu and his family was convinced that the Baronne was guilty of his murder.

This formidable woman, whose maiden name was Sophie Dawes, was English, one of several children of a drunken fisherman on the Isle of Wight. She escaped to

51. Diary, 22 April 1779.
52. Probably 1,600 hectares, although different estimates exist.
53. Arthur Young, pp. 86–7.

London where she became an accomplished prostitute. Her exceptional beauty drew the eye of the duke of Bourbon, son of the prince of Condé, and she became his mistress. He married her off with a large dowry to one of his aides-de-camp, who was under the impression that Sophie was the Duke's illegitimate daughter. He also secured for him the title of Baron de Feuchères. Eventually, the Baron discovered he had been duped and disowned his wife, whereupon the Duke took her to live with him openly. The aged duke, now the Prince de Condé, alienated by this relationship from his family, was said to have been terrified of her. Her hold on him, it was suggested was so strong, that she was able to keep him virtually a prisoner. Condé's death and the subsequent enquiry became *a cause célèbre*, so Blaikie must have known that the name of his client would have raised eyebrows. All accusations against the Baronne failed for want of firm evidence and the will was not overturned, so that she was able to hold on to her inheritance of Mortefontaine.[54] The château of Mortefontaine is still there, visible from the road behind locked and padlocked gates, its much reduced *petit parc* patrolled by guard dogs. Opposite is the entrance to the *grand parc*, inaccessible also to the public.

Blaikie lived for another two years after his final contribution to the *Gardener's Magazine* in May 1836. Henry de La Bédoyère gives us our last, sad glimpse of him in the pages of his diary. He recalls how 'in the first days of February 1838 while strolling one afternoon in the Champs Elysées, I called on the good Blaikie who lived in an isolated house, rue des Vignes, near the Arc de Triomphe. We had missed him, he had the habit of coming from time to time to have lunch with us and several months had passed since we had seen him. I found him in a sorry state, his legs swollen, his head half broken from a fall, yet in spite of the pain he was suffering and his great age, he conserved all his presence of mind. He was a decent and honest man, frank, loyal, a little rough in appearance, a real original in character, the true type of the 'English man'. Although he had lived in France for about fifty years, he had never been able to master the language, he spoke a kind of jargon, regularly mixing up the genders, making masculine words feminine and vice versa. Dear old Blaikie was very attached to us and we liked him very much, especially my dear wife, during the long stays he had made with us at various times in order to plant our parks at Raray and Nogent she had taken instruction and been trained at that time by this skillful artist in the art of the English garden, so well that she would have been capable of designing one herself … The aged Blaikie died shortly after my visit; he had unfortunately anti-religious ideas deeply rooted in his spirit, He made open profession of materialism. I hope that God had pity on his poor soul in his last moments.'[55]

La Bédoyère would have been pleased to know that among the Blaikie papers is a fragile, stained and much folded piece of paper with a prayer written in a shaky hand,

54. She became a pious and respectable woman, married off her brothers and sisters and their families well and died in London in December 1840. See L. André, *The Mysterious Baronne de Feuchères* (London, 1927).

55. Raray, Private Archive.

that resembles Blaikie's. It beseeches Jesus, Mary and Joseph to assist him in his last agony and to allow him to die peacefully in their blessed company, so it seems that, at the last, someone tried to save the soul of the 'Voltairean' spirit that was Thomas Blaikie.

Blaikie died at seven in the evening on 19 July 1838[56] in his house in the rue des Vignes among the remaining trees of the jardin Marbeuf, the garden of the chevalier Janssen. He was buried on 21 July in the cemetery of Montmartre.[57] His grave remained there until 1962 when the City of Paris followed their procedure for graves that were neglected and unclaimed, and removed his bones to the communal ossuary of the Père Lachaise cemetery.

Mrs Blaikie lived on in Paris until her death on 26 May 1850.[58] Two letters from her to her 'dearest' friends, the Burnetts, survive. In the first, dated 28 September, 1838, she writes that she is to receive half Blaikie's pension. She also tells them that this is the day that the man has come for payment for Blaikie's grave, 'which is giving me fresh tears of Despair and grief now all is Done and may very well God bless the Earthly body which lies in his last abode well covered with the green sod and as for his most precious soul I hope the lord God hath redeemed it'. Thomas Mackie is with her from Scotland and has been to visit his uncle's grave. As Burnett was Blaikie's executor, she asks him and his wife to come to see Mackie in Paris and offers to pay their travelling expenses saying that her nephew will agree to everything she proposes.[59] Her second letter to them is dated 17 April 1845. There are workmen in the house and the owner has told her that it has been sold. She is on the point of leaving. In the letter she asks after 'dear little sweet Georgina'. It was to Georgiana Christina Burnett that the Blaikies' papers were eventually left and Georgiana, in turn, left them to her god-daughter, Mrs Amy Baynham, through whose efforts Blaikie's diary was published in 1931.

Corstorphine Hill passed by a deed of trust made by Thomas Blaikie to Thomas Mackie,[60] although the rent was to be paid to Mrs Blaikie during her lifetime.[61] Thomas

---

56. Acte de décès, A de P. DQ7 3454, fol. 184v.

57. Porte Chapelle section, line 5, grave 13.

58. Archives de Paris, Acte de décès. Document no. 13296. BN Pér. V 11514 Journal Général d'Affiches, 29 May 1850 p. 12 Announcement of deaths and burials. 'Mme Blaikie 80 ans, rue du Banquet 76'.

59. She proposed to make Thomas Mackie Heir of Provision General to his uncle in November 1838, SRO, C. 22.28. The provision is explained in C. 22/15: Charlotte Letitia Lockyer to enjoy the life rent. Then the property to go to Thomas Mackie. If Thomas Mackie deceased at the time of her death, the property to go to James and Agnes Mackie to enjoy life rent. Property then to go to heirs of Thomas Mackie. Thomas Mackie had one son who registered his claim in March 1855. The census of 1850 shows that James Mackie was still living at that time.

60. SRO, C. 22.28 and C. 22/151.

61. SRO, C. 22/151. No will of Blaikie's has been found. There is an act of succession (Ade P. DQ7 3456, fol. 47v.) in favour of Letitia Lockier in virtue of a gift made to her in front of Mr Okey, English consul dated 19 July 1838. This latter document has not been found.

Mackie, however, died in April 1843, and the inventory of his estate[62] carries the notification of his inheritance of one third of Thomas Blaikie's estate. This amounted to £1176. The names of the other beneficiaries are not known. Thomas Mackie had married his housekeeper, Hannah Frazer, and they had one son, Thomas. In 1854, the nursery stock of Corstorphine Hill, then known as Pinkhill, was sold by Mackie's Trustees.[63] The land, after surviving as a nursery for a number of years, was eventually purchased by the Edinburgh Zoological Society. The house was pulled down in 1972–73[64] when the Post House Hotel was built on the site.

Through the efforts of members of the Corstorphine Trust and the Franco-Scottish Society, a small memorial was dedicated to Blaikie in the gardens of the Edinburgh Zoological Society at Corstorphine. It consists of a stone, bearing simply his name and dates, and placed at the front of a border on the hillside, dedicated to the plants he collected in Switzerland.

Blaikie's contribution to French gardening is difficult to assess since most of his gardens have vanished and in the past his achievements have often been laid at the door of others. Discriminating authorities like De Laborde and Gilly, the Swedish architect, save their highest praise for just those elements at Bagatelle and elsewhere for which Blaikie was responsible; the natural beauty, the charm of the woods and the magnificent plantings of trees which set off the buildings and cast their shadows over the wide expanses of grass. The management of the views, which he considered his greatest skill, is something else that they refer to. Contemporary comments on his planting suggest that these were innovative.[65] Blaikie's work was inspired by his love of nature; his romantic appreciation of it, advanced for his time. In the end his major achievement was probably to open French eyes to what we think of today as the English landscape style, a style that would eventually replace the picturesque garden in France during the earlier part of the nineteenth century. The much praised garden of Salm-Dyck remains as a testimony to his skills as a plantsman and a designer. He never forgot his training as a gardener, propagating thousands of plants by different methods, growing his own melons and strawberries at Bagatelle, never losing his interest in agricultural improvement.

Thomas Blaikie's diary covered only seventeen years of his life, albeit important ones, and he left out much. For the rest, it has been necessary to track him down in France, England, Scotland and America, where his papers are in private hands.

---

62. SRO, SC 70/1/71, p. 468, dated 15 October 1850, Inventory of the personal estate of Thomas Mackie. This included a ⅓ share of the principal sum of 2220 francs rentes in the French Government and a ⅓ share of £1139 18s. 3d. of 3% Consolidated Annuities of the English Government subject to his wife's life rent. The executor was a Dr Ferdinand Burnett, surgeon living in Paris. Who the two other beneficiaries were is not known.

63. *Scotsman*, 15 September 1854, carries the advertisement for the sale.

64. I am indebted to Miss A. S. Cowper for sending me a photograph of the house before its demolition.

65. He planted Bélanger's formal garden at Bagatelle with *Rubus hispidus*, a recently introduced ornamental bramble from North America, C.-L. Hirschfeld, *Théorie de l'art des jardins* (Amsterdam, 1779).

I have walked many times in the gardens of Bagatelle picturing him in my mind's eye. My personal image of him is of a tall, big-boned man, a Caledonian, with strong features and a weather-beaten skin, a rough diamond, although there is no doubt that women, from the Queen down, liked him. His conversation was interesting enough to please one as intellectually sophisticated as the princess of Salm. I cannot stroll in the orderly Tuileries gardens without recalling the massacre of those Swiss guards and every time I look up at a sophora or one of the ginkgos in the parc Monceau, I am reminded of Blaikie's love of trees. At Raincy, the ghosts of the English colony still hide beneath the surface of the modern town and any minute at Raray I expected to see his tall figure emerge through the imposing red gate crowned with its unicorn. Many of the other properties in which he worked have been swallowed up by town development or the terrible devastation of war, but in Picardy his spirit still lingers in the gardens of Arrancy. I have studied his bold signature at the foot of nursery bills in the Archives Nationales in Paris and found his entwined initials engraved on his silver cutlery set out in the dining room of a house in one American state. In a Victorian mansion in another, I have sat with his diary in my hands, surrounded by some of his possessions; his bust of Marie Antoinette, his clock that was buried at Malmaison, and books and engravings that had belonged to him, signed in his familiar hand. In the white-painted, clapboard house of an American landscape gardener, I opened a small, cool-green shagreen box and drew out the cleverly packed compasses and rules that he had used in his plans for those eighteenth-century gardens.

There are still mysteries to be solved, like the absence of a will or any likeness of him, and there are other gardens to be discovered. Nor have I found any trace of his daughter Constance Blaikie.

My enduring memory of Thomas Blaikie is of the young man who stood alone to watch the sun go down on Mont Blanc from the summit of Mount Dole and danced the night away with the herdsmen. Stubborn, charming, shrewd and outspoken, intellectually curious, with a strong sense of his own worth, what the Scots would call 'a guid conceit of himself', Thomas Blaikie was an extraordinary gardener and a remarkable man.

APPENDIX

Blaikie's Alpine Plant List

This lists the plants Blaikie collected and sent to London to the Drs Fothergill and Pitcairn before he left Geneva. It is included in his diary at the end of the Swiss section.

Written in the field without access to reference books, Blaikie's list contains many spelling errors and these have been corrected, although his species names have been left with the endings he gave them. What is remarkable about the list is how many of the best alpine plants he succeeded in collecting.

Column 1: Numerical order according to Blaikie's list

Column 2: The number of specimens collected, and sometimes the type

Column 3: The botanical name listed by Blaikie. There is no key to the starred items.

Column 4: The identifying number given to each plant by Albrecht von Haller in his *Historia Plantarum Indigenarum Helvetiae* (Berne 1769). Sometimes, when compared to the Haller numbers in the Smith and Linnean Herbaria, Blaikie's list attributes the wrong Haller number to a plant. In these cases, the number listed by Blaikie is given in italics. If the correct Haller number is known, it is given in brackets.

Column 5: The current botanical name of the plant. Where it has been a problem finding an exact modern equivalent for Blaikie's plant name, a question mark indicates a probable name. Question marks in the other columns are Blaikie's.

Column 6: Blaikie's marginal notes. These must have been added later, as they are based on W. Aiton's Hortus Kewensis (London 1789) where 40 plants are listed as being introduced by Pitcairn and Fothergill in 1775. Blaikie is given credit for three introductions. There is no key to the crosses.

1	12	*Hypochoeris maculatata v.*	2	*Hypochoeris maculata* L.	Eng
2	11	*Hyoseris foetida*	5	*Aposeris foetida* L.	75 PF
3	1	*Lactuca saligna* var	13	*Lactuca saligna* L.	Eng
4	10	*Chondrilla juncea*	17	*Chondrilla juncea* L.	1633
5	3	*Prenanthes muralis*	18	*Lactuca muralis* (L.) Gaertner	Brit
6	6	*Sonchus Alpinus*	20	*Cicerbita alpina* (L.) Wallr.	Eng
7	10	*Picris hieracioides*	24	*Picris hieracioides* L.	Eng
8	25	*Leontodon hispidum*	25	*Leontodon hispidus* L.	Brit
9	24	*danubiale* Jacq.	26	*Leontodon hispidus* L. ssp. *danubialis* (Jacq.) Simonkai	x
10	16	*Hieracium taraxacum*	27	*Taraxacum* sp.	x
11	1	*Crepis biennis*	30	*Crepis biennis* L.	Eng
12	16	*Hieracium umbellatum*	34	*Hieracium umbellatum* L.	Brit
13	12	*Sabaudum*	35	*Hieracium sabaudum* L.	Brit
14	12	*Hieracium praemorsum*	36 (51)	*Crepis praemorsa* (L.)Tausch	x
15	4	*Andryala montana*	37	*Andryala montana* L.	x
16	13	*Hieracium genevense*	39	*Hieracium genevense* Zahn	x
17	24	*Hieracium conyzifolia*	40	*Crepis conyzifolia* (Gouan) A. Kerner?	x

18		*albido magno*	41	*Hieracium intybaceum* All.	x
19		*Asperum*	42	*Hieracium asperatum* (C. France) All. ?	x
20		*Amplexicaule*	43	*Hieracium amplexicaule* L.	1739
21		*villosum*	44	*Hieracium villosum* Jacq.	Scot
22		*paludosum*	45	*Crepis paludosa* (L.) Moench	Brit
23		*Succisaefolio*	47	*Crepis succisaefolia* Tausch.	x
24		*porrifolium*	48	*Hieracium porrifolium* L.	75 P F
25		*alpinum*	49	*Hieracium alpinum* All.	Scot
26	18		?	*Hieracium* sp.	
27	8	*Hieracium cymosum*	51	*Hieracium cymosum* L., *Crepis praemorsa* (L.) Tausch	1739
28	30	*Hieracium dubium*	53	*Hieracium x dubium* L.	Eng
29	27	*Hieracium pilosella* B	55B	*Hieracium pilosella* L.	1771
30	10	*Hypochoeris pontana*		*Crepis bocconi* P. D. Sell	75 P F
31	10			*Hypochoeris* sp.?	
32	9	*Leontodon aureum*		*Crepis aurea* (L.) Cass.	1769 Rich
33	30	*Senecio incanus*	61	*Senecio incanus* L.	1759
34	14	*Cineraria alpina alata**	62	*Senecio cordatus* Koch or *S. subalpinus* Koch	Eng? x
35	14	*cordifolia*	63	*Senecio subalpinus* Koch	75 P F
36	20	*Senecio nemorensis*	64	*Senecio nemorensis* L.	75 P F
37	20	*sarracenicus*	65	*Senecio fluviatilis* Wallr.	Eng
38	14	*doronicum*	67	*Senecio doronicum* (L.) L.	1705
39	6	*Cineraria alpina integrifolia*	68	*Senecio cordatus* Koch or *S. integrifolia* (L.) Clairv.	Eng
40	2	Solidago Virga aurea minor	69B (69)	*Solidago virgaurea* L.	Wales
41	34	*Inula*	73	*Inula helvetica* Weber	
42	3	*Inula hirta*	75	*Inula hirta* L.	1759
43	20	*britannica* B	78	*Inula britannica* L.	1759
44	16	*Aster Alpinus*	82	*Aster alpinus* L.	1759
45	15	*Erigeron acre*	85	*Erigeron acer* L.	Brit
46	20	*alpinum*	86	*Erigeron alpinus* L.	1759
47	10	*uniflorus*	87	*Erigeron uniflorus* L.	75 P F
48	25	*Arnica scorpioides*	89	*Doronicum* sp.	1759
49	12	*montana*	90	*Arnica montana* L.	1759
50	4	*Doronicum bellidiastrum*	92	*Aster bellidiastrum* (L.) Scop.	1759
51	25	*Chrysanthemum corymbosum*	95	*Tanacetum corymbosum* (L.) Schultz Bip.	1759
52		*alpinum*	96	*Leucanthemopsis alpina* (L.) Heywood	1759
53	2	*Achillea nobilis*	109	*Achillea nobilis* L.	1640
54	10	*atrata*	111	*Achillea atrata* L.	1774 P F
55	30	*Genipi moschata*	112	*Achillea erba-rotta* All. ssp. moschata Wulfen. Rchd.	1775 P F
56	12	*macrophylla*	115	*Achillea macrophylla* L.	1759
57	6	*alpina*	116	*Achillea sibirica* Ledeb.?	1731
58	9	*nana*	(113)	*Achillea nana* L.	x
59	25	*Artemisia glacialis*	125	*Artemisia glacialis* L.	1748
60	5	*rupestre*	*127*	*Artemisia rupestris* L.	1748
61	5	*vallesiaca*	128	*Artemisia vallesiaca* All.	75 P F
62	12	*campestris*	131	*Artemisia campestris* L.	Eng x
63	20	*Carpesium cernuum*	*134*	*Carpesium cernuum* L.	1768
64	16	*Conyza squarrosa*	135	*Inula conyza* DC.	Brit

65	3	*Cacalia Alpina*	137	*Adenostyles alpina* (L.) Bluff & Fingerh.	1739
66	1	*Tussilago frigia paradoxa*	141	*Tussilago* or*Petasites* sp.	1758
67	5	*alpina*	142	*Homogyne alpina* (L.) Cass.	1731
68	10	*Gnaphalium Supinum*	148	*Omalotheca supina* (L.) DC.	x
69	6	*Alpinum*	150	*Antennaria alpina* (L.) Gaertner	75 P F
70	12	*Filago Leontopodium*	152	*Leontopodium alpinum* (L.) Cass.	76 Jacq(?)
71		*Gnaphalium dioicum*	157	*Antennaria dioica* (L.) Gaertner	Brit
72	11	*Centaurea Rhapontica*	160	*Leuzea rhapontica* (L.) Holub	1686
73	6	*Arctium personata*	162	*Carduus personata* (L.) Jacq.	76 Jacq
74	10	*Serratula tinctoria minor* alpina	163	*Serratula tinctoria* L.	x
75	11	*Carduus defloratus*	164	*Carduus defloratus* L.	1775 Jacq
76	12	*eriophorum*	168	*Cirsium eriophorum* (L.) Scop.	Brit
77	16	*Carduus palustris*	170	*Cirsium palustre* (L.) Scop.	Brit
78	10	*Cnicus spinosissimum*	172	*Cirsium spinosissimum* (L.) Scop.	x
79	14	*pinnatiffidis*	174	*Serratula pinnatifida* (Cav.) Poiret in Lam.	x
80	8	*Erisithales*	175	*Cirsium eristhales* Scop.	87 Mon Var
81	7	*Carduus tataricus*	176 (173)	*Cirsium oleraceum* (L.) Scop.	75 Jacq
82	1	*rigens*	176B	*Cnicus rigens* Willd. (?)	75 P F
83	5	*acaulis*	178	*Cirsium acaule* Scop.	Brit
84	20	*Serratula alpina*	179	*Saussurea alpina* (L) DC	Brit
85	21	*Carlina vulgaris montanus*	182	*Carlina vulgaris* L.	Brit
86		*acaulis*	183	*Carlina acaulis* L.	1640
87		*Doronicum Bellidiastrum rubrum*	92	*Aster bellidiastrum* (L.) Scop.	x
88		*Centaurea phrygia*	188	*Centaurea phrygia* L.	1727
89		*Scabiosa Alpina*	200	*Cephalaria alpina* (L.) Rhoem. & Schult.	1570
90		*columbaria*	202	*Scabiosa columbaria* L.	Britain
91		*fl. alba*	202B	*Scabiosa columbaria* L.	Var x
92		*Sylvatica*	204	*Knautia drymaea* Heuffel	1748
93	15	*Pterocephala*	207	*Pterocephalus perennis* Coult.	x
94	2	*Valeriana tripteris*	211	*Valeriana tripteris* L.	1739
95	20	*montana*	212	*Valeriana montana* Jacq.	1739
96	30	*Globularia cordifolia*	216	*Globularia cordifolia* L.	59 Mill
97	15	*nudicaulis*	217	*Globularia nudicaulis* L.	39 Mill.
98	6	*vulgaris*	218	*Globularia vulgaris* L.	Europ
99	6	*fl. alba*	218B	*Globularia vulgaris* L. var. *alba*	Br x
100	20	*Mentha Sylvestris Alpina*	227	*Mentha sylvestris* L.	Brit
101	6			*Mentha* sp.?	
102		*Origanum vulgare fl. alba*	233B	*Origanum vulgare* L. var. *alba*	Br x
103	8	*Thymus alpinus*	238	*Calamintha alpina* Lam.	1731
104	10	*Clinopodium alpinum*	239	*Acinos alpinus* (L.) Moench	x
105	12	*Melissa calamintha*	241	*Calamintha nepeta* (L.) Savi ssp. glandulosa (Req.) P.W. Ball	Eng
106	4	*Dracocephalum Rhyuschianum*	254	*Dracocephalum ruyschiana* L.	1758
107	7	*Stachys germanica*	255	*Stachys germanica* L.	Eng
108	28	*Sideritis hyssopifolia*	260	*Sideritis hyssopifolia* L.	1731
109	23	*hirsutus*	262	*Sideritis hirsuta* L.	1731
110	2	*Betonica officinalis alba*	264B	*Stachys officinalis* (L.) Trevisan var. *alba*	Br
111	14	*Alpina*	265	*Stachys alpina* L.	x
112	20	*Lamium laevigatum*	270	*Lamium maculatum* L.	75 P F
113	1	*laevigatum album*	270B	*Lamium maculatum* L. var. *album*	x

114	10	Stachys sylvatica	275B	Stachys sylvatica L.	Br x
115	10	Prunella laciniata	279	Prunella laciniata (L.) L.	1713
116	10	fl. alba	279B	Prunella laciniata L. var. alba	x
117	40	Ajuga genevensis	283B	Ajuga genevensis L.	1759
118	10	Teucrium montanum	285	Teucrium montanum L.	1711
119	10	Pinguicula Alpina	293	Pinguicula alpina L.	x
120	12	Erinus Alpinus	302	Erinus alpinus L.	1759
121	12	fl. alba	302B	Erinus alpinus L. var. alba	x
122	13	Bartsia alpina	312	Bartsia alpina L.	x
123	10	Pedicularis flamula	315	Pedicularis flammea L.	75 P F
124	13	comosa	317	Pedicularis comosa L.	75 P F
125	2	verticillata	318 (3896)	Pedicularis verticillata L.	x
126	2	Scrophularia ruta canina	328	Scrophularia canina L.?	1683
127	5	Digitalis ferruginea	331	Digitalis ferruginea L.	1597
128	34	Antirrhinum alpinum	338	Linaria alpina (L.) Miller	1570
129	12	Polygala Amara 2 varieties	343	Polygala amara L.	75 P F
130	12	chamaebuxus	345	Polygala chamaebuxus L.	1658
131	25	Genista pilosa	351	Genista pilosa L.	Eng
132	19	germanica	352	Genista germanica L.	1773
133	3	sagittalis	353	Genista sagittalis L.	1758
134	14	Spartium decumbens	355	Cytisus decumbens (Durande) Spach	75 P F
135	3	Ononis spinosa fl. alba	356	Ononis spinosa L. var. alba	Brit
136	2	rotundifolia	357	Ononis rotundifolia L.	1570
137	20	natrix	358	Ononis natrix L.	1683
138	30	minutissima	359	Ononis minutissima L.	1739
139		Tozzia Alpina		Tozzia alpina L. (Bl.notes give this as H.No. 298)	x
140	10	Trifolium alpinum	369	Trifolium alpinum L.	75 P F
141	6	Alpestre	376	Trifolium alpestre L.	Scot
142	8	Medicago Lupulina	380	Medicago lupulina L.	Brit
143	5	Lotus siliquosus	386	Tetragonolobus siliquosus (L.) Roth	1683
144	4	Coronilla coronata	388	Coronilla coronata L.	1776 Jac
145	1	minima	390	Coronilla minima L.	1683
146	15	Hypocrepis multisiliquosa	391	Hippocrepis multisiliquosa L.	1739
147	4	Hedysarum onobrychus	396	Onobrychis viciifolia Scop.(?)	Brit
148	25	Anthyllis montana	397	Anthyllis montana L.	1759
149	2	Phaca alpina	401	Phaca alpinus Wulf., Astragalus penduliflorus Lam.	1759
150	7	valesiaca	402	Phaca or Astragalus species	x
151	3	australis	403	Astragalus australis (L.) Lam.	1779
152		Astragalus tragacantha	405	Astragalus sempervirens Lam. ssp. sempervirens	1640
153		campestris	406	Oxytropis campestris (L.) DC.	78 Thou(in)
154		montana	408	Oxytropis jacquinii Bunge	x
155		monspessulanus	414	Astragalus monspessulanus L.	Pit(cairn)
156		depressus	415*	Astragalus depressus L.	1772
157		Orobus luteus	419	Lathyrus gmelinii Fritsch	1757
158		Vicia onobrychioides	425	Vicia onobrychioides L.	x
159	13	Arabis pendula	444	Arabis pendula L.	1759
160	16	Cheiranthus polyceratus	446	Sisymbrium polyceratum L.	x
161	10	Cheiranthus Sulfurinus	449	Erysimum sp.	x
162	13	erysimoides	450?	Erysimum sp.	Eng
163	13	Turritis hirsuta	456	Arabis hirsuta Clav.	Brit

164	3	*Sisymbrium tanacetifolium*	460	*Hugueninia tanacetifolia* (L.) Reichenb.	1731
165	2	*Dentaria pentaphylla*	469	*Cardamine pentaphyllos* (L.) Crantz	1656
166	6	*Cardamine bellidifolia*	476	*Cardamine bellidifolia* L.	x
167	4	*resedefolia*	(476B)	*Cardamine resedifolia* L.	x
168	10	*Myagrum saxatile*	490	*Kernera saxatilis* Rchb.?	
169	12	*Draba Alpina*	498	*Draba alpina* L.	x
170	2	*Lunaria rediviva*	500	*Lunaria rediviva* L.	1597
171	13	*Biscutella dydima*	501	*Biscutella laevigata* L.?	x
172	12	*Lepidium Alpinum*	516	*Pritzelago alpina* (L.) Kuntze	75 P F
173	13	*Iberis rotundifolia*	517	*Pritzelago rotundifolia* (L) Kuntze	1748
174	10	*Thlaspi montanum*	518	*Thlaspi montanum* L.	Eng
175	3	*Isatis tinctoria Alpina*	523	*Isatis tinctoria* L. ssp. *tinctoria*	Eng
176	10	*Veronica latifolia*	535	*Veronica austraca* L.	75 Jacquin
177		*aphylla*	541	*Veronica aphylla* L.	75 P F
178	3	*spicata alba*	542B	*Veronica spicata* L.	x
179	3	*Veronica s. incarnata*	542	*Veronica spicata* L. ssp. *incana* (L.) Walters	x
180	30	*bellidioides*	543	*Veronica bellidioides* L.	75 P F
181	10	*alpina*	544	*Veronica alpina* L.	Scot
182	8	*fruticulosa Saxatiles*	545B	*Veronica fruticulosa* L.	68 Saussure
183		*Viola hirta*	559?	*Viola hirta* L.	Eng
184		*palustris*	560	*Viola palustris* L.	Brit
185	10	*canina*	562	*Viola canina* L.	Brit
186	10	*biflora*	563	*Viola biflora* L.	1739
187	10	*cenisia*	564	*Viola cenisia* L.	x
188		*calcarata*	566	*Viola calcarata* L.	1739
189	2	*Atropa Belladona*	579	*Atropa bella-donna* L.	Brit
190	2	*Verbascum lychnitis fl. alba parva*	583B	*Verbascum lychnitis* L.	Brit
191	4	*Pulmonaria angustifolia*	598	*Pulmonaria angustifolia* L.	1731
192	16	*Onosma echioides*	601	*Onosma echioides* L.	1683
193	25	*Primula decora*	613	*Primula* sp.	x
194	10	*Diapensia helvatica*	617	*Androsace helvetica* (L.) All.	75 P F
195	20	*Aretia Alpina*	618	*Androsace alpina* (L.) Lam.	75 id
196	20	*Androsace carnea*	619	*Androsace carnea* L.	68 Sauss
197		*Aretia villosa*	620	*Androsace villosa* L.?	68 Sauss
198		*Androsace lactea*	622	*Androsace lactea* L.	68 id
199	32	*Primula farinosa*	623	*Primula farinosa* L.	Brit
200	25	*Swertia perennis*	626	*Swertia perennis* L.	Eng
201	7	*Gentiana punctata*	638	*Gentiana punctata* L.	75 P F
202	12	*purpurea*	639	*Gentiana purpurea* L.	68 Saus
203	18	*asclepedia*	640	*Gentiana asclepiadea* L.	1629
204	25	*pneumonanthe*	641	*Gentiana pneumonanthe* L.	Eng
205	2	*cruciata*	643	*Gentiana cruciata* L.	1596
206		*bavarica*	645	*Gentiana bavarica* L.	75 P F
207	13	*ciliata*	653	*Gentianella ciliata* (L.) Borkh.	x
208	15	*alpina*	657	*Plantago alpina* L.	74 P
209	20	*cynops*	662	*Plantago cynops* L.	1596
210	6	*Azalea procumbens*	666	*Loiseleurea procumbens* (L.) Desv.	Scotl
211	cuttings	*Sambucus racemosa var.*	672	*Sambucus racemosa* L.	1596
212	1	*Lonicera caerulea*	674	*Lonicera caerulea* L.	1724
213	6	*Phyteuma pauciflora*	679	*Phyteuma pauciflorum* L.	x

214	8	*orbicularis*	681	*Phyteuma orbiculare* L.	Eng
215	5	*spicata*	684	*Phyteuma spicatum* L. ssp. *spicatum*	Europe 1683
216	2	*coerulea*	684B	*Phyteuma spicatum* L. ssp. *coeruleum* R. Schulz	x
217	2	*Campanula rhomboides*	693	*Campanula rhomboidalis* L.	75 P F
218	2	*Trachelium*	690	*Campanula trachelium* L.	Brit
219	11	*barbata*	694	*Campanula barbata* L.	75 P F
220	12	*uniflora*	696	*Campanula uniflora* L.	x
221		*rotundifolia*	701	*Campanula rotundifolia* L.	Britain
222		*Campanula rotundifolia alba*	702B	*Campanula rotundifolia* L. var. *alba*	x?
223		*Galium Sylvaticum*	712	*Galium sylvaticum* L.	1713
224		*Alpinum*	713	*Galium* sp.	x
225		*Galium rubioides*	720	*Galium rubioides* L.	75 P F
226		*rotundifolia*	727	*Galium rotundifolium* L.	x
227	3	*Asperula cynanchica*	730	*Asperula cynanchica* L.	Eng
228	12	*Eryngium campestre B var.*	735	*Eryngium campestre* L.	Eng
229	10	*Alpinum*	736	*Eryngium alpinum* L.	1752
230	17	*Athamanta cretensis*	746	*Athamanta cretensis* L.	x
231	6	*Chaerophyllum hirsutum*	751	*Chaerophyllum hirsutum* L.	1768 M
232	2	*Athamanta meum*	761	*Meum athamanticum* Jacq.	Brit
233	13	*Phylandrium (Phellandrium) mutillman*	763	*Ligusticum mutellina* (L.) Crantz	1774 P F
234	14	*Aethusa Alpinum*	765	*Aethusa cynapium* L.?	x
235	3 tuf	*Bupleurum longifolium*	768	*Bupleurum longifolium* L.	1713
236	30	*angulosum*	770	*Bupleurum angulosum* L.	1759
237	12	*Stellatum*	771	*Bupleurum stellatum* L.	75 P F
238	23	*falcatum*	776	*Bupleurum falcatum* L.	1739
239	4	*Sium falcaria*	782	*Falcaria vulgaris* L.	1759
240	3	*Pimpinella magna rubiola*	785	*Pimpinella major* (L.) Huds.	E
241	8	*Astrantia minor*	791	*Astrantia minor* L.	1759
242	4	*Laserpitium latifolium*	792	*Laserpitium latifolium* L.	1640
243	5	*Panax* Gouan	795	*Laserpitium halleri* Crantz	x
244	22	*mutellinoides*		*Ligusticum mutellinoides* (Crantz) Vill.	x
245	8	*lucidum*	796	*Ligusticum lucidum* Miller	75 P F
246	12	*Peucedanum alsaticum*	798	*Peucedanum alsaticum* L.	74 Rich
247	6	*Selinum carvifolium*	802	*Selinum carvifolia* L.	1774 Rich
248	12	*Athamanta cervaria*	804	*Peucedanum cervaria* (L.) Lap.?	1597
249	1	*Heracleum alpinum*	810	*Heracleum sphondylium* L. ssp. *alpinum* (L.) Bonnier & Layens	1739 M
250	8	*Ribes alpina*	817	*Ribes alpinum* L.	Brit
251	1	*Rhamnus Saxatilus*	822	*Rhamnus saxatilis* Jacq.	75 P F
252	3	*alpina*	823	*Rhamnus alpinus* L.	x
253	10	*Linum narbonense*	837	*Linum narbonense* L.	1759
254	8	*tenuifolium*	838	*Linum tenuifolium* L.	Eng
255	3	*Telephium imperatoria*	841	*Telephium imperati* L.	1739
256	tufts	*Cherleria sedoides*	859	*Minuartia sedoides* (Pers.) Cumino ex Loisel.	Scot
257	10	*Moerhingia muscosa*	860	*Moehringia muscosa* L.	75 P F
258		*Spergula Saginioides*	862	*Spergula* or *Spergularia* sp.	Eng
259	18	*Arenaria saxatilis*	867	*Arenaria* sp.	x

260	20	*laraxifolia*	869	*Minuartia laricifolia* (L.) Schinz & Thell.	Brit
261	4	*biflora*	877	*Arenaria biflora* L.	x
262	4	*Stellaria dichotoma*	886	*Stellaria* sp.	1774
263	12	*Cerastium alpinum*	888	*Cerastium alpinum* L.	x
264	13	*Dianthus Superbus*	898	*Dianthus superbus* L.	1629
265	3	*carthusianorum*	899	*Dianthus carthusianorum* L.	71 Rich
266	10	*Gypsophylla saxifraga*	902	*Tunica saxifraga* Scop.	74 Rich
267	19	*repens*	905	*Gypsophylla repens* L.	74 Rich
268	6	*Silene rupestre*	917	*Silene rupestris* L.	71 Rich
269	16	*Silene Quadrifida*	918	*Silene quadrifida* L.	x
270	7	*acaulis*	919	*Silene acaulis* (L.) Jacq.	Britain
271	tufts	*Oxalis acetosella var.*	928	*Oxalis acetosella* L.	Br V
272	9	*Geranium pheum*	934	*Geranium phaeum* L. var. *lividum* L'Herit.) Perse.	Eng
273	8	*Serratum aconitifolium*	935	*Geranium rivulare* Vill.?	75 P F
274	8	*Striatum*	936	*Geranium versicolor* L.	1629
275	tuf	*Sempervivum arachnoides*	952	*Sempervivum arachnoideum* L.	1699
276	10	*Sedum anacampseros*	956	*Sedum anacampseros* L.	1596
277	T	*Sexangulare*	965	*Sedum sexangulare* L.	Eng
278	12	*Saxifraga bryoides*	969	*Saxifraga bryoides* L.	75 P F
279	10	*aspera*	970	*Saxifraga aspera* L.	48 Mil
280	10	*autumnalis*	971	*Saxifraga* sp.	x
281	T	*hirculus*	972	*Saxifraga hirculus* L.	Eng
282	T	*Stellaris*	973	*Saxifraga stellaris* L.	Brit
283	T	*Saxifraga oppositifolia*	980	*Saxifraga oppositifolia* L.	Brit
284	10	*biflora*	981	*Saxifraga biflora* All.	x
285	10	*caesia*	982	*Saxifraga caesia* L.	x
286	12	*Androsace*	984	*Saxifraga androsacea* L.	x
287	12	*caespitosa*	988	*Saxifraga caespitosa* L.	Engl
288	20	*Epilobium alpinum*	999	*Epilobium alpinus* L.	Brit
289	16	*Angustissimum*	1001	*Epilobium dodonaei* Vill.	75 P F
290	10	*Monotropa Hypopitys*	1002	*Monotropa hypopitys* L.	x
291	20	*Adoxa moschatellina*	1005	*Adoxa moschatellina* L.	Brit
292	30	*Pyrola Secunda*	1008	*Orthilia secunda* (L.) House	Brit
293	3	*minor*	1009	*Pyrola minor* L.	Brit
294	40	*rotundifolia*	1010	*Pyrola rotundifolia* L.	Brit
295	T	*uniflora*	1011	*Moneses uniflora* (L.) A. Gray	1748 Mil
296	16	*Erica herbacea*	1014	*Erica herbacea* L.	1760
297	18	*Rhododendron ferrugineum*	1015	*Rhododendron ferrugineum* L.	1739
298	15	*Rhodendron hirsutum*	1016	*Rhododendron hirsutum* L.	1739
299	30	*Arbutus alpina*	1019	*Arctostaphylos alpinus* (L.) Sprengel	Brit
300	16	*Daphne alpina*	1026	*Daphne alpina* L.	1750
301	30	*Cistus fumana*	1032	*Fumana procumbens* (Dunal) Gren. & Godron	1739 M
302	2	*Serpyllifolia*	1034	*Cistus* sp.	1759 M
303	15	*hirsutus*	1035	*Cistus hirsutus* Lam.	x
304	23	*polyfolius*	1036	*Helianthemum polifolium* DC	Eng
305	10	*Euphorbia cyparasius*	1047	*Euphorbia cyparissias* L.	1640
306	10	*dulcis*	1051	*Euphorbia dulcis* L.	1759
307	10	*paralias*	1055	*Euphorbia paralias* L.	Engl
308	1	*Althea hirsuta*	1073	*Althaea hirsuta* L.	1683
309	1	*Mespitus chaemaemespilus*	1090	*Mespilus germanica* L.?	1683
310	5	*Rubus aeduis*	1108	*Rubus idaeus* L.	Britain

311	10	Potentillla norvegica	1115	Potentilla norvegica L.	x
312	8	Sibbaldia procumbens	1116	Sibbaldia procumbens L.	Br
313	10	Potentilla verna	1119	Potentilla verna L.	Brit
314	3	recta	1121	Potentilla recta L.	1648
315	15	aurea	1122	Potentilla aurea L.	1739
316	20	caulescence	1123	Potentilla caulescens L.	1759 M
317	8	Geum Montanum	1131	Geum montanum L.	1597
318	16	reptans	1132	Geum reptans L.	75 P F
319	30	Dryas octopetala	1133	Dryas octopetala L.	Scot
320	4	Spirea Aruncus	1134	Aruncus dioicus (Walter) Fernald	1633
321	6	Thalictrum	1140	Thalictrum foetidum L.	x
322	7	Anemone vernalis	1147	Pulsatilla vernalis (L.) Miller	x
323	22		1149	Pulsatilla alpina (L.) Delarb.	
324	10	alpina luteo	1149B	Pulsatilla alpina .(L.) Delarb. ssp. sulphurea L.	1731
325	18	Alpina minima	1151	Pulsatilla alpina (L.) Delarbr. ssp. alpina	x
326	10	narcissiflora	1155	Anemone narcissifolia L. ssp. narcissifolia	1773
327	42	Ranunculus glacialis	1166	Ranunculus glacialis L.	75 P F
328	16	alpestre	1167	Ranunculus alpestris L. ssp. alpestris	x
329	15	nivalis L	1168	Ranunculus nivalis L.	75 P F
330	7	lanuginosus	1172	Ranunculus lanuginosus L.	1683
331	16	thora	1178	Ranunculus thora L.	1710
332		amplexicaule		Ranunculus amplexicaulis L.	1633
333		Potentilla rupestre		Potentilla rupestris L.	Eng
334	16	Aquilegia Alpina	1196	Aquilegia alpina L.	1731
335	8	Aconitum	1198	Aconitum lycoctonum L.	
336	30	Anthora	1199	Aconitum anthora L.	1596
337	T	Anthericum calyculatum	1205	Tofielda calyculata (L.) Walhend.	Scotl
338	20	ramosum	1208	Anthericum ramosum L.	1597
339	6	serotinum	1209	Lloydia serotina Reichenb.	
340	11	Ornithogalum pyrenaicum	1210	Ornithogalum pyrenaicum L.	Eng
341	12	luteum	1213	Gagea lutea (L.) Ker-Gawler	Brit
342	16	Allium Sphaerocephalum	1220	Allium sphaerocephalum L.	1759
343	8	petraeum	1227	Allium sp.	x
344	2	Allium ursinum	1228	Allium ursinum L.	Brit
345	1	Uvularia amplexifolia	1237	Streptopus amplexifolius (L.) DC.	1752
346	1	Iris germanica	1258	Iris germanica L.	1596
347	3	Ophrys anthropophora	1264	Aceras anthropophorum (L.) Aiton f.	Brit
348	15	insectifera moyedes	1265	Ophrys insectifera L.	Brit
349	8	arachnites	1266	Ophrys holoserica (Burm.f.) Greuter?	Brit
350	5	Satyrium viride	1269	Coeloglossum viride (L.) Hartman	Brit
351	6	nigra	1271	Satyrium nigrum L.	1779 (or 4) x
352	4	Orchis globosa	1272	Traunsteinera globosa (L.) Reichenb.	x
353	6	ustulata	1273	Orchis ustulata L.	Eng

354		odoratissima	1274	Gymnadenia odoratissima (L.) L.C.M. Rich.	x
355		millittaris	1275	Orchis militaris L.	Eng
356			1277	Orchis militaris L.	
357		maculata alba	1278	Dactylorhiza maculata (L.) Soo.	Brit
358		incarnata lutea	1280	Dactylorhiza sambucina (L.) Soo.?	x
359		incarnata	1280B	Dactylorhiza incarnata (L.) Soo.	x
360		Chamaeorchis	1281	Orchis sp.	x
361		bifolia	1285	Platanthera bifolia (L.) L.C.M. Richard	Brit
362		abortiva	1288	Limodorum abortivum (L.) Sw.?	x
363	6				
364	2				
365	3				
366	4				
367	4	Ophrys cordata	1292	Listera cordata (L.) R.Br.	
368	40	Spiralis	1294	Spiranthes spiralis (L.) Chevall.	Brit
369	20	Satyrium repens	1295	Goodyera repens (L.) R.Br.	Scot
370	3	Serapias palustre	1296	Epipactis palustris L.	x
371	10	latifolia	1297	Epipactis latifolia (L.) All.	Brit
372	8	longifolia	1298B	Cephalanthera longifolia Rich.?	Brit x
373	2	Damasonium	1299	Cephalanthera damasonium (Miller) Druce	x
374	1	Cypripedium calceolus	1300	Cypripedium calceolus L.	Eng
375	16	Triglochum palustre?	1308	Triglochin palustris L.	Brit
376	T	Juncus trifidus	1315	Juncus trifidus L.	Scot
377	T	articulatis	1322	Juncus articulatus L.	Brit
378	T	pilosus	1325	Luzula pilosa (L.) Willd.	Brit
379	T	rufescens Alpinus	1326	Juncus alpinus Vill.	1
380	8	niveus	1328	Luzula nivea (L.) DC.	1770 Rich
381	T	campestris	1330	Luzula campestris (L.) DC.	Brit
382	7	Straminius		Juncus sp.	x
383	T	Scirpus cespitosus	1334	Juncus cespitosus L.	Brit
384	4	Schoenus compressus	1342	Blysmus compressus (L.) Panzer ex Link	Brit
385	4	Cyperus flavescente	1348	Cyperus flavescens L.	76 Thouin
386	4	fuscus	1349	Cyperus fuscus L.	77 Black(?)
387	T	Carex muricatus	1365	Carex muricata L.	Brit
388	T	Alpina	1371	Carex ericetorum Poll. (acc. to Blaikie's notes)	x
389		flavescente	1380	Carex flava L.	Brit
390		id	1383	Carex fulva Good.	x
391		id	1386		x
392		id			
393		id			
394		id			
395		id			
396		id			
397		Andropogon Ischaemum	1414	Bothriochloa ischaemum (L.) Keng.	Blai
398		Poa Gerardi	1470	Festuca paniculata (L.) Schinz & Thell. ssp. spadicea (L.) Litard.	75 P F

399		*Panicum*	1527	*Cynodon dactylon* Pers.? (Bl's notes give *Panicum dactylon* L.)	x
400		*Phleum Alpinum*	1529	*Phleum alpinum* L.	x
401					
402	2	*Scleranthus perennis*	1550	*Scleranthus perennis* L.	E
403	4	*Herniaria glabra*	1552	*Herniaria glabra* L.	Eng
404		*Alchemilla pentaphylla*	1568	*Alchemilla pentaphylla* L.	1748 M
405	6	*Thesium Alpinum*	1573	*Thesium alpinum* L.	x
406	4	*Rumex alpinus*	1587	*Rumex alpinus* L.	1597
407	6		1598		
408	cuttings	*Salix Laponica?*	1642 (1643)	*Salix lapponum* L.	Scot
409	do	*nova*	1643	*Salix* sp.	x
410		*rosmarinifolius*	1644	*Salix rosmarinifolia* L.	Eng
411		*retusa*	1648	*Salix retusa* L.	1763
412		*herbacea*	1649	*Salix herbacea* L.	Brit
413		*reticulata*	1650	*Salix reticulata* L.	Brit
414		*Myrsinitis*	1645	*Salix myrsinites* L.	Scot
415		*incubacea*		*Salix repens* var. *incubacea*	75 P F
416					x
417		*Osmunda Lunaria*	1668 (1686)	*Botrychium lunaria* (L.) Swartz	Brit
418		*crispa*	?	*Cryptogramma crispa* (L.) R.Br. ex Hooker	Brit
419		*Lycopodum Selago*	1716	*Huperzia selago* (L.) Bernh. ex Schrank & Mart.	Brit
420		*Alpinum*	1719	*Lycopodium alpinum* L.	x
421		*clavatum*	1722	*Lycopodium clavatum* L.	Brit
422		*Astragalus uralensis*	(420)	*Oxytropus uralensis* (L.) DC.	Scot
423		*Sempervivum montanum*		*Sempervivum montanum* L.	1759
424		*Heracleum novum*		*Heracleum* sp.	
425		*Centaurea alba*	(196)	*Centaurea alba* L.	1773
426		*Draba incana*	(495)	*Draba incana* L.	Brit
427		*Primula*	610		E2 x 2
428		*Gentiana Verna*	644	*Gentiana verna* L.	x
429		*verna alba*	644B	*Gentiana verna* L. var. *alba*	x
430		*Campanula cenisia*		*Campanula cenisia* L.	75 P F
431		*thyrsoides*	(688)	*Campanula thyrsoides* L.	85 Pitcairn
432		*Pimpinella glauca*	788	*Trinia vulgaris* DC.?	x
433		*Ophrys Alpina*	1263	*Chamaeorchis alpina* (L.) L.	x
434		*Asplenium*	1690		
435			1709	*Polypodium alpinum* All.?	
436			1690		
437		*Chrysanthemum atratum*	(98)	*Leucanthemum atratum* (Jacq.) DC	75 P F
438		*Lycopodium helveticum*	(1718)	*Selaginella helvetica* (L.) Spreng B.	79 M fr
439		*Galium aristatum*		*Galium aristatum* L.	78 Bla
440		*Nepeta incana*		*Caryopteris incana* (Thun.) Miq.	78 Bla

Bibliography

Manuscripts

Archives Nationales (AN)
R1 309, 310, 311, 312, 315, 317, 318, 320, 321, 322, 333, 338, 339, 340, 341, 342, 361, 371, 379, 435, 513
O1 1581, 1876, 2111
O2 344, 1238
O3 1237, 1238
AJ 15 511
NIII Seine 586
MC ET XVIII 951 LVIII 806

Archives Privées
3 AP, 134, 341 fonds Nicolay
95 AP 70, 72, fonds Caulincourt
137 AP 17, 18 fonds Ney
349 AP 1, 7, 8, fonds Montesquiou-Fezenac
300 AP I 24, 185, 308, 317, 2110, Maison de France

Archives de Paris (A de P)
Acte de décès, Document no. 13296. Acte de décès, DQ7 3454, fol. 184v. Acte de déces. Document no. 13296. Acte de Succession DQ7 3456, fol. 47v

Bibliothèque de l'Union Centrale des Arts Décoratifs
MS De Ganay, *Les Jardins à l'anglaise en France au XVIIIeme siècle.*

Bibliothèque Historique de la Ville de Paris (BHVP)
Papiers Jean Stern, 2825, 2827, 2830, 2831

Bibliothèque du Muséum National d'Histoire Naturelle, Paris
MS 126 306, 315, 1308, 1353, 1984

Bibliothèque de l'École Nationale Supérieure des Beaux-Arts Paris
MS. PC 12760

Fondation pour l'Histoire de la Haute Banque, Paris
41AQ 7

Archives Départementales de Calvados
8E 16086

Musée Municipale de la Toile de Jouy, Jouy-en-Josas, France (MMTJ)
Gottlieb Widmer, *Mémorial de la famille*

Cambridge University Library (CUL)
Brand MS Add 8670

Edinburgh Botanic Gardens Library (EBL)
Professor Daniel Rutherford (1749–1819), *Miscellaneous papers and correspondence.*
Thomas Blaikie, Catalogue of the plants in the Jardin du Roi, 1777.
Lectures in Botany by John Hope in the Royal botanick garden Edinburgh, 1777–1778.
Correspondence of Patrick Neill.

Memoirs of the Caledonian Horticultural Society 4 vols.
Hope Papers.

Public Record Office, Kew (PRO)
SP47.

Royal Botanic Gardens, Kew
B.C. 1 67, B.C. 1 86–87, B.C. 1 91.

Scottish Record Office, Edinburgh (SRO)
RS 27 \959 ff 155R–159V; C.22.28; C.22/15; C.22/151; SC 70/1/71.

Royal Botanic Gardens, Kew
Kew: B. C. 1.67, BC 128.

Archives de Raray (Private Archive).
Ambroisine de La Bédoyère, *Journal des champs*.
Henry de La Bédoyère, *Diary*.
Eighteenth-century plan of the château and gardens of Raray.
Plan of 1861 showing the *jardin anglais*.
Plant lists for the *jardin anglais* at Raray.

Blaikie Papers (Private Archive)

Published Works

ABRANTÈS, L., Duchesse d', *Memoirs* 8 vols (London, 1831–35).
ADAMS, William Howard, *The French Garden 1500–1800* (London, 1979).
AITON, W., *Hortus Kewensis* (London, 1789).
ALGER, John G., *Paris in 1789–94. Farewell Letters of Victims of the Guillotine* (London, 1902).
ALPHAND, A., *Les Promenades de Paris, histoire, description des embellisments etc.*, 2 vols (Paris, 1867–73).
ANDRÉ, L., *The Mysterious Baronne de Feuchères* (London, 1927).
ARNETH, Ritter von, ed. *Marie-Antoinette Joseph II und Leopold II, der Brief Wechsel* (Leipzig, 1868).
ARNEVILLE, Marie-Blanche, *Parcs et jardins sous le premier Empire* (Paris, 1981).
ARNOTT, H., *History of Edinburgh* (Edinburgh, 1779).
ASTRUC, Jean, *Le Raincy* (Paris, 1969).
AVRILLON, Mademoiselle d', *Mémoires de Mademoiselle Avrillon*, ed. Maurice Dernelle (Paris, 1969).
BACHAUMONT, Louis. Petit de, *Mémoires secrets pour servir à l'histoire de la République des lettres en France, depuis MDCCLXII jusqu'à nos jours, ou Journal d'un Observateur* (London, 1780).
BARBER, Peter, *Switzerland 700* (British Museum, 1991).
BARRIER, J. and MOSSER, M., *Sur les terres d'un jardinier* (Besançon 1997).
BARTRAM, William, *Travels through North and South Carolina etc.* (Philadelphia 1791; Penguin edn, 1988).
BATEY, Mavis and LAMBERT, David, *The English Garden Tour* (London, 1990).
BEAUCHAMP, A. de, *An authentic narrative of the Campaign of 1815, comprising a circumstantial detail of the Battle of Waterloo. By a Staff Officer in the French Army. Forming a sequel to the History of the Campaigns of 1814*, 2nd edn (London, 1815).
BECKFORD, William, *The Travel Diaries of William Beckford*, ed. G. Chapman, 2 vols (London, 1928).
BERRY, Miss Mary, *Extracts from the Journal and Correspondence of Miss Berry*. ed. Lady Theresa Lewis (London, 1865).
BIELSCHOWSKY, Albert, *The Life of Goethe*, trans. W. A. Cooper, 3 vols (New York 1905–08).
BLACK, Jeremy, *The British Abroad: The Grand Tour in the Eighteenth Century* (Stroud 1992).
BLACK, R., *Horse Racing in France* (London, 1886).
BLAIKIE Thomas, *Diary of a Scotch Gardener at the French court at the end of the 18th Century*, ed. Francis Birrell (London, 1931).
BOMBELLES, Marquis de, *Journal*, 3 vols (Paris, 1977).
BONNIER G. and LAYENS, G. de, *Flore complète portative de la France de la Suisse et de la Belgique* (Paris, 1986).

B(ORDIER), M., *Voyage pittoresque aux glacières de Savoie fait en 1772* (Geneva, 1773).

BOSWELL, James, *Boswell on the Grand Tour; Switzerland and Italy*, ed. E. A. Pottle (1953).

BOURRIT, M. J., *Description des Cols ou passages des Alpes* (Geneva 1803).

——, *A relation of a Journey to the glaciers of Savoy* (Dublin 1776).

BOUVIER R. and MAYNAL, E., *Aimé Bonpland, explorateur de l'Amazonie, botaniste de Malmaison, planteur en Argentine, 1773–1858* (Paris, 1950).

BRAHAM, Allan, *The Architecture of the French Enlightenment* (London, 1980).

BRETONNE, Rétif de la, *Les Nuits de Paris*, folio edn (Paris, 1986).

BRITSCH, A., *La Jeunesse de Philippe Egalité* (Paris, 1926).

BROGLIE, Gabriel de, *Madame de Genlis* (Paris, 1985).

BROWNING, Oscar, *Despatches of Lord Gower containing the Paris diary of Henry Temple, second Viscount Palmerston (1739–1802) for the period July 6–Aug. 31 1791* (London, 1885).

BROWNING, Oscar, *Despatches from Paris, 1784–1790*, 2 vols (London, 1909–1910).

——, *Despatches of Earl Gower* (London, 1885).

BRUCE, Evangeline, *Napoleon and Josephine, an Improbable Marriage* (London, 1991).

CALMON-MAISON, M., *L'Amiral D'Estaing (1729–1794)* (Paris, 1910).

CAMERON, H. C., *Sir Joseph Banks: the Autocrat of the Philosophers* (London, 1952).

CAMPAN, Mme de, *Mémoires sur la vie privée de la Reine Marie Antoinette*, 2nd edn (Paris, 1823).

CARMONTELLE Louis Carrogi, *Jardin de Monceau, près de Paris, appartenant à son Altesse Serenissime Monseigneur le duc de Chartres* (Paris, 1779).

CARR, Sir John, *Stranger in France* (London, 1803).

CARTER, H. B., *Sir Joseph Banks* (London, 1988).

CASTELOT A., *Philippe Egalité le Régicide* (Paris, 1991).

CAUMONT, A de, *Statistique monumentale de l'arrondissement de Pont l'Eveque* (Pont l'Evêque, 1859).

CAYEUX, Jean de, *Hubert Robert et les Jardins* (Paris, 1987).

CHASE Isabel, *Horace Walpole Gardenist* (Princeton, 1943).

CHASSANGE, Serge, *Oberkampf. Un entrepreneur capitaliste au siecle des Lumieres* (Paris, 1980).

CHATEAUBRIAND, *Mémoires de l'outre-tombe*, trans. A. A. Teixeira de Matos (London, 1902).

CHEVALLIER, Bernard, *Malmaison Château et domaine des origines à 1904* (Paris, 1989).

CHRISTISON, Sir Robert, *The Life of Sir Robert Christison*. 2 vols (Edinburgh, 1885).

COCKBURN Henry, *Memorials of His Time* (Edinburgh, 1856).

COLIN-BLEUWEN Michel and MEYNAL Corinne, *Inventaire des parcs et jardins digne d'intérêt historique, botanique ou paysager en région d'Ile de France* (Paris, 1987).

COLLET, Henri, *Notes pour servir à l'histoire de Ris-Orangis*, n.d., vol. I, pp. 18–22.

COOLIDGE, W., *The Alps in in Nature and History* (London, 1900).

COWPER, A. S., *Historic Corstorphine and Roundabout* (Edinburgh, 1992).

COXE, William, *Sketches of the Natural, Civil and Political State of Swisserland* (London, 1779.)

——, *Travels in Switzerland in a Series of Letters to William Melmoth Esq. from William Coxe*. 2 vols, Dublin 1789.

COULOMB, Pierre et GONON, Maurice, *Histoire de Neuilly* (Paris, 1966).

CROY, Emmanuel, duc de, *Journal inédit du duc de Cröy (1718–1784)*, ed. Grouchy and Cottin (Paris, 1906–07).

CURL, James Steven, *The Art and Architecture of Freemasonry* (London, 1991).

DAICHES, JONES and JONES, *The Scottish Enlightenment 1730–1790. A Hotbed of Genius* (University of Edinburgh, 1986).

DAWSON, Warren R. ed., *The Banks Letters; a calendar of the manuscript correspondence of Sir Joseph Banks, preserved in the British Museum, the British Museum (Natural History) and other collections in Great Britain* (London, 1958).

DEBEER, G. R. and ROUSSEAU, A. M., *Voltaire's English Visitors* (Geneva, 1967).

DEBEER, G. R. *Early Travellers in the Alps* (London, 1930).

DELILLE, Jacques, Abbé, *Les jardins; ou l'art d'embellir les paysages* (Paris, 1782).

DENTAN and DELUC, *Relations de Différents Voyages dans les Alpes de Faucigny* (Maestricht, 1776).

DEFFAND, Mme du, *Lettres à Horace Walpole (1766–1788)* ed. Paget Toynbee (London, 1912).

DESJARDINS, Gustave, *Le Petit Trianon* (Versailles, 1885).

DESMOND, Ray, *Dictionary of British Botanists and Horticulturists* (London, 1994).

——, *Kew: The History of the Royal Botanic Gardens* (London, 1995).

DOHER, Marcel, *Charles de La Bédoyère 1786–1815 Aide de Camp de l'Empéreur* (Paris, 1963).

DOHNA, Countess Ursula, *Private Gardens of Germany* (London, 1986).

DOSQUE, Pierre and RICHARD Yves, *Au coeur de la Brie, Mauperthuis, Pézarches* (1982).

DUCHESNE A.-N., 'Les voyages d'Antoine-Nicolas Duchesne à Ecouen, Chantilly, Ermenonville, Choisy, Brunois etc. en 1780, 1786 et 1791,' ed. E. de Ganay, *La revue de l'histoire de Versailles et de la Seine-et-Oise* (année 1921).

DUCHESNE, H-G., *Le château de Bagatelle (1715–1908)*, Paris, 1909.

DUCREST, Georgette, *Mémoires sur l'Impératrice Joséphine*, 3 vols (Paris, 1828).

DULAURE, *Nouvelle Description des Environs de Paris* (Paris, 1786).

EBEL, J. G., *Manuel du Voyageur en Suisse*, 4th edn (Zurich, 1819).

ENGEL, C. E., *A History of Mountaineering in the Alps* (London, 1948).

FLEURY, Y., *Le département de l'Aisne en 1814* (Laon, 1858).

FLEURY, Maurice, *Louis XV intime et les petites maîtresses* (Paris, 1909).

FONTAINE, Pierre François Leonard, *Journal 1799–1853*, 2 vols (Paris, 1987 edn).

FORESTIER J. C. N., *Bagatelle et ses jardins* (Paris, 1910).

FOX, Richard Hingston, *Doctor Fothergill and his friends: chapters in eighteenth century life* (London, 1919).

FRENILLY, A. F. F. de, *Souvenirs du Baron de Frenilly, Peer of France* (London, 1909).

FUNK-BRETANO, Frantz, *The Diamond Necklace*, trans. H. Sutherland Edwards (London, 1901).

GAILLY, Gerard, *Promenade sur le Mont Canisy. Bénerville, Tourgeville, Deauville, Saint-Arnaut* (Brussels, 1960).

GALLET, Michel, *Les architectes parisiens au XVIIIe siècle Dictionnaire biographique et critique* (Paris, 1995).

——, *Demeures parisiennes, l'époque de Louis XVI* (Paris, 1964).

GANAY, Ernest de, *Les Jardins de France et leur décor* (Paris, 1949).

GAUTIER Théophile, *Mademoiselle de Maupin* (Paris, 1835–36).

GENLIS, Mme de, *Mémoires* (Paris, 1825).

GIAMATTI, A Bartlett, *The Earthly Paradise and the Renaissance Epic* (Princeton, 1966).

GIBBON, E., *Miscellanea Gibboniana*, ed., G. R. de Beer and G. A. Bonnard (London, 1951).

GIRAUD, P., *The campaign of Paris in 1814* (London, 1815).

GONCOURT, E. and J. de, *Sophie Arnould d'apres sa correspondanc et ses mémoires inédites* (Paris, 1877; Geneva 1967–68 edn).

GRAY, Thomas, *Correspondence of Thomas Gray*, ed. Paget Toynbee and L. Whibley, 3 vols (Oxford, 1971; reprint of 1935 edn).

GREATHEED, Bertie, *An Englishman in Paris, 1803: the journal of B. Greatheed*, ed. J. T. B. Bury and J. C. Bury (London, 1953).

GRIEDER, J., *Anglomania in France 1740–89, Fact, Fiction and Political Discourse* (Geneva, 1985).

GROSLEY, M., *A Tour to London or New Observations on England and its inhabitants*, 2 vols (London, 1772).

GRUBER, Alain-Charles, *Les Grandes Fêtes et leur Décor à l'Epoque de Louis XVI* (Geneva, 1972).

GUILLOIS, A, *Le Salon de Mme Helvétius* (Paris, 1894).

GUY, Basil, *Coup d'Oeil at Beloeil and a Great Number of European Gardens* (California, 1992).

HALLER, Albrecht von, *Poésies de M. Haller*, trans. V. B. Tscharner 2 vols in one (Berne, 1760).

——, *Historia Stirpium indigenarum Helvetiae* (Berne 1768).

——, *Nomenclator ex Historia Plantarum Indigenarum Helvetiae Excerptus* (Berne, 1769).

HARRIS, John, *A Garden Alphabet* (London, 1979).

HASLIP, Joan, *Marie Antoinette* (London, 1987).

HARVEY, John, *Early Gardening Catalogues* (Chichester, 1972).

——, *Early Nurserymen* (Chichester, 1974).

HEITZMANN, Annick, *Trianon La ferme du hameau* (Paris, 1991).

HENDERSON, D. M., and DICKSON, J. H., *A Naturalist in the Highlands* (Edinburgh, 1994).

HILLAIRET J., *Dictionnaire historique des rues de Paris*, 2 vols (Paris, 1963).

HIRSCHFELD C. C. L., *Théorie de l'art des jardins*, 5 vols (Leipzig, 1779–85).

HORTENSE, La Reine, *Mémoires de la Reine Hortense, publiés par le prince Napoléon* (Paris, 1927).

HOUGH, Richard, *Captain James Cook, a Biography* (London, 1994).

HOURTOULLE, F. G., *Ney, le brave des braves* (Paris c. 1981).

HOUSSAYE, H., *1814* (Paris, 1899).

HUNT, John Dixon, *William Kent Landscape Designer* (London, 1987).

——, *The figure in the landscape: poetry, painting and gardening during the 18th century* (Baltimore 1976).

HUSSEY, Christopher, *English Gardens and Landscapes 1700–1750* (London, 1967).

——, *The Picturesque* (London, 1927).

JONES, Colin, *The Longman Companion to the French Revolution* (London, 1988).

KARAMZIN, N. M., *Letters of a Russian Traveller 1789–90: an account of a tour through Germany, Switzerland, France, and England*, trans. and abridged by F. Jones (1957).

KETCHAM, Diana, *Le Désert de Retz* (MIT Press edn, 1994).

LABORDE, A. de, *Descriptions des Nouvelles Jardins de la France, et de ses anciens châteaux* (Paris, 1808).

LA BÉDOYÈRE, Comte de, *Le Maréchal Ney*, 2nd edn (Paris, n.d.).

LABLAUDE, Pierre-André, *The Gardens of Versailles* (London, 1995).

LABOUCHÈRE, Alfred, *Oberkampf (1738–1815)* (Paris, 1866).

LA BUTTE, A., *Essai historique sur Honfleur et l'arrondissement de Pont l'Eveque* (1840).

LABOUCHÈRE *Oberkampf* (Paris, 1874).

LAURAGUAIS, Louis Brancas, comte de, *Mémoire pour moi par moi* (London, 1773).

Lettres du Cn B. Lauraguais à l'occasion du contrat de vente que le Deptnt de l'Aisne lui a passé du Presbytère et de l'Eglise à Manicamp; et de surcis que le Ministre des Finances a mis à l'exécuter de ce contract (Paris, 1797).

LAW, A., *Education in Edinburgh in the 18th Century* (London, 1965).

LAWRANCE, Mary, *A Collection of Roses from Nature* (London, 1799).

LE BRUN, Madame Vigée, *Memoirs*, trans. Sian Evans (London, 1989).

LESCURE, A de, *Correspondance secrète inédite sur Louis XVI, Marie Antoinette, la cour et la ville*. 2 vols (Paris, 1866).

LE ROUGE, G. L., *Jardins anglo-chinois à la mode ou Detail des nouveaux jardins à la mode* (Paris, 1776–1789).

LE ROUGETEL, Hazel, *The Chelsea Gardener Philip Miller 1691–1771* (London, 1990).

LE TEXNIER, *Notice sur les jardiniers célèbres et les amateurs de jardins* (Paris, 1907).

——, *Les Jardiniers célèbres: Soulange Bodin* (Paris, n.d.).

LETTSOM, J. C., *The Works of John Fothergill*, 3 vols (1783–84).

LETOUZY, Yvonne, *Le Jardin des Plantes à la croisée des chemins avec André Thouin 1747–1824* (Paris, 1989).

LIZIER, Henri, *Marboué, cité historique, site touristique* (Marboué, 1979).

LOUDON, J. C., *Arboretum et Fruticetum*, 8 vols (London, 1838).

LOUDON, J. C., *Encyclopedia of Gardening*, various editions.

MANSEL, Philip, *The Court of France 1789–1830* (Cambridge, 1988).

——, *Louis XVIII* (London, c. 1981).

MARTYN, Thomas, *Sketch of a Tour through Swisserland* (London, 1787).

MASSON, F., *Madame Bonaparte* (Paris, 1920).

——, *Joséphine répudié* (Paris, 1901).

MÉNÉVAL, C.-F., Baron de, *L'Impératrice Joséphine* (Paris, n.d.).

——, *Mémoires pour servir à l'Histoire de Napoléon depuis 1802 jusqu'à 1815* (Paris, 1894).

MERCER, Cavalié (General), *Journal of the Waterloo Campaign*, 2 vols (Edinburgh, 1870).

MERCIER, L-S., *Tableau de Paris* (Hamburg, 1781).

——, *Le Nouveau Paris* (1798).

——, *The Picture of Paris before and after the Revolution*, trans. W. and E. Jackson (London, 1929).

METRA, F. (ed.), *Correspondance secrète, politique et littéraire*, 18 vols (London, 1787–90).

MORTON, A. G., *John Hope 1725–1786 Scottish Botanist* (Edinburgh Botanic Garden Trust, 1986).

MONTAGUE, Lady Mary Wortley, *The Complete Letters*, ed. R. Halsband (Oxford, 1965–67).

MOORE, Dr John, *A View of Society and Manners in France, Switzerland etc.* (8th edn, London, 1793.

MOORE, John M.D., *A Journal during a Residence in France from the beginning of August to the middle of December 1792*, 2 vols (London, 1793).

MOREL, J., *Théorie des Jardin; ou l'art des jardins de la Nature* (Paris, 1774).

MORNET, Daniel, *Le sentiment de la Nature en France* (Paris, 1907).

NOLHAC, P. de, *Peintures de Hubert Robert 733–1808* (Paris, 1910).

NEILL, Patrick, *Journal of a Horticultural Tour through some parts of Flanders, Holland and the North of France in the Autumn of 1817* (Edinburgh, 1823).

OBERKIRCH, H. L. Baronne d', *Mémoires*, 3 vols (Paris, 1853).

OUDIETTE, Charles, *Dictionnaire topographique des environs de Paris* (Paris, 1812).

PEMBROKE, Henry Herbert 10th Earl of, *Henry, Elizabeth and George (1734–80); letters and diaries of Henry, tenth Earl of Pembroke and his circle*, ed. by Lord Herbert (London, 1939).

PEMBROKE, Sidney Charles Herbert 16th Earl of, *Pembroke papers, 1780–94: letters and diaries of Henry, 10th Earl of Pembroke and his Circle*, ed. by Lord Herbert (London, 1950).

PENNINGTON, Rev. Thomas, *Continental Excursions or Tours into France, Switzerland and Germany in 1782, 1787 and 1789*, 2 vols (London, 1809).

PERCIER and FONTAINE, *Résidences des Souverains* (Paris, 1833).

——, *Le château de Malmaison* (Paris n.d.).

PESVNER, Nikolaus (ed.), *The Picturesque Garden and its influence outside the British Isles* (Dumbarton Oaks 1974).

POISSON, G., *Evocation du Grand Paris; La Banlieue Nord-Ouest* (Paris, 1960).

——, *Evocation du Grand Paris; La Banlieue Nord-Est* (Paris, 1961).

PONTIEUX Alfred et BOUZARD, Jules, *Notice historique sur Manicamp (Aisne) d'après les notes de Monsieur l'Abbé Carlet* (Chauny, 1937).

PRADE, Guy de la, *L'Illustre société d'Auteuil 1772–1830; ou la fascination de la liberté* (Paris, 1990).

QUELLERN, L. de, *Le château de Bagatelle, étude historique et descriptive* (Paris, c. 1910).

REMUSAT, Comtesse de, *Mémoires*, 3 vols (Paris, 1880).

RIBEIRO, Aileen, *Dress in 18th Century Europe 1715–1789* (London, 1984).

RICE Howard C. Junior, *Thomas Jefferson's Paris* (Princeton, 1976).

RIGBY, Dr Edward, *Dr Rigby's Letters from France in 1789*, ed. Lady Eastlake (London, 1880).

ROBIN, Pierre, *Le sequestre de biens ennemis sous la Révolution française* (Paris, 1929).

ROSENBLUM, Robert, *Transformations in Late Eighteenth Century Art* (Princeton, 1970).

ROUSSEAU, Jean-Jacques, *la Nouvelle Héloise* (Paris, 1761).

RUDÉ, George, *The French Revolution* (London, 1988).

RUTLAND, Elisabeth Duchess of, *Journal of a Short Trip during the Summer of 1815* (London, 1815).

SALAMAN, R. N., *The History and Social Influence of the Potato* (Cambridge, 1949).

SAUSSURE, Horace Benedict de, *Voyage dans les Alpes*, 4 vols (Neuchatel, 1779).

SCHAMA, Simon, *Citizens* (London, 1989).

SEYLAC, L., *Excursions d'un botaniste écossais dans les Alpes et le Jura* (Neuchatel, 1935).

SHENSTONE, William, *Works in verse and prose*, 2 vols (London, 1764–69).

SHUCKBURGH, Sir George, *Observations made in Savoy in order to ascertain the height of the mountains by means of the barometer* (London, 1777).

SIMO, Melanie Louise *Loudon and the Landscape. From Country Seat to Metropolis* (Yale University Press 1988).

SINCLAIR, Sir J., ed. *The Statistical Account of Scotland*, 21 vols (Edinburgh, 1791–99).

SIREN, Oswald, *China and the Gardens of Europe of the 18th Century* (New York, 1950).

SMITH, Sir James Edward, *A Sketch of a Tour on the Continent in the years 1786 and 1787*, 3 vols (London, 1793).

Memoirs and Correspondence of the late Sir James Edward Smith MD, ed. Lady Smith, 2 vols (London, 1832).

SMOLLETT, T., *Travels through France and Italy* (London, 1796).

SMOUT, T. C., *A Social History of Scotland* (London, 1969).

SOMERVILLE, Thomas, *My Own Life and Times* (Edinburgh, 1861).

SOUTHEY, Robert, *Journal of a Tour in Scotland in 1819* (London, 1829).

STERN, J., *A l'ombre de Sophie Arnould, François-Joseph Bélanger, architecte des Menus Plaisirs. Premier architecte du comte d'Artois*, 2 vols (Paris, 1930).

STROUD, Dorothy, *Capability Brown* (London, 1975 edn).

STRUTHERS, John, *Historical Sketch of the Edinburgh Anatomical School* (Edinburgh, 1869).

SWITZER, S., *Iconographia rustica: or, The nobleman, gentleman and gardener's recreation: containing directions for the surveying & distributing of a country seat into royal and extensive gardens*, 2nd edn, 3 vols (London, 1742).

TAIT, A. A., *The Landscape Garden in Scotland* (Edinburgh, 1980).

TAYLOR, B., *Stubbs* (London, 1971).

THACKER, Christopher, *The History of Gardening* (London, 1979).

THEIBAULT, General, Baron P., *Mémoires* (Paris, 1894).

THIERY, Luc-Vincent, *Guide des amateurs et des étrangers voyageurs* (Paris, 1787).

THOMAS, Graham Stuart, *The Rock Garden and its Plants* (London, 1989).

THOMPSON, *English Witnesses of the French Revolution* (Oxford, 1938).

THOMSON, James, *The Seasons* (London, 1746).

THOUIN, Gabriel, *Plans Raisonnés de Toutes les Espèces de Jardins* (Paris, 1819).

THRALE, H., *The French Journals of Mrs Thrale and Doctor Johnson*, ed. Tyson M. and Guppy H. (Manchester, 1932).

TOUR DU PIN, Madame de la, *Escape from the Terror. The Journal of Madame de la Tour du Pin*, ed. and trans., Felice Harcourt (London, 1979).

TOURZEL, Duchesse de, *Mémoires* (Paris, 1883).

TROUILLEUX, Rodolphe, *N'oubliez pas Iphigénie. Biographie de la cantatrice et épistolaire Sophie Arnould (1740–1802)* (Grenoble, 1999).

WALPOLE, H., *Letters*, ed Paget Toynbee (London, 1935).

VASSAL, Philippe, *Les eaux de Paris en Révolution 1775–1825* (Paris, 1997).

VELLA, Christina, *Intimate Enemies: The Two Worlds of the Baroness de Pontalba* (Louisiana, 1997).

WATKIN, David, *The English Vision. The Picturesque in Architecture, Landscape and Garden Design* (London, 1982).

WEIBERSON, Dora, *The Picturesque Garden in France* (Princeton, 1978).

WESTON, S., *Letters from Paris* (London, 1793).

Two Sketches of France Belgium and Spain (London, 1817).

WHATELY, Thomas, *Observations on Modern Gardening* (London, 1770).

WILDENSTEIN, Georges, *Un peintre de paysage au XVIIIe Louis Moreau* (Paris, 1922).

WILLIAMS, H. M., *Letters on the events which have passed in France since the Restoration in 1815* (London, 1820).

——, *Letters written in France in the summer of 1790 to a friend in England*, 2 vols (London, 1790).

——, *A Tour in Switzerland or a view of the present state of the Governments and Manners of those Cantons, with comparative sketches of the present state of Paris* (Dublin, 1798).

——, *A Narrative of Events* (London, 1815).

WILLSON, E. J., *James Lee and the Vineyard Nursery, Hammersmith* (London, 1961).

——, *West London Nursery Gardens* (London, 1982).

WILMOT Catherine, *An Irish Peer on the Continent 1801–1803; being a narrative of the tour of Stephen 2nd Earl Mount Cashell, through France, Italy etc. as related by C. Wilmot*, ed. Thomas V. Sadler (London, 1920).

WOOD, J., *Scotland – Town Plans 1818 to 1823* (Edinburgh, 1823).

YORKE, Henry Redhead, *Letters from Paris in 1802*, 2 vols (London, 1804).

YOUNG, Arthur, *Travels in France during the Years 1787, 1788, 1789* (Bury St Edmunds, 1792).

Articles and Essays

ANON, 'Réunion du 10 janvier 1946', *Societé d'Histoire et d'Archaeologie de Senlis*, comptes rendus, 8ème série, (an 1946–47).

ARNAUD, Claude, 'Le comte d'Artois et son coterie', *Folie d'Artois* (Paris, 1988).

ASTRUC, Jean, 'Les Anglais au Raincy', *Bulletin de la S.H.R.P.A.*, no. 31, (January 1964).

ASTRUC, J., 'Des boutons d'habit extraordinaires', in *En Aulnoye Jadis*, no. 3 (1974).

AVEZON, R., and DUMOLIN, M., 'La Maison de Madame de Lamballe à Passy', *Bulletin de la Société Historique d'Auteuil et Passy* vol. XL.

BAILEY, Colin, 'Artois, mécène et collectionneur,' in *La Folie d'Artois* (Paris, 1988).

BAILLIO, Joseph, 'Hubert Robert's Decorations for the château de Bagatelle,' *Metropolitan Museum Journal*, 27 (1992).

BALTRUSAITIS, Jurgis, 'Jardins et pays d'illusions', *Aberrations. Essai sur la légende des formes. Les perspectives dépravées-I* (Paris, 1995 edn).

BARRIER, Janine, 'Bélanger et l'Angleterre', *Bagatelle dans les jardins* (Paris, 1997)

BATCAVE, 'Le Seizième arrondissement', *Société Historique d'Auteuil et Passy* SHAP XIV (1923–1930).

BAULEZ, Christian, 'L'Ameublement du comte d'Artois', *Bagatelle dans ses jardins* (Paris, 1997).

BLAIKIE, Thomas, 'Excursion Horticole' par un Anglais, *Annales de la Societé Horticole* (Paris, 1835).

BRACCO, Patrick et LEBOVICI, Elizabeth, 'Les vestiges du parc du Raincy', *Monuments historiques, Ile-de-France*, no. 129 (October–November 1983).

BRIDEL, Doyen, 'Excursions de Bex à Sion', *Conservateur suisse* (1786).

BOUGON, J., 'Des boutons d'habit extraordinaires', *En Aulnoye Jadis*, no. 13 (1983).

BUGON, J. and GAULARD, M., 'Le parc de Raincy', *En Aulnoye jadis*, vol. I, no. 3 (1974).

CHENNEBENOIST, J., 'St Arnoult', *Athena sur la Touques* (May 1969).

CHEVALLIER, Bernard, 'Les jardins secrets de l'Impératrice', *Historama*, no. 64 (June 1989).

COATS, Alice M., 'The Empress Josephine', *Garden History*, vol. 5, no. 3 (1977).

CONSTANS, Martine, 'L'architecte-décorateur François-Joseph Bélanger. L'énigme d'une carriére brizée', *Les cahiers de Maisons*, no. 23 (eté 1994).

——, 'Le château du comte d'Artois', *Bagatelle dans ses jardins* (Paris, 1997).

DACIER, Emile, 'Le parc Monceau avant la Révolution', *Société d'iconographie parisienne* (1910).

DENEF, J. P. 'Le parc de Mauperthuis. Ledoux, Brogniart, Hubert Robert', *Le Temps des Jardins* (Paris, 1992).

FARA, Patricia, 'Images of a Man of Science', *History Today*, vol. 48 (10) (October 1998).

HARVEY, John, 'A Scottish Botanist in London in 1766', *Garden History*, vol. 9, no. 1 (1981).

HÉNARD, Robert, 'Les Jardins de Bagatelle', *La Grande Revue*, 10 May 1907.

JACQUES, David, 'On the Supposed Chineseness of the English Landscape Garden', *Garden History* 18, vol. 2 (Autumn 1990).

JANVRY, Olivier Chopin de, 'A much visited Solitude', Rosemary Verey and Katherine Lambert, *Secret Gardens Revealed by their Owners* (London, 1994).

——, 'MÉRÉVILLE', *L'Oeil*, 1969, t. 2.

JOUDIOU, Gabrielle, 'Saint-James', in *Cent jardins a Paris et en Ile de France* (Paris, 1992).

JOUVE, Jean -Pierre, 'La maison avant le comte d'Artois', *Bagatelle dans ses jardins* (Paris, 1997).

LEFEVRE, E., 'Le parc de Méréville', *Gazette des Amateurs de Jardins* (Paris, 1921).

LEROUX-CESBRON, G. C., 'Le Baron de Sainte-James et sa folie de Neuilly', *La Revue de Paris*, 1 February 1925.

LOUDON, J. C., 'Notes and Reflections made during a Tour through Part of France and Germany, in the Autumn of the year 1828', *Gardener's Magazine* vol. 9.

MAZEL, Geneviève, 'Le château et les jardins du marquis de Girardin. Le souvenir de Jean-Jacques Rousseau', *Groupe d'étude des Monuments et Oeuvres d'art de l'Oise et du Beauvaisis*. 1996 Bulletin no. 73–5.

——, 'Ermenonville L'histoire et la vie du village', *Groupe d'étude des Monuments etc.*, 1996 – Bulletin no. 73–5.

——, 'Raray et son château', *Groupe d'etude des Monuments etc.* 1999 Bulletin 90–1.

MINAY, Priscilla, 'Early Improvements in the Eighteenth Century Lothians', *Bulletin of the Scottish Georgian Society*, vol. 2 (1973).

MOLIN, J. B., 'Nogent l'Artaud pendant la Révolution', *Mémoires de la Fédération des sociétés d'histoire et d'archéologie de l'Aisne*, vol. XXXVIII.

MIDDLETON, R., 'The Château and Gardens of Mauperthuis; The Formal and Informal', *Garden History Issues, Approaches, Methods*, ed. J. Dixon Hunt, (Dumbarton Oaks, 1992).

MONTAGNIER, H., 'Thomas Blaikie and Michel-Gabriel Paccard', *The Alpine Journal*, no. 246 (May 1933).

MOSSER, M., 'Histoire d'un jardin', *Folie d'Artois* (Paris, 1988).

——, 'Le Rocher et la colonne: Un thème d'iconographie architecturale au 18e siècle', *Revue de l'Art* 58/59 (1983).

MOULIN, Jacques, 'Le Château d'Aunoy et l'apparition en France du Jardin à l'Anglaise', *Bulletin Monumental*, Tome 149, vol. II (1991).

MWS, 'The Story Behind the Buttons', *Bulletin of the Button Society of America* (February 1986).

OLAUSSON, Magnus, 'Freemasonry Occultism and the Picturesque Garden towards the end of the 18th Century', *Art History*, vol. 8, no. 4 (December 1985).

OTTOMEYER, H., 'Autobiographies d'architectes parisiens', *Bulletin de la Société de l'Histoire de Paris*, vol. 98–100.

PERROT, Victor, 'Communication sur le château, le domaine et le site de Bagatelle', *Procès verbaux de la Commission du Vieux Paris* (Paris, 1923).

POISSON, G., 'Un transparent de Monceau', *Bulletin de la Société de l'Histoire de l'Art Français* (1984).

PONS, Bruno and FORRAY-CARLIER, Anne, 'Hotel de Segur puis Salm-Dyck, 97 rue de Bac', *Le faubourg Saint-Germain La rue du Bac* (Paris, 1990).

RANCH, M. F., 'Gardening Tour in Germany made in the spring of 1836', *Gardener's Magazine*, vol. 12.

SABATTIER, J., 'Méréville', *100 Jardins à Paris et en Ile-de-France* (Paris, 1992).

SCHOMMER, Pierre, 'Joséphine amateur de jardins', *Revue de l'Institut Napoléon*, no. 92 (July 1964).

SIREN, O., 'Le désert de Retz', *Architectural Review*, CVI (November 1949).

SCOTT, Barbara, 'Bagatelle Folie of the comte d'Artois', *Apollo*, June 1972.

SYMES, Michael, 'Charles Hamilton's Plantings at Painshill', *Garden History*, vol. 11.

TAYLOR, Patricia, 'Les plantations du parc 1778–1830', *Bagatelle dans ses jardins*, Paris, 1997.

WALTER, Rodolphe, 'Le parc de Monsieur Zola', *L'Oeil*, no. 272 (March 1978).

WEDEPOHL, E, 'Le Château de Bagatelle description de Frédérich Gilly, *L'Oeil*, 126 (June 1965).

WILLIS, Peter, 'Rousseau, Stowe & le Jardin Anglais', *Studies on Voltaire and the 18th Century*, XC (1972).

WOODBRIDGE, Kenneth, 'Bélanger, Son Carnet de Voyage', *Architectural History*, 25 (1982).

YRIARTE, Charles, 'Mémoires de Bagatelle,' Part 1, *Revue de Paris*, 4 (July–August 1903); Part 2 (September–October 1903).

WATKINS, David, 'Architectural Education, Patronage and Practise in Ancien Regime France,' *Georgian Architectual Practice*, Symposium of the Georgian Group, 1991.

Newspapers and Magazines

Edinburgh Advertiser, 9 August 1822.

Journal de Paris, 14 October 1779, 20–23 May 1780.

Gardener's Magazine, vols 2–13, 1826–1838.

Le Moniteur Universel, June 1792, 26 November 1815.

Galignani's Messenger, Paris, 3 May 1819.

Journal Général d'Affiches, 29 May 1850.

Scotsman, 15 February 1854, 26 December 1998.

Edinburgh Evening Courant, 14 September 1822.

Edinburgh Evening News, 26 December 1998.

The Times, 31 December 1998.

Le Figaro, 18 May 1965,.

Le Monde, 26 May 1965.

Toutes les Nouvelles de Versailles, 28 December 1964 and 14 July 1965.

Exhibition Catalogues

De Bagatelle à Monceau, 1778–1978: les Folies du XVIIIe siècle à Paris, Domaine de Bagatelle and Musée Carnavalet, Paris, 1978–79.

Elisabeth Louise Vigée LeBrun 1755–1842. Catalogue by Joseph Baillio, Fort Worth 1982.

Grandes et petites heures du parc Monceau. Hommage à Thomas Blaikie (1750–1838) jardinier écossais du duc d'Orléans, Musée Cernuchi, Paris, 1981.

Jardins en France 1760–1820. Pays d'illusion, Terre d'expériences, Caisse nationale de Monuments Historiques et des Sites, Hôtel de Sully, Paris, 1977.

Les Anglais à Chamonix aux 18ème et 19ème siècles, Musée Alpin-Chamonix, September 1984.

Les Jardins de Versailles et de Trianon D'André Le Nôtre à Richard Mique, Musée national des châteaux de Versailles et de Trianon, June–September 1992.

Les joies de la nature au 18e siècle, Bibliothèque Nationale, Paris, 1971.

Index